CW00921693

SAVED TO SERVE

The Story of the
Wesley Deaconess Order
1890-1978

E. Dorothy Graham

ISBN 1 85852 224 2

Printed by Stanley L. Hunt (Printers) Ltd

Dedicated to
all members of the
Wesley Deaconess Order –
past and present

If truth were wholly contained in Matthew Prior's words, that 'Variety alone gives joy', then we in our vocation should be the most joyous people in the world, although the greater part of the change we experience is brought about by the sin and suffering of those around us. It would be somewhat strange for us to depend upon such variety for our joy, nevertheless, I feel that we are among the happiest folk, because we do not depend on outward circumstances for happiness. We draw our joy from an unseen source, having taken of that 'well of water which is springing up into Everlasting Life'.

In dwelling in thought upon the subject, 'How best can we fulfil our calling', it seemed to me to be better for us to be women of many resources than adepts at one or two particular accomplishments.

Life is short at the longest, and our task is great . . .

We who desire not only to be *called,* but also to *be* 'Sisters' to those around us, can see plainly, before setting out on our task, that we shall be wanted to give advice and assistance on very many subjects.

Remembering, also, that we have set aside our own wishes and interests, and desire only to serve our Lord, we render help (primarily spiritual, and after that in whatsoever way we may see it possible) to our brothers and sisters in distress . . .

Sister Erica Marley: Address at Convocation
Friday 25th April 1902, Oxford Place, Leeds
(*Flying Leaves* June/July 1902 p.103)

Teach me, my God and King,
In all things Thee to see,
And what I do in anything,
To do it as for Thee.

George Herbert

Foreword

The deaconess was some 30 years my senior, and she looked me firmly up and down. Then with humour in her eyes she said: 'I have been accustomed to Wardens who were fathers in God. I have known those who were brothers in Christ. But now it seems that I must get used to one who is a son in the gospel.' She was to become a firm and supportive friend to the new Warden, conscious of his comparative lack of years; and it is worth setting on record how warmly all the members of the Wesley Deaconess Order welcomed Una and me, with our two young children (as then they were). The Order was a closely-knit organisation, but we felt accepted as part of a family, and were privileged to share something of the unique spirituality of this group of women who contributed so significantly to the life and work of Methodism.

Dorothy Graham has delved deeply into the original records, and has done a magnificent job in bringing shape to a story which must at times have seemed confused to those who lived through it. Just as Methodism took so long to make up its mind that it was right for women to be presbyters, so it could never quite decide what work it wanted its deaconesses to do. But perhaps that is in essence the greatness of the story. Here were women willing to do virtually anything if it seemed right to the Church and relevant to God's Kingdom. They asked for little in return, and indeed for decades resisted attempts to increase the allowances paid to them, on the grounds that they did not want to price themselves beyond the means of the poorer circuits. Some were activists like Martha, others more reflective like Mary; and there were those who were greatly gifted who would have shone in any sphere or profession. At last the story is set out worthily, so that – if a little tardily – Methodism may sense something of its debt to a remarkable band of women.

Rev. Brian J. N. Galliers
Warden of the Wesley
Deaconess Order (1972-80)

Commendation

In a time of rapid change it is easy to devalue the past, or indeed to forget it altogether. Diaconal ministry in the Methodist Church has changed more rapidly than many other parts of our common life in recent years, with the opening of the Methodist Diaconal Order to men as well as to women and with the recognition of deacons as an order of ministry within the Church as well as a religious order with its own rule of life. There are exciting times ahead. But it would be wholly mistaken to look only to the future of diaconal ministry. In its past lie the roots of that spirit of disciplined service which the Wesley Deaconess Order cherished and guarded throughout its 88-year life, and which is its great gift to the Church. It is not only the Methodist Diaconal Order which enters into a goodly heritage; we all do.

This book is rightly an honouring of the past. But it is more than that. In the people whom you will meet in these pages, we have example, challenge and encouragement for the ministry of service to which every Christian is called. May our Wesley Deaconess forebears inspire the deacon in all of us.

Rev. Dr. Christina Le Moignan
President of the Methodist Conference, 2001-02

Acknowledgements

The idea for this history of the Wesley Deaconess Order originated from a conversation with Sister Christine Walters when she was Warden of the Order and I rashly promised to try to record its story. Her interest and support, and also that of her successor, Margaret Matta, has been a great source of encouragement: to them I extend grateful thanks. With her 'Postscript' Christine has also kindly brought the story of the Order up to the present time. I am also indebted to countless people: deaconesses, former deaconesses, people associated with the Order, and other friends, too many to mention by name, have given me valuable assistance, advice and information.

However, special thanks are due to the Rev. Brian J. N. Galliers, the last Warden, who not only 'endured' long telephone conversations, but also kindly read the script in its various stages with deep interest and insight. Then to the Rev. Gerald M. Burt I offer my very sincere appreciation – without his careful scrutiny of my grammar and every comma (!) there would have been many more stylistic errors – and but for his help, advice and encouragement this project would probably never have reached the publishing stage. The time he expended on it was surely past the call of duty of an Editorial Secretary!

Yet again a Methodist author is indebted to Dr. John A. Vickers not only for generously sharing his wide knowledge of Methodism, but also for another admirable index. Finally, much expertise and advice was provided by Brian Thornton, Susan Hibbins, Sue Gascoigne and the staff of the Methodist Publishing House: so to them and all, including my own family who 'sorted me out' when my inexpert computer skills gave up, who helped in any way, my thanks.

E. Dorothy Graham
Autumn 2002

Abbreviations

Bradfield	Bradfield, William, *The Life of Thomas Bowman Stephenson* (1913)
Chambers	Chambers, Wesley A., *Not Self – But Others: The Story of the New Zealand Methodist Deaconess Order* (Wesley Historical Society (New Zealand), Proceedings No. 48, August 1987)
Cope	Cope, Thomas J., *The Hand of God in the History of the Deaconess Institute of the United Methodist Church* (n.d.)
FL	*Flying Leaves from the Wesley Deaconess Institute of the Wesleyan Methodist Church* (1901-15)
HH	*Highways and Hedges and Children's Advocate: organ of The Children's Home* (1891-1901)
Mins. of Conf.	*The Methodist Church: Minutes of Conference* (1932-78)
Mins. of Conv.	Minutes of Convocation (1892-1969)
MSS Cuttings	MSS Cuttings Book (compiled by R. W. Gair)
RConv.	Record of Convocation (1892-1935)
Smith	Smith, Henry, *Ministering Women: The Story of the Work of the Sisters connected with the United Methodist Deaconess Institute* (n.d.) [1st and 2nd editions]
Smith, Swallow and Treffry	Smith, Henry, Swallow, John E., Treffry, William, *The Story of the United Methodist Church* (1932)
UMDI Report	*United Methodist Deaconess Institute Reports* (1905-10)
UMFC Mins. of Conf.	*United Methodist Free Churches Minutes of Conference*
UM Mins. of Conf.	*United Methodist Minutes of Conference Methodist Church* (1949-59)

UMDIMins I	United Methodist Deaconess Institute Minutes (1906-17)
UMDIMins II	United Methodist Deaconess Institute Minutes (1917-32)
UMDIMins III	United Methodist Deaconess Institute Minutes (1932-38)
WDIMins I	Wesley Deaconess Institute Minutes (1890-1910)
WDIMins II	Wesley Deaconess Institute Minutes (1911-33)
WDMag.	*The Wesley Deaconess Magazine of the Methodist Church* (1949-59)
Wm Mins. of Conf.	*Wesleyan Methodist Minutes of Conference* (1885-1932)
WDOMins III	Wesley Deaconess Order Minutes (1933-47)
WDOMins IV	Wesley Deaconess Order Minutes (1948-78)
WDO Stations	*Stations (or Appointments) of the Wesley Deaconess Order* (1892-1961)

Contents

Wesley Deaconess College, Ilkley

Introduction

In 1914 a Wesley Deaconess reported that a woman had told her she preferred Missions to church services because they 'told you more antidotes in the sermons'.[1]

This account offers some anecdotes and word pictures of the work and history of the Wesley Deaconess Order from its inception in 1890 until it ceased recruiting in 1978. As far as possible the first chapters about the actual work undertaken by the deaconesses use their own words or accounts as recorded in the various magazines or reports. From these stories questions inevitably arise: How did it all begin? Who started the Wesley Deaconess Order? What was the vision/inspiration behind its establishment? How did it develop? How were the deaconesses trained? What did they wear? How did things change? How did the various Wardens influence the Order? Why did the Order cease recruitment? The second part seeks to provide answers to some of these queries.

Many more stories could be told and much more information given of the wonderful work done: much self-sacrifice, commitment, devotion and an incaluable contribution made to the life and ethos of Methodism and indeed the wider community and the world. Hopefully this account will strike a chord and make the Methodist people thankful for, and inspired by, the dedication of the Order through all these years.

Today, to all intents and purposes, the Order is still alive and well, albeit in a very different form. After a break of eight years the Wesley Deaconess Order 'reopened' as the Methodist Diaconal Order, accepting both women and men, but that is another story.

October 1902 saw the centenary of the official opening of the Wesley Deaconess College in Ilkley and this book is offered in tribute and celebration of that event and of nearly 90 years' work (1890-1978) and witness of the Wesley Deaconess Order.

---

1. *Flying Leaves from the Wesley Deaconess Order* (hereafter *FL*) (June 1914) 'Jottings' p.91

In November 1901 the Warden, the Rev. Dr. Thomas Bowman Stephenson, issued a 'Report Number' of *Flying Leaves* in which he commented:

> Of the seventy-one Deaconesses and Probationers now in active service two are in charge of Training Houses, two are Deaconess-Evangelists, and two have devoted themselves to the establishment and management of a Convalescent Home for poor women and children. Three are Deaconess-Nurses, of whom one is connected with Calvert House, one is on the staff of a Circuit, and one is labouring in connection with a great Mission. Five Deaconesses hold appointments beyond the seas: one of whom is establishing an affiliated Order in New Zealand; two are in the Transvaal, and two are toiling amid the darkness of a thoroughly heathen village in Ceylon. Fourteen Deaconesses are working in connection with Home Mission Enterprises in England, Scotland, and Ireland; and forty-three are connected with Circuits. Nearly all of these last are engaged in work of a missionary character. They are seeking to revive decayed causes, or to nurse young ones. In a few cases they are strengthening the pastoral work needed amongst large congregations.

He went on to note that there were also 15 Student-Probationers in training.[2] This early report indicates the scope of deaconess work achieved in the first decade of its existence. This range of work was extended through the following years as more women offered for the Order and more opportunities opened in circuits, churches and the wider community and requests from overseas were received and answered.

One confusion which arose early, and continued for many years, was the use of the phrases 'Wesley Deaconess Institute' and 'Wesley Deaconess Order'. Stephenson sought to explain the phrases as early as 1902, saying that 'the Conference has sanctioned the "Wesley Deaconess Institute" ' and that many people assumed that this meant that 'Institute' referred to the building in which the 'Order' was trained. However, that was a rather simplistic explanation and really the connotation was much wider.

---

2. *FL* (November 1901) p.5

'Institute' and 'Order'　　　　　　　　　**The Warden**

By many people the word Institute is supposed to apply to a building, and the chief training house of the Wesley Deaconess Order is taken to be the Wesley Deaconess Institute . . . but it may be much greater than any building, or, indeed without a building . . . a voluntary association . . . (meeting), say in a room in a hotel.

Usually, however, the word means both property and persons . . . In like manner the Wesley Deaconess Institute means the Warden, Officers, and Members of the Wesley Deaconess Order, their training houses, or other buildings which they may possess, as their centres of operation . . . It is in this wide sense of the word that it is used among us . . .

What then, is meant by an Order? This is an ecclesiastical term . . . An Order in the church is a body of workers recognised by the church, having their own distinctive work and place . . . So the Deaconesses, recognised by the Church and authorised by it, are an Order of women, set apart for such work such as is particularly suitable to their sex. It is *an* Order . . .

Source: *Flying Leaves* (March 1902) pp.37-8

Two articles in *Flying Leaves* in 1906 entitled 'All in Brief about the Wesley Deaconess Institute' set out to provide answers to 37 questions, ranging from 'What is a Deaconess? (1) and 'What is a Wesley Deaconess?' (2) through such topics as uniform (9), candidature (10), training (11-12, 29), probation (13-14, 30), discipline (15), work in Missions and circuits (16-19, 21-27), overseas work (20), finance (28, 33-36), and consecration (31-32) to 'How is more information to be got?' (37).[3]

In April 1907, just a few months before his retirement through ill-health, Stephenson explained how candidates were selected from the applicants and that in many ways this selection was 'the most anxious and difficult part of our work. After all it is the personality that tells in all such enterprises. The personality should be governed by high motives, trained to accurate and appropriate effort, and baptized with holy fire, but the personality must be there, or little can be done. Sometimes it reveals itself in an illiterate woman, sometimes in one who has received high

---

3. *FL* (November 1906) pp.170-71, (December 1906) pp.186-87

literary culture; and therefore we receive candidates belonging to all ranges of society, and all varieties of culture. If they have force and grace, they will find their appropriate work, and will do it.'[4]

One Qualification in a Deaconess   The Warden

One excellent qualification in a Deaconess is that she has a quick eye for things worth learning and worth teaching. To stimulate interest in all that belongs to the Kingdom of Christ amongst men, is an object kept constantly before us. At the college we take pains to provide the mental excitements which help in this direction. One lecture each week is delivered by some sympathetic outsider, who brings to the student's mind knowledge of men, and modes of places and things, of which they might otherwise hear but little. The mind is broadened and the relish of life and work is sharpened, if fresh subjects, or subjects freshly treated, are brought before minds receiving discipline.

Source: *Flying Leaves* (April 1907) p.51

Later that year the new Warden, the Rev. William Bradfield, wrote 'An Open Letter to Intending Candidates' in which he listed some of the desirable attributes they should possess – good health, clear voice, sound understanding, 'willing obedience', 'dauntless faith', 'boundless hope', lack of 'bigotry', ability 'to understand and practise the principle of Christian freedom, that we must in love serve one another', willing to show 'humility and courtesy to all', and to give 'respect and honour to age and authority'. Practical preparations were important too, as well as was being able to read and pronounce correctly in order to read the Bible aloud clearly. 'School knowledge' was valuable, and applicants should be able to write well and legibly, while singing and playing music should be practised. Any opportunity to gain nursing experience should be taken, so that, at the very least, first-aid could be given when necessary. Finally, Bradfield insisted that one of the most important subjects was 'the study of the Bible and of Christian Theology. The Bible should become so familiar that 'you cannot bear to hear it quoted wrongly and till you can tell the children the stories without misrepresenting them or spoiling them'. The Revised Version of the Bible, with Revised References and Maps, Cloth Boards, costing 5s.3d., was the

---

4. *FL* (April 1907) p.51

recommended edition: 'Be sure you do not try to use smaller print than this. It not only injures the eyes, but it obscures the meaning of the Bible very seriously to read it in tiny print.' When it came to the study of Theology he felt that the best thing was to learn the Second Catechism thoroughly, while another useful study would be to take each phrase of the Apostles Creed and then find appropriate biblical references. Then Wesley's sermons, works by the great English authors, travel, history, biographical books and some lighter, but worthwhile literature, should be read. However, Bradfield, sensibly, commented:

> Don't attempt the impossible; to do so has daunted many a brave beginner. But having prudently chosen something inside the compass of your time and strength, be sure you go through with it and don't leave it half-done.
>
> And so may God help you to prepare yourself for the service of Christ and his Church.[5]

Advice on practical preparations for becoming a Wesley Deaconess   Rev. William Bradfield

I am often asked . . . what is the best preparation you can make for becoming a Candidate for the Order of Wesley Deaconesses . . .

. . . let us begin with some things that are very near at hand. Do you know how to make beef-tea? to boil a potato properly? to lay a fire so that it will certainly light? It is a most valuable preparation to practise, as far as possible, all the arts of good housewifery. They are all wanted, and cannot be learned anywhere so well as at home. If you can learn them now and learn them well, you will be making very good use of your time.

Source: *Flying Leaves* (November 1907) pp.156, 157

Bradfield's wise words of 1907 seem just as applicable today as they did at the time and surely provide a fitting introduction to this story of the Wesley Deaconess Order and indeed for all who wish to serve Christ in his Church.

---

5. *FL* (November 1907) pp.156-58

Sister Florence Thornton, Church and Circuit work

Chapter 1

The Wesley Deaconesses – 'Maids of all Work'

The Employment of Women in the Work of the Methodist Church is no longer an open question. They **will be** employed: successful experiment both demands and justifies their employment. The only question is, will the Church employ them, under the most favourable conditions, and with best possible guarantees against failure in character and in efficiency?[1]

So read the 1902-03 report to the Wesleyan Methodist Conference, thereby reiterating the importance of the Church making full use of the talents of women rather than ignoring this important resource. It also noted the fields in which Wesley Deaconesses were already at work or in which they could serve, thus illustrating the vision of Stephenson.

Report to the Wesleyan Methodist Conference, 1902-3

The Work of the Deaconess is very varied. She may be a *Church Deaconess*, aiding in the Pastoral work of a great congregation. She may be a *Mission Deaconess*, taking part in the manifold activities of a Central or other Mission. She may be a *Deaconess-Evangelist*, mainly devoted to Special Services. She may be a *Deaconess-Nurse*, bringing to her work, not only skill, but the character and influence of a devoted Christian woman. She may be a *Deaconess-Teacher*, carrying on School Work in neighbourhoods, where Schools cannot be established on the ordinary commercial principles, but where they are greatly needed to counteract Romish and 'High Church' influence. She may be a *Slum Deaconess*, caring for the very lowest; or she may be the *trusted friend*, and, humanly speaking, the saviour of women who are lost in the midst of wealth and fashion. She may be engaged in *Rescue* work for women or for

---

1. Wesley Deaconess Institute Minute Book (1895-1910) (hereafter WDIMins I) inserted between pp.157 and 158

> the prisoner, working at the prison-gate, or within the prison. And lastly she may be a *Foreign Missionary Deaconess*, carrying out all the above ideas, amid the special circumstances of Christian work in heathen lands. Several of these departments are already being wrought by the Order; others have yet to be undertaken.
>
> *Source:* Wesley Deaconess Institute Minute Book
> (1895-1910) (between pp.157 and 158)

The variety of work in which the deaconesses engaged was such that it seems best to let them tell their stories in their own words. At the beginning the Wesley Deaconess Institute did not have its own magazine, but was given a few pages in *Highways and Hedges: The Children's Advocate*, the magazine of The Children's Home. Then in September 1901 came the first issue of the Order's own magazine, *Flying Leaves*. Numerous accounts of the work of the deaconesses are recorded, but sadly in its later years and also in the second magazine, *The Agenda*, which commenced in 1922, there are fewer, so perforce most of the stories come from the earlier period of 1891-1915. Although many of the stories seem rather stereotyped and repetitive, they do give some idea of the work undertaken.

> **Address to Convocation 1902   Sister Erica Marley**
>
> We are often the only representative of the Wesley Deaconess Order for miles around, and it is then necessary for us to be 'Multum in parvo'. In such a position we are called upon to be sometime preacher, class leader, adviser, doctor, nurse, cook, housekeeper, organist, soloist, banker, secretary, organiser, friend, reprover, temperance advocate, dentist (!), head of labour bureau, creator of new workers, and helper in such other ways as opportunity and necessity present!
>
> Our calls being so many, and varied, it is necessary for us to make ourselves the possessors of all kinds of general information. We must be in touch with every Institution, Society, Dispensary, Hospital, Convalescent Home, Infirmary, Charity, doctor, nurse, Christian worker, that can aid us in our multitudinous needs.
>
> *Source: Flying Leaves* (June 1902) p.103

The early years

Sister Rita, the Sister-in-Charge at Mewburn House, the training house in London, wrote of the first year's work that in 'the first few months of its existence my work has seemed to lie more in the direction of nursing than in direct evangelistic effort', but even so she had been able 'to tell them of the love of God'. She felt that often her nursing skills had led to openings which would not have otherwise occurred.[2]

Early Deaconess work   **Sister Rita Hawkins**

Although the work is sometimes laborious and exhausting, I have never before realised so much of the joy of living, for as a poor woman whom I visited said to me when I remarked that I was tired, 'Ah, yes, but it's a blessed tired.'

I might say we do not go where we are needed; but where we are needed most. A large number of the cases visited are amongst the very poor, some amongst the artisan class, and a few, in special circumstances, in a still higher grade.

In this work great tact is required, to avoid hurting the feelings of the poor, and to show as much refinement and nice feeling as possible. We want to gain their confidence, and to prove to them that we are really what we call ourselves – 'Sisters'.

Source: Highways and Hedges (August 1891) p.146

Sister Freer gave an account of her eight months at Hackney Road Wesleyan Chapel where she started a Ladies Sunday afternoon Bible Class and a Society Class which was 'composed of those who had "ceased to meet", some who had formerly attended other places, some who had been converted, and visitors who have not yet formally joined us'. District visiting in the homes of children gave opportunity for arranging a mothers' meeting, which proved to be a great success, leading to two baptismal services for about 20 children. She spoke at Band of Hope Meetings and 'also occasionally conducted services in the chapel'.[3]

---

2. *Highways and Hedges* (hereafter *HH*) (August 1891) pp.145-46
3. *HH* (September 1891) pp.178-79

Work at Hackney Road   **Sister Freer**

Another woman in my class who has been converted, said that in the past she would have nothing to do with 'religious saints' as she called God's people, but after my first visit she counted the days that would elapse before I called again. . . .

When inviting the husband of one of our mothers to a service, he said, 'Well, Miss, you have been so kind and friendly to my wife that I'll come, if only to please you.'

Source: Highways and Hedges (September 1891) pp.178-79

That the work at Hackney Road was not confined to women is shown by Sister Charity's report that her evening evangelistic meeting for men was well attended, that the change in many of the men had had great effect on their families and indeed a number of them had undertaken to visit other men. The men had also organised a tea, invited their wives to it, and altogether a hundred people sat down to the meal.[4]

Sister Hilda was working at the Leysian Hall Mission, which she described as being 'in the midst of a poor and densely populated neighbourhood' where she found that there was much to be done: 'district visiting, sick nursing, medical mission and Sunday School, Band of Hope Meetings and, last but not least, the Enquiry Room and the Methodist Class Meeting'. The work was hard, but encouraging and opportunity was found to tell 'of the Saviour's love and power to save'. The Leysian Mission deaconesses regarded their district visiting as very important because there they could try to improve the home conditions of the families. Another interesting part of their work was the Medical Mission which was held every Tuesday and Friday afternoon and where advice, medicine and a visit, if necessary, could be obtained for one penny. A half-hour service was held and many who came for medical advice or treatment were converted.

---

4. *HH* (June 1892) pp.119-20

Sunday at the Leysian Mission　　　　　**Sister Hilda**

We commence in the afternoon, for it is arranged that we shall meet together for public worship at the Morning Service at The Children's Home Chapel, in order that none of us may teach others, while yet ourselves untaught. In the afternoon my Sunday School Class is one of boys, numbering ten scholars. School over, I visit my tract district, and then after a short rest, we take part in an open-air meeting, followed by the evening service, where many opportunities are afforded of welcoming weary men and women who gladly come to our bright, happy service. Our work in itself is a real training for even larger service.

Source: Highways and Hedges (October 1891) p.200

Sister Karis was attached to the Methodist Church at Lady Margaret Road, London, N.W. which she described as being 'in a flourishing condition' and so her work was mainly visiting and assisting at the church's many meetings. Each Monday there was a large 'Slate Club' for men and women and visiting its members was her special responsibility. Soon after her arrival she went to see 'a poor man' who was very ill, but because of her efforts he was cured and converted. She wrote:

> Poor fellow! he was exceedingly ignorant of all about God. His great trouble now was his wife, who had always treated him badly, and who in addition to being a *drunkard,* was strongly opposed to religion. One day as he and I knelt in prayer he prayed for his wife . . . 'O Lord, she has bin a sore fret to me these five and twenty years, I've tried to make some'at out of her, but I couldn't; Sister says Thee can, so Thee'd best try Thee hand on her, I donna mind Thee trying, and I shallna mind if Thee doesna manage after all, for she's a real bad un.

Later, being asked how things were going, he said 'that he thought the Lord was managing the job very well'.[5] There are many such stories – of poverty and illness – often caused by drunkenness and unemployment. Sister Rita commented on the latter, 'They don't want charity, but work. I have been trying to get employment for them, but meet with so many discouragements. Who has work, or

---

5. *HH* (February 1893) p.39

will make work for people like these.' Similar reports are given by deaconesses working in Norwich, Leicester and elsewhere, but of particular interest is the work of Sister Thirza Masters whose handwritten diary covering the years 1892-1911 survives. In it she recorded some of the incidents she encountered while working in Truro (1892-93); Cardiff (1893-97); Camborne (1897-99); Wolverhampton (September 1899-January 1900); The Leysian Mission (1900-04); resting because of health and home claims (1908-10) and it closes with her time in Hednesford, Staffordshire (1910-11). In Truro and Camborne she delighted in being in Methodist towns, but in Cardiff, particularly in the Docks area, she was deeply saddened by much drunkenness and great poverty. Sister Thirza was especially concerned for the young girls who were in danger of falling into prostitution, but, although she gave them as much help and support she could, in many cases it was all in vain. There is a telling entry for 10th November 1894 which gives some idea of the strain of the work:

> 10th Missed train to Penarth, walked through boisterous wind & rain, arriving in a not very prim condition at my friends house. What a relief to body & mind, – to sit around the fire & chat with genial friends! I have been taken out of myself, & come back to the dreary Docks refreshed.[6]

As soon as she arrived in Wolverhampton Thirza had to give the address at the Floral Service during the Harvest Festival

celebrations on 3rd September 1899. Again, she was faced with extreme poverty and had to act as nurse and cleaner for several very sick members of the church. Then, just as she had got to grips with her task in Wolverhampton, on 31st January she was: 'Ordered to take an appointment at London by Dr. Gregory'. Unfortunately she wrote little, just 17 pages covering 1900-03, about her time in the Leysian Mission. By now

Sister Thirza Masters,
Church and Circuit Deaconess

---

6. MS Diary of Sister Thirza Masters

Thirza's health was giving cause for concern and she left, on 1st July 1904, to go home to Evesham for a three-month rest, but after consulting a specialist she was diagnosed with 'one of the worst cases of Nervous Prostration' and the 11th found her in the General Hospital in Birmingham in a 'Private Ward. Here I spent a Solitary existence for 9 weeks – not permitted to see a soul save Doctor & Nurses & no conversation with either. Neither did anyone stay in my room longer than was necessary . . . God only knows what that awful loneliness was to me. Sometimes I felt I should go mad.' She described her feelings of isolation, her diet, treatment, the staff and her weight – she had been only 6 stone 9lbs when she entered the hospital. Eventually on 10th September she was allowed to go home and, although there are no entries, she must have been well enough to have resumed her work at the Leysian Mission until 11th July 1908 when she again had to take a break for health reasons and then for 'home claims'. However, on 1st September 1910 as her sister had come home from 'S. Army Work I am able to take up harness again'. So she went to Hednesford in Staffordshire a 'Mining District – practically a new town, more like a large village' for about two years. The diary ends rather abruptly in January 1911, when health and home claims seem to have forced her retirement from the active work.[7] This first-hand account gives a graphic account of the strains and stresses of deaconess work, her dedication which had caused, in the doctor's words, 'damage (to be) done by continuing on at work in an unfit condition, that could never be undone' and also a rather terrifying picture of medical treatment at the time!

The following report is interesting for two reasons: one, it shows that the deaconesses were willing to try all means to reach people and secondly, that the local minister, William Bradfield, later to be the second Warden, was very supportive of the Institute well before he was officially connected with it. Sister Sylvia Pryce-Jones was working in Leicester in 1894 where she comments, 'There is much distress . . . and our Soup Kitchen is in full swing. God put it into my heart to have a series of Lantern Services . . . We have had the first, and . . . those who are difficult to attract to any place of worship (came). Mr. Bradfield spoke to

---

7. MS Diary of Sister Thirza Masters; *Stations of the Wesley Deaconesses* (hereafter *WDO Stations*) 1892-1961. They were at times entitled *Lists of Appointments*.

them simply and beautifully, and Mr. Alcock lent him his lantern and himself exhibited the slides.'[8]

Sister Elise Searle, who was in charge of the branch house in Norwich, was elected to the Board of Guardians and was able to carry out her Christian service in a different way. She described the Board Meetings as resembling 'miniature House of Commons' and said that, as she did not want to favour either the Progressives or Conservatives, she sat as an Independent. She visited the workhouse and was able to institute various changes for the inmates such as an adequate supply of towels, brushes and combs and better meals.

When Sister Edith Booth was sent to Dublin the work there proved very different and also difficult because of the influence of the Roman Catholic Church. Most of the people with whom she worked lived in tenement blocks where she found two families, numbering 14, living in one room, while it was common to find families of 'seven, eight or nine living and sleeping in the one room'. She also got the impression that 'there was a great tendency to go about from one place of worship to another'. She felt that there was a great restlessness and love of change among the Irish and this, along with much intemperance, presented the greatest difficulty.

The deaconess working at Acton Green in 1898-99 found that the children of working mothers were 'often left in undesirable places'. So she, the minister and some friends decided 'to start a creche'. They received financial encouragement and in June were able to rent a house, from a Wesleyan landlord, just four doors from the Mission church. Furniture and linen was acquired and a lady 'volunteered for a very small salary to act as nurse'. The creche opened with three children, but by January 1900 14 children were being cared for each day.

8. *HH* (May 1894) pp.98-99

The Acton Green Creche

Our work does not tend to pauperise, but to help a hardworking class. The mothers have been accustomed to pay 8d. or 9d. per day, exclusive of food, and often the children were wholly uncared for. We charge 6d. per day, and provide suitable food, and the children are under the constant care of a Christian nurse. Their changed surroundings soon show the effect. Instead of singing the low songs of the public house, they learn to sing and to enjoy our simple Gospel hymns. The mothers greatly appreciate the blessings of the creche, and by means of it we are enabled to reach them in a way that would otherwise be impossible. Several of the mothers now attend our Sunday evening services.

Source: Highways and Hedges (January 1900) p.21

Another deaconess in London gave a very brief but telling account of the life of one family, living in 'a clean, but scantily furnished room', where a mother supported herself and six children by 'brush-making'. She was paid a halfpenny for a hundred knobs of hair fastened into a brush. For each brush, which took about three-quarters of an hour to make, she earned 'a penny farthing'.[9]

Lucy Hawken in Leicester wrote about how they had started a fund to provide a week's holiday at Mablethorpe in June 1899:

> During the month we had fifty guests, each of whom spent a week, and it is difficult to say who enjoyed it most. Tired mothers, some of whom told us they had *never* had such a complete rest and holiday before; madcap maidens, whose frolics were difficult to keep within bounds, and whose exuberance of animal life and spirit did us all good; and staid gentlemen, for this year our *clientele* included two of these, all joined in the glad chorus of gratitude for a happy holiday, and we felt that He who came to give life and give it more abundantly, was the companion and giver of our joy.[10]

---

9. *HH* (February 1900) p.94
10. *HH* (October 1900) p.236

Perhaps realizing that much deaconess work seemed to concentrate on the women and girls, the Sisters at Mewburn House decided to have a social for some of the boys from the Bonner Street Boys' Club. Although, at first, a little overawed at finding themselves in such a large house, the boys were soon playing a game of Parlour Football with their hostesses – with the honours equal at eight goals each! – and were very loath to go home at 9.30 p.m.

One of the stories told at the 1901 Convocation illustrates the dangers faced by young girls. Sister E. (either Ethel Harris in St. Helen's or Edith Booth in Dublin) had gone down to the seaport (either Liverpool or Dublin) to see off a young girl, who had been in her class, and was going abroad to seek work. At first, all seemed well as she, along with 12 others, were travelling in the care of 'a respectable-looking elderly woman, who . . . had promised them good situations, with high wages', but somehow the deaconess' suspicions were aroused. So, as soon as the boat had sailed, she went to the Police Station and told of her concern. The Police Chief wired the ship's destination where detectives met the ship and arrested the woman, who was well known to them, as a 'procuress'.[11]

In January 1902 a deaconess gave details of her week's timetable:

Sunday –	10.00	S. School
	11.00	Divine Service
	1.30	Take it in turns to get a dinner for a poor member
	3.00	Society Class
	6.00	Prayer Meeting
	6.30	(In turns) Children's Mission
	8.00	After-meeting in Church
Monday –	10.00-12.30	Visiting
	2.30-4.15	Mothers' Meeting
	6.30	Junior Class
	7.45	Women's Own Meeting
	9.00	Numerous Committees

---

11. *HH* (August 1901) p.171

Tuesday –	10.00-1.00	Visiting
	3.00	Visiting
	6.30	Children's Service
	7.30	Band of Love Prayer Meeting
	7.45-9.45	Factory Girls' Club
Wednesday –	10.00-1.00	Visiting
	7.00	Band of Hope
	8.00	Guild
Thursday –	10.00-1.00	Visiting
	3.00	Visiting
	7.00	Senior Society Class
	8.00	Prayer Meeting
Friday –	10.00-1.00	Visiting
	3.00	Visiting
	6.30	Visiting
	8.00	Class (Senior)
Saturday (Free) –	8.00	Pleasant Saturday Evening[12]

Each day was fully occupied! Not only was there little time for rest and relaxation, but little for any further study or training: it is easy to understand why a more organized and extensive training was required.

Sister Kate Christie, stationed at Scarborough in 1903-04, described an '*all-night*' visit from the navy and the welcome prepared by the local church:

> We got fifty beds and blankets from the Barracks . . . the men just rolled themselves up in their blankets and 'cuddled doon'. We arranged to give them coffee and bread and butter at night, and coffee, tea, and sandwiches in the morning before going back to the ship. We had *no* idea as to the number of men to expect . . .
>
> Our workers (mostly young men) met at 10.30 p.m. on Saturday night, and went down the principal street and on the pier 'fishing' (for men). They kept bringing them in, and we gave them coffee &c., and a

---

12. *FL* (January 1902) p.9

warm welcome. At 1.30 a.m., all was quiet, and we had 88 men, sleeping in our large Schoolroom . . .

I was up and ready when the whistle blew at 5.30 a.m., and in half an hour or so all the men were off the premises. Before they left us, one of their number, an officer, made a speech, thanking Queen Street friends for all their kindness.[13]

Many of the London Missions, including the South London Mission at Bermondsey, made full use of the Wesley Deaconesses and many stories of changed lives and dedicated service are recorded in the pages of *Flying Leaves*.

Men's Meeting

It was very encouraging to hear one of my members say: "We have never had such a happy Christmas since our marriage as this one has been, for since my husband came to your meeting, and then got converted, our home has been changed. He always made fun of me going to meetings, but now he goes more than I do."

Source: Flying Leaves (January 1905) p.183

Sara Weddell wrote of her experiences in the County Council Lodging House in London. There were 14 lodging houses within a stone's throw of Great Queen's Street Chapel and they were notorious for swearing and drinking. In spite of being warned off she went to hold a service in one and, although 'some of the young ladies who went with us were in tears and said they could never go again', her service was appreciated and there was no more trouble. In fact she became known to the men as 'Nurse Sara' and they came to regard the Wesleyan services as 'Our services'. One day she found a tract giving details of the lodging house in which it stated 'Sister Sara, from a neighbouring Chapel, is very popular, and her presence always increases the audience.' She went on to explain how she managed to get to the lodging house fairly often, 'I go to Chapel and see the people in, then to the lodging house to

---

13. *FL* (January 1904) p.13

hold the service, and back to Chapel in time to see the people out.'[14]

Another problem one deaconess found and tried to resolve was that of an elderly unmarried couple who could not afford to marry. She took the woman to the Registrar to 'get the notice in', measured her finger for a ring and undertook to get a 'bit of a coat' – 'a fashionable one' for the man. The date was set for three weeks ahead, with the minister and chapel steward promising to conduct the ceremony without charge. The Society Steward got them a ring and the deaconess obtained a 'whole suit, "fashionable ones" and a bonnet for the old lady. So the couple were married on 2nd January 1905 and 'Their gratitude and thanks were very touching, and I have wondered since how many are living together too poor to marry, and no one to undertake for them.'[15]

Sing a Sermon [Tried by the young folk of the Albert Hall Mission, Nottingham, under the leadership of 'Sister Minnie'.]

Sing a sermon. A sermon may be sung as well as preached. Sometimes the people prefer the sermon sung. Many a one can sing a sermon who cannot preach one. And twenty people can sing the same sermon at the same time, though only one can preach it. Yet more, the singing preachers may all be women and children, and can do without a man at all. A group of earnest souls with sweet voices can go into a back street and begin singing. Nobody will stone them or curse them, and everybody in the streets will listen. The women will come to the doors, windows will be thrown up to make hearing easier, and the Gospel will fly to many on the wings of song.

Source: *Flying Leaves* (January 1906) p.12

Eastbrook Hall, Bradford, had four deaconesses attached to it and the work of the Mission was extensive. Many women's meetings, much visiting, including prison cells and lodging houses, and rescue work filled the deaconesses' days. Both the men's 'Brotherhood' and the Women's Meeting were the largest

---

14. *FL* (February 1905) pp.198-99
15. *FL* (May 1905) p.255

in the country. Tuesdays found one or two of the deaconesses in one of the woollen mills, holding 25 minute services for the girls during their dinner hour. Another feature of the Eastbrook Hall work was the summer open-air services: a portable pulpit, like a waggon with four wheels and rubber tyres, no sides, but a book rest, two large carriage lamps and a harmonium, usually played by one of the deaconesses, was made and pulled to the chosen site. Often a cornet player added to 'the brightness and carrying power' and a crowd soon gathered.

Lizzie Cumberland in Stratford, London, was very concerned about the local factory girls, including those working at the local brewery, who were such a rough lot that she was advised to get some policemen near at hand when she arranged a meeting for them. However, she 'conscripted' the superintendent minister, the circuit steward and a few others to help. The doors opened at 7.30 p.m. and a noisy crowd flocked in:

> The room was decorated . . . 'My! ain't we going to have a time?' 'Not 'alf,' was the reply from somewhere across the room. We had a fine musical programme. 'By Jove, this licks the Empire' – such was another exclamation. During the evening our plans for the session were disclosed. We should teach dressmaking, cooking, nursing, and musical drill. Up to Christmas we had some excellent meetings for three hours every Monday evening: a busier hive could not have been found throughout Stratford.[16]

The More Unusual Enterprises

One of the more unusual accounts shows, along with a picture, how deaconesses could minister 'in fields of toil, outside the reach of regular husbandmen'. By virtue of their work it was difficult for men in occupations like the police, the railway and the fire service to get to church regularly:

> Not far from Mewburn House is a large and nobly equipped fire station. From the conning tower, watch is kept over a wide district, against the fire demon.

---

16. *FL* (December 1906) pp.181-82

At a moment's notice, night or day, Sabbath or week-day, the corps of the fire fighters have to be ready for the struggle . . . they are not irreligious. Their hearts respond to the truth, especially when it is presented with kindness and sympathy. Subject to a break-up of the congregation at any second's notice, simple services may be held, and are welcome by the men. Our Deaconesses are reckoned prime friends of these brave fellows: and their unpretentious ministry is far more welcome than anything more imposing could be.[17]

Then there were devotional meetings organised by Dorothy Hindle in Wigan for the members of the Brass Band at their request and meetings for the 'Ballet Girls' in Leeds arranged by Emily Martin.

'Ballet Girls' in Leeds   **Sister Emily M. Martin**

I well remember, soon after I commenced my work in Leeds, being asked to make arrangements for a tea for the Ballet Girls, and we gave them two during that season.

Last winter . . . I asked permission of the managers to allow me to meet the girls in the dressing rooms. I thought it would . . . give me an insight into the life of the girls behind the scenes . . . Up to this time I was, practically speaking, ignorant of this kind of life, and had never been inside a theatre in my life . . .

I have been several times since, and have been cheered by the knowledge that the girls were glad to see me there. I have wondered again and again whether it is possible for girls to live lives of high morality under such conditions . . .

Source: Flying Leaves (November 1907) pp.154-55

Sister Edith Wrench delighted in her fortnightly meeting with the Caister Fisher and Lifeboat men where, for obvious reasons, the attendance fluctuated, but where there was always plenty of singing. As she comments, 'In the main they are a class untouched by any religious workers.' This shows again how the deaconesses were going into new fields of service.

---

17. *HH* (September 1898) p.212

Yet another unexpected venue was at the Derby, where Nan Keers found herself with a group of helpers from Stepney Central Hall, singing the Gospel to the racegoers. The year was 1913, the suffragettes were active, and Emily Davison was killed when she threw herself under the King's horse. Nan referred to this incident and gave a vivid description of the scene on Epsom Downs, as, dressed in her Wesley Deaconess uniform, she stood on a chair and 'sang for hours and hours', accompanied by a concertina:

> We left the Stepney Central Hall in a motor car, on every side of which were emblazoned texts . . . such as 'I came not to call the righteous but sinners to Repentance.' 'He is able to succour those that are tempted.' . . .
>
> It was my first experience of a Race Meeting. How is it possible to describe adequately that motley crowd of people of all classes, estimated at more than a quarter of a million – from the King and Queen in the Royal Box to the tattered gipsy children turning somersaults for coppers? The memory of the sight will live with me all my life. Sin abounded, yet we were confident that 'Grace did abound more exceedingly', and to one and all as they gathered round our stand, and passed in rapid kaleidoscopic variety, we declared the Saviour's boundless Love.
>
> Amid all the distractions and worldliness of the course, we were upheld by the thought of praying friends at home . . .
>
> We made it a point while the actual races were being run, to kneel down on the grass and commit ourselves and all the vast multitude to God, and strange were our feelings as we lifted our hearts in intercession, whilst, near by, the thunder of the horses' hoofs beat past us. Truly we felt like Christian in 'Vanity Fair'.
>
> When each race was over we started singing and got the people to stand and listen. Then came our opportunity to proclaim salvation for lost men and women; and we feel sure that by our efforts much good seed was sown, though we shall never know the result until Christ comes to judge the world.[18]

18. *FL* (August 1913) p.118

It does not take much imagination to appreciate the courage and faith of this little band from the East London Mission singing among the great crowds on Derby Day.

The Deaconess as Nurse

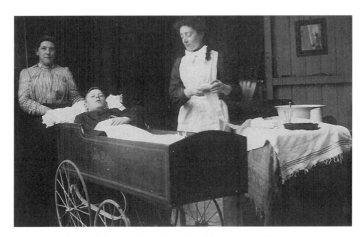

Sister Marian Braithwaite, Deaconess Nurse

By the very nature of their work those deaconesses with qualifications or a special interest in nursing often had to deal with infectious illnesses to which some succumbed. For example, Lucy Hawken, who had been working in Maidstone, Kent, during a typhoid epidemic in 1898 fell victim to the fever herself. In the 1899 *Highways and Hedges* she gave an account of conditions in the town at the height of the outbreak:

> The intense sadness and overwhelming sense of sorrow that appeared to brood over the town was depressing . . . the little one could do for those who were its victims was gratefully accepted . . . My own work lay almost entirely among our own people, and I soon found that night duty would in many cases relieve tired relatives, and prove the most acceptable help I could render. On turning to my diary I find that I stayed twenty-three nights, paid seventy-three visits, and did various other fragments of work as I was able, during the time I was at work in Maidstone from 22nd October to 28th November.'[19]

---

19. *HH* (March 1899) p.68

Two other deaconesses contracted scarlet fever and diphtheria. A deaconess, working in a suburban area, wrote:

> I find my knowledge of nursing invaluable in my visiting. One woman said when I called, 'Oh, Sister, if I had known you were coming to-day I should not have taken my little boy to the doctor's last night.' It is a joy to have their confidence, but at the same time I don't feel equal or desirous of taking the doctor's place.[20]

and another commented:

> I returned from my holiday about a month ago, and since then I have been very busy. One case especially has taken up much time and thought. The poor woman is dying with cancer, the father in the asylum, and there was no one to care for the four children. The 'Home' has taken three and the eldest has gone to an aunt's. The whole of the nursing, home and children has been on my shoulders for a month. The mother I took to the Infirmary last Wednesday. How thankful I am that I have been able to help this poor sister. But, above all, I believe she has found her Saviour and is now trusting in Him.[21]

Nursing in Birmingham, 1902   **Sister Erica Marley**

We are well supplied in Birmingham with hospitals and dispensaries . . . but there are often many who . . . find it more convenient to come to me. . . . If they go to the hospital it means waiting three or four hours each visit, and consequent loss of much work and wage . . . Or, children get burnt, scalded or cut . . . both parents go to work, and can ill afford to lose the time . . . the little ones come to me . . . During the last year over 200 were helped in this way . . .

Source: Flying Leaves (June 1902) p.106

---

20. *HH* (October 1900) p.236
21. *FL* (January 1902) p.10

A probationer deaconess working in a large hospital found when she went on night duty that there were six empty beds as patients had been discharged during the day. However, it turned out to be anything but a quiet night as admission after admission filled up the beds and at the end of her shift she commented:

> Never was I so thankful I was of a calm nature. Had I been excitable, I think I should have lost all self-control . . . I retired to my room, and I can tell no one how I felt. The best illustration of my feeling was, when a firework has been fizzing, then goes bang! and all is silent and over. I felt really *flat* . . . The next night, as the Sister came round . . . she said, 'Your beds are all occupied, so you need not fear another night like the last'; and said, 'I think you are capable, after last night, of anything.'[22]

Slum, Prison and Rescue Work

Deaconesses were appointed to circuits to assist the minister with work, particularly among the women and children. In many cases they were practically acting as social workers, but were also able to do nursing and evangelistic work. Often their appointments were in the larger missions or town circuits, though they also worked in rural situations where the minister could only visit occasionally. Another aspect of the city circuit and mission work, especially in the large industrial cities, was visiting and helping in slum areas. Sister Mildred Homer told the 1901 Convocation of her morning in the Old Town Mission in Hull:

> Rise at 6.20; walk through the cold about two miles to the Mission Room. There, amid surroundings of bread, jam, cocoa, soup and dirt, she feeds starving and clamouring children of the very poorest class, in an atmosphere into which she would not send her worst enemy! Then home again to breakfast at 9.30. Out again almost at once to return to the Hall, to deal out soup to the poor women for their dinner. It depends on the size of the oftimes strange vessels they bring as to how much soup they get, or, as Sister Mildred put it: 'They are supposed to be served

---

22. *FL* (March 1904) pp.40-41

according to the family; really, it is according to the faith!' She told her story of hard work, lasting until 9.30 at night with many flashes of humour, which relieved some of the sombre pictures she drew. We scarcely knew, towards the end of her address, whether to be depressed or gladdened at her story; but she herself spoke so earnestly of the compensations to all the unpleasantness of work in the slums . . .[23]

There is an interesting account of the problems in 'a manufacturing village', which was probably Hinckley in Leicestershire. Having pointed out that the country is 'delightful' in summer, but in winter the country worker has to come home from work by walking or cycling along dark, muddy, slushy roads the writer continues:

Life . . . is very different from what is ideally thought of as living in the country. Here we have the surrounding of the country with the work, and none of the conveniences of the town. The people work in large factories in the winter from eight o'clock in the morning to seven o'clock or half past at night with intervals for meals, and in the summer from six-thirty in the morning until half past five in the evening. The women also go to work so visiting in the homes is a difficulty, especially as the housework has to be done in the evening . . .

There are the same temptations to materialism, immorality and drink in the manufacturing village as in the town. The great temptation is to make as much money as possible, and, as life is so monotonous, spend it on dress and pleasure. Accordingly on the Saturday afternoon holiday, there is a general rush to the nearest town.

The Deaconess coming to work in one of these centres for the first time finds the work and conditions altogether different from those to which she has been accustomed. But the work needs to be done, and it is better to save people from ever entering the slum, than to rescue them from the slum.

---

23. *HH* (June 1901) p.139

She pointed out the need for Girls' Parlours and also the difficulties – water had to fetched from a pump in a bucket, kettle boiled on a stove and washing up done in the bucket or a tin bowl, to say nothing of bad weather! Then, although one might have thought country life would be healthier it was not so with consumption, scarlet fever and typhoid common, probably due to the long hours worked, inadequate clean water supply and poor sanitation. She concluded that the work was not exciting, but there was a wide sphere of usefulness and people in the village needed spiritual help and uplifting just as much as those in the town.[24]

Much of the what the 1902-03 Report called 'rescue' work had to do with intemperance, poverty, unemployment, poor housing, too many children and ill-health and deaconesses met all these conditions. They were often the only source of help for some and the sight of their distinctive dress brought a measure of hope, thus bearing out Stephenson's belief that a uniform served a vital purpose. One deaconess visited Holloway prison and spent several hours in the police courts supporting a drunken woman who was eventually committed to 'an inebriates' home' for three years, under the Habitual Drunkards Act, where the deaconess visited her and wrote to her weekly. Another deaconess in Leigh visited an injured drunkard in the workhouse. He was horrified to see her and even more so when she suggested going onto his ward to talk to the other men, saying 'we are all past redemption', but as she was leaving he asked her for her New Testament. A few weeks later, after she had addressed a meeting in the Market Place, he came up and told her that the other 50 men in the ward had asked him to read it to them and had stopped all their cursing and swearing.[25]

In Prison – M. G.   **Sister Maude Gent in Hull**

Place: The waiting room of a prison in a Yorkshire city.

Time: Sunday 4 p.m.

Occupant: A Wesley Deaconess waiting for admittance to the cells!

The Sergeant was long in coming to admit the visitor. She whiled away her time by counting the long rows of tiled bricks of which the

---

24. *FL* (April 1912) pp.54-55
25. *FL* (February 1902) p.25; (November 1912) p.161

walls were composed. She counted them singly; then in fours –
'This year, next year, sometime, never!'

The door opened: the voice of the Constable was heard, 'Sister, you
may come in now, but she doesn't want to see you. It isn't your
fault. You see it's this way,' continued the Sergeant, 'She's too
ashamed.' This was good news. She had been in prison monthly
for nearly two years: the Sister had helped her again and again,
and at last the woman had begun to feel ashamed. Come into the
cell and look at her. A woman of good education, forty years of
age, well built, but saturated with drink and sunk into depths of sin.
Is there any hope? There is an old word to be told once more.
'Thy sins which are many are all forgiven, go in peace.' Like Mary
of old she listens and says, 'Can he forgive me?' And she was
answered.

Source: *The Agenda* (May 1924) p.22-33

Lottie Hudd was a Prison Visitor at Holloway Prison, but she
realised that the scope of her work was limited as she could only
visit individuals and only those who were non-conformists,
whereas an 'Instructress' had 'a much wider field for service'.
The opportunity was offered and accepted, and so for more than
two years a deaconess gave weekly instruction in handcraft, which
meant that

> the women may purchase from their own earnings the
> things they themselves make and may send them out
> to their children or to friends. Other things are sold at
> the Annual Sale held at the Prison, and the proceeds
> go to their own branch of the Discharged Prisoners'
> Aid Society. It was a wise and happy decision which
> made it possible for the women to work for their own
> interests.

This work had been appreciated so much by the prison authorities
that the Deputy Governor wrote asking if there were any other
suitable teachers who would be willing to take classes at
Holloway. The Governor asked if Sister Lottie knew of any
'Christian girls with a sense of vocation who would like to train as
officers'.[26]

---

26. *The Wesley Deaconess Magazine* (hereafter *WDMag.*) (November 1950)
pp.6-7

Emily Bird wrote, in 1913, that nearly three years ago she had been asked to take charge of a small Rescue Home in Bournemouth. She recognised that not many people would think a place like Bournemouth would have need for such a Home, but one only had to visit the public gardens between 8.00 p.m. and 9.30 p.m. to realise that many girls, who were chiefly domestic servants, were in danger of becoming prostitutes. The girls were taken into the Home and trained to do housework so that they could obtain good situations, but the Rescue Work did not stop there, for the girls kept in touch with the Home after they left. Florence Archer was also doing Rescue Work in a Home in Birmingham, where some girls were taken off the streets and others sent by the Police courts. Again she kept in touch with the girls when they left and counted it a special 'joy and privilege to stand by one of our girls a few days ago at her Baptismal service'.[27]

Visiting and Meetings

However, apart from these more specialised types of work, the day-to-day district visiting and taking of meetings continued. A deaconess in the Midlands reported:

> We have been very busy since September. Many times work done in fear and trembling has brought forth grand results. The Gospel Social is growing. We have now a membership of over one hundred. A few weeks ago nine of the mothers took entire management of the meeting; three gave brief addresses, solos were sung by three, two recited, and one presided. It was quite a red-letter day in their lives, they never having done anything of the kind before. A savings bank is held in connection with our meeting, also a visiting committee, the visitors having been selected from the meeting. This has been a great blessing keeping many interested and busy.

and

> Our Mission Band is doing a glorious work. Since May (when the Mission Band was organised) we have not missed one Sunday evening going out into

---

27. *FL* (May 1914) pp.69-70, 73

the open air. The membership is now one hundred. This winter a Fairy Organ had been purchased; also two beautiful large lamps, which are carried on two long poles . . . we now get crowded congregations. Sunday evening it was my appointment; a large number stayed to the prayer meeting, at which we had nine conversions, afterwards sixty were seeking reconsecration.[28]

Another report from 1902, this time from the Bishop Street Circuit, Leicester, where, in an effort to get women and girls off the streets, a Girls' Guild was started on Wednesday evenings when cookery, and nursing courses with practical demonstrations alternated with social games, dressmaking and doll dressing competitions. Mothers' Meetings, missionary meetings, Wesley Guild activities, cottage services, Workers' Leagues and sales of work to raise money to help the needy all had their place too.

Jumping a decade there are reports from the Bolton, Wigan and Bradford areas. Many are concerned with the evil of drink and its effect on family life – unemployment, poverty, cruelty, destitution – and how the deaconesses faced danger in order to protect the women and children from drunken fathers or to rescue children from women who had fallen prey to the bottle. Many women found a few hours' relief from their family problems in attending Mothers' or Women's Meetings or Pleasant Afternoon gatherings. Although the deaconesses' work was largely with the women and children in a number of cases the change in them rubbed off on the men and so the whole family situation was improved.

Teaching would be part and parcel of the deaconesses' life as they took Sunday School, Society and Bible Classes and ran all the various Women's and Girls' meetings and probably gave ordinary school lessons at times. For example, Sister Edith Passmore in Sheffield found that some people would not come to her class because they could not read, so this decided her to start a 'reading class' for adults every Wednesday night an hour before the Society Class.

---

28. *FL* (March 1902) p.43

Many of the deaconesses found themselves in special mission situations, where not only did they face the same problems as their colleagues in the circuits, but had a wider rôle in trying to bring people into the church by visiting and organising special services and visitations. Much work done, through personal contact and helping families in time of sickness, bereavement or difficulty, persuaded a member to attend a service and then to bring others of the family along too. Missions were held in a variety of places, for example, – 'We meet in a large mess-room, lent . . . by the proprietor of some large iron works . . . the room seats about 400 and is generally three parts full . . . this mission was a new departure in a very needy neighbourhood . . . we began a small Sunday School, gathering the children in from the streets. We now have more than sixty scholars . . . we began a weeknight service . . . a weekly prayer meeting.' But the work was not restricted to towns, as the outlying villages, farms and cottages were visited and society classes formed.[29]

One of the deaconesses, appointed to the Mantle Memorial Schools in Leicester, described it as a comparatively new Mission situated in one of the most densely populated areas with the people belonging mainly to the artisan class, but added that there had been a great response. As well as helping with all the usual mission activities she had managed to develop close contact with the girls who attended her class.

Mission Work in Leicester

During the summer months I have taken the members of my class for rambles in the country; this has been a source of great enjoyment. One gets to know and understand them better, for it gives the opportunity of a chat about their homes and factory life. Most of them work in either the boot or hosiery factories. These girls need to be very soundly converted to be able to stand all the scoffs and jeers to which they are exposed every day. It is often most pathetic to hear them in our Class pray for grace and strength to keep true.

Source: *Highways and Hedges* (March 1899) p.70

---

29. *HH* (July 1894) pp.138-39; *FL* (February 1902) pp.24, 26-27

In April 1907 Huddersfield Mission opened a Women's Home to help women and girls and it proved to be a very necessary refuge for many in all sorts of distress. Much of the work was confidential, but a few stories tell of helping orphaned young girls, drunken women, the homeless, young unmarried mothers, deserted wives and prostitutes. Sister Emmeline Downing painted pictures of some of the work done by the Women's Home:

> Let me contrast two pictures in closing, and ask you if you think our work is really worth the doing:
>
> I.   The Workhouse Ward! A girl sent there by the police. Such a weak, frightened ignorant lassie. Next week she is to be charged with manslaughter. But listen now as she shudders and wails, 'Oh! I didn't kill my baby! I never killed my little baby! I was so frightened. Do somebody help me.'
>
> II.   One of the bedrooms in the Home! By the side of one of the beds is a little white crib, and the mother of the baby bending over it.
>
> 'Not asleep, dear?'
>
> 'No. I'm just praying to be made good, I must be good now Sister, for baby's sake, and because you have helped me.'[30]

Christmas 1910 looked like being a miserable one in one of the large Missions, situated in one of the poorest districts of London, as there were no funds available to help the local slum dwellers. Much prayer was offered and it was decided to try to give a small parcel of groceries to the poorest members of the Women's Meeting and have faith that they would be provided. Next evening the Boy Scouts of the First Hatcham Troop, belonging to Aske's School, Pepys Road, offered gifts for 18 families. The deaconess comments:

> This meant a good deal, for, besides the time spent in making up the large parcels, the boys themselves pulled a heavy waggon, for an hour, in a misty drizzle, in order to bring their goods to the Mission, and alth' the district was quite unknown to most of

---

30. *FL* (November 1909) p.161, (December 1910) pp.176-79

them, they delivered the parcels at the various homes in some of the poorest streets in London. We saw the lads at 9.45 p.m., ready for their hour's tramp home again – a tired, mud-splashed, weary-looking lot, but with radiant faces, for they had been experiencing the joy that comes from 'giving', and had done better even than they promised, having taken parcels to twenty-three homes, instead of eighteen.[31]

At Carver Street, Sheffield, Sister Clara Nicholls, noticing women and girls standing in the streets in all weathers during their lunch hour, realised their plight, and the church agreed to set aside a room for their use at that time, so that they could eat their food in a safe place. For the price of one penny per week they were supplied with milk, hot water, teapots, cups and saucers so that they could make themselves tea or cocoa. Magazines, papers and table games were provided to encourage the girls to stay rather than wander the streets till it was time to go back to work. About 30 girls used these facilities and when any were sick they were visited.[32]

Mabel Fielder describes Saturday nights in the Attercliffe Road area of Sheffield when the deaconesses visited the local public houses 'offering friendship and leaving invitations'. At 'turning out time' they attempted to help those in need. To people who queried whether this work was worthwhile, they replied, 'We believe that the time has come when we must take our message to the people and not wait for them to come to us. As the people are to be found in their hundreds in the public houses, we go to them to offer them Christ and friendship in his Name.'[33]

In 1929 the Rev. Dr. W. Russell Maltby, the Warden at this time, pinpointed an important dilemma which faces all who serve, not just the Wesley Deaconesses, when he wrote:

> I find myself wondering more and yet more at the courage and patience with which our Sisters are facing difficulties and discouragements, and at the bewildering variety of the things they are expected to do. They must take services, preach sermons, address

---

31. *FL* (February 1911) pp.22-24
32. *FL* (April 1913) p.54
33. *The Agenda* (December 1928) pp.6-7

women's meetings, superintend Sunday Schools, teach scholars, lead classes, captain guides, visit the sick, sit up with the dying, make beds, smooth pillows, companion the lonely, haunt the prison gates, take drunk people home, raise money, run Jumble Sales, oil the ecclesiastical machine, and know everybody, as well as, read, think, pray and keep their peace of mind. All needing to be done? Yes, and it is weakness to grouse about it. Yet I am in a strait betwixt two. I believe we must not decline the tasks of service in all their variety, and we must do what we can to fill empty lives with rational and healthy interests of many kinds. But often those who are busy with these activities are half dismayed with the fear that the real message is not being conveyed, but only *drowned* in all this serving.[34]

The United Methodist Free Churches/The United Methodist Church

At the same time as deaconess work was becoming established, known and used in the Wesleyan Methodist Church, the United Methodist Free Churches were exploring the rôle women could play, and, though in rather a different format, so was the Primitive Methodist Connexion.

The emphases of the United Methodist Free Churches Deaconess Institute were evangelism, district visiting and sick nursing. The evangelistic work will be covered in a later chapter, but with evangelistic missions usually taking place during the autumn and winter months the deaconesses were available to help elsewhere as district visitors, often at 'reduced terms'. This meant that churches were able to take advantage of the services of 'capable preachers' and 'the opportunity . . . to increase the effectiveness of their ministry'.

Sisters, who were stationed in circuits, often had to take charge of the village causes because the minister needed to concentrate on the town church and circuit administration. She would go to one church after another for about a fortnight or

---

34. *The Agenda* (June 1929) pp.3-4

month, but many felt that, while some good was done, the time was too short to make a great impact on the neighbourhood.

Besides the missions the Sisters did much work in the districts to which they were assigned, leading Bible Classes, Girls' Guilds, Band of Hope meetings, Mothers' Meetings and meetings of the Young Peoples' Society of Christian Endeavour. However, much of their work was carried on in people's own homes and with the family where confidentiality was strictly observed. So apart from comments such as 'theirs . . . is a much needed and blessed ministry. Many who never attend Church or chapel have been impressed by these "deeds of weekday holiness" ', no

Sisters Maude and Florence,
United Methodist Deaconesses,
Katherine Road Church,
Forest Gate, London

further details are given. That intemperance was often a cause of family disruption, bringing misery and poverty to many, can be inferred from the 1901 Report which comments:

> All the sisters are total abstainers. Many were temperance workers before they joined this sisterhood. In their deaconess work they have been brought face to face with the demon drink, and the issue has stirred them to do their utmost to save the people from its cruel power. They carry a pledge book with them and urge converts to sign . . . During the past year they have brought nearly 800 people to sign the temperance pledge.[35]

As noted the aim of the Institute was evangelistic and missions served two purposes – fostering the spiritual welfare of the people and engendering income for the Institute from the collections. Statistically, in the nine months from September 1901 – April 1902 191 special missions were conducted and from 185 of these 4,081 conversions were recorded, but more important was the impact felt on the life of the churches. As with the Wesley

---

35. *The United Methodist Free Churches Minutes of Conference* (hereafter *UMFC Mins. of Conf.* (1901) p.250

Deaconesses, the United Methodist Sisters backed up their missions with permanent organisations in the churches, especially Christian Endeavour Societies for young people. Unfortunately, the evangelical work of the United Methodist Deaconesses fell victim to its own success in two respects. First, the Warden, the Rev. Thomas J. Cope, reports:

> The success of the evangelistic branch of the work was so much before the churches that there was danger that the Institute would be regarded as a Women's Special Mission Agency. This we wished to avoid, for many influential ministers and members, whose sympathy and help we needed, were strongly prejudiced against women preaching. Favourably to impress these friends it was necessary to bring to their notice the good work which was being done by the visiting deaconesses. But this was one of our difficulties. The ministry of the deaconess evangelist was in public and its success proclaimed itself, but the ministry of the visitation deaconess was to the people in their homes . . .[36]

Obviously, this latter work was confidential, and therefore not so high profile, but neverthless it was a very important side of the deaconesses' work. For example, Sister Kathleen, stationed at Lady Lane Central Mission in Leeds, described her work:

> She had factory meetings, market meetings, class meetings, and also a girls' parlour as well as visitation work . . . Around the Mission there are a large number of Jews, Roman Catholics, and Irish . . . One woman lived in a street where she was the only Christian or Englishwoman . . . In connection with their factory meetings they [she and her women helpers] went to different factories during the dinner hour . . . On Sunday evening they held open-air meetings in the Market Place, largely attended by men.[37]

Sister Irene, working at Lower Wortley, Leeds, found that the members of the 'Women's Bright Hour', which was well-attended both by the women in the church and also those in the

---

36. T. J. Cope, *The Hand of God* [hereafter Cope] (n.d.) p.19
37. *United Methodist Deaconess Institute Reports 1905-10* [hereafter *UMDI Report*] (1906-07 Report) pp.18-19

neighbourhood, were interested in the same topics used in the recently started Men's Adult School on the previous Sunday. This, she felt, had the advantage that both knew the topic taken and could presumably discuss the same subjects together.

Rotherhithe was one of the poorest areas in London and Sister Clare was extremely concerned about the children and started several more unusual activities for them, including 'play' hours, and guilds for both boys and girls where they could use books and games and see lantern shows. She also provided clothes for some of the boys, but was wary enough to realise that if they took the clothes home they would end up in the pawn shop, and so the boys put on their 'Sunday' clothes when they arrived in the morning and changed when they went home at night.

Poverty in Rotherhithe   Interview with Sister Clare

'We suppose you come into contact with much distress and poverty in Rotherhithe?'

'Yes, the needs of the children in such a neighbourhood are not only spiritual. We have during the past winter given 2,570 breakfasts to boys and girls who would otherwise often go breakfastless to school.'

Source: United Methodist Deaconess Institute Report (1907-08) pp.25-29

The United Methodist Church in Shernhall Street, Walthamstow, where Sister Constance had been stationed from its very beginnings, had a magnificent set of buildings and had become a very busy centre for Christian work in the area. Her endeavours there had contributed greatly to the success of the church. A brief list of some of her weekly activities was highlighted in the 1909-10 Report:

Monday:	'Women's Own', and some evening meeting.
Tuesday:	The Young Women's Meeting.
Wednesday:	Junior and Senior Bands of Hope.
Thursday:	To act as secretary to the doctor who conducts the nursing classes, and attend the preparation class.

Friday: Conduct the Scripture class, and attend Committee Meeting.

Saturday: Act as secretary to Women's Club, with one hundred and fifty members.

Sunday: Senior Bible class; conduct prayer-meeting, and be in the vestibule to welcome the people to both services.

. . . in addition to the above. She is in much demand for sick visiting and has many calls to visit the homes of the people.

Usually the mornings are spent in visiting and attending to sick people in the district . . .

The Sister's day is mapped out for her work. From 2.30 to 5.30 she does ordinary visiting and calls on any sick ones who do not require special attention. Often the Sister is called to the death-bed of some sufferer, and the people look upon her as their friend when in trouble.[38]

Many of the reports from all over the country show how the Sister in question gave herself to the people among whom she worked. So it is good to learn from Sister Constance that, much as she

loved her work at Shernhall, when, after 12 years, she had begun to feel 'the work was getting beyond her, and she was very much run down', the church gave her six months' leave and sent her on an all expenses paid trip to Australia. She realised she was fortunate and that most churches could not afford to do anything like that, but she pleaded with them to help their Sister with consideration and by prayer.

Sister Constance,
United Methodist
Deaconess, Shernhall St.,
Walthamstow, London

---

38.   *UMDI Report* (1909-10) pp.24-26

In an article on 17th April 1924 the Warden commented:

> The sisters are fulfilling a big place in the life of our
> churches. They visit the sick and the poor, they
> befriend the young, they teach in the schools, they
> work among women, and by their sympathetic help
> brighten the lives of others and win many for the
> Saviour; while some of them are working bravely in
> down-town churches.[39]

The Deaconess Institute always held a meeting at the Annual
United Methodist Conference and in 1924 Sister Lillie Sweet
described how a church in a northern mining village recovered
from near closure when the people decided 'as a last resort to
engage a Sister'. After a difficult period the church underwent a
great transformation and many young men were converted, giving
hope of great strength for the future.

Public opinion about the position of trained women in the
Church was undergoing a change during the 1920s as is shown
when an Armistice Day Service was held at Box in Wiltshire.
Sister Lillian, then stationed in the Bath Circuit, was invited by the
vicar to read the lesson in the service at the parish church and later
to lead the prayers at the Memorial.

Women in the Church – 18th December 1924

In the pioneer days of our movement such a thing was almost
unthinkable. Now, however, under the change of opinion with
regard to women's work in general, and by the service and ability of
the Deaconesses themselves, they have won distinct recognition
and confidence in the churches.

Source: MSS Cuttings Book (compiled by R. W. Gair) 18th December 1924

Many churches and individuals collected and made up parcels
of clothing which they sent to the deaconesses to distribute to
needy families, where they were received delightedly and with
much gratitude. Just before Christmas 1925 parcels apparently
were received at Bowron House, the training house, and the
students were able to take them out as 'Christmas' presents. The
senior student described the heart-warming experience:

---

39. MSS Cuttings Book (compiled by R. W. Gair) 17th April 1924

If those who sent the box of garments could have helped to distribute them, they would have felt well repaid for their labour of love. To note the smile of pleasure, the flush of joy as one poor mother fitted on the black winter coat was most gratifying. The same woman was so very pleased with the woolly coat and hat left for baby and I watched her stow them away in a drawer until Christmas Eve, when they will be put in baby's stocking as a present from Santa Claus.

A big white scarf gladdened the heart of another poor woman whose home is darkened by the curse of drink. 'That's the only Christmas present I shall get, Sister, and I would like those who sent it to know how pleased I am with it.'

Several parcels were left at homes where there are many children, and the mothers were so grateful for the beautiful warm garments which will protect their kiddies from the bitter cold winds.

One little old lady, who received a beautifully-lined black coat, fell in love with the smart lining, and when we returned the next day we found the coat spread out upon the bed, the lining uppermost. 'I have never had anything so pretty before,' was her remark.[40]

The Sisters sometimes stood in police courts as character witnesses for prisoners and very often were able to persuade the magistrates that the person in the dock was really 'trying to be better' and she and the church members would do all they could to support her, so that the case was adjourned. Sisters Rhoda and Lillian appeared before the Licensing Benches of their Districts to oppose the granting of fresh licences and spoke of their experiences with the results of intemperance. The Warden commented that he thought the word of a deaconess working daily among the people went a long way in influencing a decision.

A more unusual experience fell to Sister Dulcie in Rotherhithe, during floods which hit that part of London in January 1928. She was able to help people who had lost

---

40. MSS Cuttings (9th January 1926)

practically all their belongings, by distributing clothing and other items and 'in conjunction with other workers, and by the aid of a tradesman's motor-van' meals were taken to wrecked homes.

Scrubbing at 75 – 1928

In South East London an old soul of 75, who still has to clean offices morning and evening, recently said to one of our Sisters stationed in a poor district after the Monday afternoon meeting, 'I'm just off to my little bit of work, Sister, and God bless you for that meeting. It does make me feel lovely and bright like to get through my scrubbing.' The Sister says 'She has not a relation in the world and one feels so glad to have found her. I feel this is a Sister's work, and to me it is glorious.'

Source: MSS Cuttings Book (compiled by R. W. Gair) 11ᵗʰ October 1928

The Wesley Deaconess Order of the Methodist Church (1932-78)

Sister Clarice Slater in Kingston, Hull, gave an insight into one of her days. It started with prayer, an hour's study of 1 Corinthians, when 'in imagination I am in a deaconess's appointment at that time in Corinth when the clock reminds me that in reality I am in Hull, and out I must go'. Three visits followed, then an early dinner as it was Sisterhood Day, after that, another visit: this time to a young mother whose nine year old boy was suffering from cancer and only expected to live a fortnight. Then came the Sewing Meeting Tea and at half past seven the Girls' League Surprise Supper – 'Little did I think that at the end of the day I should be sitting under an African palm tree with coconuts, etc., spread before me, but a deaconess's life is full of surprises of one kind and another, and, best of all, are those in other people. So the day ends . . . and there is tomorrow with all its hope.'[41]

---

41. *The Agenda* (April 1938) pp.11-12

The End of a Day, Kingston, Hull

Sister Clarice Slater 1938

Then into bed, with the hope that the man who first invented beds has now a Somnus mattress in heaven, which, according to advertisements, if not to the experiences of lodgings, cures insomnia and ensures perfect sleep.

Source: The Agenda (April 1938) pp.11-12

Edna Peters, the deaconess at Leeds, Brunswick, in 1938, having noted that she and the Sunday School Primary Leader had arranged for a 'christening' on the Sunday afternoon, remarked, 'The minister christens the elect, but to me is given the honour and joy of christening those of lowly birth.'[42] What does this tell us about Methodism at that time? Were ministers beginning to let deaconesses have a greater share in presbyteral ministry? Was the performing of the christening or baptismal service being opened out to people other than ministers? Had this developed because of the ideas and practices of the non-Wesleyan denominations? How class-ridden or class-conscious was the Methodist Church?

An interesting appointment must have been that of Helen Herd who was stationed in Cupar, Fifeshire, as 'Welfare Officer to the Blind' from whence she describes not only the beautiful scenery, but the courage and resourcefulness of the blind people she and her collie dog, Fleet, visited – a man with half his face, including both his eyes and left arm, blown away in a quarry accident, who was helping a friend more recently blinded; a 98 year old man whose ambition was to reach his 100th birthday; a gipsy encampment, giving Braille and handicraft lessons, and finally the pair went to see three blind ladies who were full of the joys of life.

Among the Blind, Flintshire   Sister Helen Herd, 1939

. . . in Miss M.'s house we [Helen and Fleet] find Mrs G. and Miss H. Miss M. is the only survivor of a family of five, all blind. She gets up every morning at six although she is 74 years old. She does all her own housework . . . Mrs G. is a German lady also blind and Miss H. is deaf. When I go in Miss H. is busy reading a chapter of Isaiah.

---

42. *The Agenda* (April 1938) p.14

> When she finishes Mrs G. is reminded of a hymn and sings it straight away, then all three begin in turn to witness to some special bit of help they have received . . . They laugh at the mistakes they make. Miss M. found she had been trying to cut her dish-cloth, thinking it was tripe, and Mrs. G. chuckles when she tells of her sighted husband coming to her to thread a darning needle for him.
>
> So ends our day . . . in this day . . . we have met more conquerors than conquered. And the conquerors are those who have believed that He is able, even for such a calamity as blindness.
>
> *Source: The Agenda* (June 1939) pp.11-12

In 1941-42 Madeline Shipp was appointed as Girls' Club Leader and Organiser in Sheffield. She found the work very demanding as her 'family' grew to about '330 boys and girls, all between the ages of 14 and 18'. Each night around 100-150 came to the Club, she had little help and with such a large number to control, at times she got 'scared as to what they will be up to next'. They were full of mischief and boundless energy, and difficult to keep interested in anything for long. After hearing the problems she encountered, the Warden commented that 'Perhaps some of those who are talking freely about the new opportunities and Youth centre work may begin to realise that it isn't going to be everybody's work, or at any time easy work, and that the Methodist Church may have to change its outlook in some ways if it is to be a serviceable instrument.'

> **Club Work in Sheffield 1941-42   Sister Madeline Shipp**
>
> We have the usual activities like dramatics, handicrafts, physical training, cricket, swimming etc., also a Girls' Training Corps, and Boys' Army Cadet Unit. There are 50 girls in the Corps, who are interested (at least for a week or so) in Child Welfare, Morse, First Aid and drill – they like lots of drill. One girl told me quite seriously that she thought strong discipline was what the Club needed (I quite agree!) but the next moment sulked like a child because her favourite record was not played on the radiogram . . . The Sunday evening service is not compulsory but we always have a good attendance.'
>
> *Source: The Agenda* (August 1942) p.10

In 1946 Sister Clare Powers was appointed as a Moral Welfare Officer by the Women's Fellowship. Many people questioned the need for such an appointment within Methodism – 'surely we do not need a Moral Welfare Officer for Methodists'! However, within the first 12 months she noted that she had had 'forty strictly moral welfare cases, mostly illegitimate children, and all but six of them are Methodists from respectable homes'. She was also a prison visitor to two of the largest women's prisons in England. From the stories she heard from the inmates Clare concluded that much of the delinquency came from the breakdown of family life. Another concern she had was for babies and she was looking forward to the opening of a Mother and Baby Home. The job of Moral Welfare was a new, but very necessary, venture.

Ethel Beckett, in 1947, found herself in Preston at the Clubland Church, which had been started around 1942 in a redundant Methodist Church. The building was very unprepossessing, but it was a 'second home' to many young people between the ages of 14 and 18. A good number of the young folk, mostly factory or mill workers, came from broken or overcrowded homes and felt frustrated. The Club was open every night of the week and offered educational classes of various sorts and a canteen. Outdoors games were played on Saturday afternoons and a service held on the Sunday evening, followed by refreshments, a film, concert or discussion. A group met on the Sunday afternoon to discuss Christianity and its practical application. Many of the young folk who became Christian faced derision from family, friends and workmates. It was hard, but rewarding, work.

Clubland Church, Preston   **Sister Ethel Beckett, 1947**

It is an achievement to get most of the youngsters to come to church, when the custom is Sunday cinema, and they are not slow to criticise if the service is long or boring. A threat came to me once just before service, 'You'd better be good, miss, or I'm walking out.' This boy stuck it through and graciously commented afterwards, 'Not bad, Miss.' I was greatly encouraged!

Source: The Agenda (July 1948) pp.4-5

A very different appointment lay in store for Nora Trineman when, after 20 years in the Order, chiefly in city missions, she found herself 'in the midst of Rural Methodism, with the whole of Cornwall and a good slice of Devon thrown in!' as she became Warden of the Camborne Community Centre (1944-47). After wandering 'all over the place seeing where she could be of use', Sister Nora decided that the word which suited Methodism there was 'Family'. Obviously, the usual structures of Sundays or Methodism in general did not fit in a village where the total child population was nine, ranging from the ages of three to fourteen years. She described her visits to various small villages, for example, taking a Guild evening where the pianist was 'a small boy of nine [and] the lesson was read by his smaller brother of seven!'

Rural Methodism   **Sister Nora Trineman**

The chapel stood alone at the end of the lane, which seemed to me to lead to nowhere, but I was told that there were nine families who lived within two miles of the place and this was their chapel. The membership was 17, children 6, Sunday School 23; in fact, everybody! The fact that their ages ranged from 3 to 83 didn't worry anybody. The family is happy together and the spirit here was one that many a larger church might envy.

Source: The Agenda (April 1949) pp.4-5

Marjorie Maltby was an Industrial Chaplain in Manchester and each week she visited a factory which made brake linings and employed 1,500 people. During the lunch hour, as she passed between the tables in the canteen, she touched on a multitude of different topics with the 500 gathered there. Then it was on to the Staff Canteen where she ate while she talked, answering all sorts of questions about religion and its relevance to life. After that the Doctor's Room was put at her disposal for personal interviews with people who had problems or just wanted to talk. Lastly she would visit the factory floor, showing interest in the product and helping anyone who needed it. When the 'buzzer' went and she left with the workers her day was still not finished as there were visits to pay or house groups to attend and more discussions. A tiring, but exciting, appointment.

Around 1964 a 'new town' was established at Livingston, about 15 miles west of Edinburgh and Sister Joan Ryeland joined the Ecumenical Experiment in 1974, working with colleagues from the Scottish Episcopal Church, the Church of Scotland, the

Congregational Union of Scotland and the Methodist Church. From the beginning both buildings and worship were shared, with the team ministry sharing in the leading of worship and being pastorally responsible for allocated areas of the town and certain hospital wards and schools.

New Town Work: Livingston, Scotland

Sister Joan Ryeland

There is always something thrilling about treading new pathways, opening up new territory. Here in this town of promise away north of the Border, God has called and is using the Church to do just that, and it is a joy to be in the Team here at this time.

Source: A Way of Serving (Autumn 1974) pp.4-5

Dorothy Carey became a Community Worker in an experimental partnership between the Church and Corporation in the Stonehouse area of Plymouth. At first the few elderly church members who had struggled to keep the church open were very dubious about the experiment, but as time passed and things began to improve they were delighted in spite of various set-backs, such as vandalism. In addition to her work at the church, Sister Dorothy became very involved with social work in the area, finding out what was needed in the community and endeavouring to help provide the amenities required. It is interesting to note that she felt her 'uniform identified [her] as someone available and ready to serve', thus endorsing, over 80 years later, Stephenson's insistence of the value of a distinctive uniform for his deaconesses.

Stonehouse, Plymouth, 1974   **Sister Dorothy Carey**

There has been horror . . . at the damage done to our premises by the very youngsters we are trying to help and serve. I am not sure if horror or delight triumphed on the Saturday on which our float appeared in the Lord Mayor's Day procession to advertise our church and its work, but the youngsters thought it was great. They sang and sang for nearly three hours on Plymouth Hoe and around the city and at least their joy got across.

Source: A Way of Serving (Autumn 1974) pp.21-23

The girls Joyce Wakeley met, in the Assessment and Remand Home in Bristol, provided a great challenge as she tried 'to get through to them (by working alongside them, sharing their leisure, their games, their walks etc.); to try to understand them, to assess them, so that, together with a team of educationalists, psychiatrists, field social workers, doctors and so on, we might come to an agreement about the future of the girl'. She found that almost always the underlying problem of their behaviour was that 'they had been made to feel that *they did not matter to anybody* – and therefore it did not matter how they behaved or what they did'. Sister Joyce admitted that all endeavours were rarely very successful, but at least the girls benefited from the more stable routine they were forced to live in the Home and eventually some came to realise that the staff accepted them for what they were without condemning them or condoning their actions and that they had within themselves the possibility of leading a better life. So it was a great joy when a girl had 'made good' and could return proudly to tell of her success.[43]

Sister Dora Dixon had been a social worker before she became a Wesley Deaconess, but after 22 years' work in 1972 she sought permission to be trained and employed as a psychiatric social worker. She felt that there was a great need for such workers and that 'the changing shape of the Order with the entry of women into the Ministry of the Word and Sacrament, [which] gave the Order freedom to explore anew what is meant by being a service arm of the Church in today's world', and a third reason related to the contribution the Order could make to the thinking of the Church about lifestyles. After her training at Manchester University Dora took up an appointment at All Saints Hospital, Birmingham, as a member of a multicultural team, where not only did she deal with the mentally ill patients, but also with the families who had to cope with the problems this caused.

The Villa Road Methodist Church, Birmingham, where Sister Yvonne Hunkin found herself, was in a run-down area with a great racial mix. A few years before, a Methodist Commission had recommended its closure, but the local people said 'No'. The Rev. Michael Ward arrived and together they began 'Christian Neighbourhood Centre' – aiming to serve the neighbourhood, opening the church premises to local groups and generally

---

43. *A Way of Serving* (Autumn 1975) pp.9-12

improving the life of the area. Extra finance from various sources made it possible for Sister Yvonne to be stationed there. She

realised that on her own she could have little impact, so she set about building up the life of the church and persuading people from very different backgrounds to train and work together so that they could go out into the community.

Sister Yvonne Hunkin, 1948. In 1977 she became Associate Warden and took the Wesley Deaconess Order into the Methodist Diaconal Order in 1986.

Villa Road, Birmingham   Sister Yvonne Hunkin

In fact everything we do at Villa Road is geared to training, and this is one of the things which makes it so fascinating, like a teenager growing up, because although the building is old, the church is in a new phase of its life, full of ideas, experimenting, making mistakes, being exasperating, learning to laugh at itself, getting up and going on. If sometimes I envy a smoothly efficient church I know I would miss the bouncy life and warmth and the challenges of Villa Road.

Source: A Way of Serving (Autumn 1976) pp.3-6

The cathedral city of Canterbury in 1976 had, during the previous 10 years, changed as the University of Kent, the Christ Church College of Education and the College of Technology had been established. This meant an increase in population with the student population moving on each year. Sister Jill Bowden was one of an ecumenical team of chaplains and one of the ways they tried to encourage a search for a true Christian way of life was to open a Student Christian Community House. Here she lived with eight students, male and female, of all denominations and from the various colleges. She explained:

> We are seeking to live in openness to God and each other and those around us . . . We have created a community liturgy which we use each Tuesday before breakfast at 7.30 a.m.; we would like it to be a eucharist but must live with the harsh reality of division in the Church and experience the pain as

others do . . . Community life is not always enjoyable and some find it easier than others, but all have felt the venture worthwhile.[44]

Two accounts in the Wesley Deaconess Magazine in 1976 paint very different pictures. Ellen Whalley, in Northern Ireland, described her life and work against the background of 'The Troubles' (the activities of the I.R.A.), while Margaret Jones wrote of the beauties of the Welsh Border, around Clun, with long journeys through the countryside and the agricultural year affecting church activities. In spite of the problems facing the farming community, dwindling congregations and other hardships there was a great sense of community and spirit of fellowship.

> **Travels in Rural Methodism, 1976   Sister Margaret Jones**
>
> Finding the way along the narrow, twisting, and often steep, lanes is quite an adventure. On one early occasion, my passenger said, 'Don't get up too much speed. You have to turn right at that tree.' I wondered how I should ever be able to navigate by trees – but it works surprisingly well, and I still look out for that particular tree! Every local inhabitant is able to direct the stranger to any house he wants, because everybody knows everybody else (or will do his best to find out!).
>
> *Source: A Way of Serving* (Autumn 1976) pp.14-17

A Wesley Deaconess was first appointed as a resident Assistant Chaplain at the Methodist College, Belfast in 1969 with special responsibility for the pastoral oversight of the girls, especially the boarders. Sister Sheila Parnell, in 1977, was also the Senior Mistress in the girls' Hall of Residence and taught full-time in the Religious Education Department, plus helping with games and counselling. She commented that, in spite of all the upheavals caused by the security measures in place because of 'The Troubles', it was amazing how little the normal routine of the College had been affected.

The areas in which the deaconesses have been involved has changed and developed over the years. At the beginning the emphasis was more on the rescue type of work due, to a large extent, to poverty and intemperance and along with that went the

---

44. *A Way of Serving* (Autumn 1976) pp.9-12

importance of pressing home the Gospel message. Social change and conditions forced redirection of the deaconess work in fields which were newly opened to women, so the Sisters were to be found in the forces and caravan missions. Then, latterly, they were allowed to remain in the Order, but to work in the sector ministry as social and psychiatric workers, teachers, and industrial chaplains. The scope is endless.

A Caring Ministry

In September 1893 Sister Dora (Stephenson) read a paper at 'The Congress on Women's Work, held in connection with the World's Fair, at Chicago' on 'Deaconess-Work in England' in which she gave details of the establishment, training and work of the Wesley Deaconesses. At one point she quoted a remark made by one of the deaconesses which seemed to sum up the nature and variety of their work 'a Deaconess must be equal to any emergency from 'making a poultice to preaching a sermon . . .'[45]

'Variety of names' given to a deaconess, 1907

I am rather amused at the variety of names they give me here. 'Singing Nurse', 'Praying Nurse', 'Preaching Nurse', 'Wesleyan Nurse'. Sympathy has twice been misplaced, as I have been taken for a 'young widow.'

Our own people, many of them farmers, pay a very undeserving compliment, and say, 'The Sister is a "Tommy Owt" in the Church.' I must explain that a 'Tommy Owt' is a man employed on a farm, a man good at anything, and to whom nothing comes amiss.

Source: Flying Leaves (October 1909) p.138-39

Many ministers, some of whom had been a little sceptical of women workers, gave witness to the usefulness of the deaconesses:

> It has been my joy to have several of your Deaconesses in our Circuit. I am a convert to the Institute. I have seen so much splendid, cheerful service rendered by the Sisters.

and

---

45. *HH* (October 1893) pp.187-191

I have had working with me four Deaconesses or Probationers. If these may be taken as fair specimens of the Order, I think you have done a splendid work in training and sending out such workers. 'So may the bright succession run.'[46]

The 1910 issue of *Flying Leaves* printed a selection of reports from ministers about the deaconesses who were 'fully received' into the Order during that year's Convocation at Bristol. All were very favourable, paying tribute to their work.

Comment on Deaconess Work, 1910

She lives in a chronic state of over work (sic) and does not take sufficient care of herself. The idea of having a Deaconess here was criticised at first by many of our own people. One hears nothing of that sort now, and she has so commended herself and her work to our people that £70 was raised for the Deaconess Fund last week, and the local Mayor sent us a contribution as the 'town's recognition of Sister's work'. He said she was worth six policemen.

Source: Flying Leaves (June 1910) p.91

In 1974 the last Warden of the Wesley Deaconess Order, the Rev. Brian J. N. Galliers, wrote: 'Just what a deaconess *is,* and what she *does,* is not easy to answer these days.' So, in order to try to answer these questions, a number of deaconesses were asked to write about their own ministry and their attitude to it in *A Way of Serving* (Autumn 1974). These articles give a picture of their work in the latter half of the 20th century and show how, although much had changed since 1891, the basic principles and ideas were still the same and the need for such a caring ministry still just as vital. Mr. Galliers rightly commented:

The result is a picture of care for people, and of dedication to Christ. It is a story of women reacting to the places and situations in which they find themselves. They dare believe that those places and situations have been offered to them by God, and that in them they must proclaim by deed and word the working of the Holy Spirit and the challenges of the Kingdom.[47]

---

46. *HH* (July 1901) p.164
47. *A Way of Serving* (Autumn 1974) p.1

Chapter 2

Three Wider Spheres of Work

Three areas of work demand special consideration in the life of the deaconess organisations. In some ways they either broke new ground within Methodism or, at very least, helped to widen the popular conception of the traditional rôle of women. The first was that of the deaconess evangelist, the second, the caravan missions and the third, the part played during the wars and afterwards as Chaplains' Assistants. Again, we shall rely particularly on the deaconesses' own words to tell their stories.

The Deaconess Evangelists of Wesleyan Methodism

The rôle of the Deaconess Evangelist was a rather specialised one and particularly interesting as, at that time, officially Wesleyan Methodism did not approve of women preaching, though undoubtedly women did preach.[1] The 1803 Conference regulation to this effect was still in force and it was only in 1910 that the phrase 'address only her own sex' was removed and equal official recognition with men given in 1918 to women local preachers and the following year to deaconesses.

In 1891 the minister of the Hackney Road Mission, the Rev. Samuel Wilkes, reported that of the two deaconesses attached to the Mission, 'one is provided with opportunity for public addresses and exposition of God's work, by which many have been blessed'. The same year Sister Ruth gave some idea of the work in which she and Sister Annette engaged, including giving addresses at the monthly 'Evangelistic service', whilst Sister Freer wrote of her 'impressions and memories of eight months' work at Hackney Road Wesleyan Chapel'.[2]

---

1. See chapter 11 cf. John Lenton 'Women Preachers of Wesleyan Methodism' (paper given at W.H.S./W.M.H.S Conference, Easter 1996); *Workaday Preachers* (ed. Milburn & Batty, 1995) pp.165-190
2 *HH* (February 1891) p.39, (March 1891) p.60, (September 1891) p.179

Hackney Road Wesleyan Chapel, 1891   Sister Sarah Freer

It has been no small part of my duty to render assistance in the more public work by speaking at our Band of Hope Meeting and religious gatherings. I have also occasionally conducted services in the chapel, and upon these efforts God's power and blessing have rested.

Source: Highways and Hedges (September 1891) p.179

A few months after this Sister Freer went to Bowman House, Norwich, with the object of devoting herself to evangelistic work in the villages, and the minister, the Rev. George Graves, testified to the value of her work in the churches:

> Sister Freer has been at work for six months in Norfolk and Suffolk. Her headquarters are at Bowman House, our Branch Deaconess House at Norwich. Her work is chiefly evangelistic; in this respect differing from that of the majority of the Sisters. We do not expect, or even desire, that every Sister shall be able to speak in public. This is a great gift; but there are many forms of useful work in which the Sisters may be happily engaged that have not that special power. None the less we are thankful when God gives us consecrated women who can speak with power and persuasiveness to the people.[3]

Sister Louie Harpur, a trained singer, having studied at the Royal Academy of Music, had been connected to the North Birmingham Mission, but left when the minister, the Rev. J. G. Mantle, had to retire through ill health. Her singing of 'the Gospel' had touched many hearts and so after the 1892 Conference she was attached to the Wesley Deaconess Institute and was available 'for work as a Song Evangelist in various parts of the country'. When the second branch house, Calvert House, was opened in Leicester Sister Louie was to 'have her "abiding place" there in the intervals of the Missions in which she takes part'. Sister Louie's services were obviously in demand as her appointment diary for 1893 shows:

Hastings	Jan 6th to 20th
Belper	Jan 26th
Grimsby	Jan 29th to Feb 5th
London (Home Missionary Meetings)	Feb 12th to 17th
Wednesbury	Feb 19th to Mar 2nd
Bolton	Mar 5th to 10th

---

3. *HH* (January 1892) p.13, (December 1892) p.234

Further requests for her services were invited.[4] However, after this there is no further mention of Sister Louie, so one must assume that she withdrew for some reason.

Sister Ruth Northcroft reported that, while she was based in Truro (1891-92), there had been no great call for her to 'give public addresses' and in fact she had only given nine since Christmas – two at Juvenile Missionary Meetings, three Gospel addresses, and four Temperance ones. It seems that from 1893 some deaconesses were used in more organised evangelistic work, for that year *Highways and Hedges* notes that:

> It is hoped that during next year one or two of our Sisters, whom God has greatly blessed in addressing meetings of an evangelistic character, and for the enriching of the spiritual life, may be able to hold Missions here and there. Generally speaking, these Missions ought to extend for a month. The services should not be held every day, but at intervals, which would allow of the ordinary services, particularly the Class Meetings, to be maintained without interference. Such Missions we have found from experiment to have been greatly blest; they seem likely to leave more permanent results than those in which a great disturbance is necessarily made in the ordinary work of the Church. Ministers desiring the services of one of our Sisters for this purpose, should make early application.[5]

Sister Alice Hull had been 'set aside' for 'Special Mission Work' in Luton. So in a different situation she had been doing the same type of work among the young women workers in the straw-plaiting industry. It was also reported, after she had worked in Bristol for six months, that 'her public ministrations will be always be remembered with gratitude, and for her soul-probing addresses and quiet heart-searching utterances many will bless God throughout eternity'. Sister Alice preached her farewell sermon from Romans 6:23, 'The wages of sin is death, but the gift of God is eternal life through Jesus Christ our Lord.' The sermon was described as 'most eloquent and impressive reasoning of righteousness, temperance and judgement to come'. From Bristol she went to Birmingham to hold

---

4. *HH* (July 1892) p.138, (November 1892) pp.216-17; (January 1893) p.16
5. *HH* (August 1893) p.158

a two month mission.[6]   In March 1894, Sister Ruth Northcroft, reported from Leicester that since the last Conference she had given 11 addresses and felt 'increasing joy in the work, and especially in the purely evangelistic speaking'.[7]

Sometimes deaconesses had to step into the breach, especially in the villages, if the appointed preacher failed to arrive, but deaconesses like Sylvia Pryce-Jones, at Leicester and later in the West Country, and Elise Searle, in charge of Bowman House in Norwich, often spoke at mission services and Pleasant Sunday Afternoon meetings of other denominations as well as local Methodist Church functions.   Many Sisters, over the years, gave addresses at Convocation on a variety of subjects related to their work.   However, Convocation of 1894 is interesting in that on the Sunday morning Sister Freer spoke from Psalm 118:14, 'The Lord is my light and my salvation; the Lord is my strength and my song' and Sister Florence Thornton gave an address, taking as her text, Romans 8:8, 'And we know that all things work together for good to them that love God, to them who are called according to his purpose.'[8]

The 1898 report from the Salford Deaconess House mentions that for several months Sister Erica Marley 'held weekly Dinner Hour Services in a cigar factory in her district and several girls working there' then joined her Gravel Lane Girls' Club:

> I am to take three services on this plan; last plan I had four – three evenings, one morning, and the Watchnight service. Next Tuesday I give the address at the Mission Band meeting.[9]

There are two fascinating reports from Sister Charlotte Vinson, who in 1913 was stationed at Witney, Oxfordshire, in which she describes Carterton, 'a sort of "Garden Village" ' whose inhabitants come from many parts of the world, going on to say:

> Our little Wesleyan Chapel is the only place of worship . . . I have come across Agnostics, Christadelphians, Unitarians, Roman Catholics, and almost every variety of Noncomformist.   There are only three real

6. *HH* (October 1893) pp.191, 198, (November 1893) p.218
7. *HH* (April 1894) p.78
8. *HH* (September 1894) p.168
9. *HH* (June 1900) p.142

Wesleyans in the place, and our membership is only five, including myself. As far as congregations go, I am thankful to report a real increase . . .

There was a Sunday Morning School . . . Now the numbers have grown . . .

My time is very fully occupied, for I need to do a lot of studying. On our present plan I have sixteen appointments on Sundays, beside seven weeknight services. The preaching part of the work is not easy, for my hearers are mostly very well-read men and women, and of such various shades of opinion. Then I have a Society Class, and a Children's Service on Sunday mornings, and there are two villages four miles away to each of which I go fortnightly to take either a Bible Class or a Temperance Meeting. I should not think that there are many Methodist Societies in England that can boast of a chapel-keeper who can read Hebrew, but we can! I was quite startled one night in class, when he began to expound to us the literal meaning of a passage in the Hebrew version . . .

I have mentioned our Class. That is as unique as the rest of things. We usually have two Congregationalists, a Primitive Methodist, a Baptist, and two Church people present, in addition to three or four Wesleyans.[10]

So a number of deaconesses did take services, but from 1901 some were especially designated as Deaconess Evangelists in the *Stations*. The Warden, in his capacity as editor of *Flying Leaves*, wrote in January 1905:

Many of the Wesley Deaconesses are good speakers: they say their say, and do not say anything merely for the sake of saying it. A few of them preach with power and success. But ours is not an order of women preachers. Yet when the Spirit of God touches with fire a woman's lips, we dare not bid her be silent. Two of our number are wholly devoted to mission preaching. They can command large audiences or small in large chapels and halls, or in little village sanctuaries. Their work is very wearying and exhausting, and we desire to

---

10. *FL* (January 1914) pp.7-8, (May 1914) p.80

commend them specially to the sympathetic prayers of our friends.[11]

Here, surely, Stephenson was following in the footsteps of John Wesley and Hugh Bourne in believing that if God had chosen a woman as his instrument they dare not deny her the right to preach whether they approved or not.

The first so called was Sister Jeanie Banks. Eliza Jane Banks was the daughter of the Rev. Matthew Banks (1798-1878), a missionary in the West Indies (1826-1837) and sister of the Rev. John Shaw Banks, DD, Tutor of Systematic Theology at Headingley College (1880-1910) and President of Conference (1902). She records that she was brought up on stories of her parents' experiences there, which influenced her and made her feel that

> To preach the Gospel and save souls was . . . the chief thing worth living for; and my first sermon (a very short one) was made and given away when I was fourteen years of age.[12]

Certain that this was her mission in life, but, having elderly parents whom she could not leave, she started to teach from home and also gave music lessons in the evening in a boys' boarding school, where a number of her pupils were converted. Jeanie also did much 'visiting of the sick and dying, the aged and lonely, the drunkard and forlorn' and regarded this as good training for her future work. Her experience in nursing her parents also stood her in good stead.

Sister Jeanie had been a Sister with the Rev. Peter Thompson in the East London Mission for eight years, before transferring to the Wesley Deaconess Institute in 1896.[13] Her previous years of service were taken into account and she was excused the usual period of probation, being consecrated in April 1896. She was 'wholly devoted to evangelistic work' and there are many reports of her missions and tributes to the effectiveness of her work. A few of these will give the flavour of this side of deaconess work.

---

11. *FL* (January 1905) p.189
12. *FL* (February 1903) p.20
13. MS diary of Jeanie Banks (Methodist Archives and Research Centre, The John Rylands Library, Deansgate, Manchester)

In 1895 Jeanie visited Melksham and the minister, the Rev. George Clarke, in asking for a deaconess to be appointed to his circuit, paid tribute to her work, but said he would like one to 'help me to religiously educate our countryside to the supreme idea of a devoted woman's work even apart from preaching'. Obviously there was still some reservation, certainly among ministers, towards women preaching. Sister Jeanie was ready to accept any invitation to lead a mission whether that invitation came from a 'quiet country place' or 'the crowded parts of East London'.[14] The effectiveness of her work confirmed Stephenson's view that he had been right to set her aside for evangelistic efforts. There are many stories of people, strangers to religion, who were converted in her missions, but also some closely connected to the church were affected, for example, the young local preacher who declared, 'I've had a Pentecost' and another, 'I've got something I never had before.' One testimony to her work reads:

> I am very glad to bear testimony to the blessed results of the Mission recently conducted by Sister Jeanie Banks. Tomorrow evening we are giving a tea to the converts. Our roll-call now stands at 100; it was eighty-three when Sister left, and we are believing for more. Then there is the great benefit derived not only from the members of our own Church, but other Churches as well. We thank and praise God for Sister's visit, and pray that you may have many such workers. The Church and the world needs them.[15]

Sister Jeanie's Engagements list for 1898-99 gives some idea of the scope of her work:

Sep. 18 to 25	Gornal Wood (Dudley)
Oct. 2 to 9	Woodbridge
Oct. 16 to 23	Ashby-de-la-Zouch
Oct 30 to Nov. 6	Princess Alice Orphanage
Nov. 13 to 20	Uxbridge
Nov. 27 to Dec. 4	Crewkerne
Dec. 11 to 18	Broad Oak (Gloucester)
Dec. 25 to Jan 1	Malton Circuit
Jan. 22 to 29	Kirby Moorside
Feb. 5 to 12	Bakewell
Feb. 19 to 26	Moreton Hampstead
Mar. 5 to 12	Andover[16]

---

14. *HH* (April 1897) p.88, (May 1897) p.113
15. *HH* (March 1898) p.66, (April 1898) p.88
16. *HH* (September 1898) p.208

This means that in seven months she travelled from Staffordshire to Suffolk, back to Leicestershire, to Birmingham, to the outskirts of London, to Somerset, to Gloucester, to Yorkshire, to Derbyshire, to Devon, ending up in Hampshire. No mean feat.

Sister Jeanie usually gave a report on her year's evangelistic work. In these she often gives instances of conversions, but, perhaps more importantly, she emphasises that she did not just go into a circuit or church for a mission and then leave, but says:

> It is our aim after each Mission to institute a system of shepherding the new converts, and to organise a plan for having all enrolled as members on trial, or properly transferred to the care of some other church to which they may belong. The names and addresses of every enquirer are registered, and all are followed up after the Mission closes. The results are very satisfactory.
>
> ... The summary of the Year's Evangelistic Work will tell of churches quickened, congregations enlarged, new classes formed, young people gathered in, Bible Classes for men and women organised, old Methodist customs revived, and over one thousand souls found seeking Jesus.[17]

In her 1901 Report Sister Jeanie states:

> My whole soul goes out in Evangelistic work . . . In Lincolnshire, Leicestershire, Gloucestershire, Durham, Dorset, Berks, Surrey, Sussex, Devon, and Yorks., the power of the Cross has drawn many hearts, and uplifted hundreds of souls. Between three and four hundred opportunities have been given me of publicly declaring the glorious Gospel truth, in addition to visitation work in every Mission, and an extensive correspondence consequent upon success.

It is significant that the following comments were sent to her six months after the mission as they show the continuing usefulness of her ministry:

> A recognition of new members took place on Sunday. Most interesting. Both ministers present.

---

17. *HH* (October 1898) pp.233-34

'The influence of the Mission has spread to the outside villages. Mission Band formed. Classes all round aroused.'

'Cottage meetings [instituted after the Mission] splendid! Mr ---- [a convert] a devoted worker.'

'Getting on finely at ----. I do enjoy my Class Meetings; they are better than all the others.'

'A restored backslider is preaching the Word with power.'[18]

For several years Jeanie seems to have spent some time during the summer months of the fishing season in Scotland among the fisherfolk of Fraserburgh and the Hebrides and in Shetland, where she engaged in both evangelistic and medical work. A report from *The Methodist Times* described her as:

> a powerful evangelist. Small in stature – a 'shrimp' between two stalwart fishermen, as she described herself – but with every feature and action indicative of life and energy, she at once impresses her hearers with her personality . . . On Sundays she preached twice to crowded congregations, nearly all of whom were men, and on other days of the week tended to the injuries of the bodies of the much-exposed fishermen and girls. 'The doctor woman's' popularity there is consequently great.[19]

Jeanie herself summed up her 'Summer in the Shetland Isles' thus:

> August 26th – Closed the Medical Work. The fishing fleet is gradually diminishing; there is a general 'going South', and the girls, by hundreds, are following the boats.
>
> Every Sunday during the three months it has been my joy to preach the Gospel in town or country to eager listeners; 299 visits have been paid to the homes of the people; and tonight I embark again for Aberdeen, and thence to the homeland, rejoicing in the privilege of service, and feeling that if I had a thousand lives, all should be devoted to my Lord and Master.[20]

18. *HH* (March 1901) p.70
19. *HH* (October 1898) pp.234-35; (June 1899) p.138; *FL* (October 1904) pp.134-35; *FL* (September 1906) pp.124-25
20. *FL* (October 1904) pp.134-35

A quotation shows that Sister Jeanie's mission was not confined to large centres as she reported from a Village Mission, most probably Broad Oak, Gloucester, that

> Methodism in this neighbourhood was little more than a name. The Chapel is a very small one, only seating about 120 comfortably. Miss M. H. seems to be the mainstay of the Church there, and, but for her devotion, it seems as though the last spark of fire would have died out. It was she who felt it laid upon her heart to have a mission, and set to work to accomplish it . . .

> I found a Sunday School, with about fifty names on the books. Only one Society Class, and that had not met for nearly two years, excepting for the renewal of tickets (twenty members). Only two prayer leaders. I began to wonder if I might have not done more good by going to a wider sphere. I felt contracted; little to work upon. Congregations 'looked up' well on the Sundays, the chapel full, and some in the schoolroom; second Sunday, forms in the aisles also . . .

> The week-evening attendances were very encouraging. People from great distances trudged over the sodden fields, or along the muddy roads. Conversions began from the very beginning of the mission, although in limited numbers.

The response was so enthusiastic that Jeanie agreed to stay with them another Sunday and for a Christmas gathering of the Society and new converts on the Tuesday.[21]

When an invitation was given to Jeanie Banks to undertake a mission at Clydebank, Glasgow (17th February-10th March 1901) the church there made extensive preparations by organising workers into Bands to deal with various aspects of the mission and by earnest prayer for the success of the visit, so that right from the beginning great things were achieved with many being added to the churches, and not only to Methodist ones. Perhaps it is typical of the Scottish temperament that the writer of the report, 'J. B.', who must be the minister John Bennett, says that: 'There are no very striking cases of conversion to relate, but many of them are interesting.' For example, the Sunday Afternoon Bible Class for young people of 15 years of age and above increased its membership from 200 to over

---

21. *HH* (February 1899) pp.42-43

300 and gave Sister Jeanie a great opportunity for talking to them about life and faith. J. B. perhaps gives us the best account of the extraordinary evangelistic work in which Sister Jeanie Banks engaged:

> Sister Jeanie's beautiful addresses and exquisite solos will live in hundreds of hearts for many a long day. There was no straining after mere effect, no attempt to work up an unhealthy sensationalism, just an earnest and direct appeal for an immediate surrender of the will and the life, and the people came in scores . . . one word must be said of the Missioner's incessant labours in connection with her Mission. She has made scores of visits to the homes of our people. At first she devoted her attention to the sick and the aged and infirm, and latterly she made a point of seeing all our Methodist converts in their homes. The amount of time and labour which this involved were very considerable, but the conscientiousness and cheerfulness with which it was done gave us an exhibition of wholehearted Christian devotion, such as we have rarely met with before.
>
> A word also as to the thoroughness of Sister's Jeanie's methods, especially as regards the shepherding of the converts. Every Methodist convert is placed under the care of an under-shepherd, who signs a printed pledge card, undertaking to look after a certain convert for six months, and in every instance this is being faithfully and effectively done.[22]

Sister Jeanie Banks,
Deaconess Evangelist

When considering tributes like this it is important, as was pointed out earlier, to remember that officially Wesleyan Methodism frowned upon women preaching.

In a paper, 'Experiences of an Evangelist' to the Convocation in 1902 Sister Jeanie says that she always found it 'wise to get hold of the children at an early stage of the Mission, to lead them to Christ, and thus to get into sympathetic touch with Sabbath School work and workers'. After

---

22. *HH* (May 1901) pp.116-17

that she visited their homes and families and found her medical knowledge and nursing skills a great advantage. Jeanie also insisted that a Methodist evangelist must be loyal to Methodism and felt that it was part of her work to revive this loyalty in the churches and revitalize the Class Meetings, so she made a point of visiting lapsed members and encouraging other good people to become church members. Finally, rather diffidently, she outlined her methods of dealing with 'enquirers', answering their queries and encouraging them to make a commitment.

One final snippet of Sister Jeanie's travels comes from Belfast – she conducted several missions in Ireland over the years – when we read that

> . . . for the first week the Mission was confined to women, and a very gracious work was done. For the last five days men were admitted, and many of them also found pardon. The entire effect of the Mission has been most helpful and encouraging.[23]

In February 1907 Dr. Stephenson commented that

> Sister Jeanie Banks is still in Ireland. For three years she has given the bulk of her time to the Green Isle, and has had many extraordinary experiences. On the whole her work has been wonderfully successful, even when she has been toiling in the midst of Roman Catholic populations.[24]

Many more glowing reports of her work could be given but these give a snapshot of the woman herself and her work. Announcing her wish to retire at the end of August 1912, the Warden, the Rev. William Bradfield, commented to the June Committee that hers was the first deaconess superannuation and the Committee paid tribute to her.

---

23. *FL* (March 1904) pp.42-44; (June 1905) pp.266-67; (March 1906) p.39, (March 1907) pp.43-45; (April 1907) pp.59-60; (May 1907) p.70; (June 1907) pp.91-92
24. *FL* (February 1907) p.20

Retirement of Sister Jeanie Banks 1912

In giving permission to Sister Jeanie Banks to retire from the active work, the Committee desires to place on record its high appreciation of the invaluable service she has rendered to the Deaconess Order and to the Methodist Church during the sixteen years she has laboured as Deaconess Evangelist ... Her evangelistic missions have been owned of God in multitudes of converts, some of whom are now in the ministry, and many others doing great service for Christ in almost all parts of the world. She has also worthily represented the Deaconess Order on many important occasions, and striven, by speech and example, to inspire the younger Sisters with the noblest ideals of service. The Committee prays that Almighty God may bless her in her retirement, and rejoices to know that she still hopes to be useful and from time to time to conduct Missions and continue her work as God gives her strength.

Source: Flying Leaves (July/August 1912) p.102

Jeanie Banks' retirement was regarded by the Order as a sign that the Institute was no longer a novelty.[25] She died on 11th January 1932.

Sister Helen Fieldson, Deaconess Evangelist

In 1902 Jeanie Banks had been joined by Sister Helen Fieldson as another Deaconess Evangelist. Helen Louise Fieldson was brought up in the Church of England before joining the Wesleyan Methodist Church. She entered the Deaconess Institute in 1901 being consecrated at Leeds in April 1902 and the first report of her work in April 1903, while telling of its success and her improvement as a preacher, hints she had health problems. This was indeed the case as from 1913 she had to restrict the number of missions she could take and was advised only to accept engagements in the south of England. Many reports, similar to those of Jeanie Banks, were received about her work, but one in particular is of interest. She is described as a

---

25. *FL* (July/August 1912) p.109; *Wesleyan Methodist Minutes of Conference* (hereafter *WM Mins. of Conf.*) (1913) pp.80-81, 552-54

cultured, able and winning speaker, who used no sensationalism in her methods. From 3rd-14th November 1907 she conducted a mission in Northbrook Street Chapel, Newbury and the *Newbury Wesleyan Record* (December 1907) commented:

> It seemed strange at first to many of our people that a lady should undertake this particular sort of work . . . But we think that few, if any, of those who heard Sister Helen will venture to deny her call to preach the gospel. If anyone came expecting sensational or hysterical services they must have been strangely disappointed. There was in her such gentle modesty combined with quiet dignity; such an utter selflessness, such an evident surrender of herself to be (as she phrased it), simply the channel through which God's message came, that prejudices were forgotten: we felt ourselves lifted to a higher plane, and realised the direct influence of the Holy Spirit.[26]

Once the Wesleyan Methodist Conference in 1910 somewhat relaxed its stance on the preaching of women, several more deaconesses joined the list of Deaconess Evangelists. These included Sisters Florence Bucknell, Myra Lambert, Esther Bee and Mary Coles, with others, for example, Gertrude Coombs, Annie Scott, Bessie Parsons, working in various parts of the country, usually for short periods or on special evangelistic missions. Sister Florence conducted a very successful mission in the Ashton-under-Lyne Circuit with striking results, so that 'the whole spirit of the Church has been changed'. 'As a preacher and worker she has made a most favourable impression on the circuit.'[27] In the autumn of 1912 Florence visited the Rye Circuit and Rev. Walter Hudson commented that

> With a Mission we usually associate excitement and sensationalism, but these were absent from the services . . . Her addresses were well thought out, and revealed not merely care in preparation, but the ability to present old truths with a fascination that stirred the feelings and imagination of her congregation. We are very thankful for the great things achieved, and for the many young lives that have been consecrated to the service of God. The old-fashioned Lovefeast . . . was a great treat, and

26. *FL* (February 1908) p.204
27. *FL* (December 1912) p.173

an inspiration, both to the new converts and to many of
the old members . . .[28]

Sister Myra Lambert contributed to the May 1914 issue of
Flying Leaves and remarked that she had completed 12 missions
during the past winter – five in towns and seven in villages.

Missions 1913/4   **Sister Myra Lambert**

Visiting the homes of the people has brought blessing and salvation
to many. In each Mission efforts have been made to reach all classes.
Public-house visiting and open-air work has yielded good results.
Midnight Meetings in Town Missions brought us the opportunity of
preaching Christ . . . The evangelist's life is full of changes . . . for
after each Mission there is the packing up and moving on. Not always
in express train or motor-car, as I can say from experience. In
journeyings often, in perils of bad weather, in all sorts of vehicles
have I been conveyed to my appointments. Once was I taken in a
carrier's wagon; twice did I ride in a farmer's pig-cart; twice was I put
in a village grocer's cart among the packages of groceries; once was I
dragged in a trailer behind a bicycle; once did I suffer extreme
exhaustion of patience riding in a donkey-cart. To journey by train or
motor is first-class travelling.

Source: Flying Leaves (May 1914) p.76-77

When Sister Cissie Roberts joined the official list of Deaconess
Evangelists in 1915 she was already well-known in many parts of
the country from having assisted her father, Mr. H. H. Roberts of
Cliff College in his missions.

Appreciation of the work of the Deaconess Evangelists

Only those who understand the difficulties and discouragements of
many of our village causes can enter into all that it means to have the
help of a Deaconess Evangelist as a 'travelling preacher' in country
circuits. During her stay of three weeks or a month in a village she
gets into the homes of the people and personally invites them to her
first week of Services, known as Prayer Services, for the deepening of
the spiritual life of those who are members or for any desirous for
those things pertaining to spirituality. The value of the Services as a
preparation for the evangelistic work which follows is partly estimated

---

28. *FL* (January 1913) p.6

> by those who attend them. It is quite a common occurrence for eighty
> to a hundred people to be present. How mightily God's spirit has
> prevailed, and, again and again, those who never have been known to
> enter the village chapel have come to hear the old, old story of Jesus
> and His love, simply told and supplemented by song.
>
> *Source: Flying Leaves* (September 1914) p.132

Perhaps the work of the Deaconess Evangelists can best be summed
up in the prayer of a six year old boy during a mission conducted by
one of the Sisters:

> Lord, bless our Sister, make her good and keep her
> good. Help her to bring all the people in our village to
> Jesus with their sins. Help her to do her ten days' hard,
> for Jesu's sake. Amen.[29]

The conditions insisted upon by the Order for a circuit to use the
services of a Deaconess Evangelist were spelled out in 1915:

> The usual terms on which we send out Deaconess-
> Evangelists for a Ten Days' Mission are that an average
> charge of £1 for railway travelling is paid to us, that the
> Deaconess receives comfortable hospitality during the
> Mission, and that the collections on the second Sunday
> of the Mission, without any deduction, are given to the
> Deaconess Institute.[30]

After 1919, when Wesleyan Methodism finally gave official
recognition to women preachers, more deaconesses were local
preachers or regularly took services. In 1924 Sister Ellen Gould,
who was stationed in St. Albans where there were eight churches in
the circuit, remarked that she frequently visited the six village
chapels. She felt that often life in the village was lonely and that the
churches 'need us desperately, and many of them do not even know
of our existence' and suggested that one or two deaconesses might
be sent 'up and down the land' to let such places know the service
the Order could provide and so 'we should be going not only to
those who need us, but to those who need us most'.[31]

---

29. *FL* (November 1915) p.89
30. *FL* (July/August 1915) p.51
31. *The Agenda* (January 1924) pp.10-11

Service at a Village Church   **Sister Ellen Gould**

It is two o'clock on Sunday afternoon, and pouring in torrents of rain. The Sister is planned to preach at a village six miles away at three o'clock. It is a village inaccessible by bus or train, so the journey is taken on a bicycle against a strong head wind that drives the rain relentlessly against the cyclist. But Ilkley-trained Sisters are 'ready for anything', so on arrival the preacher removes her raincoat, dons a bonnet which she produces from a parcel, and is presentable and dry – save for her feet, which are soaking wet, in spite of a pair of high-laced boots. But help is forthcoming. A kindly neighbour provides dry shoes and stockings. So the Sister, who possesses size four feet, ascends the rostrum in shoes size six, and sends up a silent prayer of thankfulness for the comfort of dry feet, and another prayer of gratitude that the front of the rostrum is draped with a curtain.

Source: The Agenda (January 1924) p.10

In *The Agenda* in 1930 Ethel Fellows recounted how she had become a Deaconess Evangelist unexpectedly when the appointed one became ill. It was not a work to which she had felt any particular call in the past, rather the reverse if anything, but now she felt compelled to offer herself. With Lillie Mitchell, who specialised in singing, she went to village chapels, where at first the people were polite, but not enthusiastic about such a mission. However, they were won over and she felt 'the attempt was more than justified' as many were 'raised to a new faith in God' and there 'was a quickening of mind . . . especially in a group of young people' who 'enrolled with the Methodist Study Centre, and are now taking the Course on "The Life and Teaching of Jesus" '.[32]

The United Methodist Free Churches/United Methodist Church

As noted in the previous chapter, one of the main emphases of the Deaconess Institute of the United Methodist Free Churches/United Methodist Church was evangelism, and the Constitution contained the following objectives:

> The object of the Free Methodist Deaconess Institute is to prepare Christian Women for the service of Christ:
> (i) As Evangelists, to labour in Churches, Circuits,

---

32. *The Agenda* (March 1930) pp.10-11

Mission Centres, and Villages. (ii) As Bible Women and Nurses, to visit the people in their homes, and to minister to the sick and poor. (iii) As Missionaries, to serve on Foreign Stations. (iv) As Special Agents, to organise Societies of Women and Workers throughout our Churches.[33]

By 1894 it was felt that it would be of benefit for the Sisters to go out on short evangelistic missions and these met with much appreciation. Many village churches which could not afford a Sister for a long period had special evangelistic missions so that by 1897 180 such causes had been helped while in 1898 alone 162 special missions were undertaken.

Evangelistic Branch

Churches have been revived, wanderers restored, men and women have been brought to religious decision, and the church workers have been gladdened with the joy of spiritual harvest.

Source: United Methodist Free Churches Minutes of Conference (1898) p.227

By 1899 there were 34 Sisters in the organisation, of whom 11 were engaged in district visiting with another 18 who spent more than half their time on missions and five in training. The Report to the Annual Assembly emphasises the Institute's commitment to the evangelistic work of the Sisters:

> All are deaconesses; they are unsalaried workers whose supreme aim is to win the people to God. In serving the churches they willingly apply themselves to that particular work for which the Committee and the Church Officers think they are adapted. From September to April they conducted 180 evangelistic Missions; each extends to a fortnight, the whole making a total of two thousand five hundred and eighty public services.[34]

---

33. *Ministering Women: The Story of the Work of the Sisters connected with the United Methodist Deaconess Institute,* [hereafter Smith] (Henry Smith, n.d.) p.49
34. *UMFC Mins. of Conf.* (1899) p.222. The deaconesses were 'unsalaried' as, apart from a small allowance for expenses, those who could afford it were expected to contribute to their own support and all money received passed on to the Institute. cf. Smith pp.50-52

The importance attracted to this evangelistic work is shown by the information that 150,000 handbills, containing portraits of the missioners, printed for 120 churches to publicize the missions had been very effective. It seems that the Institute was very ready to make use of all means available to 'save souls'.

Testimony to the value of Deaconess work   **A minister**

I am quite sure if the Bowron House Committee could send such a worker as the Sister we have to all our churches, very good blessing would result therefrom.

Source: United Methodist Free Churches Minutes of Conference
(1900) p.233

Although the United Methodist Free Churches do not seem to have had women ministers in the same sense as the Primitive Methodists or the Bible Christians did a number of their deaconesses did preach. The Institute Committee, and by implication the Connexion, was open-minded enough to acknowledge their ministry:

> Some of the Sisters preach the Gospel. The committee makes no apology for this. From the first they have believed that women, as well as men, should get the pattern of their life from God, and in determining their vocation bear in mind that the talent is the call. When the Committee found that some Sisters possessed great evangelical gifts, they recognised therein the wisdom and goodness of God, and made special arrangements that each Sister might in this direction, fulfil the spiritual destiny of which God had made her capable. The results have been a joy to thousands.[35]

They were also realistic enough to note that in the 140 special missions of 1902-03 when 2,850 people had been 'consecrated to God' some would 'fall away', but, on the other hand, there would be others not included in the number who 'received good'. Another interesting comment that year is that the United Methodist Free Churches deaconesses had conducted missions for all the Methodist denominations, namely, two for Wesleyan Methodism in Lancashire; two in Yorkshire and one in Cornwall for the Primitive Methodists; two in Durham for the Bible Christians, and one each

---

35. *UMFC Mins. of Conf.* (1903) pp.254-55

for the Methodist New Connexion, (Staffordshire), and the Wesleyan Reform (Oxfordshire) while a Sister was serving the Methodist New Connexion for the summer months. In all these places they had been treated well and all the churches had 'contributed liberally to the funds'. Not only does this imply considerable co-operation between the various Methodist branches, at the grass roots at least, but it also shows that the evangelistic work of the United Methodist Free Churches deaconesses was effective and appreciated beyond the bounds of their own denomination.

When the United Methodist Free Churches, the Methodist New Connexion and the Bible Christians joined together in 1907 to form the United Methodist Church and as neither the Methodist New Connexion nor the Bible Christians had a Deaconess Institute, it was felt that Union would provide increased opportunities. With regard to the evangelistic work of the United Methodist Deaconesses T. J. Cope wrote:

> . . . we had added to the Institute an evangelistic Mission branch. Its constitution differed from that of other Deaconess Institutes in that it required all the students to be trained as deaconesses; it also provided that those who possessed evangelistic gifts should be prepared to conduct special Mission services if and when required.
>
> We secured godly and gifted women, gave them suitable training, and when the churches needed their help for special aggressive work, we sent them forth to do their best to win the people to God. We did not withdraw deaconesses from their work of visitation to send them forth to preach. We called out sufficient to meet all demands . . .
>
> A few more or less influential people expressed their disapproval of this branch of the work. They charged us with 'diverting the Institute from its original purpose', with 'manufacturing a lot of women parsons', and they told us that it did not need the vision of a seer to predict our speedy failure.
>
> Happily, we were not responsible to mere objectors . . .
> We arranged to send deaconess-evangelists to conduct special Missions of ten days each . . . [36]

---

36. Cope pp.17-18

It was agreed the churches would provide the Sisters with accommodation and that the collections on the second Sunday and the last night of the mission should go to the Deaconess Fund, while the Deaconess Committee paid the travelling expenses. Thus poorer congregations were afforded the opportunity of having a visit from 'a special agent' as collections from larger missions subsidized them. It seems that evangelistic missions usually took place between the beginning of August and the end of March, so in the other months the deaconesses were available to help elsewhere as district visitors.

As we have seen, the aim of the Institute was to be evangelistic and deaconesses with special evangelistic talents were in great demand. Missions served two purposes – fostering the spiritual welfare of the people and engendering income for the Institute from the collections. Statistically, in the nine months from September 1901-April 1902 191 special missions were conducted and from 185 of these 4,081 conversions were recorded, but more important was the impact felt on the life of the churches. As with the Wesley Deaconesses, the United Methodist Sisters backed up their missions with permanent organisations in the churches, especially Christian Endeavour Societies for young people. Unfortunately, the evangelical work of the United Methodist Deaconesses fell victim to its own success. Cope reports:

> The success of the evangelistic branch of the work was so much before the churches that there was danger that the Institute would be regarded as a Women's Special Mission Agency. This we wished to avoid, for many influential ministers and members, whose sympathy and help we needed, were strongly prejudiced against women preaching. Favourably to impress these friends it was necessary to bring to their notice the good work which was being done by the visiting deaconesses. But this was one of our difficulties. The ministry of the deaconess evangelist was in public and its success proclaimed itself, but the ministry of the visitation deaconess was to the people in their homes . . . [37]

Obviously, as this latter work was confidential, it did not attract so much general attention.

---

37. Cope, p.19

It seems that many people, apparently, while approving wholeheartedly of deaconesses visiting homes to spread the Gospel and helping with Sunday School work, objected to the more public evangelistic work. They felt it was improper for them to conduct evangelistic services and maybe even unscriptural, but others believed that if God owned the work done by the Sisters and conversions ensued then that was sufficient. It is interesting that while there does not seem to have been much opposition to the Deaconess Evangelists in Wesleyan Methodism, where women's preaching was regarded with suspicion, in United Methodism, one of whose component parts was the Bible Christian Connexion where women preachers, including travelling preachers, had been welcomed right from the very beginning, there should have been some reservations. Would this be the Methodist New Connexion influence?

A few comments about the work of the United Methodist Deaconess Evangelists will show their impact:

> Her unaffected and earnest manner of speech and her consecrated tact in the after-meetings won many for Christ.

and

> Never before has the neighbourhood been so thoroughly awakened and so manifestly interested. Seventy-five persons have come forward during the services and expressed their willingness to become disciples of Christ, forty-five of them being adults. The church is profoundly grateful to God for such wonderful blessing, and thankful to the Deaconess Institute for the services of the Sister.

and

> Our present organist, two of our local preachers, and others who are taking an active part in our work in the church and school crossed the dividing line during the mission you conducted.

and

> Two who were converted during Missions I have conducted are now in the ministry and many are local preachers.[38]

---

38. Smith, pp.119-22

The 1905 Report of the Institute perhaps gives as good a summary as any of the work of the United Methodist Free Churches Deaconesses:

> During the winter some Sisters were set apart to conduct evangelistic missions. The General Election greatly interfered with this branch of the work; nevertheless, from October to March the Sisters conducted 101 special Missions of ten days each, with gratifying results . . . Within a month the secretary received letters testifying to the value of the Sisters' work from individuals and churches in eleven different counties, from Somerset to Durham, and from Norfolk to Lancashire. These letters are gratifying to the Committee; they testified to the growing influence of the Deaconess Institute and the Churches' appreciation of the Sisters' work.[39]

The appointment list of October 1906 names 36 deaconesses with six students in training. Of these, Sisters Muriel (entered 1897), Rhoda (1898), Amy (1901), Ada (1901), Phoebe (1902), Harriet (1902), Monica (1904), Lois (1905), are listed for 'Special Mission Work' – so this means that almost a quarter were engaged in this type of work.

In 1907 Sister Muriel reported that her work had been principally evangelistic, though obviously with some visitation. For nine years she had been 'on the road', as it were, from Durham to Cornwall and had found that church attendances had fallen, although people's giving and social conscience seemed to have increased. To stem the fall she suggested that 'all seats should be free and unappropriated' and that 'more fire, both in the pulpit and pew', was needed. In the villages she felt that more concentrated work by the Sisters would be beneficial.

The 17th Report (1907-08) was the first one after the 1907 Union and the first Conference of the United Methodist Church showed its appreciation of the Sisters' work by resolving that one of the objects to which the Thanksgiving Fund should be devoted should be 'the development of the Bowron House Institute'. The evangelistic work continued and many stories could be told, but two must suffice:

---

39. *UMDI Report* (1905-06) p.9

> A most encouraging mission was held at Chase
> Terrace, Cheslyn Hay. The Sister attributes the success
> to the fact that the church was well prepared. The
> members were full of expectation and co-operated
> heartily. Other churches rendered help. The people
> crowded the chapel.

and

> At Dudley Road Church, Birmingham, there was a little
> uncertainty whether women missioners would be
> acceptable to the congregation. But arrangements were
> made for two of the deaconess evangelists to conduct a
> mission. The results were satisfactory in every
> particular. The church and congregation were
> delighted with services and the number of converts
> exceeded the expectation of the most sanguine.[40]

A ringing tribute to the effectiveness of United Methodist
Deaconess Evangelists was given at the 1908 Sheffield Conference
Ordination Service when three young ministers received into full
Connexion testified that they had been converted in Missions
conducted by the Deaconesses.[41]

The following extract entitled 'My Call to Preach' from the
United Methodist Deaconess Institute Report 1909-10 gives a good
example of the evangelistic rôle of the Sisters:

> It was a dull December afternoon and the third in
> succession of pouring rain. I was happy to be indoors
> and dry. At four o'clock a message came from the
> junior minister of our circuit, 'Will you come to me as
> soon as you leave business?' I called on the minister to
> find him suffering from severe cold and quite unable to
> go out. It was the fourth night in a week of 'special
> services,' held in a small church three miles out in the
> country. The minister said: 'I want you to go to Coaley
> tonight and take the service.' It looked impossible, and
> I said it was. He replied, 'You are able to do it and you
> must; I have no one else to depend on.' At five o'clock
> I went home to tea and prepared for the service. God
> gave me: 'I am come that ye might have Life.' As I
> walked along in the slush and rain the thoughts

---

40. *UMDI Report* (1909-10) pp.45-46
41. *UMDI Report* (1908-09) pp.10, 45-46

gathered about the text. It was a small gathering, but they had come through the rain and across swampy fields to be there. At the close one bright girl came forward and stepped into 'Life'. On the return journey it still rained, and there were no lamps to light the way, but I was borne on wings. The Lord had set his seal on me and called me to preach.

'Sister Elizabeth'[42]

There were regular reports in *The United Methodist* about the work of the deaconesses and, while many of them merely note that successful evangelistic missions had been held, there are one or two more detailed contributions. In January 1924, after briefly mentioning the places where missions had been conducted, the report continued:

It will be noticed that many of these Missions are being held in small country churches. This often makes it hard for the Sisters, for their helpers and supporters are few, but it is a form of service rendered by this department of our Home Missions which is of incalculable benefit to many of the outposts of the Denomination. Our first consideration is service to our churches, and consequently many of these remote country places which cannot receive much ministerial oversight are touched by a connexional agent, and the people often greatly uplifted.[43]

The Primitive Methodist 'Sisters of the People'

The Primitive Methodist Church did not have a connexionally settled Deaconess Order, but there were Sisters of the People, some of whom studied at Bowron House. This is borne out by the 1932 Deaconess Institute Report in the *United Methodist Minutes of Conference* which states that:

For many years the Primitive Methodist Students have attended our classes, and there are the happiest relations, together with close fellowship, between the Wesleyan Order and our own.[44]

---

42. *UMDI Report* (1909-10) p.25
43. MSS Cuttings 10th January 1924)
44. *United Methodist Minutes of Conference* (hereafter *UM Mins. of Conf.* (1932) p.176

There is no indication whether the Primitive Methodist Sisters of the People preached, but bearing in mind early Primitive Methodism's use of women as travelling preachers and their later use as missioners, evangelists and local preachers it would seem highly likely that at least some of them did preach.[45] In fact out of the 22 ex-Primitive Methodist Sisters received at the Birmingham Convocation on Friday, 13th April 1934 nine were accredited local preachers.[46] Unfortunately no detailed account of their work appears to have survived.

The Wesley Deaconess Order of the Methodist Church

After the 1932 Union the deaconesses continued with their work much as before, but with the added resources and scope which the unified enlarged Order afforded.

In August 1942 Dr. Maltby, the previous Warden of the Wesley Deaconess Order, contributed an article to *The Agenda* entitled 'Thirty Precepts for Preachers' which must have and still does strike a chord with both those who preach and those who listen!

THIRTY PRECEPTS FOR PREACHERS

1. Listen before you speak. See before you say.

2. Remember Peniel and wrestle with great themes, even if they throw you. Jacob was not Israel until he shrunk a sinew.

3. You preach the Gospel; therefore, no demand without the gift; no diagnosis without the cure. One word about sin; ten for the Saviour.

4. Be loyal to your text. Be aware of the context; if you leave it, be courteous and ask permission. Possibly the writer had bigger thoughts than your own.

5. Irrelevance is sometimes an infirmity; usually it is a sin.

6. Preachers as well as motorists should remember that the aim is not to cover the ground, but to see the country – and seeing, to love.

7. There is always water if you bore deep enough.

---

45. MS E. D. Graham, 'Chosen by God: the Female Itinerants of Early Primitive Methodism' (Ph.D. thesis, University of Birmingham 1986)
46. *Roll of Members in the Wesley Deaconess Order of the Methodist Church, March 1935* p.11 cf. *The Methodist Local Preachers' Who's Who 1934* pp.129, 154, 170, 200, 388, 423-24, 462, 504, 573

8. The well is deep and you must have something to draw with. But there is no need to make people drink out of the bucket, still less to chew the rope.

9. A teacher should know more than he teaches, and if he knows more than he teaches, he will teach more than he knows.

10. Illustrate but don't illustrate the obvious.

11. We needs must illustrate the greater by the analogy of the less, but your illustrations must not belittle the theme.

12. Aim at being independent of the concordance, but do not disdain it until you are.

13. Emotion rises out of the truth: emotionalism is poured on to it.

14. Preaching without emotion is not preaching, but beware of the cheap substitute.

15. Love simple speech as much as you hate shallow thinking.

16. Polysyllables are not the sign of profundity. Often they are the cloak of poverty, and bought at a jumble sale.

17. Never talk down to your audience; they are not there.

18. Beware of the abstract noun. The abstract puffeth up: the concrete buildeth up.

19. By your consonants people will know what you say; by your words where you come from.

20. Be audible, but it is not needful to shout. Clearness carries further than clamour.

21. In speaking, legato rather than staccato is the rule; and andante rather than presto, but none of these continuously for that is monotony. Heresy has slain its thousands, but monotony its tens of thousands.

22. Having a heavy charge, the preacher needs a light heart. Let him not look any more miserable than he must.

23. 'The joy should from our hearts arise
And speak and sparkle in our eyes (if possible)
    And vibrate on our tongues.'

24. Some preachers are like a Goods train – their sentences all tugs and stops. Glide, if you can.

25. Be sparing of gestures, but do not be a post or a robot. If your hands can talk, let them; if not, give them a rest.

26. Be not like the brook; pause sometimes.

27. (For women only) – If your speaking voice is a natural contralto, give thanks; if not do your best.

28. One cannot always finish, but one can always stop.

29. A preacher's damnation. 'He spoke of great things and made them small: of holy things and made them common: of God and made Him of no account.'

30. A preacher's Thanksgiving:

> 'I who have given to thee my best
> Rejoice thy word is unexpressed,
> And inexpressible must be
> On this side of eternity;
> And I with all my travail vast
> Am glad that I must fail at last.
> If I had found the Word complete
> No glory could I march to meet
> A pilgrim home from pilgrimage!
> A soldier with no fight to wage!
> But now my powers I still must spend
> And go on failing to the end,
> But failing I shall leave behind
> Some hints of the Eternal mind,
> And hungry pilgrims where I went
> May find a broken sacrament.'

(Edward Shillito)
W. R. M.
Source: *The Agenda* (August 1942) pp.18-19

The changed attitude of Methodism towards women preachers is shown in an article written in July 1948 by a retired deaconess, Sister Sadie Martin:

> I had gone as a very young 'grey' Sister to a new circuit, and on the first Sunday evening my very dignified Superintendent called me into his study. He looked very grave; I felt nervous. Handing me a Minutes of Conference, opened at a certain resolution relating to women's work, he said, 'I hope that you will never feel called upon to preach while in this circuit.' I assured him that I would not transgress. Forty years later I found myself with no option, for I was now in a different world. Another Superintendent sometimes expected as many as twenty-six appointments in one quarter![47]

---

47. *The Agenda* (July 1948) p.2

Caravan Work

A new opening for evangelistic work came just before Methodist Union was formally ratified. Convocation in April 1932 expressed concern about evangelistic work in villages and requested that ways of addressing this be explored. The Warden remarked that this type of work had always been part of deaconess work, but that,

Sisters Dorothy Bull and Susan Sanders with Caravan 'Epworth', Autumn 1949

at the moment, opportunities for it were probably being curtailed by lack of finance. He suggested that 'what was needed was a Caravan, and the Sisters received the idea with much enthusiasm'. Was the wish father to the thought? For in July he reported that the Home Mission Committee had offered the Order the use of the Home Mission caravan. Three deaconesses, Sisters Nora Chapman, Rene Holloway and Mary Parris would take charge of it and work in the villages. They made their first foray on familiar ground by going for a month to Hampsthwaite with encouraging results, so then they ventured further afield to Middleton-on-Tees where they found the work much harder and less successful, but the next five weeks spent in the villages of the Thirsk Circuit proved more rewarding. After a break at the College over Christmas and the New Year the caravanners planned to set out for the Oxford area.[48]

By 1938 there were three caravans, staffed by five deaconesses. The original idea of caravans being used for work in villages had been extended to cover urban 'overspill' areas for Jessie Burnett and Olive Jones took their caravan 'Faith' to a housing estate in Birmingham:

> The caravan 'Faith' is no longer in the leafy lanes of England, but is pitched in the centre of a new housing area in Birmingham. There are upwards of 3,000 houses already here, some having been occupied for 3

---

48. Record of Convocation (1892-1935) (hereafter RConv.) 1932 (12th April); Wesley Deaconess Institute Minutes (1911-33) (hereafter WDIMins II p.275; *The Agenda* (Christmas 1932) p.6

years, and as yet no church or chapel. We are holding our meetings in a big marquee erected for the purpose.'[49]

The headlines, announcing their mission, in the *Birmingham Gazette* read 'Two girls open Caravan Church in Birmingham Field' and 'Faith Crusade from Gipsy Caravan, temporary home of two gallant and happy women'. At the time the local Methodists could not manage to open a church on the estate, but in 1942 Sister Jessie was back again and 'eagerly waiting for the day in September when I can write in my journal "Beeches Estate Methodist Church opened". Yes, after four years – and in war-time – large wooden erections are being completed.'

'Call it a Night', Birmingham, June 1938
Deaconess Caravanner, Sister Jessie Burnett

11 p.m. – Heinz mushroom soup heated on a 'primus' stove . . . Yes, I know 'tis June . . . It is cold and there is a calm which bespeaks a storm . . .

11.45 p.m. – Then crash! – The first gust of wind has carried off the dust-bin lid! We hear it bowling over the Common, and finally come to rest with a clatter . . .

12-Mid. – Ooch! – Now it is really beginning. The two off-side wheels of the caravan nearly leave the ground, our feet come up to meet our heads, and doors rattle ominously . . .

12.30 a.m. – There was nothing else for it . . . each corner of the van had to be scaled and the ropes hooked on to the top four corners, then a mallet unearthed and the pins firmly buried in the cinder path . . .

3.30 a.m. – Bang! Bang! Bang! What on earth has happened now? A beam of light shines through the door, lighting up the whole caravan. An authoritative voice shouts through the letter-box, 'I'm the police! – Sorry to wake you up, but if you don't come quickly your tent will be down!' . . . All one side of the tent is down, and the 2ft. wooden stakes have been tossed aside like nine-pins. The wind is swirling under the tent and lifting it like an ungainly parachute! The 'police' is a gentleman of the first water, and he shoulders the mallet bravely, while we hang on to the ropes and his bull's-eye lantern.

Any moment we expect to be carried skyward! We feel as if a label ought to be attached to our ankles, with a message written in several languages thereon! 'Will the finder, please return to Ilkley, England,

---

49. *The Agenda* (October 1938) pp.11-12

as soon as possible – must be fed if kept longer than a week.'

4.30 a.m. – . . . we turn to tea for comfort . . .

6.45 a.m. – Our 'water-scout', a boy of 10 years wants to know if we want any water!! . . .

7.30 a.m. – The postman . . . has no sooner deposited his packet on the floor . . . than a shrill voice sounds through the letter-box (7.45 a.m.) 'I don't want to disturb you, but will you tell me what time the Women's Meeting starts, I want to bring two more.

But it is now morning and we 'Called it a Night!'

EPILOGUE

Scene: The caravan, 11 a.m. same morning.

Superintendent of the Circuit speaking:

. . . 'and you took his number of course! We should like to send him an official letter of thanks from the Quarterly Meeting.'

Source: The Agenda (October 1938) pp.11-12

Doris Chaffer's caravan too was on a new housing estate in the Leeds District in 1942, where the church had made little impact and was on the verge of closing, but after missions she could write that 'For the first time in twenty years the church is really affecting its neighbourhood. A deaconess is to be stationed here in September to cope with new opportunities.'[50]

Sisters Joan Dickenson and Jean Oglethorpe with Caravan 'Joy', Autumn 1949

The caravan 'Good News' was staffed by Margaret Horn and Beth Bridges in 1955 and the former gave a description of the missions undertaken. Each caravan stayed for 17 days in one area which gave time for the deaconesses to become known to the local people and engage in what Hugh Bourne and the early Primitive Methodists called 'conversation preaching'. The 17-day campaigns in the caravan 'Good News' began for Sister Beth Bridges on the third Saturday of every month when the caravanners set off for their appointed venue. She describes their arrival as sometimes 'easy for the caravan's coming is new, exciting,

---

50. *The Agenda* (August 1942) p.9

different, and the leaflets, complete with the doubtful help of the campaigners' photographs, are in every home, and we are NEWS! Sometimes embarrassingly so, as the night when my colleague and I sat on a bus listening to the amazing tale of our exploits in another village, and stared out of the window hoping we would pass unrecognised, vain hope!'[51]

Caravan Mission 1974   **Sister Margaret Graham**

'When I heard you were coming to our church I said, 'What on earth are they going to do here for six weeks – . . .'

It is a reaction . . . [we] . . . have often met in our work with the caravan, and part of the reason for it is that to many people the idea of 'mission' is a very narrow one, and the words Caravan Mission conjure up a picture in their minds of two very earnest women conducting highly emotional services, in an aggressive evangelistic manner for a week or so, and it is little wonder that there is apprehension at the thought of six such weeks! That our arrival and subsequent work is usually greeted with relief, we see as confirmation that what we actually do more aptly meets the need than that picture.

We see 'mission' as having a very broad definition, as being the whole activity of the whole people of God in the church and in the world, and in our work we try to interpret it as such.

Source: *A Way of Serving: The Magazine of the Wesley Deaconess Order* (Autumn 1974) pp.1-2

Caravan work was still going strong in 1974, though it was very different from the early years. Now the caravans went to Methodist Districts by invitation through the Home Mission Division and stayed in that District for two years, moving from place to place, which gave the 'missioners' independence and enabled them to become part of the community. The caravan provided not only a base for the deaconesses, but also neutral ground on which people could meet informally and 'so feel free to express their point of view'. Much work was done with young people, in Study Groups and through House Groups. Margaret Graham summed up the work that she and Joyce McCaffer did from caravan 'Promise' during the two years spent in the Oxford and Leicester District (1973-75):

---

51. *The Wesley Deaconess Magazine* (July 1955) pp.8-9, (July 1957) pp.17-18

Much of our work is the same as that of other deaconesses, except that we live in six different places each year. Six or seven weeks is a very short time for work like this, but given the co-operation and interest of the local people, it is often amazing what can be accomplished in that time. People have found renewed hope and faith, new vision and a new concern to share their life in Christ with the community in which they live as together we move out in mission to that community.[52]

So for many years the Caravan ministry of the deaconesses, supported by the Home Mission Department, served a very useful evangelistic purpose in taking the Gospel into many outlying areas and revitalizing churches and communities.

A Caravan to the Country

We have bee-hives to the left of us and bee-hives to the right of us in our present surroundings: we are hoping they won't get any ideas about swarming until we have departed. We are also living on goats' milk. We had been drinking it for a couple of days before we discovered it didn't come from a cow!'

Source: The Wesley Deaconess Magazine (July 1954) p.12

War Time Work and Chaplaincy

The work done by deaconesses during the three wars, which raged within the timescale of this book, was very significant, not only for itself, but also in relation to the whole question of women's ministry.

Much about the Boer War (1899-1902) will be found in the chapter on Overseas Work in Africa, but it is worth noting here that in the autumn of 1898 Sister Kate Christie was appointed as Lady Superintendent of the Methodist Soldiers' Home at Curragh Camp in Ireland. The Soldiers' Home was attached to the church and she was well received by the soldiers to whom she became a trusted friend and confidante. Her nursing skills were called upon by those who did not want to go into hospital. The *Irish Christian Advocate* gave a glowing report of the Camp's Christmas Party. A fountain

---

52. *A Way of Serving*: (Autumn 1974) pp.1-4

pen and 'a timepiece' were given to Sister Kate by the soldiers as 'a mark of their gratitude for her work amongst them and sympathy with them'. At the Annual Meeting of the Institute in 1899 Sister Kate convulsed her audience by telling the assembled Sisters that although there were three Homes at Curragh Camp – Roman Catholic, Anglican and Wesleyan – the soldiers voted the Wesleyan as 'the homeliest' and by appealing for reading matter, ' "If you have got any *Strand Magazine,* send them on to me, and *The Woman at Home:* the soldiers like that too." '[53]

It is clear that work with the Forces was considered important as the *Stations* of September 1908 list:

V. THE KENT DISTRICT
Chatham Mission, Garrison and Naval Port,
Sister Eva Palmer

VIII. THE PORTSMOUTH DISTRICT
Portsmouth Mission, Garrison and Naval Port,
Sister Harriet Bedmore
Salisbury Plain *(Tidsworth, Bulford, Salisbury)*
Sister Dora Stephenson (ARMY WORK);[54]

Sister Dora Stephenson

and in September 1910

V. THE KENT DISTRICT
FOLKESTONE *(Shorncliffe Camp),*
Sister Maud Westall *(Sandgate)*[55]

From September 1914 the Warden, William Bradfield makes reference in *Flying Leaves* to World War I (1914-18) and the impact it was having on the deaconesses and their work. The College enlargement scheme had to be shelved, the size of *Flying Leaves* reduced because of the cost, some appointments 'given up' as circuits could no longer afford them. In 1915 intending candidates were warned to check the trains to Ilkley as sometimes they were requisitioned by the military and they might find themselves stranded! In June 1915 concern was expressed by Convocation, and passed to the General Committee, about the rise in the cost of living. However, Bradfield emphasised

---

53. *HH* (March 1899) pp.69-70, (June 1899) p.138
54. *FL* (September 1908) p.305
55. *FL* (September 1910) p.128

that the war had meant that the work of the deaconesses was even more important. Other effects were highlighted in the Report to Conference:

> The war conditions have . . . called for some changes and adaptations . . . Very useful and much appreciated work has been done by many . . . among soldiers in the various camps throughout the country; and in a good many places where the supply of preachers for our village congregations has failed, the deaconess has been called upon to fill the gap. In a few cases she has taken the place of a minister or probationer, called away as a chaplain or enlisting as a soldier. To all such special calls, a ready response has been made. The assembling in large numbers of girls for munition work, living in huts and away from home influence, has brought the latest call for deaconess service. To meet these will tax heavily the resourcefulness and adaptability of our workers, but we believe they will prove equal to the occasion.

and the comment is added:

> The Committee recognises with much appreciation the quiet courage that has been shown . . . by those, (and there are quite a large number of them), who have had experience of Zeppelin raids in England. It is a great satisfaction that no one has failed, through personal alarm, to render the deaconess service, which has sometimes been called for in very exciting and even terrible circumstances.[56]

A Ladies Meeting, held during the 1916 Convocation, when some of the deaconesses gave first-hand accounts of their war experiences, bears out the words in that Report. Sister Edith Killick, (Nottingham Mission), spoke of her work with families of men who were away at the war and commented that as a result 20 people had joined the church, while Sister Bessie Fisher, (London Central Mission), told of her work in one of the air-raid areas.

In the December 1914 issue of *Flying Leaves* there are several anonymous extracts from the letters of deaconesses who were in appointments which brought them into close contact with servicemen and their families:

---

56. WDI Report 1915-16 in WDI Mins II between pages 78-79

Since the war broke out my work has changed very much. The visiting is very sad and terrible. I often dread going to the barracks to see the wives of men at the front, and yet I am glad to be able to comfort and help them. A few weeks ago I feared one woman, whose little baby was about ten days old, might lose her reason. Although no news had arrived, she felt convinced her husband had been killed. None of the other women could help her – they all had the same look of hopeless despair; but she was glad for me to pray, and I told her for the sake of her little children she must not give way. About a week later she heard that her husband was wounded and then she was content, and restful.

and

Among my many duties I have had to write letters to mothers for young men who were leaving for the front. The poor fellows do not feel like writing themselves and I have been so glad to be able to do it for them.[57]

In October 1915 Bradfield wrote about the danger of panic:

We have a considerable number of deaconesses . . . inside the areas that are open to the attacks of hostile aircraft. The entirely wicked plan of using these new engines of destruction for the purpose of spreading anguish and terror among the unarmed general population must be part of our appeal to the judgement seat of Almighty God against our present enemies . . . it would be 'giving place to the devil' if our people were to allow themselves to come under the domination of that most contemptible and hateful of the devils known as panic . . . it remains true that to give way to panic is worse than to die. It is, therefore, a great task that falls to our deaconesses . . . to help these sufferers to endure bravely the terrible shocks to which they have been subjected. Sometimes a letter has told me . . . of God's sustaining presence taking away all personal fear, and giving strength for the ministry of comfort to which a deaconess is so especially called. I want to ask the prayers of all who love our work for those called at this time to this special ministry.[58]

---

57. *FL* (December 1914) p.160
58. *FL* (October 1915) pp.79-80

In the very last issue of *Flying Leaves* a Circuit Deaconess wrote about the way her church was coping with the worries arising from the war, how many were thinking of others and how each week mothers brought gifts of fruit for her to take into the hospitals. She added that her Sisterhood had 'adopted an interned prisoner in Germany, and we send him a parcel once a fortnight, value 5s'.[59]

A final extract shows how Christians from various parts of the world came together during the war and found a 'home' in the local Methodist church:

> We are still busy with work amongst the soldiers. We have an average of seventy-five at the 'Soldier's Tea' every Sunday and amongst them on one Sunday we had men from England, Scotland, Ireland (Tipperary), Wales, Newfoundland and one man had travelled from Chili (sic), Peru, six thousand miles to enlist; he is the son of a missionary, and still in the city, awaiting orders for the front.
>
> At our social hour the other night, a Newfoundland man sang, with an Englishman accompanist; another Newfoundland Divinity student conducted family prayer at the close, and an Englishman reading the scriptures.[60]

All too soon again the threat of war and the worsening situation in Europe affected the Deaconess Order for in April 1939 Convocation had to face the question of National Service. It was felt that each individual sister should regard her commitment to the Church to be paramount, but then make her own judgement about any war service. The likelihood of war had an impact on the Wesley Deaconess Order as potential candidates were drafted into the forces and the Warden had numerous negotiations with the Ministry of Labour and National Service to try to get them released for training. In 1942 the deaconesses were required to register, but it was understood that, when their vocation was declared, they would then be exempted.

The work done in bombed areas is highlighted by the deaths of deaconesses, Evelyne Harrison and Evelyn Palmer, working at Bethnal Green Central Hall, and Jean McNair in Cubitt Town

---

59. *FL* (December 1915) p.97
60. *FL* (July/August 1915) p.54

(Poplar and Bow Mission) during air raids. This led to the Committee in December 1940 passing a resolution to be sent to all members of the Order and it gives some inkling of the work done at this time:

> The Committee . . . wishes to record with what pain and what admiration it has heard of the work and endurance of the Sisters in the bombed areas of London, Birmingham, Bristol, Coventry, Liverpool and other towns. For many weeks now they have shared the dangers and privations of the people among whom they worked. Some of them have not known for weeks together what it is to sleep in a bed; food and sleep they took when and as they could – or did without. Seeing death and destruction continually about them, they expected no immunities, but accepted necessary risks or avoided the unnecessary as the occasion seemed to require. Finding themselves among all the things it is natural to fear, they were lifted above fear, 'took their share of hardship as good soldiers of Jesus Christ', and were able to minister courage and good cheer in innumerable places where it was most needed.
>
> Some carried their service to the breaking point, yet after a brief respite, desired only to return. Maud Wilkinson was intending so to return, but her strength was spent and she died suddenly, universally beloved. Evelyne Harrison after 31 years of unremitting service and Evelyn Palmer after only 5 years, full of promise, were killed together in the house of the Minister who was also killed. For the life and witness of these three, who would each of them have said 'Not I but the grace of God which was in me', as well as for all those who are granted a longer day of arduous service, we give God humble and hearty thanks.[61]

In *The Agenda* of December 1940 there are six accounts of the conditions experienced by deaconesses in London.

---

61. Wesley Deaconess Order Minutes (1932-47) (hereafter WDOMins III) p.111 (letter); *Methodist Recorder* (5th, 12th, December 1940)

> **Shelters in Barking** **Sister Maud Wilkinson**
>
> Three weeks ago I started to visit some of the public shelters, and that is where the opportunity seems to be opening out. The folk have seemed glad to see me. I went into the largest shelter – I suppose about 200 sleep there at present. On Monday I got an urn of tea and 100 enamel mugs (ancient) across in a lull of firing about 9 p.m. Never have I known an urn of tea go as far or have such a welcome. Last night extra water made it go even further, and we got two urns across. The excitement of pouring tea and getting it milked and sugared, and handed out, seemed to 'pass the time' for all the shelter . . . Saturday, I walked jauntily and felt on a par with every A.R.P. Warden I passed, for was I not wearing a borrowed tin hat bearing letters meaning, I was told, 'Repair Party – Engineers'!
>
> Source: *The Agenda* (December 1940) p.13

Perhaps a good summary of the way the deaconesses coped with war-time conditions comes from the Warden in 1944 when he wrote in 'Notes and News' under the heading 'Health':

> Considering how large a proportion of our workers are in London and the South, how they have endured the ordeal of V.1 and prevailed under V.2 (debating sometimes which was the worse), how often they have done their day's work and then spent the night among tumbling houses and homeless people, and seen things which the eye of heaven should never have seen; considering all this it is wonderful that they can write as one of them did: 'P.S. I am quite well.'[62]

The outbreak of war opened many new opportunities for the Order. For example, because many women, often living in 'Munitions Hostels', were drafted into munitions factories, to take the place of men who had gone into the Forces, deaconesses were provided to be on hand to help any in need. Inevitably there would be the family crises that this new situation engendered – women working long hours, families to cope with and perhaps the loss of husband, son, sweetheart or brother.[63] The 1942-3 *Stations of the Deaconesses* include:

---

62. *The Agenda* (Christmas 1944) p.7
63. Minutes of Convocation (1936-69) (hereafter Mins. of Conv.) (June 1940) p.39; *The Agenda* (August 1942) pp.10-11

MUNITIONS FACTORY HOSTELS

Jessie Blacker	Margaret Robbins	Jessie Sharpin
Doris Elliott	Phyllis Shaftoe	Dorothy Tolson[64]

Doris Elliott outlined the problem which faced many workers of trying to reconcile their faith with making weapons:

> It is just eighteen months since I arrived here, and surely the strangest months I have ever lived . . . we began to build up Fellowship Groups, Guild Meetings and Sunday Services . . . It is only the minority who respond . . . It is not all indifference though that keeps people away . . . Sheer physical weariness prevails, and increasingly so as time goes on, and many spend most of their time working, eating and sleeping. Again, there are those who feel that religion and munitions making are incompatible, and they tell me quite frankly that they have laid aside their beliefs until such time as they can, with clear conscience, 'enjoy God', and no persuading or arguing can move some from this position.
>
> To interpret the Gospel in terms of friendship is the only way – . . .[65]

Comment by unidentified Sister Working at Munitions Hostel

I haven't even a room for my own use though I spend from 6 to 8 hours there every day. The other day I tried to talk to the General Manager. I told him if ever he felt it would be a help to the work if I lived in the Hostel, I was quite ready to do so. He got all agitated and said, "No, no, it's the last thing we want – it would give the Hostel a bad name immediately."

Source: The Agenda (August 1942) p.10

Appointments to the Munitions Factories Hostels stopped in 1945 with the cessation of hostilities.

However, there was one particular area in which the deaconesses, during the war and afterwards, made a great

---

64. *WDO Stations* (1942-43) p.8
65. *The Agenda* (December 1943) p.2

contribution and that was work with and in the Forces. The 1940 Methodist Conference confirmed the appointment of five voluntary workers to join with the other Free Churches, in co-operation with the Archbishop of Canterbury, in 'a scheme for ministering to the moral and spiritual welfare of women engaged in National Service'.[66] As shown earlier in World War I Sisters had worked with military personnel, but now they were actually appointed and recognised as chaplains' assistants in the Forces. One of the first of the 12 chaplains' assistants was Olive Jones and in the 1942-43 *Stations of the Deaconesses* she is designated as 'A.T.S. Chaplain's Assistant'. On arrival she found the camp (later identified as Catterick) extended over 25 square miles and that there was plenty to do. She described her arrival and work at 'the Camp' and then continues:

> My day starts about 9 a.m. in my office . . . Any S.O.S. by post or 'phone is collected there and correspondence attended to: then away I go on my faithful bicycle to the Company where I am needed. So the hours go by – seeing needy girls, making arrangements for coming events, attending marriages at churches and Registry Offices, discussing difficult misfits with despairing young officers, visiting the Military Hospital and the smaller hospital for minor cases, addressing the intake of new recruits, arranging a ramble or a party for that first night in a strange new camp, taking evening prayers in Y.W.C.A., and on a Sunday evening at 8 p.m. in the Y.W.C.A. – attending the dances, and doing a Slow Fox trot but avoiding the 'Big Apple'! Tonight I am meeting the Methodist girls to start a new Fellowship. So the day goes on, and how thankful I am that the good Methodist Padre and his wife have given me a lodging and that their home is right in the Camp, so my bed is close at hand.[67]

In February 1946 Sister Olive went with the Forces to the Middle East and was with the ATS in Jerusalem. She told the Warden, in a letter, 'of the tense atmosphere there, following upon the terrible outrage at the King David Hotel'.[68] Following a brief furlough early

---

66. *The Methodist Church: Minutes of Conference* (hereafter *Mins. of Conf.* (1940) p.2

67. *The Agenda* (August 1942) p.11

68. Ninety people were killed and 45 wounded, on 22nd July 1946, when Jewish terrorists blew up the King David Hotel, which housed the British government and military offices.

in 1947 she went to the Canal Zone, Egypt. In 1946 Jessie Burnett also became an ATS Chaplain's Assistant and in 1949 both are listed as WRAC Chaplains' Assistants, with Gertrude Harmes being appointed to the WRAF, as also was Eileen Furniss in 1952. Olive Jones received the MBE in 1950 and finally left this sphere of work in 1953. Deaconesses continued to be appointed as Chaplains' Assistants for many years.

Transit Hostel in Liverpool 1941

Some eighteen months ago we opened a Transit Hostel for girls in the Forces who were compelled to spend the night in Liverpool while travelling. We have twenty-two beds (or bunks) and girls come in at any hour of the night. There is always a member of the Staff on duty, but the real hospitality is offered by members of the Girls' Club, two of whom sleep in the dormitory with the Service girls and look after their comfort, making supper or hot drinks and breakfast for them. It quite frequently happens that the girls are out of bed four or five times up to two or three o'clock in the morning, often starting again with breakfasts at 5.30 a.m., and then they go off quite cheerfully to do their day's work in office or factory. This piece of service has been a revelation to us of the temptations to which girls are open in a big city such as Liverpool. The Transit Hostel is used by girls who are on short leave, and from local camps with sleeping-out passes, as well as girls in transit.

Source: The Agenda (February 1943) p.4

Yet other deaconesses worked with internees. Many foreigners were interned in the Isle of Man during the war in case they might be Nazi sympathisers and thus pose a threat to national security, and some of the women found themselves in a sorry plight. Sister Emmeline Cheshire, who had been appointed to Port Erin in 1940, became deeply involved in this situation and she wrote to the Warden:

> . . . I have been invited to take an evening service at one of the hotels here on the first Friday in every month. I went on November 8, and was given a wonderful greeting on behalf of the group of internees present from the German pastor's wife who has been in charge of the services since May. It is just what I have longed to be able to do. Yet, for many reasons, I knew that I must wait for the invitation to come from within

the hotel. Since that evening the news of my visit has travelled through the camp and I have been asked to go to two other hotels and to one of the smaller houses. The curfew is at 6 p.m. Thus the evenings are so long and I know that many of the internees will welcome me to take a Bible Class or service for them.

She also asked if the Order could help those internees who might be released:

Is it possible for you to get me any names and addresses of people who are willing to employ as domestic helps any of the internees who get their release? . . . At present there are only one or two . . . But I expect to get more requests as time goes on. Some . . . are not able to return to their former situations because of the 'protected area' restrictions, and no one can leave the Camp, even with their release granted by the Home Office, unless they have some place to which they can go and some means of supporting themselves . . .[69]

In the first issue of the new magazine, *The Wesley Deaconess Magazine*, Gertrude Harmes tells of the great change she faced on becoming a Chaplain's Assistant in the RAF. She was advised that it would be best to wear WRAF uniform from day one, but it was not ready in time so she used her deaconess 'uniform' for a month! As it turned out this had unexpected benefits as it 'established me as a representative of the Church – not just a strange "God-woman" as many C. A.'s are called, and I was accepted as such, and not at first as a "person".' She quickly became used to RAF jargon, customs and behaviour, working among the 500 WRAF personnel as a link between them and the Churches. The problem was how to 'bridge the gulf' as few had had anything to do with Christianity, but she felt it was a great opportunity to offer first friendship and then Christ. Like Olive Jones before her Gertrude, as Chaplain's Assistant, had postings both at home and overseas, before returning to circuit work in 1955. Here she found that having charge of five rural churches meant that 'her travelling days were not over'.

Eileen Furniss, in her account of a Monday in a RAF Camp, showed how her position was misunderstood by many, when she

---

69. *The Agenda* (December 1940) pp.5-6

related how a visiting officer, intrigued by her shoulder flashes bearing the words 'Chaplain's Assistant' and 'Official Duties', enquired what they meant:

> What on earth do those mean, I have never met your species before. How many are there? What is your job? Where do you work?' And the briefest of answers informs him that there are seven of us in the RAF; that we are appointed primarily to work among the women in the Forces; that we work interdenominationally and as colleagues with the Station Chaplains. But one does not linger, and by 8.15 armed with three of the great necessities, prayer, a sense of humour and a bike . . . I set out across the camp for a morning in the office, ready . . . in case anything turns up. It invariably does!

Conversation overheard by Chaplain's Assistant Eileen Furniss 1956/7

Two new lads filling in arrival chits: 'Denomination! What's that? I don't know.' 'Well, you put down the same as your father is, what does he call himself?' 'Oh, he's a rat catcher.' 'Well then, put down R. C., you clot.' It sounds funny to relate, but this pathetic ignorance is so hard to combat and yet a great challenge.

Source: The Wesley Deaconess Magazine (July 1957) p.8

In the 1950s, during Cyprus' struggle for independence, Joyce Wakely was stationed on the island with the WRAC and in the December 1957 issue of the Order's magazine she told of the Christmas festivities, but also remembered the harsher realities of life among the troops:

> Towards midnight, we became more subdued; but the underlying note of joy was still evident as we closed the day with carols. I watched them. The WRAC provost corporal still haunted by the harsh laughter of the Cypriots as a soldier lay dying from Eoka bullets . . . the young airman embittered by the tragedy of an unfaithful wife . . . the nineteen-year-old girl, jilted when all her wedding plans were completed . . . the soldier not yet recovered from the shock of seeing his pal shot in the back . . . and so many more. And all

around us, an atmosphere of disillusionment and hatred, bitterness and tension. Until the closing words of Housman's Christmas hymn became a heartfelt prayer:

O perfect Love outpassing sight,
O Light beyond our ken,
Come down through all the world to-night,
And heal the hearts of men![70]

RAF Cosford, Shropshire, was the appointment for Sister Irene Jolly in 1974 and she found it was at first 'a most shattering and bewildering experience'. However, she soon got used to service life. Cosford was part of Training Command, which trained airmen and airwomen, but one of the important areas of work was the hospital, which had 'an exceptionally high reputation'. Many of the patients were civilians who were being treated by the commissioned nursing sisters and doctors, which she felt widened the scope of her ministry. A major part of her work was in exercising 'a listening ministry' and in visiting the families who lived in the quarters or in the surrounding area as she discovered that service life often had 'a disrupting influence on family life'.

Service Life in RAF Cosford   Sister Irene Jolly 1974

My little car, which is a bronze yellow mini, has come to be known at Cosford as 'The Bronze Bombshell', and I am not infrequently referred to as 'The Military Nun'. It is when visiting the various sections at the station that I find I have always to be ready with some kind of answer for the witticisms and good-humoured ragging of the personnel. For instance, when I was asked if I would like a trip in a Varsity aircraft, it was claimed to be a very necessary exercise in order to have a more intimate word with my employer! The only way to cope is to give as much as one gets!

Source: A Way of Serving (Autumn 1974) pp.9-11

Remembering the close links the Wesley Deaconess Order had always had with the Kaiserwerth Sisters in Germany[71], perhaps an illustration of how the work of the deaconesses managed to surmount the barriers of war and nationalism provides a fitting conclusion.

---

70. *WDMag.* (December 1957) pp.9-11
71. See chapter 6

A Letter from Germany   **Dorothea Luddicke 1947**

We felt so happy to distribute the contents of your parcels. A pair of children's shoes I sent to the Russian zone, and a coat. The mother wrote back: 'After a day of disappointing and vain running about I found your parcel.' Several hours she waited . . . vainly trying to get a permit to buy children's shoes. Really worn out, she returned home, found my (or your) parcel, and when she saw the shoes . . . she was cheered up and happy and grateful that there is still a heavenly Father who helps in the uttermost need . . . Dear Sister, tell those who brought all the things which you send us: To most of the cases the gift seems to be as a help from Heaven. So it is not only the thing and its value we thank (sic) for, but it's the fact that in desperate times, under bad conditions a mother becomes encouraged to believe again in God . . . God bless you . . .

Source: The Agenda (Christmas 1947) p.11

Through their work as Deaconess Evangelists, in the Caravan Missions and in the Forces the deaconesses played an important part in reaching out to the ordinary people in these very specialised spheres of ministry.

Chapter 3

Wesley Deaconess Work
Overseas – Africa

The November 1922 issue of *The Agenda* gave a breakdown of the numbers of the Wesley Deaconess Order and where they were engaged. With regard to those 'on the Foreign Field' they are listed as:

(a) The deaconesses support two of their number at Puttur, Ceylon, as a special deaconess contribution to Foreign Missions.

(b) Deaconesses work under the direction of the W.M.M.S.[1] on the staff of Girls' Schools in West Africa, at Freetown, Cape Coast Castle, Accra and Lagos; in Hospital work in China, at Hankow and Anlu; also in Institutional and Social work in South Africa at Johannesburg.

(c) Deaconesses are employed as nurses or educational workers under the Women's Auxiliary, in Ceylon, at Trincomalie and Welimadi; in India at Haidarabad (sic), Akbarpur, and Mysore; in China at Anlu.

In other Evangelical Churches and in some exceptional appointments under special arrangements.[2]

In the account of the overseas service of the Wesley Deaconess Order we shall look at all these areas, but as the work in South Africa started so soon after the Order itself came into being that will be the first sphere surveyed.

Sisters Miriam Scriven (South Africa); Christian Hughes (New Zealand); Gertrude Nettleship (Ceylon), 1903

---

1. WMMS – the Wesleyan Methodist Missionary Society was formally constituted at connexional level in 1818, though there had been local initiatives since 1813.
2. *The Agenda* (November 1922) p.5

South Africa – Transvaal

It was not long after the Wesley Deaconess Institute started that the call came for someone to go overseas. So, on 17th March 1894, Sister Evelyn Oats sailed for Durban, Natal, arriving there safely to a warm welcome on 2nd April. This marked another milestone in the range of activities of the Wesley Deaconess Order – the beginning of Foreign Missionary work. Sister Evelyn was supposed to have had her recognition service at Convocation in July, but because of her departure to South Africa it was brought forward to 13th March. The Rev. T. Bowman Stephenson anticipated that before long other deaconesses would feel the call to overseas work, but he warned that these would need to be even more committed and trained than those working at home, presumably because of the difficulties arising from being in a different country, with a different culture, to say nothing of the weather and maybe a sense of isolation because of the distance from their home base, family and friends.

The first letter from Evelyn Oats to be published in *Highways and Hedges* described some of the conditions she met in the back streets of Durban. She was horrified at some of the things she saw, but hopeful because of the response of the people.[3] From the Executive Committee Minutes in December 1895 we learn that Evelyn had moved to Johannesburg and in a letter in *Highways and Hedges* she said she felt that this was a wise move as conditions there were similar to those she had encountered in London. She was well supported by the local people and felt that soon the work would warrant another deaconess being sent to join her. The Rev. William Hudson agreed and informed the Deaconess Committee that the friends in Johannesburg were willing to pay all the costs involved in sending and maintaining another deaconess, so it was decided 'to send a Sister as soon as possible'. However, initially the cost of the fare out would need to be borne by the Institute and so the Treasurer was empowered to increase the overdraft by £100. As overseas work was a new venture for the Institute it was decided to consult the Mission House and Mrs Wiseman (of the Ladies' Auxiliary of the Wesleyan Methodist Missionary Society) 'as to allowances, outfit and any other matters affecting Deaconesses who are appointed to Foreign Stations'.[4] Sister Evelyn described her 'Deaconess Doll's House', officially to be called 'Stephenson Cottage'. She had done most of the work on it herself with some help and gifts from a few friends and it was now a focal point for 'the poor, Ministers and doctors . . . weary, sorrowing ones . . . a common lodging house' for all needing help.[5]

---

3. *HH* (April 1894) p.78,(June 1894) p.120, (November 1894) p.219
4. WDIMins I pp.16, 21, 24, 28
5. *HH* (October 1895) pp.198-99

'Stephenson Cottage', Johannesburg   Sister Evelyn Oats

'It has required no little energy and push to carry the matter through in a place where Deaconess work is practically unknown, and I have worked almost single-handed, but already the step taken has been fully justified by the results. 'Stephenson Cottage' consists of three brick and iron rooms, all letting into each other; it is very centrally situated, just below our principal church, and easily accessible to the people. The Committee voted me the magnificent sum of £20 to furnish – my bedstead and bedding cost about £10, leaving a very small amount to be spent on the sitting room, and kitchen necessaries. However, there is such a thing as sanctified ingenuity, and a cosier little place than I am now writing in it would be hard to find.

Source: Highways and Hedges (October 1895) pp.198-99

Sister Evelyn Oats'
Cottage,
Johannesburg,
South Africa

Sister Miriam Scriven, having been consecrated just prior to her sailing in May 1896, went out to join Evelyn Oats. Towards the end of that year Evelyn went to Australia 'on a mission of extraordinary delicacy and difficulty' about which Stephenson refused to give any details, but while she was there she managed to make contact with some old boys of the Children's Home and visit 'Sisterhoods' associated with the central missions in Melbourne and Sydney.[6] Once back in Johannesburg Evelyn wrote about her 'work among the natives'. There seems to have been a 'dynamite explosion' which wrecked the church, but within three months it had been rebuilt.

Evelyn Oats took part in the afternoon reopening service, speaking through Zulu and Dutch interpreters. She described the colourful scene the following Sunday – the clothes of the men, women and children, the singing and the service. Then the church transformed itself for a 'gift service' with people putting coins on the table and having their names listed. It was a noisy, exuberant occasion, which she described as 'fun, sanctified fun', while the pile of money grew, with many people giving out of their poverty to help finish the re-building until £17.17s.9d. was raised.

---

6. *HH* (January 1897) pp.10-11, (February 1897) p.41, (March 1897) pp.64-66

Miriam Scriven gave a report in the President Street Church on 18th October 1896 in which she told how she came to be in Johannesburg. She continued that in the four months since her arrival she had paid 300 visits and had met with a great variety of experiences helping needy people. For example, one Sunday she visited an ill woman in an 'indescribable' room. She made the invalid as comfortable as possible and looked after her all day, managing to clean and tidy the room a little. She found on one visit that the family 'had been sponging her head with brandy instead of water, and tied up the poor woman's feet in tar and linseed oil. I did what I could for her relief, sometimes going late at night, a most dangerous journey, as it was in the brickfields. She, however, grew worse and died.' As part of her appointment Miriam worked in Fordsburg, a 'suburb 15 minutes' train ride from Johannesburg'. Here the population was chiefly miners and the Methodist Church quite strong, but she found the nursing and visiting quite heavy as there were a number of typhoid cases. It seems that many of the miners were immigrants and on their deaths their widows and children were left destitute, so that Miriam longed for a 'Home for the fatherless children'. Life in the 'Golden City' (Johannesburg) was uncertain as the work and employment fluctuated, so that many found themselves at times in dire straits. She had managed to start a Women's Meeting and a Society Class and felt that the work was progressing.

Evelyn Oats had started a small Convalescent Home in Johannesburg, which was proving to be a very valuable project and through it she met all sorts of people and she hinted at good co-operation with other denominations – the Presbyterians, Salvation Army and Church of England.[7]

At Market, Johannesburg   **Sister Evelyn Oats**

I had a fine time (at the market) this Saturday. First, the auctioneer was selling bunches of flowers, and he smiled and threw some at me. Then a working-man shared his cabbage with me. Next a gentleman said, 'What, you here, Sister! what do you want?' and bid for turnips, taking no money. 'No; it is a contribution to your Home.' And then another man gave me lots of carrots. I like going to market like that.

Source: Highways and Hedges (July 1897) p.162

---

7. *HH* (May 1897) pp.114-15, (June 1897) p.140, (July 1897) pp.162-63

By late 1897 Miriam Scriven had moved to Fordsburg, where she found many poor people and much nursing to do. Many of the miners were on their own and it fell to her to pack up the things of those who died and send them with letters to relatives far away. As time went on things got worse in Fordsburg: both there and in Vrededorp there was much sickness and distress caused by unemployment.[8]

The citizens of Johannesburg celebrated Queen Victoria's Golden Jubilee by establishing a fund to help worthwhile projects. Sister Evelyn had received the offer of a valuable piece of land which was very suitable for building a large and permanent Convalescent Home. She was anxious to accept the offer, so she put her case to the subscribers to the Jubilee Fund and was so persuasive that she received a resounding majority in its favour.[9] So in 1898 she was able to present a report of the Convalescent Home to the Johannesburg Quarterly Meeting. The home had opened on 11th January 1897 and during the year had catered for about 100 folk. People were sent there by 'certificate' and their individual needs met. The charge was two guineas a week, but the friendless and penniless were never turned away. She told the stories of some of the convalescents, all of whom had benefited from the nursing care and good diet provided.

News of the effectiveness of Sister Evelyn's and Sister Miriam's work must have spread because in the spring of 1897 the Rev. Isaac Shimmins, who had been in the Transvaal (1885-91) before moving to Rhodesia, wrote to the Deaconess Committee requesting the help of a deaconess. Then the Rev. Ezra Nuttall asked for one for Cape Town. Unfortunately, as no deaconesses were available, it was impossible to fulfil these requests at that time.[10]

In March 1898 both deaconesses sent a letter to the Warden and other deaconesses as they met in Convocation. They felt that, although there were 'drawbacks and discomforts' in deaconess life abroad, there was much work to be done and indeed six Sisters could be usefully employed. The area was teeming with young men, many of whom had come out alone to work in the mines, hoping to make their fortunes. They needed much care and attention. Then there were many young girls and women who had followed the 'rush'. Hence there arose numerous social problems, much sickness, often followed by many funerals at which the deaconesses were often the only mourners.

---

8. *HH* (September 1897) p.211, (January 1899) pp.19-20
9. *HH* (November 1897) p.256; (March 1898) pp.66-67
10. WDIMins I pp.41, 43, 46

Another area was 'search work' as they often received letters from all over the world asking them to trace loved ones. So letter writing took up a great deal of time – passing on news of the illness or death to a mother or wife. Then last, but not least, 'Stephenson Cottage' was an ever-open door for callers.[11]

Callers at 'Stephenson Cottage'

'The number of callers taken daily for a fortnight were as follows: 8, 9, 17, 10, 12, 23, 13, 21 (6 before 9 a.m.), 35, 17, 20, 16, 26.'

Source: Highways and Hedges (May 1898) p.116

Unfortunately, Sister Evelyn had to write in October 1898 that 'Stephenson Cottage' had been burgled again when she had lost her watch and chain and also a 'beautiful little loaded revolver', given to her after the previous burglary. Now the local men had brought her £10 and 'a big old bull-dog revolver, which is too heavy for me to fire, but which may serve to intimidate'. At the same time she told how she had managed to escape being sent to 'the lazaretto' or getting smallpox when she looked after a family, ostracised by everyone else, who had been suffering from the disease. In addition to her nursing she was also taking many services.[12]

After five years working in the Transvaal Evelyn Oats was able to travel back to England, arriving in time for the 1899 Convocation where she gave a detailed address to the assembled audience, telling of dangers and stories of 'heroism and pathos, of joy and sorrow'. The Rev. William Hudson, on furlough from the Central Johannesburg Circuit, gave testimony to the effectiveness of her work, mentioning in particular how she had managed to get the money for the Convalescent Home.[13]

In the autumn disturbing news came from South Africa, where Miriam Scriven found herself in the midst of chaos as the prospect of war between the British and the Boers drew near. Once she heard of the situation, Evelyn abandoned her furlough and hurried back, although it was uncertain whether she would be able to get through to Johannesburg. The Warden was very concerned about her returning as her health was not too good, but he understood her anxiety to be with

---

11. *HH* (May 1898) p.116
12. *HH* (October 1898) pp.235-36
13. *HH* (June 1899) p.139, cf. pp.280-83

Miriam and the people there and realized that her services in nursing the sick and wounded would be invaluable in Cape Town if she could not actually reach the Transvaal. While Evelyn Oats was on her way news came that Miriam Scriven had had to leave Johannesburg and was going to Durban, so it seemed likely that Evelyn would have to go there too and together they would work with the sick and wounded. In the event both were working in Durban caring for refugees, though they were prepared to go to the front if required to work with the military.[14]

A letter from Evelyn Oats, dated 11th November 1899, told of the plight of many in Durban, the shortage of coal as the mines were in enemy hands and how at last troops arrived 'to relieve the beleaguered towns'. She remarked that the 'Revs. Scott, Briscoe and Thompson' were 'shut up in Kimberley!' and that England was being condemned for her slowness in reacting to the situation. Meanwhile Miriam had taken on the maternity work at the barracks.[15]

Relief work in Durban 1899/1900   **The Warden**

The relief work seems to be well organised, and as efficient as can be expected. The rate of pay is one shilling a day for each adult, and sixpence for each child under fourteen. Many of the refugees suffer so in having to come for their money, that on entering the office they are speechless, while some shrink as though struck with a blow. In some instances, knowing this, Sister Evelyn acts as almoner. They are wondrously patient, though occasionally self control is lost, and hard and bitter words are said.

Source: Highways and Hedges (February 1900) p.44

In the March issue of the magazine Evelyn mentioned the heart-rending work among the refugees, added a few items about the soldiers, including the escape of Winston Churchill, the arrival of 300 stretcher bearers, stories of individual soldiers and how lonely she and Miriam had felt at spending Christmas, almost as refugees themselves, so far from their base in Johannesburg.

---

14. *HH* (November 1899) p.260; (January 1900) p.20
15. *HH* (February 1900) pp.37, 44; (August 1900) p.188

Escape of Winston Churchill	Sister Evelyn Oats

Lieutenant Churchill has escaped and landed here yesterday, borne aloft amid plaudits, hundreds seeking a hand-shake. He is only twenty-six. At the Town Hall he stopped, someone produced a Union Jack, and he spoke, concluding by an assurance of final victory, and a prophecy that we should yet hold a Cape of GOOD HOPE. He was cheered at almost every sentence. You will read of how he went sixty hours without food, and lay among coal sacks thirty-six hours. Not an hour did he wait, but was off to the front like a shot. You may be sure I was there cheering and glorying in a brave Englishman.

Source: Highways and Hedges (March 1900) p.69

The Methodist Times paid tribute to Evelyn Oats' work with the Transvaal Refugees Committee where, at all hours of the day or night, she would meet the steamers carrying troops or bringing refugees from Lourenco Marquez – 'Whenever she could get tidings of the landing of troops she was sure to be found on the quays.' *The Natal Mercury* gave an account of the Volunteer Convalescent Home in Durban, started, after the relief of Ladysmith, when it was realised that there was no organisation in Durban to cope with the volunteers from the front who were in need of convalescent care. A committee was formed, a house in Aliwal Street rented and Sister Evelyn agreed to become the supervisor. Sister Miriam, meanwhile, had moved from Durban to Cape Town at the Rev. G. Lowe's request, where she found plenty of work among the refugees and soldiers. She commented that, although both she and Evelyn had been keen to go to the front or engage in some capacity with the military, as they were not 'certified nurses' it had not been allowed. Both Sisters hoped to be able to return to Johannesburg, but as so far it had proved impossible, they were still working in Durban and Cape Town with the refugees and wounded.[16]

At last Evelyn Oats managed to get back to Johannesburg as a letter told Dr. Stephenson: this was dated 7th December 1900, when she wrote from the Wesleyan Soldiers' Home. Here she was acting as 'Jack of all trades', but happy to be back. Unfortunately, 'Stephenson Cottage' had been devastated and all her personal belongings, nursing equipment and most of her books had either been destroyed or were missing altogether. She noted that so far Miriam Scriven had not been able to get a permit

---

16. *Methodist Times* from *HH* (April 1900) p.91; *Natal Mercury* from *HH* (July 1900) p.166 cf.p.213, (August 1900) pp.188-89, (December 1900) p.278; (January 1901) pp.21-22

to return to Johannesburg. When Evelyn had a little more time, in March 1901, she wrote about the Wesleyan Soldiers' Home, describing in particular the refreshment bar where the soldiers could 'buy a cup of tea for a penny, and for another a thick slice of bread and butter'. Post Office workers, Fire Brigade men, Military Hospital staff and the Military Police dropped in too and all were made to feel at home.[17]

In spite of all the troubles which beset South Africa during the war the Methodist churches there still had collections on Christmas Day for the Children's Home and a total of £11.14s.3d. was forwarded by Evelyn Oats.

Watchnight Service Greeting Card, 1901　　　　**The Warden**

. . . she [Evelyn Oats] encloses an interesting greeting card announcing the First Watchnight Service held under British rule in the mother Church of Rand Methodism. A curious addition to the announcement of a Watchnight Service is the following note: — 'By the permission of the Commissioner of Police this is a duly recognised pass for this occasion from 10 p.m. 31st December, to 1 a.m. 1st January.'

Source: Highways and Hedges (March 1902) p.43

In February 1901 the Deaconess Institute commenced its own magazine, *Flying Leaves,* and the deaconesses in South Africa continued to correspond with the Order at home, so that it is possible to see how the work there was progressing. The February 1903 issue contains a letter from Evelyn which had been sent to the Warden 12 months earlier. It had not been intended for publication, but Stephenson now felt that it would be appropriate to include it. In the letter she described waiting alone, except for her dog, Maxim, each night for the attack on Johannesburg by the Boers, who are 'all around us', with 'the alarm to be given by three blasts on the hooter, a thing used to call the men to mine work'. Stories of encounters with soldiers on their way to the front or returning wounded are told, but the most touching is that of her visit to the cemetery.

---

17. *HH* (March 1901) pp.6, 115-16

Cemetery in Johannesburg   Sister Evelyn Oats

I was at the cemetery this morning. Ah me, what a sight! – almost countless rows of soldiers' graves. My tears dropped as I stood in the midst and thought of the homes of sorrow represented. 'Erected by his comrades' – this simple expression of devotion on very many. They seem to have adopted a different style of stone to mark each regiment; for instance, a wooden cross represents the East Lancs., and a black one, much lower, the Staffords. The New Zealand Rough Riders have a cross in black wire, with a brass heart or shield with the inscription. Of course there are far more nameless, and we are going to plant flowers on them. While there, a double funeral came, led by the mournful strains of the bagpipes – two of the Scots Fusiliers borne to their rest; and the wail of the pibroch, the salute of the guns, added to the solemnity.

Source: Flying Leaves (February 1903) pp.30-31

By the beginning of 1902 Miriam Scriven had been able to return to her home in Fordsburg, only to find that some of her belongings had been stolen or destroyed, but the church had managed to stay open during the war. So she had been doing a great deal of visiting and had restarted her classes and Women's Meeting.[18] Evelyn Oats wrote to the 1902 Convocation and referred to the work she and Miriam were still doing among the refugees. She was a member of the Refugee Aid Committee.

Refugee Aid Committee, Johannesburg   Sister Evelyn Oats

Two members meet every incoming train. Offices are open all day, with a number of clerks and messengers always at work. Furnished houses are waiting, and every homeless one, or any whose houses are dirty, looted, or wrecked are welcomed there for 48 hours, or longer if necessary. We have 36 cottages, of three rooms and a kitchen, furnished with every necessary, for those who need a few weeks' housing ere they can straighten out their difficulties. A men's shelter of 40 beds is also in waiting for single men. A doctor attends daily at a given hour, and all medicines are charged to the Refugee Aid Committee. Special arrangements for all maternity work are under my direction.

Source: Flying Leaves (June/July 1902) pp.94-95

---

18. *FL* (April 1902) p.52

Educational work, religious work, clothing and furniture depots, and a labour bureau were all functioning and the facilities of telephone, telegraph, railways and police force were put at their disposal. Unfortunately, martial law and the need for permits hindered progress and many heart-rending stories could be told.[19]

Miriam Scriven sailed for England, arriving on 18th April 1903, and was, therefore, able to attend Convocation. Her address at Convocation is described:

> Sister Miriam Scriven gave her experiences in a Boer Concentration Camp. She first traced the general anxiety before the war began, then described the hurried exodus from the Transvaal, the congested state of the railway traffic, the hardships endured until East London was reached, and afterwards Durban. It was a story thrilling with interest from first to last. We followed her step by step through all her camp life, her duties, difficulties and illness, and felt a welcome relief when all was over, and she was again in work and safety as before the war.[20]

While she was away the local people had furnished a two-bedroomed cottage for her, which delighted her as it meant that more people were now able to visit her in private.[21]

Letter from Mrs C. Rogers [a South African Associate]

DEAR SIR — I herewith enclose Money Order for twenty shilling, with Collecting Card. Sister Miriam Scriven, our Wesley Deaconess in Fordsburg, is doing a splendid work, and is beloved by all who know her ... Sincerely yours, [Mrs] C. Rogers.

Source: Flying Leaves (May 1903) p.76

A very excited letter came from Evelyn Oats in May 1903 in which she wrote of the upheaval caused in her own tiny house as she had had to take in a young man suffering from enteritis and she had also been nursing the Superintendent's wife who was very ill with dysentery, but, in particular, she had, unexpectedly, had the chance to work among 'the Arabs'. A lady who had been working 'among the Syrians at Beyrout

---

19. *FL* (March 1902) p.36; cf. (May 1903) p.70; (September 1903) p.122
20. *FL* (June 1903) p.88
21. *FL* (January 1904) p.8 cf. (October 1904) p.136

(sic) and Tyre' had come to Johannesburg and the chance was too good to miss, so Sister Evelyn had 'spanned her in':

> We took copies of two hymns, Nos 117 and 16 in Sankey, and got out notices of a meeting in red and black, printed in Arabic. Then I went prospecting in fear and trembling. My first visit was discouraging; my second met with a cordial and courteous welcome. We borrowed a timber yard, arranged planks, took down my baby organ, and had our first meeting for the Arabs. And what do you think? One man offered to send to Beyrout (sic) for hymn books, and pay for them: another said when he heard of the service his heart felt as large as Johannesburg. Truly the Lord works.[22]

Another deaconess was on her way to South Africa: on 10th May 1903 Nellie Cooper sailed from Tilbury for Cape Town before going on to Pretoria. In March 1904 she commented on how the work there had developed since her arrival and that now they were holding services in three of the new townships as well as doing hospital and prison visiting.[23] It seems, from the Deaconess Institute Minutes, that there was trouble in Pretoria over the payment of Nellie Cooper. The general rule of the Institute was that all money from the churches and circuits should be paid to the Institute which would then pay the Sisters. However, in spite of a long correspondence, the authorities in Pretoria refused to pay the Rev. Amos Burnet, who was recognised Sub-Warden of the Wesley Deaconesses in South Africa, and insisted on paying Sister Nellie directly. The President of Conference, the Rev. Marshall Hartley, offered to write to the Superintendent of the Pretoria Circuit to see if he could resolve the matter. Nothing further is recorded, but as Nellie Cooper continued at Pretoria, presumably the matter was settled satisfactorily.[24]

In April 1904 Evelyn Oats was encouraged because the British and Foreign Bible Society was doing a roaring trade in selling Bibles. Her native services were very well-attended, but she wished she was 'a native linguist' and did not have to rely on a translator. However, the wonderful thing was that the Christian natives became 'missionaries' to their own people, for when they went back to the kraals they gathered the villagers together and passed on the message. She lamented that there were endless opportunities if only there were enough teachers.

---

22. *FL* (May 1903) p.76
23. *FL* (March 1904) p.42
24. WDIMins I pp.180, 190

Open-air work, Johannesburg   **Sister Evelyn Oats**

We have a stand on the Market Square, right under the Post Office. I am very proud of our Mission Band, a ring of fine young fellows, miners, mechanics etc. The leader is an old Scotchman (sic), once a drunkard, now on fire for God. The lightbearer is an ex-soldier of the Coldstream Guards, a manly type of Christian, and a continual joy and inspiration to me. I play for them a baby organ, which had taken an immense share in the work for many years, doing its level best everywhere and always, in heat and cold, moist and dry, within and without, and yet never out of tune. It got carried off during the war, and was found in pieces at Maraisburg, but was rescued and brought back to service.

Source: Flying Leaves (April 1904) p.59

For many years Sister Lucy Hawken had been anxious to work overseas, especially in West Africa, but bouts of typhoid, while serving in Maidstone, precluded an appointment there. However, in 1904 she was able to go to Cape Town. In the 1905-06 *Stations* she is listed as:

SOUTH AFRICAN CONFERENCE
1. THE CAPE OF GOOD HOPE DISTRICT
CAPETOWN
Sister Lucy Hawken.[25]

*Sister Evelyn Oats,
before departing for
her third tour in
South Africa, 1905*

In 1905 Evelyn Oats was able to reach home in time to get to Convocation, returning to Johannesburg for the third time.

---

25. *FL* (October 1904) pp.137, 147 cf. (January 1905) p.186; (September 1905) p.319

Tribute to Sister Evelyn Oats   **The Warden**

Two periods of five years she (Evelyn Oats) has spent in South Africa. Ten years she has given to the Transvaal, particularly to Johannesburg. And what a time it has been! The gold fever has been raging all the time. The Jameson Raid and the South African war have created an electrical atmosphere for all who lived within their influence. Scores of thousands of young Englishmen have been poured into that region, and a great political and social revolution has been effected. And through all this time our dear Sisters at Johannesburg have kept the flag flying; have turned their hands to whatever was urgently needed, without distinction of Englishman or Boer or Native. And in Johannesburg itself, amongst all classes Sister Evelyn has won affection, admiration, and respect.

Source: Flying Leaves (September 1905) p.331

The following year the Sisters, both the Wesley Deaconesses and those of the Children's Home in the Transvaal, not being able to be at Convocation in Bolton, decided to hold one of their own. They met together in the morning for Bible study, led by Sister Isabel Hunt, and prayer, then after lunch went to the Post Office to send 'telegrams to Sisters Lucy Hawken and Grace Carr – "We, in Convocation assembled, greet you – Mizpah." ' The afternoon session, at Sister Miriam's house, was spent in reflection, prayer, Bible study and conversation on 'the Work of God'. Fortuitously, during the day letters arrived from the Warden and from the deaconesses in Ceylon, so as Evelyn Oats remarked, 'Blest be the tie that binds.' In future years as many sisters as could get together continued to observe Convocation.[26]

Evelyn Oats gave an account of the death of one of the ministers in her circuit, the Rev. George Maddison. Apparently, as he was cycling to a Sunday School Anniversary service he heard cries for help and going to investigate found a group of native men 'molesting' another man. Trying to intervene he received a stab wound in the neck and when it worsened had to have an operation during which he died. She commented that everyone was very disturbed because recently there had been quite a few such incidents and no one felt safe.[27]

In 1907 Sister Evelyn left Johannesburg after 14 years and went to be Principal of the newly established Kilnerton Institute 'for the training of native girls'.

---

26. *FL* (July/August 1905) p.113; (July 1907) p.106
27. *FL* (October 1906) p.153

> ### Kilnerton Institute, 1907   The Warden
>
> A Principal of unusual gifts and influence was wanted for this work; and those most responsible earnestly desired the appointment of our Sister. She has been appointed, and has taken charge of the work.
>
> *Source: Flying Leaves* (June 1907) p.94

Her description of arriving, on a Saturday midday, at Kilnerton, finding the place absolutely empty and trying to make it habitable and of how she had to 'tackle floors, clean furniture (after three days' travel on an open waggon), wield a hammer . . . make blinds and a score of other similar tasks, to say nothing of digging and planting' show that 'those most responsible' had indeed chosen rightly! For three days she, and another woman who had accompanied her, more or less lived on bread, which they had to make and bake. They also had to make and wash everything they wore – 'I really don't know whether my head or my hands will be of the most use,' she remarked. She had two teachers, both in their 20s, to help her – one white and the other black. So the Institute was ready to open its doors:

> My first nine come in on Monday, and are all Native Ministers' or Evangelists' daughters, with the daughter of a Mine Compound Manager (native), who comes on condition that she learns music. They are from Johannesburg chiefly. Then comes twenty from all parts. The building will accommodate forty pupils.[28]

Sister Miriam Scriven, (South Africa) – taken later in life, 1910

Unfortunately in January 1908 it was reported that both Miriam Scriven and Evelyn Oats were ill. Sister Miriam sailed for home and it was hoped that she would recover sufficiently to be able to take a home appointment in due course. This she did for a number of years and died on 14th March 1924, leaving her estate to the Order.[29] Sister Evelyn was resting from her work at Kilnerton and it was undecided whether she should return to England, but eventually she arrived on 8th August when she spent some time with friends in Cornwall and in a sanatorium in Devon. Sister Evelyn's ill-health meant that she was

---

28. *FL* (July 1907) p.102
29. *WDO Stations* September 1915; WDIMins II pp.203, 206

unable to return to South Africa or take a home appointment, so she retired in 1908-09 and died on 13th August 1937. Sister Nellie Cooper was also expected home from Pretoria and in 1908 she was stationed at Leeds Mission. She was not replaced at Pretoria. Meanwhile Lucy Hawken in Cape Town was working actively against the Cheap Wines Licences Bill, which would allow light wines to be sold in cafés, shops and business places. She, representing 3,000 women who had signed a petition against the Bill, was a member of a deputation which went to see the Premier. She returned to England on furlough for four months in 1909 and attended Convocation. Returning to Cape Town she continued her temperance work. She acknowledged that it was a very

Sister Lucy Hawken, South Africa, 1904

difficult situation because so many of the farmers were dependent upon the wine industry.[30] Lucy Hawken must have left Cape Town in mid-1910 as in the September appointments list she is recorded as 'resting'.

After this first period of work in South Africa there seems to have been a break between 1910 and 1920 when the Deaconess Minutes state that 'arrangements had been made for Sister Donna Levy to take up special work in Johannesburg'. It is now described as being in South Central Africa, Transvaal and Swaziland District. She was joined there in 1924 by Sister Marion Doughty. Sister Donna came home in the summer of 1926 and in 1927 is listed as without appointment because of 'home claims'. Marion came home in 1929-30 and underwent a serious operation, so was unable to go back to Johannesburg. However, Dorothy Teare, currently at Bermondsey, volunteered to take her place. She left on 14th November 1930 and stayed there till 1935-36, when she was stationed to London (Bow Street) and the Johannesburg appointment was given up.[31]

Later there were appointments for a short time in South Africa, chiefly in Johannesburg Central Mission from 1938-39 until 1956-57 and in Cape Town, from 1951-52 until 1954-55, but there is little information about these. For example, 'Grace Woolcott who came into our work from Overseas Missions, was ordained . . . She will be sailing

---

30. *FL* (January 1908) p.188; (February 1908) p.200;(April 1908) p.232; (May 1908) p.248; (September 1908) pp.304, 305; (October 1908) p.324; (April 1909) p.52, (December 1909) pp.174-75
31. WDIMins II pp.158-59, *The Agenda* (September 1924) p.8; (November 1924) p.12, (November 1930) p.3; *WDO Stations* et al.

any day for South Africa, where she will be joining the staff of the Johannesburg Central Mission.'[32]   While, in July 1956 'to celebrate the 150th Anniversary of Methodism in South Africa' Sister Winifred Woods recalled her time in Johannesburg from 1948 and especially the thrill of being in the Conference which accepted the formation of the South African Deaconess Order.[33]   Sister Unez Smuts recorded: 'The Birth of a New Deaconess Order in South Africa' in the *The Wesley Deaconess Magazine* explaining how first the idea had grown of finding 'our own girls' and sending them to Ilkley for training. So Mary Caley, Yvonne von Hagen and Unez Smuts became Wesley Deaconesses, but then the South Africans 'wanted an Order of their own'. After 'a long battle and uphill struggle' the South African Conference of 1953 established the Order and the Rev. E. W. Grant was appointed as the

*Sister Unez Smuts, 1951
South African Deaconess*

first Warden. Then Mary Caley, Yvonne von Hagen and Unez Smuts were transferred to the new Order. Beryl Alexander was the first deaconess to be ordained in South Africa in October 1954 at the Conference in Queenstown, but students from South Africa still came to Ilkley to be trained; for example, Constance Oosthuizen was, in 1955, received on probation from the Wesley Deaconess Order of South Africa and Ursula Zerbst, a student from South Africa, was welcomed at Convocation in 1957.[34]   So the work of the British Wesley Deaconess Order, as such, closed after 60 years, but in a very real sense the work there found its fulfilment with the creation of its own Order.[35]

South African Wesley Deaconess Order   Sister Unez Smuts

What of the future? There are still many problems confronting us; but we believe that the Order has been established by God Himself, and we know that under His guidance all will be well. Our plans include the other branches of our great multi-racial Church, and an establishment of our own training centre. In the meantime we are deeply grateful that the doors of Ilkley are still open to us.

Source: The Wesley Deaconess Magazine (December 1954) pp.12-14

---

32.   *The Agenda* (December 1943) pp.6-7
33.   *WDMag.* (July 1956) pp.3-5
34.   Mins. of Conv. (1955) p.161, (1957) p.184; *WDMag.* (July 1954) p.1, (December 1954) pp.12-14, 16
35.   Mins. of Conv. (1954) p.157

Rhodesia

As noted earlier, in 1897 the Warden reported that the Rev. I. Shimmin, (Rhodesia District 1891-98), had expressed a wish for two deaconesses to go out to Bulawayo and hoped to communicate with the Council shortly.[36] Mr. Shimmin had been in the Transvaal prior to going to Rhodesia and doubtless his request was prompted by his experience of the work of Evelyn Oats and Miriam Scriven.

In 1925 Muriel Pratten went out to Nenguba in the Rhodesia District and worked there until her retirement in 1952. One of the few reports from Rhodesia came, in 1938, from Dorothy Teare who had gone there following her departure from Johannesburg and after a one year home appointment. She explained that it was 'a lone appointment, the possibilities of which I have to explore'. Learning the language was providing quite a challenge, but she was making gradual progress. Although Dorothy was dealing largely with African women's work she had found a friendly reception from both the women and men. One of the men had explained it by saying, 'Sister, if you help our women you will be helping us.' So she helped with sick people and simple dress-making as well as 'singing and praying' with them. Having visited the homes in a kraal Sister Dorothy was struck by the difference to be found in the homes of Christians and non-Christians. She read Gospel stories to them and talked and answered questions through an interpreter.

A Village Kraal, Rhodesia, 1938   **Sister Dorothy Teare**

In the afternoon the church bell was rung and we had a service before I left. The road was difficult, the wind strong, and my bicycle hard to manage, but I returned to town with a song in my heart. I will master that language, and then I will be some real use. (But this was in August. Now no doubt? – Ed.)

Source: *The Agenda* (December 1938) pp.7-8

Sister Dorothy was responsible for establishing the 'Junior Manyano', which became the Girls' Christian Union. In 1977 its membership had grown to 23,000 with over 900 branches.[37]

When she returned from furlough in 1939 Margaret Dry was delighted to find that, although the new hospital was not completely finished, progress had been much greater than she had expected and

---

36. WDIMins I p.41
37. *A Way of Serving* (Autumn 1977) pp.6-10

there had been a great influx of patients. The new Maternity Ward had not got any doors, so she had had to use curtains to give some privacy, but 'two little girls made their first appearance into the world on Easter Sunday'. The regular Sunday services which they had started in the hospital were beginning to have an impact and 'it is our desire that we shall not only heal men's bodies, but that souls shall be saved for the Kingdom of God'.[38]

Sister Muriel Pratten sent a lengthy account from Rhodesia of the Vungwi Bible School – the preparations and the journey, the actual Bible School and the return home. A very long journey of 250 miles was eventually completed and the missionaries met the students who came, on foot, by train or by lorry from four circuits to the fortnight's Bible School. The age range was from 'bright young women in their late teens to elderly grandmothers who had little or no schooling' and the days passed in studying the Bible, considering the work of the church, how to conduct meetings, teach in the Sunday School, fellowship, prayer, preaching and witnessing. After a procession of witness to the chief's village the chief, a non-Christian with 16 wives, was impressed with the preaching and teaching and later in the week visited the school to express his thanks verbally and in kind – for he sent 'a fine ox as his contribution to the food problem'! At the close of the fortnight Muriel commented: 'Who can tell what the outcome of such a Bible School will be in the lives of the women who have attended it? The knowledge gained, the enthusiasm engendered from the rich fellowship, as women have studied, sung, prayed, talked around the camp-fire together, will be taken into four wide circuits, over hundreds of miles of country, into mining compounds, locations and heathen kraals.'[39]

VUNGWI – a Bible School   **Sister Muriel Pratten**

A box of provisions (enough to last a fortnight) has to be carefully packed, a camp-bed to be stitched up in a hessian cover, blankets, etc., in a hold-all; books, pictures, etc., to sell and to give away, all yet another case, and lastly, the personal belongings of the missionary. At last all is packed, the house locked up – the cook-boy instructed in looking after the dog and cats – and away we go in the 16-year-old Austin to the station, seven miles away.

. . . we jolt along for 200 miles . . . we are hurriedly deposited at a junction

---

38. *The Agenda* (June 1939) p.6
39. *The Agenda* (July 1947) pp.11-13

> to wait two and a half hours for another train . . . Only another 23 miles, but the train takes three hours to accomplish the journey; but why hurry, for (as the African proverb has it) 'Tomorrow is also a day.'
>
> . . . an African minister arrives with an ancient car to take us the last twenty miles to Vungwi; so we pile in with all the luggage, plus the African minister, his daughter, a teacher, a bicycle, a sack of mealie meal, a frying pan, new boots etc., etc. All goes well for the first 15 miles – . . . [then] . . . A *puncture.*
>
> *Source: The Agenda* (July 1947) pp.11-13

In 1949 Muriel Pratten wrote her last letter from Rhodesia just before she retired in January 1950, after 25 years' service there. The Warden commented that her work had been particularly with running 'Bible Schools where women from the villages are trained to be leaders in their little communities'. Muriel confessed that she was looking forward to 'a less strenuous life, but it will be hard to leave my beloved African 'children' and 'grandchildren'.[40] Muriel died in 1978.

In 1949 the Rhodesia District became known as the Southern Rhodesia District. Sister Margaret Dry received the MBE in the King's Birthday Honours list in 1951 for her work in the hospital in Nengubo. She retired in 1956 after 29 years working in Southern Rhodesia and died in 1974.[41] Margaret Randall went out to Salisbury in 1957, serving there until 1970. In June 1964 she wrote a letter which was both encouraging and sad: she had just had a happy week at Chiunye in the hills near Mount Darwin at a Bible School for Local Preachers and Ruwadzano leaders, but then returned to many problems in Salisbury. The Chiunye area had been very primitive, but then was opened up to Africans possessing 'the Master Farmer's Certificate' and Methodist farmers had settled there. The Bible School had been 'a very mixed company . . . Master Farmers and their wives and a number of the local Makorekore who were totally illiterate. One fine old chap with a white beard and lively eyes had walked 20 miles to get to the school . . . Here at Chiunye I was in a different world from that of Salisbury and it was good to have the change.' All too soon she was back in town, where she found 'that this week two members of my preachers' classes have had their homes stoned, and I have this afternoon been surveying the damage – broken windows and furniture – at our Old Highfield Church. Classes of the Community School use our church buildings and two

---

40. *WDMag.* (July 1949) pp.11-13, (July 1951) p.18
41. *WDMag.* (December 1951) p.13, (December 1956) p.12; *A Way of Serving* (Autumn 1974) pp.30-31

days ago they were attacked by a gang believed to be members of one of the political groups. This morning the school children are reported to have retaliated by beating up a teacher belonging to that party. It is not surprising that political frustration plus extensive unemployment has led to this continuous violence in the townships . . . The serious unemployment problem is hardly likely to be remedied until the political deadlock is resolved, and the church is actively concerned with this. But in the meantime we do what we can in the way of relief . . .'[42]

In 1955-56 the first deaconess, Sister Dorothy Quantrell, was sent out to Northern Rhodesia. The Southern and Northern Rhodesia Districts two were combined as the Rhodesia District in 1965-66 and deaconesses continued to be stationed there until 1978-79 which is the end of the period covered by this account of the Wesley Deaconess Order. Sister Joan Stockley served in Rhodesia from 1972 when she had 'special responsibility for work among women' in the lay training team. This was a very loose description of her rôle as within the seven circuits of the Bulawayo Area, about 39,000 square miles, she also ran courses for Sunday School teachers, Youth Leaders, Local Preachers and so on. She commented that the people had got used to her speaking their languages in 'a Dorset accent'. She described the Girls' Christan Union meetings, the work of the Women's Association, the 'preaching places' and class meetings, and hinted at the 'difficult situation', presumably following from Rhodesia's unilateral declaration of independence from Britain in 1965 and moving towards black majority rule in 1980. A comment from Joan provides a fitting conclusion.

Rhodesia/Zimbabwe, 1977　　　　　**Sister Joan Stockley**

Once a month, African and European youth leaders of both Bulawayo circuits meet in my flat to share ideas, plan united services and joint meetings. To give and receive fellowship and hospitality like this means much, at a time when, and in a country where, there is so much division. Pray that the Christian church of every denomination may respond in humility and obedience to God Who alone can work the miracle of reconciliation and heal our land.

Source: A Way of Serving (Autumn 1977) pp.9-10

---

42. MS letter from Margaret (Meg) Randall (12th June 1964)

Kenya

It seems that the United Methodist Church had had women missionaries stationed in Meru, Kenya since 1920 as 'educationists', 'nurses' and 'nurse-evangelists'. So a number of Sisters of the United Methodist Church either worked on the Foreign Mission field or wished to do so, but the denomination seemed to find it difficult to maintain some of the appointments at various times. For example, Sister Ethel Simpson was all prepared to go to Africa, but was disappointed in February 1923 when the Foreign Missionary Secretary, the Rev. C. Stedeford, wrote to say that the Foreign Mission Committee 'had decided to discontinue the appointment of lady missionaries to Africa'. A home appointment was found for her, but apparently she decided to leave the Sisterhood and become a nurse. However, in 1929, Sister Muriel (Martin) was interviewed by the Women Auxiliary Council 'in connection with her offer for service in Africa', so it looks as if the Foreign Missionary Committee was now prepared to have 'lady missionaries' in Africa again. The General Committee, on 20th December 1929, learned that the Foreign Missionary Committee had voted a grant of £75 towards Sister Muriel's training at Kingsmead College, Birmingham. It also expressed 'its joy and appreciation that Sister Muriel has been accepted for service in Africa, and requested the Warden to send a letter of thanks and good wishes to her'. She would be 'set apart' at the forthcoming Anniversary. The Foreign Missionary Committee asked the Deaconess Committee in 1930 'to loan Sister Lilian Bartholomew to the Mission Field of Africa for a term of four years and allow her to resume service again at home, during which period the F. M. Comt. would pay all charges on the Retiring Allowance Fund'. The Committee agreed, but resolved that if there was 'any breakdown or injurious effect on the Sister's health owing to her work in Africa, the F. M. should deal generously & sympathetically with her'.[43] So both Sister Muriel (Martin) and Sister Lilian (Bartholomew) were appointed to the East Africa District in 1930. Sister Lilian was a qualified 'handcraft' teacher and she combined teaching domestic skills with religious teaching. 'Education in the upbuilding of the home and of Christian character is the valuable contribution made by these lady workers in the Meru Mission' in Kenya states *The Story of the United Methodist Church*.[44] Two deaconesses continued there after Union, but there is little information about their work or indeed other work in Kenya where deaconesses served until 1970-71.

---

43. United Methodist Deaconess Institute Minutes (1917-32) (hereafter UNDIMins II) pp.340, 365-66, 370, 375-76
44. H. Smith, J. E. Swallow and W. Treffry (eds.), *The Story of the United Methodist Church* (1932), (hereafter Smith, Swallow and Treffry) p.135

West Africa

In early 1900 the Colonial Nursing Association, apparently at the suggestion of Mary Kingsley, contacted Dr. Stephenson about the possibility of the Wesley Deaconess Institute supplying Deaconess Nurses for hospital work in West Africa. Unfortunately the Institute was unable to comply with the request at that time. In February 1903 Stephenson reported that the Secretary of the Colonial Nursing Association, Mrs. Piggott, had sent an urgent request for nurses for a hospital in Sierra Leone. However, before the request could be granted, suitably qualified deaconesses willing to go to West Africa had to be found and many practical issues settled. A sub-committee was convened and at its first meeting on 7th May the Warden explained the background:

> The Colonial Nursing Association is an organisation very closely connected with the Colonial Office . . . Its object is to maintain hospitals in the Crown Colonies and certain other places where Englishmen are in danger of being left in illness without proper care. But the Association finds a difficulty in obtaining Nurses of sufficiently trustworthy character, and they plainly say to us that they believe that Methodist Deaconess-Nurses could be trusted to behave themselves with propriety where persons who are merely selected on a commercial basis break down. The Association also represents to us that along the coast the Methodist Church has strong Mission Stations, and that Deaconess-Nurses would be in friendly touch with our other Mission workers and under the supervision of our general Superintendents.

A draft scheme for the services of the Wesley Deaconesses, prepared by the CNA, was carefully considered and a 'proposed arrangement' was adopted and forwarded to the CNA together with a 'draft financial scheme'. The CNA meeting on 9th June received the proposals, studied them and suggested some amendments. The Wesley Deaconess Council accepted several and reworded others. The main difficulty seems to have been the Wesley Deaconess Order's insistence on maintaining its authority over its own deaconesses which it was not willing to relinquish to anyone else.[45]

---

45. WDIMins. I pp.71, 137, 138, 139-41, 153, 159-66

Colonial Nursing Association and Wesley Deaconess Order Arrangements

The Wesley Deaconess Order proposed:

4. The selection of the Deaconesses shall be made by the Officers of the W.D. Order, subject to the approval and Medical Examination of the C.N.A.

The C.N.A. amendment:

4. The Officers of the W.D. Order shall submit Candidates for selection and medical examination by the Officers of the C.N.A.

The WDO replied:

4. Our Committee are unable to accept this modification, but are willing to accept the following form of words:-

   'The Nurse-Deaconesses selected by the Officers of the W.D. Order shall be subject to the approval and Medical Examination of the C.N.A.'

In reference to this point we submit to you that the W.D. Order is a community having its own government and itself subject to the Wesleyan Methodist Church. It is vital to the Order that it should retain to the full its authority over its members. It is through that authority, and the character of the members thereby guarded and promoted, that we are able with confidence to place Wesley Deaconesses in positions of trial, where others not so strengthened would be more likely to fail. If the authority of the W.D. Order over its members were in any way weakened, the very end which the Committee of the C.N.A. has in view would in our judgement be imperilled.

Source: Wesley Deaconess Institute Minutes (1895-1910)
pp.139, 160, 164 cf. pp.138-66

After all these negotiations, on 9th July 1903, the Assistant Secretary of the CNA, Miss M. E. Dalrymple, wrote to say that 'As the Committee was sitting a communication was received on Tuesday afternoon from the Colonial Office which informed them that in view of a dispatch just received from the Governor of Sierra Leone, the Colonial Office could not see their way at the present moment to make any change in the existing Nursing arrangements' and therefore the CNA felt that for the moment the negotiations with the Wesley Deaconess Institute should cease, but that all the papers would be filed 'in the hope that it may become available in the future'.[46]

---

46. WDIMins I between pp.167-68

On 25th September 1903 the Wesleyan Methodist Missionary Society Secretary, the Rev. William H. Findlay, wrote to Stephenson urging the Order to consider work in West Africa. As a member of the sub-committee which had been involved with the CNA negotiations Findlay had been made aware of the 'wider views of Missionary usefulness for the Deaconesses in West Africa'. The WMMS Finance Committee had endorsed his opinion and so he wrote:

> To you I need not enlarge on the urgent need there is for women missionaries in our West African work. Our progress is in many respects one-sided and unsatisfactory because women and girls have not the example and training of English Christian womanhood. I do not hesitate to say that at this moment women missionaries are more needed than men in our Native Churches . . .
>
> The Deaconess Organisation appears to me to be in several respects eminently fitted to occupy this sphere of usefulness . . .
>
> I do not mean to suggest that Missionary work in West Africa can be anything but difficult and costly, even with the most favourable arrangements of organisation. All that I suggest is that the Deaconess organisation may perhaps render possible of achievement a Missionary task there which has long been desperately needed, but has hitherto seemed impossible.[47]

The General Committee replied enthusiastically and appointed a sub-committee to confer with the Missionary Committee. A joint meeting, held at the end of October, stated that there were four types of Women's Work which needed to be done:

(a) Educational work. The native Church realises (sic) the need for the education of girls:-
　　1. *Cape Coast Castle School* . . .
　　2. *Lagos High School Building* . . .
　　3. *Freetown Girls' High School* . . .
(b) Regular Itinerant Evangelistic Work by Women . . .
(c) Medical, Nursing and Dispensary Work.
(d) Pastoral Work . . .

Just before Christmas 1903 arrangements for administration, rotation of period of service and finance were agreed − Wesley

---

47. WDIMins I pp.181-82

Deaconesses were to act under the direction of the General Superintendent who would be regarded as the Sub-Warden for his District, that any withdrawal of deaconess service would normally be subject to six months' notice on either side, three deaconesses would be allocated to each station, meaning that two would be working and the third on furlough, and the length of service was not to be more than 18 months at a stretch. With regard to finance the WMMS would accept the financial obligations and pay £10 per annum per deaconess into the Superannuation Fund because of 'the nature of the climate'.[48]

In the *Flying Leaves* of May 1904 Stephenson spelt out the difficulties of working in West Africa. The climate meant shorter terms of service there and longer furlough periods, hence a greater number of workers were required for a satisfactory rotation. He also emphasised that the deaconesses who went overseas had to be volunteers; that only those who passed a stringent medical examination would be allowed to go, although developments in housing, diet, medicine, drainage and communications meant that there was now a better understanding of how to mitigate the risks involved, and that two deaconesses would go together. The 'Resolutions of the General Committee of the Wesleyan Methodist Missionary Society on the Employment of Wesley Deaconesses in West Africa' were reproduced, so that any deaconess feeling a call to such service could see what was involved.[49]

Work in West Africa   **The Warden**

. . . beyond question, the nature of the climate makes West Africa emphatically the land of Christian adventure. Heroic souls are wanted there. Men and women who 'count not their lives dear unto them,' should be sent thither, for the risks are more than ordinary. Yet that is surely no reason why the perishing people of West Africa should be left to die in darkness. If Christianity is to save the world, if Methodism is to take its share in that splendid achievement, and if the Wesley Deaconess Order is to be worthy of its name and profession, there must be no shrinking from a holy crusade like this.

Source: Flying Leaves (May 1904) p.67

The Rev. William Findlay spoke to the 1904 Convocation and issued an appeal for deaconesses to volunteer to go overseas, particularly to West Africa. He was conscious that the WMMS had

---

48. WDIMins I p.188 cf. pp.199-202, 203
49. *FL* (May 1904) pp.67-69

only male missionaries there and that most of those were young and unmarried. The status of women and girls was very low and the situation needed to be addressed as quickly as possible. He said that the Rev. A. T. R. Bartrop, General Superintendent of the District, who was on furlough, was hoping that two deaconesses might be able to go back with him after Conference to work in the Cape Coast School. Findlay explained that Mrs. Ellis, the widow of the Chairman of the District, had started a boarding school after her husband's death 'where the daughters of our Christian men on the Gold Coast were gathered, and she taught them cleanly ways and purity and kindness. She had wonderful success; the leading natives in that part of the Coast gladly sent their children. She was *by herself* for more than 12 months . . . but her health gave way and she came home and could not return.' The Women's Auxiliary had tried unsuccessfully to find a successor and had managed to keep going with native teachers, but desperately needed someone to go out there. Discussion followed his address in which it was emphasised that the deaconesses should be able to prepare pupils for 'the College of Preceptors' Examination; but the teaching of the scholars in Christian household ways was one of the most important works. One of the deaconesses should be a good housekeeper, the work is not all educational. There is scope for every kind of Deaconess Work.' Mr. Findlay added that 'English would be spoken in the school. There were certain varieties of dialect spoken throughout West Africa, but all is easy; a knowledge of French would be an advantage.' Mrs. Stephenson said that several deaconesses had already volunteered. Indeed, on 17th September, Sisters Annie McVicker and Ethel Worthington set sail for Cape Coast Castle.[50] Sister Annie wrote her first letter home on Sunday 4th October telling of their safe arrival and warm welcome. On the Wednesday they had gone to the school and were delighted to sing familiar hymns as 'they use our Sunday School Hymn Book'. She described the Sunday service at which Mr. Bartrop gave the sermon which was translated into Fanti. Work in earnest at the school was due to start on the Monday with 24 scholars. Later she reported the numbers had increased to 28 and the boarders would arrive after Christmas. Annie gave some idea of the work at the school:

> There are three native teachers, who require a good deal of training; consequently I have to leave my class, whenever possible, to superintend and teach. When Sister Ethel takes my girls for French, I am quite free to take another class. It is impossible at times to take things quietly, but I do my best, for I find you are tired out here so much more sooner

---

50. *FL* (June 1904) pp.89-91; (September 1904) p.116; (October 1904) p.131

than at home. Sister Ethel will take the music pupils as soon as we get a piano! She also takes the school for Catechism and Scripture every Thursday morning and I am free that morning till 9.25.[51]

It is obvious that Stephenson was very concerned about how his deaconesses would stand up to the climate in West Africa, because in many issues of the magazine he notes 'the health of our Sisters continues good' or the work has 'so far has been uninterrupted' or again they have 'suffered little from the climate'. In accordance with the rotation arrangements it was necessary to have a third deaconess ready to go out to relieve Sisters Annie or Ethel in the autumn of 1905. So Mabel Robinson was prepared to go as and when necessary. She left in September and arrived safely.[52]

Sisters Annie McVicker and Ethel Worthington before departing to Cape Coast Castle, West Africa, 1904

In June 1905 the Warden reported that three additional Wesley Deaconesses were required by the Missionary Society for West Africa. In Sierra Leone the missionary wife of the Rev. W. T. Balmer had 'carried on the school through a successful experimental stage', but now two Deaconess-teachers were needed. The Report of 1904-05 stated that

Of the 12 who are engaged in Foreign Missionary Work,
3 are employed by the Foreign Missionary Society.
1 is employed by the Women's Auxiliary, and
8 are engaged by local authorities.

During the coming year, 3 will be working in Ceylon, 5 on the West Coast of Africa, 1 in China, 3 in the Transvaal, 1 in Cape Colony, 1 in Natal, and 2 in New Zealand, total 16.[53]

At the request of the WMMS Sister Helen McLean and Minnie Maud(e) went out to Sierra Leone with a third one ready to go 'should necessity require it' – if one of the others fell ill.[54] Helen wrote just

---

51. *FL* (December 1904) pp.169-70; (January 1905) p.18
52. *FL* (January 1905) p.187, (February 1905) pp.195-96, (May 1905) pp.244-45, (August 1905) p.293, (October 1905) p.331, (November 1905) p.339, (December 1905) p.355
53. *FL* (September 1905) p.306
54. *FL* (November 1905) pp.339-40

before Christmas, a month after their arrival, reporting that, as the school had been without a European teacher for six months since Mrs. Balmer left and there had been alterations in the building, 'there will be a good deal of pulling up and re-organising to do'.

High School, Freetown, Sierra Leone   Sister Helen McLean

Our present idea is to divide the school into three divisions, Junior, Intermediate, and Senior. Sister Minnie will take the Intermediate with one native teacher, and I the Junior and Senior with two native teachers. My idea in having Junior and Senior under my own charge is particularly that I may endeavour to teach the older girls, amongst other things, how to teach, they having the younger ones to practise upon.

Source: Flying Leaves (February 1906) pp.24-25

The High School and Mission House, Sierra Leone

Mabel Robinson, writing from Cape Coast Castle, gave details of her teaching work particularly with the native girls where she had realized the language problems. She ended with the telling comment – 'Whatever else my short stay out here has done for me, it has made me believe in the negro. Give him a chance, and give him time, and there is no despising him.'[55]

After her furlough Annie McVicker was to return to Cape Coast Castle whereupon Ethel Worthington would leave for her vacation and then when she got back Mabel Robinson would depart. So Stephenson commented, 'We have got the rota-system into good working order.' There is a delightful picture of Sisters Ethel Worthington and Mabel Robinson with the native teachers and pupils of the Cape Coast Castle

---

55. *FL* (February 1906) p.25

High School in the October 1906 *Flying Leaves.* It is all the more poignant because the photograph was taken just before Ethel left for home. Unfortunately, within days of her arrival, her mother died and because she was needed to care for her father and the family she was unable to go back to West Africa.[56]

In *Flying Leaves* in May Minnie Maude reported that in addition to their school work they had held 'a sort of "At Home" at the bungalow' during the District Synod which had been much appreciated. There had been a service for the 'Recognition of New Members' during Synod which she had found 'very interesting and new' and 'a very good way of making new members feel their responsibility in becoming members of the Church and professing Christianity'.

Recognition Service of New Members, Sierra Leone, 1906

First of all they received their tickets of membership and the 'right hand of fellowship', and afterwards they all took the Communion for the first time. Some of our girls were admitted, and some poor Mendi women who had only been baptized the year before. They came in their native dress, but all in white, and with pretty coloured silk head-ties on, they looked very nice.

Source: Flying Leaves (May 1906) p.77

The letter of Annie McVicker, dated 19th May 1906 from Cape Coast Castle, makes rather depressing reading. She had been unwell and the climate, together with various local customs, was making life difficult. She also, perhaps understandably, seemed a little homesick. Such letters are unusual, but indicate just how wearing was the work so far from home in a rather hostile environment and a very different culture.[57] However, the Cape Coast deaconesses were able to enjoy a well-deserved holiday, doubtless during the school holidays, and they gave a vivid description of their travels by boat, 'go-cart, pulled and pushed by four boys' and, rather bumpily, in 'hammocks, each carried by four boys' from the Cape Coast to Accra and then on to Aburi, where they rejoiced in 'the quiet of the Mission House, in a veritable Garden of Eden'.[58]

---

56. *FL* (April 1906) p.59, cf. (July/August 1906) p.103, (October 1906) p.151
57. *FL* (July/August 1906) p.111
58. *FL* (October 1906) pp.148-49

On 19th September, after a valedictory service at the Leysian Mission, London Edith Le Masurier journeyed to Sierra Leone to relieve Minnie Maude.[59]   Soon two more deaconesses were on their way to West Africa – one, Sister Bessie Shearn to relieve Mabel Robinson at Cape Coast Castle and the other, Evelynne Beer, subject to medical examination, would replace Helen McLean in Sierra Leone. In spite of all the health precautions Mabel Robinson suffered two bouts of fever, but recovered well.   Stephenson emphasised that foreign mission deaconesses' furloughs were to be times of relaxation and refreshment and they should not be expected to speak at meetings until fully rested.[60] Helen McLean's journey home was not without incident for her ship, the *Jebba*, was wrecked on the south Devon coast just before arriving in Plymouth. Helen gave a vivid account of the foundering of the ship, the feelings of those on board, her escape by 'bo'sun's chair' to the foot of the cliffs, the scramble up the cliff, the kindness of the villagers of Hope Cove, the drive into Kingsbridge and finally the train journey to London.[61]

Wreck of the *Jebba*   **Sister Helen McLean**

By this time daylight was beginning to break, and we saw that some brave fellows on shore had climbed down the cliff and set a 'bo'sun's chair' agoing. As this saved climbing the rigging and the risk of being scraped against the cliff it was suggested that the ladies should go ashore on it . . . somewhere about six o'clock, I think, I found myself being assisted on to the chair – really just a strip of wood like a swing – I was told to hold tight and shut my eyes, and a few minutes after, I felt myself being seized hold of and deposited somewhere on the rocks. There we women sat huddled together till the men got off . . . The waves were breaking over the ship more and more . . . Then came the ascent of the cliff, which was, to say the least, a dirty and difficult undertaking. The first half I managed with only the assistance of a rope, along which I pulled myself hand over hand . . . About half way up a burly coastguardsman met me and tied a rope round my waist . . . As far as I can remember the coastguardsman got behind me and pushed, the rope round my waist was pulled from the top, two others came down and got hold of my arms, and the top was gained. I was thrust into the arms of some ladies who poured brandy down my throat, and finally set on the ground, feeling not a little amused . . .

Source: Flying Leaves (May 1907) pp.71-72

---

59. *FL* (October 1906) p.149; (December 1906) p.180; WDIMins I p.261
60. *FL* (February 1907) p.20, (March 1907) p.36, (May 1907) p.74; WDIMins I pp.261, 283, 287
61. *FL* (April 1907) p.52, (May 1907) pp.71-72, 73, (June 1907) p.94

At the invitation of the Warden, Helen McLean described the work in West Africa in order to recruit volunteers. Teachers, who would spend 'several hours each day in the ordinary routine work of a school, teaching any ordinary school subject from the alphabet to Elementary French and Mathematics, and superintending the native teachers', were required, but also housekeepers for the domestic side of caring for and training the boarders so that they would 'develop into capable, reliant women'. The appeal was all the more urgent as it was hoped to open a third school in West Africa in Accra. Sister Winifred Haigh sailed on 14th September 1907, arriving in November 1907, to take the place of Annie McVicker, who was in charge of the Girls' Wesleyan School in Cape Coast Castle, during her furlough.[62] Then, subject to medical examinations, Helen McLean and Mabel Robinson were due to return to West Africa in December. However, the Medical Advisor recommended that Mabel should not go back immediately, but eventually she was well enough to sail on 25th September 1909. On account of this Annie McVicker cut short her furlough, while Sister Edith Le Masurier and Beatrice Shearn were making ready to return for a well-earned rest. However, disaster struck, as Beatrice

Sister Winifred Haigh before departing to West Africa, 1907

wrote, hoping her letter would get through, explaining that after she and Helen McLean had been in Accra for a week getting the school ready to open they were told that the plague was rife in the native quarter of the city and soon it and the port would be put into quarantine. So the 'European doctor' sent them away 'to Aburi, a health resort 24 miles distant, at once'. She described their journey in 'hammocks' and two stops *en route*. A note by the Editor at the end of the account said that the Sisters had now been allowed to return to Accra.[63]

During the Christmas vacation the Sisters in Sierra Leone were able to have a holiday at Cape Coast Castle where they enjoyed 'a typical West African picnic'. Food, a hammock and deck chairs had been sent on ahead, then at daybreak the party set off in 'go-carts' or 'rick-shaws' along the coast to the Mission House before exploring the town and arriving at the chapel. In the afternoon they went to the Castle, where they were given tea and a guided tour by the commissioner, which included visiting the prisoners in the dungeons and in the Fort.[64]

---

62. *FL* (October 1907) pp.135-36, 137; (December 1907) p.174
63. WDIMins I pp.309, 316, 345; *FL* (December 1907) p.167; (February 1908) p.200; (April 1908) pp.232, 236-37
64. *FL* (May 1908) pp.254-55

Visit to the Chapel at Accra

We soon arrived at our chapel, which was a delightful surprise to us, with its quaintly tiled floor, handsome rostrum, and comfortable seats, and pipe organ. The collection boxes were specially quaint, being made from the half of a coconut shell, gilded inside, and ornamented with suitable texts outside, the whole being attached to a very long handle.

Source: Flying Leaves (May 1908) p.254

Perhaps experience determined the resolution in February 1908 that Wesley Deaconesses serving in West Africa should have 'twelve months' work, four months' furlough' implying that the original 18-month period had proved to be too long. This was borne out when evidently West Africa had taken the toll of Helen McLean's health as Bradfield commented that she had 'come home in much better health than was feared, and there is every reason to hope that after a good rest, she will be able to take up active work at home'. Her return, however, meant that a trained teacher was now required to fill her position. In September 1908 Bradfield pointed out the need for another deaconess to assist Annie McVicker at Accra and said that, as a Miss Rose Draper had volunteered and the need was pressing, he had received her as a probationer, so she would be sailing on 26th September. On account of her health the furlough of Evelynne Beer had been extended. The Warden further indicated that 'he hoped to make an amended agreement with the Mission House relative to the West African work'. Rose Draper arrived and was well-received and Myra Russell and Lucy Solomon offered for work in West Africa.[65] Lucy Solomon left Birkenhead on 1st May 1909 to go to work at Freetown High School. In the privacy of her MS Diary she expressed her feelings rather more forcefully than many of the published accounts recount: her sadness at leaving home, family and friends, but also the conviction that God had chosen her for this work, the boredom of being at sea and as they approached Freetown the 'strange sensation to be gradually getting near a foreign country that is to be the scene of your life's work'. Her first few days at the school proved to be a rude awakening:

> Monday 17 [May 1909] The first day at school. Can I ever describe my horror at the undisciplined state of the girls? Perhaps I expected too much & they did not understand me very well. When I rang the bell, few noticed it & many

---

65. WDIMins I pp.316, 325, 326, 330, 331, 333; *FL* (October 1905) p.319; (July/August 1908) p.279, (November 1908) p.335 cf. (December 1908) p.357

whispered not only to others but to themselves. The natives all have a trick of muttering to themselves. Teachers & children were alike late. Another native failing. They laughed at nothing, also natural to them. The teachers realise no sense of responsibility.

One day during the first week a teacher left school before the close. I asked her next day why she had done this and she said she was tired. I explained that that was not excuse enough.

Another day during the first week I settled all the classes to work & began my own teaching. Presently I heard a noise from Class IV & asked what it was. The teacher who was sitting with a blackboard between her & her class, (in a geography lesson) calmly answered my question 'What are they doing?' with 'They are quarrelling Sista' (sic). Oh the grace & patience that will be wanted to understand the people & to train the girls.

Her diary is full of descriptions of life in Freetown: the markets, the bargaining, the weather (rain and yet more rain!), visits to the Free Library, the Botanical Gardens, and the Cathedral, church services, the surrounding countryside, the native religion and practices and the longing for the ship to arrive with letters from home. It is obvious that the school situation was making her very 'despondent' as 'there seems absolutely no order & therefore no chance of doing much good'. For example, on 1st June two girls were expelled for a week for fighting and when 'the school girls do what they know is wrong & when punishment is given they come so sweetly to beg off'. Sister Lucy also seemed to feel that she did not always get the support she might have expected from her deaconess colleague, in fact it appears fairly evident that she and Sister Edith (Le Masurier) did not get on at all well. This incompatibility with colleagues was yet another stress for deaconesses working overseas, far from home, family and friends, where colleagueship would have been so important.

Sister Lucy Solomon, West Africa

Visits from missionaries and other deaconesses, such as Annie McVickers, working elsewhere in West Africa, provided welcome exchange of news and different conversation. Sister Lucy was distressed, on 15th August, when she attended a service at the Cathedral and 'sat in the white folks' pew & when a coloured man came to sit in the end seat he was turned out. This made me feel sad for surely a creole has equal rights in the Father's House'. A brief entry that 'This [death of Mrs. Tunley, a friend] is the second white person's death in 8 days here & both might have been prevented by taking it (blackwater fever) in time' brings home the very real dangers of working in West Africa.

On 8th January 1911 Sister Lucy started her second tour of duty in Freetown and, although her diary entries are briefer, she was evidently much happier, often giving light-hearted descriptions of events and incidents; for example, her description of trying to ascertain the ages of the local staff for the census was hilarious and eventually she remarked in laughing despair, 'we are as far off as ever from the truth'. It is possible that the departure of Sister Edith and the arrival of a more compatible colleague in Sister Elsie Dukes had quite a lot to do with her better frame of mind and also, most probably, the school organisation had settled down over the years and that had also made life easier. As a complete contrast to the lighter moments Lucy was rather upset on Good Friday:

> Good Friday was an awful day. The bells began tolling early in the morning congregations assembled attired in black. At our Wesley Chapel the pulpit, lecture & prayer desk were in mourning – the Dead March was played & the hymns were sung as funeral dirges. All because our Redeemer had suffered & so had triumphed over sin and death. It was most oppressive to think of a funeral service for our exalted Lord who is at the Right Hand of the Father. No sorrow for sin that caused the suffering seemed present. How can we teach the people that forms & ceremonies do not count as do lives of the professing Christians?

The last entry in the diary is, however, heart-warming: 'August 9th 1912. When telling the boys about Moses seeing the Glory of the Lord I said "We no able to see God." Ynbassu replied, "No, but we can feel him in our heart!" His face had brightened as he said it that I felt he really could.'[66]

Lucy Solomon finally left the West African work in 1914, having served there for five years.

---

66. MS Diary of Sister Lucy Solomon 1909-12

On 3rd January 1909 Mabel Robinson wrote to Mrs. Bradfield from the Wesleyan Mission House in Coomassi (Kumasi). She had left Cape Coast Castle and at Sekondi had said 'good-bye' to Sister Winifred, who was setting off for England, before travelling on a 12 hour train journey to Coomassie, 'the capital of Ashanti'. Coomassie was 'still under semi-military law, and even the Watchnight service could not be held without permission'. She remarked that the little chapel was always full and the feeling 'homely', and 'that the bell that calls to the service is hung on a tree, which was formerly an execution tree.'

Camp Meeting, Coomassie   **Sister Mabel Robinson**

Under the shade of two tall trees, a long shed had been erected on a framework of bamboos, and roofed with palm branches. Here there were services all day, and the people flocked to them. From nine to eleven we had short sermons – 'no preacher to exceed fifteen minutes', the programme said. Half-way through, two chiefs came in state, attendants to carry their stools, and wave their gorgeous umbrellas over them. One of them wore a rich and gorgeous silk cloth, and the massive gold rings and bracelets. The other is President of the Chief's Council, and speaks and reads English fluently. These men are not members, but they attend our services, and it is a great joy to know they are so favourably disposed to Christianity, as they are men of great influence, and in a country where the people readily follow the example of the powers that be, the influence of these men naturally tells in favour of our work.

Source: Flying Leaves (March 1909) p.38

Bradfield commented that the West African work continued with 'constant comings and goings' and that soon another volunteer might be needed for the work was developing rapidly and he was anxious to have a good number of deaconesses willing to serve there, both as new opportunities opened and as those already serving needed to be relieved.[67] Now that the pattern of work and furloughs is well established in West Africa note will only be taken of points of special interest.

The Rev. W. T. Balmer, whose wife, as we noted earlier, had been instrumental in developing the Girls' High School in Sierra Leone, wrote at Bradfield's invitation about the school. Mrs. Balmer, a trained teacher, had carried on almost single-handed for about 18 months, in spite of having several bouts of fever, so it was a considerable relief

---

67. *FL* (April 1909) p.52, (February 1910) p.21

when the Wesley Deaconesses arrived and they had been very successful and the school and its influence had grown considerably. Balmer explained that 'the Hinterland' was being opened up and even more opportunities were arising, so he wished for 'a rota of at least four Sisters for that one school alone'. Looking to the future, Balmer envisaged 'a chain of schools . . . properly established all along the coast, including Lagos', which would be well-equipped with apparatus to stimulate the scholars in a 'hands-on' way rather their just learning 'parrot fashion', and a good wide-ranging syllabus with suitable annual testing. Then, because there were many women in Freetown, an extra deaconess, who could do 'a great and worthy work' among the Mendi women, was needed.

Work with Mendi women, Sierra Leone   Rev. W.T. Balmer

It would be a work that would soon tell, owing to the peculiar position of women among the Mendis . . . In fact, I count the work done for heathen women as quite of the same rank and importance as that of training the ministry.

Source: Flying Leaves (February 1910) p.25

In the summer of 1910, when she reached Sierra Leone, Frances Hunt found the port in quarantine because of yellow fever. Sister Flora Harris and the local missionaries sent her a note advising her to go straight to Cape Coast Castle, otherwise she might find herself in quarantine and unable to proceed on her journey.[68]

At last in June 1910 the Warden was able to report the revised arrangements for the Wesley Deaconess work in West Africa:

1. That in future the Society [W.M.M.S.] shall only pay £25 a year, instead of £30, as coast allowance for Deaconesses who have been more than one year in the work; but shall pay the Wesley Deaconess Institute an allowance of £5 a year for every Deaconess engaged in West African service; it being understood that out of this sum the Wesley Deaconess Institute will pay the cost of obtaining and, when necessary, supporting candidates, and of other expenses incidental to the work of providing a supply of Deaconesses for the West Coast.

---

68. *FL* (September 1910) p.124

2. That all the Deaconesses employed on the West Coast, to wit, at Freetown, Cape Coast and Accra, shall be regarded as employed by the Wesleyan Missionary Society, and paid for at the above rates; and that the same conditions prevail with regard to the proposed new school at Lagos if Deaconesses are sent there.[69]

Towards the end of 1911 Mabel Robinson contributed an excited and exciting article to *Flying Leaves* about a Missionary Centenary Meeting. September 1911 marked 100 years since the first missionary had been sent to the West Coast of Africa – to Sierra Leone – so the Methodist Church in the Gold Coast was planning to extend its work into the Northern Territories, and as the Africans themselves would mainly do this it was important for them to be educated and trained. So a school or college was needed and money to build it required. The District had pledged itself to raise £3,500 in September, with each church being assessed in proportion to its membership, and the Missionary Committee in London had promised to give £3,000 when this had been achieved. As well as the school and college, it was proposed to build two Mission Houses in the interior and also new premises for the Girls' School in Accra. This seemed a wonderful way to celebrate the Missionary Centenary. Mabel gave an account of the week-long celebrations at which £380 was raised.[70]

The First Missionary Centenary Meeting, West Africa
Sister Mabel Robinson

In October, the Chairman sets out to travel to the utmost limits of the Northern Territories to see where the great centres of population are, which places are most suitable for Mission Stations, and to obtain grants of land for building purposes. Almost immediately the erection of suitable premises for our Boys' Secondary School, Teachers' and Ministers' Training College, will be established at Cape Coast, so that we may have trained and tested Africans to be pioneer missionaries. In urging the people to give liberally so that these schemes may be carried out, the Chairman did not forget to make plain to the people that they must first give themselves to the Lord, and then their gifts would be acceptable to Him.

Source: Flying Leaves (November 1911) pp.160-61

---

69. WDIMins I p.361
70. *FL* (November 1911) pp.160-61

Two volunteers, Sisters Gertrude Coleman and Jessie Holloway, left on 20th March 1912 to staff the new school in Lagos and the Warden commented that two more could well be required. By May 1912 the Wesley Deaconess Order was responsible for staffing two schools. It is interesting to note that Mr. J. Calow, who had often sent medicines to Ceylon, also did the same for West Africa. The June 1912 issue of *Flying Leaves* conjures up an interesting picture when the Warden wrote that 'a piano, specially built for the tropics, is badly needed at the Girls' School at Cape Coast Castle'. Apparently during her furlough Winifred Haigh had found a firm which had some good second-hand ones for sale, but £30-£40 was needed to buy one and then 'she would be able, on her return to the Coast at the end of the summer, to take one back with her'.[71]

On 14th May 1913 Sister Agnes Reed, BA sailed to Accra on the *SS Falaba*. She arrived a day earlier than expected, but soon settled into her new situation and took charge of the school when Marianne Malings left for England. Agnes Reed was a Manchester University science graduate who had taught at the Ministers' Daughters' College in Edinburgh while waiting to be accepted for work in West Africa. It had been planned that, having left Edinburgh, she would have a term or two at Ilkley, but the need in Accra was pressing and so she went straight there. On 12th June, within a week or two of her arrival in Accra, she contracted yellow fever, as did her fellow deaconess, Nellie Hopewell. At the Committee Meeting on 17th June the Warden read a telegram from the Mission House: ' "Cable just received Hopewell Reed yellow fever condition grave deep sympathy Perkins" '. Prayers were said for their recovery. Although ill herself, at first, Nellie was able to nurse Agnes, but then Dr. Le Fanu sent both of them into hospital for specialist nursing. Unfortunately, Agnes died at 1.00 a.m. on Tuesday 17th June and was buried in the cemetery at Accra.[72] Nellie was too ill to be told of her death for a fortnight, but when she had recovered she wrote:

> . . . Almost without any exception, yellow fever means death; and on my recovery Dr. Le Fanu informed me that there were only two or three cases in the whole of the Gold Coast that had ever recovered from a virulent attack of yellow fever. People called it a miracle.

---

71. WDIMins II p.24; *FL* (February 1912) p.19, (March 1912) p.37, (April 1912) p.52, (May 1912) p.68, (June 1912) p.85, (September 1912) p.126
72. *FL* (June 1913) p.84, (September 1913) pp.125-26, 128 cf. WDIMins II pp.38-39, 48

... For a week I was in a kind of stupor. Towards the end of the week the stupor began to pass away, and the next week I remember only too vividly. The days were like years and the nights like centuries. On the Saturday my temperature suddenly went down to normal. On the Sunday I was no worse, and every day after that I got a little stronger.

On the Wednesday of the following week I learned that Sister Agnes was dead.

... After being in hospital four weeks, I went to a bungalow outside Accra for a week, and from there Dr. Le Fanu brought me to the 'Akabo'. The voyage has done me great good and I feel much better.

I cannot describe the love and kindness I received while I was ill, especially from Dr. Le Fanu and Miss Stanton, the Sister at the Hospital. The whole of the Gold Coast and Nigeria seemed to know, and the sympathy expressed almost overwhelmed me.[73]

Mabel Robinson, writing in late 1913, reminisced about how attitudes had changed over the nine years the Wesley Deaconesses had been in West Africa. At first the African men had been sceptical of white women trying to teach their women and girls, but now 'not only have they the utmost confidence in the Sisters, but they are learning to believe in the possibilities of their own women, and to thoroughly appreciate the training given them in our schools'. Even so words of appreciation were few and far between 'from those outside the Mission circle'; however, recently the newly appointed Governor of the Gold Coast visited the school at Cape Coast and was very impressed.[74]

Visit of the Gold Coast Governor   **Sir Hugh Clifford**

I visited the Wesleyan Girls' School this morning, and was introduced to the scholars and shown specimens of the work done by the Sisters. I venture to offer my congratulations to these ladies upon the admirable work which they are doing in affording a sound education and a genuine training of character and mind to so many girls – the portion of the community which is above all others is, on the Gold Coast, that which stands most sorely in need of such mental and moral training and education.

Source: Flying Leaves (November 1913) p.162

---

73. *FL* (September 1913) pp.128-29
74. *FL* (November 1913) p.162

Sister Ethel Fellows sailed to Sierra Leone on the *SS Appan* on 10th June 1914 after her furlough and was delighted the following year to be able to report that the new Secretary of the Wesleyan Methodist Missionary Committee (the Rev. William Goudie) had visited them in Freetown, after touring the Mission Stations of the Protectorate, and said how impressed he had been to find that many of the native ministers' wives 'had been trained in this school'.[75] Sister Jessie Holloway, writing from the *SS Dakar en route* to Lagos after her furlough, gave a graphic account of a very bad storm at sea and also hinted at the hazards World War I had posed to travellers:

> We have steamed a hundred miles out of our course, another thing which has delayed us. The captain has been receiving S.O.S. messages for several days, which he believes to be a decoy. There are rumours too, that the *Karlsruhe* is about, so we have gone a long way into the Atlantic, and only seen one vessel since leaving the Irish Sea.[76]

In November 1915 there came a cable from the Rev. Harry Webster of Ibaden, that Sister Jessie Holloway had been suffering from 'Blackwater fever', but was recovering and hoped to be fit enough to travel home in early December.[77]

Sister Jane Theopold wrote with news that the school at Accra had moved temporarily to Aburi, 25 miles away, in January 1914 and there was some doubt as to whether it could be carried on successfully there, but all went well in spite of the different tribal affiliations. Later she gave a graphic account of the Sunday School there which was held, rather chaotically, in the boys' school, and she commented that it was 'all very different from home. One never knows what part one may have to take, and the mind of the negro is a totally unknown quantity.' Her hope was that the children would take the message home and that the 'work would bear fruit in years to come'.[78] At a special examination committee meeting on 4th July 1914 Miss Evelyn Lily Bellamy of Worcester, a trained teacher, volunteered to go out to West Africa and sailed on 2nd September for Cape Coast Castle. This was very unusual, but the need was urgent and so she went immediately without going to Ilkley. There was to be a special consecration service for her on her return from West Africa.[79]

---

75. *FL* (February 1915) p.12
76. *FL* (February 1915) p.12
77. *FL* (December 1915) p.96
78. *FL* (September 1914) p.129, (March 1915) p.20
79. *FL* (October 1914) pp.143-44 cf. WDIMins II pp.65, 69, 110, 125, 144, 148

World War I caused a shortage of paper and so *Flying Leaves* was discontinued. Thus, apart from brief references in the Wesley Deaconess Institute Minutes, mainly connected with appointments and sailings, little information can be gleaned about the progress of the work in West Africa until *The Agenda* started in 1922.

The Minutes reported in July 1917 that Marianne Malings had been ill and the school at Accra had been opened, but there was little news because of the war, which made communication difficult.[80] At the Committee Meeting on 28th June 1918 the Warden reported that he had heard from the Rev. William Goudie that the Government would probably grant permission for three Wesley Deaconesses in West Africa to travel home in the near future. Obviously the war had affected the work in West Africa where the workers had been for more than two years and unable to come home on furlough. If they were able to travel it might also mean that, because of the difficulty of supply, the school would have to be closed for a time. However, at the same meeting two candidates, Miss J. E. Johnson from Manchester and Miss Clara Churchill from Fishponds, Bristol volunteered for work in West Africa, so the problem was eased. They were accepted and in December Sister Mabel Fielder also offered to go out.[81] Clara resigned when she married a missionary, the Rev. J. R. S. Law of Freetown.[82]

Sister Elsie Dukes who, as we saw earlier, went out to teach in the Girls High School in Freetown in 1910, gave an account of a 17 day trip she and Sister May (Hatchard) took with missionaries up the Scarcies River to Kambia and Forracarriah in April 1918. She describes the eventful boat trip, beset by adverse tides and tornadoes, the overnight stops in all sorts of makeshift accommodation, often with unwelcome rats as uninvited house guests, and the services, usually conducted in the local dialect. Land travel was either on foot or by being carried in hammocks through difficult terrain in great heat and heavy rain storms, plagued by mosquitoes and sandflies. Several of the party became ill, including Sister May, but Elsie managed very well. The local people often presented them with gifts which sometimes caused embarrassment, but were accepted in the spirit in which they were given. After another eventful voyage home they duly arrived back at the Cline Town Wharf and she concluded with the words 'Thus ended a pleasant trip.' ![83]

---

80. WDIMins II p.120
81. WDIMins II pp.127, 129, 134-35, 149
82. *The Agenda* (December 1924) p.16, (February 1925) p.12
83. MS copy of an account 'A trip up the Scarcies River to Kambia and Forracarriah 10-27 April 1918' by Sister Elsie Dukes

> ### Mission Trip (with gifts), 1918   Sister Elsie Dukes
>
> . . . the head man of Fouracarriah (sic) brought us some rice and kolas (nuts), then Mr and Mrs Pratt presented us with a sheep. Jusu stayed at home to act as butcher and cook and the rest of us started off. Sister May and I had hammocks. It was a very hot open road and we were very glad to get there. (Herimakonnah) The Paramont (sic) Chief was a very old man – not at all handsome or imposing and rarely seemed to smile. He gave us a reception in his verandah (sic) and after wards (sic) presented us with rice kolas, eggs and a young bullock. What to do with the bullock became a question of the moment. It was suggested that Mr. Williams should ride it home, and that it be made to swim and tow the boat against wind and tide. However after a little trouble we persuaded the people to accept the animal as a gift from the V. Chairman. They were to kill it and hold a festival in our honour. We had breakfast in a tumbled down mosque, and later a service which was very good and seemed to be appreciated by the people.
>
> *Source:* MS 'A trip up the Scarcies River to Kambia and Forracarriah.
> 10th-27th April 1918

Sister Elsie Dukes left West Africa in 1922, having served there for 12 years.

In October 1920 Miss Gertrude A. Flower of Barry, who had volunteered for West Africa work, was accepted as a Probationer Deaconess and at the same meeting it was reported that there were vacancies at Cape Coast Castle and Accra for two teachers at Christmas and that an extra worker had been requested for Lagos. By December, after just a short while in College, Gertrude Flower was on her way to West Africa. At the same time it was reported that a Miss A. Hall had volunteered to do a year's supply work at Accra 'without any question of joining the Order at present' as also did a Miss Edwards who went to the Lagos school. Later both Miss A. M. Hall (Sister Mary) and Miss B. M. Edwards (Sister May) offered and were accepted into the Order. The latter resigned when ill-health forced her return from Lagos.[84] From these examples it is obvious that the need in West Africa was urgent and so women, who would normally have spent time in College when they volunteered for West Africa, were quickly accepted and almost immediately sent out. This does not necessarily imply that the Order lowered its very high entry standards as all the volunteers were

---

84. WDIMins II pp.159, 163, 165, 171, 180; *The Agenda* (July 1922) p.10, (March 1924) p.19

interviewed and underwent a stringent medical examination. It simply shows the importance placed on the West African work, the awareness of the arduous conditions there with the need to have a rota of deaconesses, so that all could have regular furloughs, and the care and concern afforded to the 'Foreign Mission' Sisters. It is also likely that the volunteers were already trained nurses and teachers and therefore considered suitable for immediate appointment in hospitals or clinics and in schools. In April 1926 four probationers, who were either home on furlough or preparing for foreign appointments, were consecrated, even though their probation was not completed.[85]

In February 1922 Ethel Johnson and Alice MacDonald, new volunteers for the Women's Auxiliary, sailed to the Coast to serve respectively in Accra and Lagos, while Sister Gertrude Joy and Winifred Shovelton went in March 1922. Miss Hall, who had been supplying at Accra for the past year, Marianne Malings and Miss Edwards from Lagos and Clara Churchill from Freetown were expected home. The fact that Wesley Deaconesses were specially trained for overseas work is shown by the report that Sister Alice Burroughs was sent to the Hull Royal Infirmary in February 1923 to undertake a full course in Hospital Nursing in order to qualify for special missionary work in West Africa.[86]

In the spring of 1923 the Warden, quite unexpectedly, got the chance to go to West Africa and was able to pay a 'flying visit to the Girls' High School at Wilberforce', Freetown, before proceeding to Seccondee and on by train to Kumassi. The experience gave him an insight into the country, the conditions and the work being done by the missionaries and the Wesley Deaconesses.[87]

'The Bush'　　　　**The Warden, the Rev. Dr. W.R. Maltby**

I never knew what 'The Bush' was like until that day. There is something menacing and even fearful in this surge of silent vegetable life. The grasses rise 12 ft. high and wall you in. Palms and bamboos seem to grow while you watch, and shut out the sky. Mankind seems an intruder in a hostile kingdom . . . Such a country seems to say to men 'Live here if you dare.' And they dare. Wherever you go, you come on clearings in the midst of the Bush, and villages, and men, women, boys and girls. You

---

85. WDIMins II p.226
86. *The Agenda* (February 1922) p.9, (March 1922) p.8, (May 1922) p.11, (January 1923) p.14
87. *The Agenda* (June 1923) pp.3-5, (July 1923) pp.2-5

look at the poor little mud-walled huts, the squalid and comfortless surroundings, and ask yourself 'Is life worth living here?' But you get your answer in the human faces before you. In the end I found myself thanking God for their mysterious cheerfulness.

Source: The Agenda (June 1923) pp.3-4

Kumassi	The Warden, The Rev. Dr. W. R. Maltby

Kumassi is a name that will be familiar and famous among Methodists in a few years' time. We have a wonderful site there . . . Already the walls of our splendid College, which is to be the School of the prophets, are up to the second storey . . . Boys' School and Girls' School are to follow, and all that can help to build up a great Christian community and furnish Missionaries for West Africa from the Africans themselves . . . There is a work of God in Kumassi.

Source: The Agenda (June 1923) pp.4-5

Qualifications for Work in West Africa	The Warden

. . . an enchanting land if it were not for the heavy air and the humid heat . . . If any English girl is thinking of going to West Africa, and wonders whether she will like it, she should look out for a very warm and sultry day with thunder about, then put on all the clothes she has, do a morning's ironing, spend the afternoon in calling on people who don't want to see her, or an afternoon's sick visiting. If she feels cheerful and can eat as much as she drinks, she has some of the qualifications for West Africa. Seriously, we ought to consider the heavy handicap that these tropical climates lay upon our workers. It is a hard thing for many eager spirits to feel that the climate drains them of half their vitality before they even begin. Yet they prevail!

Source: The Agenda (July 1923) p.4

On his return trip Maltby was able to spend longer at the Girls' High School and to appreciate the wonderful work being done by Sisters Florence Chislett and Gertrude Flower, commenting that 'it is hard to think of any work that is better worth doing'. In May 1923, when arrangements made for supplying the Freetown School broke down, Sister Persis stepped into the breach to relieve Gertrude Joy until

November. It was arranged that Miss Minnie Burns, who was teaching at Ilkley College, would go to Freetown in November and Sister Persis would return to her post at Ilkley College. She eventually returned on 3rd August 1924, but in 1926 she was back in the Gold Coast for another year. Minnie was received as a member of the Order before she sailed.[88]

The work in West Africa was expanding rapidly, with many volunteers offering to go, but in December 1923 the Warden was particularly anxious to have the services of a 'woman graduate or Certificated Teacher with a Missionary Call' for the High Schools as the educational work there was deemed so important. The Wesley Deaconess Order had a special interest in West Africa, as it had in Ceylon. Sister Jessie Rapson, writing from Segbwema, gave an account of her 'first month in Mendi-land'. Her sphere of work was 'nursing' and her introduction to it memorable, for, having opened the Dispensary on the Monday morning 'with fear and trembling, as the native minister had asked the whole town to come, and I knew I hadn't a great stock of medicine' the Paramount Chief arrived and pledged his help. Tragically that afternoon he suffered a cerebral haemorrhage from which he never recovered. Jessie visited him and his family several times a day for a week and he was baptised 'Constantine' before he died and his was 'the first Paramount Chief round here to have had a Christian burial. He was buried at dead of night in his own compound, but without the usual heathen customs. The following day there was a most impressive Memorial service round his grave, 1,000 people being present, including many tribal authorities and Mohammedans. Mr. Law had walked twenty miles the previous day in order to get here, and was just in time fortunately. One felt the circumstances attending the death of "Momo Jimmy" marked an important epoch. The steady sowing of previous missionaries had brought this about.' The medical course which Jessie had undertaken was now proving extremely valuable as she became involved in all sorts of nursing emergencies. In addition to this work she also took part in conducting services in the villages and helping in the Mission Boarding School.[89]

Sister Persis wrote of a Kru service she attended at Freetown where she spoke through an interpreter and was not as inhibited as she had expected.

---

88. *The Agenda* (June 1923) pp.5, 16, (July 1923) p.12, (September 1924) p.8
89. *The Agenda* (December 1923) pp.6-7, 10-11

> **Kru Service, Freetown**   **Sister Persis M. Beer**
>
> The minister who introduced us had to be interpreted, but his introduction ran something like this: 'We very glad to see big man (Mr. Bethell) with us tonight and dem ladies. They come for love of Christ teach all dem picannin. Big man no preach, but one of dem ladies will. I tell you one secret - Big man go over sea to see all – (comprehensive wave of hands) – all the big people. You all pray he go safe.' The hymn 'There is a fountain filled with blood', Sister Winifred sang the verses in English, and they the chorus in Kru. I am glad to have had the opportunity of going to that Kru service. I did want to make them see Him, but I feel like an infant with a stammering tongue when I try . . .
>
> Shall I finish with a West African 'howler'?
>
>   'I must close my letter now as time is aspiring.'
>
>   *Source: The Agenda* (January 1924) p.13

A letter from Evelyn Bellamy gives some indication of the valuable work the school at Cape Coast was doing by teaching the girls, both theoretically and practically, to be good home makers, Sunday School teachers and class leaders. The influence of the school and its students spread widely as visitors to the school testified when speaking of the native homes they had visited, and, when senior girls, during their vacations, taught in Sunday Schools and helped in day schools. One ex-student wrote asking for a testimonial so that she could accept the invitation of a Government Inspector to teach needlework in a school in the northern Territories. She also noted that the school had had successes in the College of Preceptors' examinations and that 'this term we have sent some of our ordinary school work to the British Empire Exhibition, where we hope many of our English friends will visit and see the work of their little black African sisters'.[90]

Gertrude Joy paid tribute to the work of Sister Jessie when she reported the opening of the temporary house and the Girls' Boarding House in the 'Mende Country'. She realised that it would be some time before the school got on its feet and said that they were labouring under difficulties at present:

> . . . as our sole furniture consists of some benches (no desks), a blackboard and easel, and a very dirty ricketty [sic] table. That combination, together with bare whitewashed walls, on which is displayed one solitary text,

---

90. *The Agenda* (February 1924) pp.12-13

is not exactly inspiring for teaching, but we are hoping to have a transformation shortly.[91]

There was sadness in 1927 when Sister Gertrude Joy died suddenly on 18th July from fever. Probably the difficult climatic conditions had also taken their toll of Sister Ellen Johnson, who was not well enough to return from her furlough, but once again a volunteer, though not a deaconess, came forward in the person of Miss Lilian H. Quilliam, a certificated teacher, whose offer was accepted and who sailed immediately on 24th June 1925 for Accra.[92]

The development of the work and the co-operation between the Wesley Deaconess Order and the Women's Department of the Missionary Society is shown when two deaconesses were accepted by the Women's Department for work overseas. So Dorothy Platts was destined to go to the Gambia District to specialise in Girl Guide work and Edith Spears in educational work.[93] The Women's Auxiliary was sending its candidates to be trained at Ilkley before they went abroad and in due course some of these workers applied to join the Order. In 1928 agreement was reached with the Women's Department of the WMMS that it should contribute £10 per head to the Superannuation and Retiring Funds for all deaconesses in its service and also make a grant of £125 per year towards the cost of training. Then in 1930 it was decided that deaconesses appointed from 1st January 1930 to serve overseas for the Women's Department should be included in its Pension Fund, unless they retired before completing 25 years' service when the Order would take over the responsibility from the 1st September following retirement and the Women's Department would transfer all payments made into the Order's Annuitant Fund. For those appointed earlier who had served 25 years and reached the age of 55 the Women's Department would pay up to £30 per annum.[94]

As we have seen Sister Persis Beer was a tutor at the College, but the autumn of 1928 found her again on her way to West Africa to help establish the school at Kumassi. However, as the building was not completed she remained in Accra where she reorganised the Sunday School work and trained teachers. Once the school, Wesley College, was opened she seems to have taken charge of it.[95]

91. *The Agenda* (September 1924) p.10
92. WDIMins II p.237; *The Agenda* (May 1925) p.14, (June 1925) p.6, (October 1926) p.13
93. *The Agenda* (June 1928) p.15, (Christmas 1928) p.4
94. WDIMins II pp.220-21, 224, 228, 238, 241, 249, 266
95. *The Agenda* (Christmas 1928) pp.4, 7-9, (November 1930) p.13, (October 1933)

From 1930 the publication of *The Agenda* was very spasmodic and so little detailed information is available. A Monthly Letter seems to have taken its place. This presumably was a cyclostyled sheet which was circulated to the deaconesses, but unfortunately few survive and those that do give scant information. Some extracts from these Monthly Letters were given in those copies of *The Agenda* which did appear. So, from the September 1936 letter, we learn that Evelyn Bellamy began her 22nd year in West Africa, returning on furlough in December 1940 prior to beginning her last tour of duty in the overseas work. In 1944 she received the MBE in recognition of her 30 years' service in West Africa.[96]

Award of MBE in 1944 to Sister Evelyn Bellamy

Sister Evelyn was summoned to Buckingham Palace for the investiture . . . and this was followed by a luncheon of a family party of Gold Coasters and other friends. As the Warden said . . . 'Honours may mean little or much. This one recognises nothing less than a sanctified and successful ministry, and so the Order itself is honoured in the King's decorating Sister Evelyn.'

Source: The Agenda (Christmas 1944) p.8

The plea for more overseas candidates was evidence that this work, in which the Wesley Deaconess Order, was involved was expanding rapidly. Sister Dorothy Farrar, in 1938, highlighted the 'need for more Overseas Candidates. They wanted two doctors, two teachers, two teacher-evangelists, one evangelist and four nurses. There were at present in training no doctors, four teachers, no teacher-evangelists, five nurses who had not yet finished their training, but ought to be sailing in September.'[97]

Sister Elsie Walters, who had been with Persis Beer at Kumasi, moved from there to Cape Coast and reported on her journey.

---

p.5, (October 1936) p.2

96. *The Agenda* (October 1936) p.3, (December 1940) p.12, (July 1944) p.12, (Christmas 1944) p.8, (July 1945) p.10. Deaconesses have kindly lent me some later Monthly Letters.

97. *The Agenda* (May/June 1938) p.19

From Kumasi to Cape Coast   **Sister Elsie Walters**

I came in the College car and was thankful for that. The lorries that run between Kumasi and Cape Coast are not tempting. They are driven at a furious rate, uphill and down, hairpin bends or straight roads, usually with a suitable text such as 'The Lord is my helper' over the driver's seat, and 'O.K.' on the windscreen.

Source: The Agenda (December 1938) p.9

Winifred Shovelton had given 29 years to the overseas missionary work of the Order and in 1949 she returned to Western Nigeria 'to do part-time work among the people who have become her people'. After returning home in 1952, she went out again in the October to Badagry, finally coming back in July 1954.[98] In December 1951 Iley Carrington went out for her first term in French West Africa.[99]

The July 1952 issue of *The Wesley Deaconess Magazine* has a letter from Sierra Leone which is both exciting and rather pathetic telling, as it does, of the struggles of 'this young church' which required many workers, 'both European and Native'. The need for work to be done among the women was particularly urgent as they tended to 'cling to the old ways and hold back advance and hinder the men'. She (unidentified deaconess, probably Sister Celia Cotton) remarked that:

> Of the six workers I have met in this trek, three have been left by their wives for no other reason than that they preferred a polygamist household. Where one finds Christian homes they are, I think, the most powerful of all witnessing agencies . . .[100]

In 1957 the Gold Coast District became the Ghana District and went on to be The Methodist Church in Ghana in 1963. Wesley Deaconesses continued to serve there until 1971. In 1965 Rebecca Okyne attended Convocation and was welcomed by the Warden as 'the first, and, so far, the only deaconess of the Methodist Church in Ghana' and Convocation sent its good wishes to the Church there. Sister Rebecca replied with greetings from the Church in Ghana and told of her call and training.[101] The two Nigeria Districts united in 1964 to

---

98. *The Agenda* (April 1949) p.13 cf. *WDMag* (November 1945) p.14, (July 1952) p.15, (October 1952) p.17, (July 1954) p.13
99. *WDMag* (December 1951) p.13
100. *WDMag* (July 1952) p.15
101. Mins. of Conv.(1965) p.8

become the Methodist Church in Nigeria where deaconesses worked until 1977. Sierra Leone District, which became the Methodist Church in Sierra Leone, still had a deaconess appointed there when the Order ceased recruitment in 1978. The work of the Wesley Deaconess Order in the Gambia District closed in 1974-75 and in the Ivory Coast, formerly French West Africa, in 1971.[102]

A fitting conclusion to the involvement of the Wesley Deaconess Order in West Africa is provided by the obituary of Sister Rose Little, who died on 26th April 1952, which not only gives the bird's-eye view of the woman herself, but indirectly pays tribute to the work done there by so many others like her. As indeed, does an article by Persis Beer recalling her early days in the Gold Coast in which she tells of her arrival in 1923, encounters with all sorts of insects, speaking at meetings through interpreters, dealing with tribal customs, and observing nursing dispensaries being held on missionaries' verandas. Persis' main work was educational and in particular the establishment of the Boarding School for Girls (Mmofraturon – meaning 'Children's Garden') in Kumasi. As we have seen she was also involved with the training of teachers. The early days were hard work as there was a cocoa slump and many people found it difficult to raise even the modest school fees, especially for girls. However, progress was made and teachers trained by the school were in great demand. Sister Persis ended her account by writing that 'Looking back I feel that the enduring value of our work was the personal work.'

Obituary of Sister Rose Little	**Sister Persis Beer**

There will have been many sorrowful hearts in the Gambia and the Gold Coast when the news reached them of the death of Sister Rose Little, for she had loved and served in West Africa for thirty-three years, and she had hoped to end her days out there.

Sister Rose first went to West Africa in 1915 after only a few weeks as a student at Ilkley and she regretted missing her student year. But there was need in the Gold Coast and she went gladly. She had a great gift in her understanding of African people and one mark of her interest and friendship was shown in her learning the Ga language. She gained facility in hearing and speaking it as few if any others of our missionaries have done. She learned Ga, as she did so many other things, with real enjoyment.

For most of her time in West Africa Sister Rose was in charge of the Girls'

---

102. *WDO Stations* up to 1978

School in Accra, with a few years' break when she did similar work at Bathurst, in the Gambia. She was concerned to raise the academic standards of her school, but not only this; she worked to make it a training ground for character and a place where the girls learned to know God and to take their share of responsibility as members of the Church. In recent years her interest went increasingly to evangelistic work among women . . .

I think Sister Rose will be remembered by Africans and Europeans alike for three outstanding gifts – her sanity and common sense, her strong faith in God, her radiance and joy.

Sisters who were in College, was it 1919? may recall a time when Sister Rose was due to return to the Coast after furlough but no passage was available in those post-war days. Then came news of a colleague's illness in Accra and she felt it urgent to get back and felt sure that it was God's will. Students joined in prayer and after ten days a telegram came from Elder Dempsters offering a passage in the next boat, sailing almost at once. 'Can you be ready in time?' she was asked. She smiled. 'I am ready. I can go in half an hour. I did my packing ten days ago.' Next day she sailed. Her faith was like that, sure and practical.

Source: The Wesley Deaconess Magazine (July 1952) pp.22-23

The work in West Africa was demanding, but rewarding. The fact that there were so many volunteers offering to serve there, facing difficult conditions, and that so many served for a considerable number of years is a tribute in itself to the Order and the dedication of its members.

Sisters Faith Hunter, Annie Capper and Gertrude Nettleship, Puttur, Ceylon, 1904

Chapter 4

Wesley Deaconess Work Overseas – Asia

Ceylon

The Rev. and Mrs G. J. Trimmer had been missionaries in Ceylon from 1877 and in *Flying Leaves* he gives an account of the start of the work in Puttur. When they returned home on furlough in 1896 the people in Puttur and Jaffna asked them to 'bring two ladies to live in Puttar'(sic) when they returned. The request was simple, but the solution difficult. The Women's Auxiliary could not help, but Miss Ireson offered to go on as a voluntary worker. Next, the Warden, Dr. Stephenson wrote to Mrs. Trimmer asking if she would speak at the session on Foreign Missions at the Wesley Deaconess Convocation. Having accepted the invitation Mrs. Trimmer appealed for financial support, so that another worker could go to Ceylon. The appeal was successful and soon plans were made for the appointment of a Wesley Deaconess.

Arrangements were made by which the Women's Missionary Society accepted the offer of the Wesley Deaconess Order and agreed to pay the 'necessary expenses of passage and outfit', while the Order would raise money for her maintenance for five years. However, Stephenson said he would prefer two deaconesses to go together for mutual support and encouragement. Needless to say, the Trimmers and the people of Ceylon were delighted at the prospect. Donations flowed in and by June only £150 was still needed to enable a second deaconess to go to Ceylon. Meanwhile Sister Gertrude Nettleship had finished her medical training and set sail, arriving at Colombo on 21st August 1897 on her way to Jaffna.[1] The Order took Ceylon under 'its wing' and thereafter supported the work there financially – by donations, subscriptions, appeals and special events for 'The Ceylon Fund'.

---

1 *FL* (Jan 1903) pp.8-10; *HH* (January 1897) p.17, (February 1897) p.41, (March 1897) p.64, (June 1897) pp.137-38, (October 1897) p.232

Start of Wesley Deaconess work in Ceylon
Rev. George J. Trimmer

We had spoken of Puttar (sic) as a suitable centre for such work. We had a house there, built for the residence of a Tamil minister, which could, at small expense, be adapted for a Deaconess Home. The village is the head of a circuit. We had four schools, with about 1,000 children learning in them, and there was a population of 10,000 people within easy reach of the Home.

Source: Flying Leaves (January 1903) p.9

In her first letter home Sister Gertrude described her arrival and gave her first impressions of Ceylon where she visited a women's hospital, went to a Baptist Sunday School treat, to a Girls' School, and spoke, through an interpreter, at the Singhalese Missionary meeting.

First Tiffin in Ceylon   Sister Gertrude Nettleship

We had tiffin at the native minister's house. There were some of the funniest dishes. One looked just like a mould of dripping, but turned out to be rice and honey and other things cooked, and was very nice. We sat in a verandah (sic), round a little compound, with a tree in the middle, into the branches of which came a lovely humming-bird.

The old minister is very anxious that the second Deaconess should come there.

Source: Highways and Hedges (November 1897) p.257

He is such a nice old man, with a very black face and very white hair. He had pictures of many English Methodist notabilities on the walls, and I was pleased to recognise your face among them, smiling down on me. This minister – Mr. Mendis – is a very loyal Methodist. He has named his youngest son Garrett Champness! He is most anxious for a Deaconess.

Source: Highways and Hedges (December 1897) p.279

After a 10 day wait in Colombo for a boat to Jaffna Gertrude finally arrived and started getting acclimatised. She had Tamil lessons for three hours a day and on the first two Sundays went with Mr. and Mrs. Trimmer and Miss Ireson to Puttar, 12 miles away, but because of the long journey she was longing for a second Sister to come so that they could go to live there. There seems to have been good co-operation between the Christian denominations in the district with 'The Monthly Meeting' being held in different houses where everyone shared their experiences and someone gave a paper on 'a subject of common interest', which was followed by a prayer meeting and a shared meal.[2]

Joys and Troubles at Puttur   Sister Gertrude Nettleship

Mail day is one of the greatest enjoyments of missionary life . . . One of my greatest troubles just now is mosquitoes. My room . . . makes me think of Pharoah's palace, because of the different plagues I get in it. There are frogs and locusts hopping about the floor every night; then I get moths (some of them most lovely colours), bats, beetles, ants, and swarms of mosquitoes. Then I have had a huge scorpion and a centipede. Mr. Oliver, when he was here, grumbled because he saw nothing! They must have all come out for my special initiation into Ceylon life!

Source: Highways and Hedges (December 1897) p.280

Evidence of co-operation between the Children's Home and the Order is shown when Gertrude wrote to Mr. Horner, one of the Treasurers, suggesting that a few toys would be welcome for the Tamil children, explaining that they had to learn around 200 Scripture texts during the year and were rewarded with 'the gift of a penny English doll' when all were said correctly. Immediately the Children's Home organised a toy service and about 500 children brought all sorts of toys.[3]

Sister Gertrude was a good correspondent, as was her colleague Faith Hunter who joined her at the end of 1898, and they wrote frequently usually making sure that a letter arrived for Convocation. In the first one from Puttur Gertrude described her work and the reception she received from various people, especially when she was introduced as the 'doctor Ammah'. Her medical skills were in great demand and she was extremely thankful for the 'medicine chest' 'Mother' (Miss McDougall, Treasurer of the Mission to Ceylon) had helped her to get together. However, as her stock of medicines was running low she hoped more supplies might be sent out. She listed some of the items needed urgently – '. . . a really good stock of

---

2. *HH* (December 1897) pp.279-80
3. *HH* (April 1898) p.83

Castor Oil, Livingstone Rousers (Burrough's and Welcome's Tabloids), Quinine and Chlorodyne, etc.'.[4]

Both Gertrude and Faith had to learn Tamil before they could do a great deal of work as few of the local people understood any English. However, they were able to do some visiting each week, assisted by a 'Bible woman' to act as interpreter. Once they were fairly at home with the language the deaconesses settled in Puttur where their real work began. Mr. Trimmer described their work as 'principally evangelistic' as they visited the women in their homes, held meetings for them and visited schools. Sister Faith described her day when she travelled in the 'bandy' (a sort of trap) as she had to take a Bible woman interpreter with her. They visited some schools, checking on absent pupils, and treating sick ones. She found that as she travelled from 'compound to compound' she gathered 'an ever-increasing train of followers' and so most of her interviews were conducted sitting 'on a mat on a sort of verandah (sic) step'. Faith was very amused at the reactions to her medical skills of 'looking at tongues, feeling pulses, enquiring into symptoms, advising, prescribing, ordering, with a weight of authority and an air of wisdom no fully fledged MD could surpass, all the while making my very scanty stock of tonic go as far as it possibly would, to the great delight of the people . . .'[5]

The bungalow in which Gertrude and Faith eventually settled had a 'bedroom, bathroom and a tiny study each, with a fair-sized sitting room and dining room in common' set in a compound with trees where they hoped to make a garden. The normal routine of learning Tamil, visiting and taking meetings and services continued. Often they

'Off to a meeting': Sister Faith Hunter (bicycle); Sister Gertrude Nettleship (bandy), 1903

travelled to outlying areas in 'bullock carts'. They decided to hold their own Convocation at the same time as the one at home, 'by making a vigorous raid upon the women of as many of our villages as we could, taking a village each day, and having a magic lantern

4. *HH* (May 1898) p.114
5. *HH* (May 1899) pp.114-18

meeting in the evening, where we had been working during the day'. Their Convocation lasted a week and was very successful, so they continued the practice.[6] Mr. Trimmer gave an account of this 'raid'. Three girls from the village of Chempadu asked if they could go to the Boarding School at Jaffna and after about four years there they wanted to be baptised. Family objections were overcome and 'these three children are the "First-fruits" in the way of definite conversion and baptism of the Sisters' work'.[7] He also said that Magic Lantern shows had been a great attraction.

Magic Lantern Attraction   **Rev. G. J. Trimmer**

Many open-air lantern services have thus been held and largely attended. With the sheet slung between palmyra trees, and well damped, the picture is clearly visible on both sides of the sheet. One of the Sisters works the lantern on one side of the sheet; the other, with a baby organ and some of the workers, is on the other side. There, in the comparative shadow, the women of the village creep quietly up and are able to enjoy the pictures, the singing, and the preaching, as well as the men who gather on the other side of the sheet.

Source: Flying Leaves (February 1903) pp.24-25

In September 1899 Sister Faith was unexpectedly asked to take over at the Girls' English High School in Jaffna because Miss Ireson, the Principal, had to leave to nurse her brother in Kandy. Although Faith did some teaching much of her work was administrative which gave her many opportunities of contact with the girls.[8] Both Gertrude and Faith wrote to the 1900 Convocation. Gertrude, in particular, told of sick visits to families who were strict Hindus, where their medical skills were appreciated even though she was not allowed to touch the patient or any of the family's belongings because of pollution. Again, the shortage of medicine was a problem in spite of gifts from home, and she remarked that the people often paid in kind rather than currency which meant that she was unable to buy supplies locally. Sister Gertrude, as a trained nurse and midwife found great call for her services, which helped to overcome prejudice. The result of this was that the veranda of their house virtually became a dispensary. Obviously, this was not acceptable and she longed for a small separate dispensary. Ill-health

---

6. *HH* (October 1899) pp.237-38
7. *FL* (February 1903) pp.24-27
8. *HH* (February 1900) p.47

forced Mrs. Trimmer to return to England for six months, and Mr. Trimmer, who was Chairman of the District, promised that if £50 out of the £100 needed for such a building was raised then he would get work started on it. In the September issue of *Highways and Hedges* Stephenson was delighted to announce that the money had been sent and work commenced. More money was raised locally by 'Christian, Hindu and Mohammedan' friends and the dispensary, named 'Jevons Dispensary', was opened on 26th October 1901. It consisted of a meeting room, used as a surgery waiting room and for various meetings, a tiny consulting room, the dispensary, a dressing room and a ward with two beds. It met a great need as in the first three months 600 cases were treated and seldom was the two-bed ward empty. In their annual letter to the 1902 Convocation the deaconesses pleaded for the 'support of a Nurse-Bible woman' who could live in the dispensary and help with the nursing and dressing and after-care of patients.[9]

Puttur Dispensary

In the autumn of 1900 Sister Faith was able to start a little school in one of the houses in the village of Eevenay and was hopeful that, if it was a success, they would be able to build a proper school.

First Sewing Lessons at Eevenay   Sister Faith Hunter

It was such fun; their grimy little paws, their bewilderment over the right end of a needle to hold, and their delight with the thimbles, which they thought were jewels or playthings, and could hardly be made to see that they were of any possible use. Some of them were very bright and quick, and will soon learn. Some bright patches of

9. *HH* (August 1900) pp.189-90, (September 1900) p.212; *FL* (April 1902) p.58, cf. (February 1903) pp.24-27

> print that I took pleased them greatly, and they were very proud to get a piece to try what they could do. It is such a delight to watch them gradually learning to take in thoughts and ideas so utterly novel, and to see how even already they are developing.
>
> *Source: Highways and Hedges* (October 1900) p.238

When Sister Gertrude sailed for home on 9th March 1903, arriving in early April, the Order hoped another deaconess could be sent out to cover her furlough, and also Faith's the next year, and ideally stay on altogether. A Mr. Thomas Firth offered to provide half of the cost of a third deaconess for one year and therefore the challenge was to find the other half. One way of raising money was for the students at Ilkley to hold a Summer Sale and this continued for many years.[10]

Sale of Work

Early in September we hope to hold at the College, Ilkley, a small Sale of Work on behalf of our Puttur Mission. We want to raise at least £50, and shall be very grateful if our Lady Associates and other friends will send us each some plain or fancy article for this occasion.

Our Wants

Wanted *for Puttur, by* 1st August:
  1 Lady's Bicycle.
  1 Baby Organ.
  1 Small Camera.
  House-linen.
Any friend who would like to give, or assist in giving, one or other of these articles, should please write to Sister Dora Stephenson.

Source: Flying Leaves (July/August 1903) p.98

Sister Annie Capper started medical training at the Salvation Army Maternity Hospital, Hackney in preparation for going to Ceylon and on 31st October 1903 she wrote from on board the *RMS Ortona* describing her voyage to Colombo.[11] However, in November 1903 the Order's work in Ceylon faced a financial crisis when the Children's Home, which had been jointly supporting the two deaconesses there, withdrew its support as it wanted to send out

---

10. *FL* (March 1903) pp.36-41; (April 1903) p.54
11. *FL* (July/August 1903) p.115, (January 1904) pp.7-8

someone officially connected with the Home. Gertrude Nettleship was on furlough and money was urgently required if she was to be able to go back and a third deaconess sent. So it was decided to hold a special 'gathering' with a 'bring and buy sale' in the College Hall at which she would explain her work and show lantern slides.

Advertisement for Ceylon
Fund, Flying Leaves
(November 1903) p.162

Sister Faith's letter to Dora Stephenson in August 1903 shows the variety and extent of her daily work and one is amazed at all she managed to cram into a day:

> Wednesday was an average day: up about 6, tea, attending to domestic affairs, giving out stores and orders for the day, seeing the animals fed, putting my bedroom in order etc, until 7, then over to the dispensary, where I was on duty more or less constantly until 9.30, then off to two school meetings . . . After school, breakfast between 11.30 and 12. Tamil prayers with the servants, over to the dispensary again, where I was kept busy until about 2, when there was just time to bathe and change, have a hurried cup of tea, and get off in the bullock bandy with the Bible-woman to a village 2 miles drive, where I have a very interesting women's meeting every fortnight . . .
>
> . . . on this particular day, as the moon was good . . . we had a magic-lantern meeting in another village about 1 mile from Puttur, in quite the opposite direction, so I had to hurry back after the women's meeting, get the lantern, sheet, table, stool etc., etc., packed into the bandy, and off to the scene of action with . . .

Chinnappu, our-man-of-all-work, who can manage the lantern now as well as I can. We were soon joined by the Catechist and teachers who did the speaking, and had a very good meeting . . . [description of the scene]. Then the packing up, talking to those who came round, seeing a few sick folk, etc., etc., and getting home about nine to an empty little house, where my three dogs give me the warmest of welcomes and do their best to make up for the lack of any other society. My 'family' consists just now of three dogs, two bulls, four pigeons, and ten rabbits . . .[12]

Faith was also concerned that native 'Bible women' were not being properly trained and that the old idea that 'anyone can do Mission-work' was becoming dominant. So she was anxious that a Home or College should be set up 'where *educated young native women* can receive a good and careful training in 'systematic Bible-study, in practical application of it to the needs they meet, and in nursing sufficient to make them at least not a hindrance in time of need . . . When such a trained Tamil woman is available she can hope to accomplish in one year what no European can do in five. From her own life she will be familiar with the details of the lives of the women amongst whom she works.'[13]   A very forward looking comment!

Sisters Faith and Gertrude, Puttur, 1903

The 1904 Convocation said goodbye to Sister Gertrude as she prepared to go back to Puttur and reminded all present that the Wesley Deaconess Order work in Ceylon was now wholly supported by the Order. By the end of the year, when Faith was on furlough, the worry again was whether enough money could be found to send her back and then maintain the work in Ceylon. While she was at home Faith spent some time, largely at her own expense, getting more training at a medical college in London, so that she could be of most use to the women in Puttur. The Mission in Puttur received a glowing report from the Rev. W. H. Findlay

---

12. *FL* (November 1903) pp.165-66
13. *FL* (December 1903) pp.182-84

(Wesleyan Methodist Missionary Secretary) and his wife after the official inspection.[14] Apparently the Rev. G. J. Trimmer asked Annie Capper to go to Batticaloa to fill a vacancy for a few weeks, but her stay extended to three months. There she found a fever epidemic raging and also much general sickness and as 'the Moors' were very prejudiced against male doctors she found plenty to do. Faith Hunter was not returning to Puttur after her furlough because of 'several circumstances', but, she was going to Batticaloa and the people there were looking forward to her arrival. Stephenson explained this development. Apparently, the financial crisis during her furlough made it seem likely she would not be able to go back at all as the Order could only manage to support the two sisters at Puttur and the Women's Auxiliary was short of funds. However, 'Mrs. Wiseman and her committee agreed that Sister Faith should go out to one of their posts', if the Order could find half the cost. Sister Dora Stephenson undertook to be personally responsible for raising £35 per annum. This was forthcoming and so Faith went to Batticaloa:

> For the first time, **a Wesley Deaconess** is going to foreign work **in connection with 'Women's Auxiliary'** to the Wesleyan Missionary Society. Sister Faith Hunter . . . is to go to Batticaloa to fill an important vacancy there. But her support will be provided by the Women's Auxiliary, and she will act under the direction of the Auxiliary's Committee. She will none the less continue to be a Wesley Deaconess. This is as it should be. The support of the Sisters at Puttur, by contributions given or collected by the Wesley Deaconess Order is altogether an exceptional thing. It is not the business of the Institute to support workers, but to train them. As the Circuits or Missions at home support the workers with which we have supplied them, so the Missionary Society or the Women's Auxiliary will maintain the Deaconesses whom we place at their disposal . . .[15]

As time went on the arrangement between the Wesley Deaconess Order and the Women's Auxiliary was formalised with the Executive Committee, December 1910, insisting that 'where Wesley Deaconesses are employed by the Women's Auxiliary

---

14. *FL* (June 1904) p.92, (October 1904) p.140, (February 1905) p.198, (April 1905) p.228, (June 1905) pp.266, 271, (September 1905) p.327
15. *FL* (October 1905) p.325, (December 1905) pp.358-59, (January 1907) p.13

Society' the terms should be the same as they were for any other 'agents', with the deaconesses being paid directly and only £5 being paid into the Superannuation Fund. Bearing in mind that Puttur was the special concern of the Order the same meeting spelled out financial arrangements for them, which shows its care and concern:

> That the payment for Deaconesses at Puttur shall be £75 each per annum, payable quarterly, in advance.
> That if satisfactory arrangements can be made, the money shall be forwarded direct to the Deaconess.
> That in addition to this, a grant of £10 shall be made every second year for holiday expenses,
> That in cases where a Deaconess is alone at her post, her allowance shall be at the rate of £90 a year.
> That claims for medical attention shall be considered as they arise.
> That at the end of five years' service, a furlough allowance of £12.10.0 a quarter shall be paid for one year, provided the Deaconess is returning to her work.
> If a Deaconess is not returning to the work, no furlough shall be paid except by a special decision of the Committee in each case as it arises.
> In the case of a Deaconess on furlough who is returning to her work, a grant of £4 worth of uniform shall be paid at the beginning of the furlough, and £10 renewal of outfit at the end.[16]

On 25th August 1905 the Governor, Sir Henry A. Blake, and Lady Blake visited Jaffna and Puttur and actually inspected the dispensary, asked many questions, expressed appreciation of the work of the Mission and signed the Visitors' Book.

Viceregal Entries in Visitors Book at Puttur – 25th August 1905

I am delighted with what I see of the arrangements of this Dispensary. No institution is more useful than such as this, which reaches the women and children.

HENRY A. BLAKE, *Governor, etc.*

I am much pleased to find a lady doctor so far afield.

EDITH BLAKE.'

Source: Flying Leaves (November 1905) p.343

---

16. WDIMins I pp.371, 372

Faith Hunter, as she wrote from the Jevons Dispensary, Batticaloa, quickly settled down there and was amused to be addressed as 'doctor' and consulted on almost everything. However, she delighted in the medical work as it brought her into contact with so many different people. She longed to be able to help the Mohammedan women and was hoping to study Arabic in order to do this. Her work at Batticaloa was 'entirely medical' and she had charge of four dispensaries, one being a hospital which was training three nurses. One of the other dispensaries, at Kattancudy, 'the great Moor settlement' was a Goverment-run one and the situation was very unsatisfactory, as the women would not go to a man, so she longed to have one of her own to which the women would come. This was reinforced as, when the Government male dispenser could not be there, many more women came to see 'Doctor' Faith.

Visit of 'Amma' to Kattancudy   Sister Faith Hunter

The Government dispensary at Kattancudy, the great Moor settlement, is reached about 9.30, and four busy, breathless hours follow. The dispenser is away ill, the dispensary has been closed since the Amma's last visit a week ago, and is now being besieged by an anxious crowd, pushing and jostling and squabbling in eagerness to secure first turn. To write (and Government requires much writing), prescribe and dispense for 115 patients of all sorts and conditions in the short time at command gives little room for pause . . . It is quite a field day for the Moor women. No dispenser being there the masculine element is absent, leaving them free to come as they will – a freedom they take full advantage of. Names and ages have to be entered in the Government register. Name they usually manage to tell - though frequently not at all sure of their children's – 'Asiayatamma', 'Ismailmommathupillai', 'Mommachiepillaikundu', are amongst the short and easy ones to write! The attempt to discover age gives rise to much amusement. 'Look at me', – 'Look at her teeth' – 'I have three children' – three or four as the case may be, are the answers given. Description of their ailments is but little less vague as a rule, and ingenuity and patience are sorely taxed to unravel the story.

Source: Flying Leaves (October 1907) p.142

Eventually, in July 1907 Faith was able to have her Mission Dispensary at Kattancudy, which the women greatly appreciated. She continued training native girls to be nurses, but felt unable to leave them in sole charge of the In-patient Department and so could only accept 'the most urgently necessary cases'. She lamented that the openings she made through her medical work could not be followed up:

> And there is one special sorrow – to see so constantly doors open that cannot be kept open because there is no one to go in and follow up what the medical work has begun! The medical worker is called into homes of all classes and creeds and races . . . But when the particular need for which she has been called is over, she must pass on to others. And so the open door is closed again! Medical work that is to have its full evangelistic value cannot be done by one worker.[17]

Each year *Flying Leaves* contained a copy of her report to Synod, but, as she remarked of the 1906 one, it was 'a very bald statement of what had been done during the year'. For example, that year, over 8,000 patients had been seen, weekly meetings held regularly at all the dispensaries and various other activities as the opportunity offered.[18]

Gertrude Nettleship wrote very interestingly about the candidates' examination papers which had been sent to her and which Mary, her Bible woman, attempted to answer verbally. Her answers on the Scripture paper were very good and some of her answers on the General papers were illuminating to say the least!

Candidate's's' Examination Answers   by Mary – at Puttur

For question 6 I had to find as near as possible the Tamil equivalents for 'Policeman', 'Guardian', 'Sanitary Inspector', etc., and I could not help but think that if the gentlemen holding the 'headmanships' of this district could have heard Mary's descriptions of their supposed duties (gathered by observing what they *did*), and had they thought these descriptions would reach the ears of the Government officials . . .

---

17. *FL* (April 1908) pp.239-40 cf. (December 1908) pp.354-55
18. *FL* (April 1907) p.58; (April 1908) p.239 et al.

these 'Tamil gentlemen of position' would rather tremble at the thought of the next election for these honourable and remunerative posts!'

Source: Flying Leaves (September 1908) p.311

Mary had a very bright little daughter, Rachel Gnanamma (Wisewoman), who had passed through all the standards of her village school and ought to go on to the Girls' Boarding School in Jaffna, but her parents could not afford the fees of £5 a year. So Gertrude appealed to her readers for support.[19]

In 1908, Elizabeth Spence, who went out to cover Annie Capper's furlough, soon settled down well and was able to manage when Gertrude Nettleship became ill in December with 'enteric fever'. It seemed likely that Gertrude would have to return to England when she came out of hospital and her illness exacerbated the financial problems of the Ceylon Mission. The cost of Annie Capper's furlough, Elizabeth Spence's passage and tropical outfit, plus Gertrude's illness had meant an extra £250 expense, which was more than the Order could afford. The difficulty was not just to deal with the immediate problem, but also to ensure that it did not arise in the future. Again, the Warden emphasised that it was the function of the Order to train deaconesses and not to support mission workers.[20] Annie Capper married the Rev. William C. Bird, a missionary in the North Ceylon District (1906-23), in the autumn of 1909 and left the Order, but continued to work in Ceylon as a missionary's wife and kept in touch with the deaconesses in Ceylon. In the autumn of 1911 her husband conducted special mission services in the Jaffna District and wrote to the Warden:

> During a week's Mission at Puttoor (sic) we had the splendid co-operation of the Sisters there. The Mission was the most striking, from many points of view, of the whole series. Each night the Sisters brought from fifty to eighty Hindu women to the big meeting, and squatted down on the floor with them at one end, in a building otherwise full of men. Such a thing would have been considered incredible only a few years ago.

---

19. *FL* (September 1908) pp.310-11
20. *FL* (February 1909) p.19, (April 1909) p.53

> The villages around Atchelu (Puttoor circuit) are tremendously influenced by Christianity, and I can truthfully say, mainly through the agency of the Sisters.[21]

After her convalescence furlough Sister Gertrude returned to Puttur in May 1910 and Sister Elizabeth had a brief holiday in the hills before going to Batticaloa in July to replace of Sister Faith who was leaving the Order on her marriage to the Rev. Edgar Thomas Selby, a missionary in North Ceylon District (1907-33). They were married on 3rd June 1911 at Colpetty Wesleyan Chapel, Colombo. Sister Elizabeth's first letter from Batticaloa on 30th October 1910 showed she was happily settled in her new job and surroundings.[22]

Easter Hayden, who went to Puttur, was a trained nurse and midwife and her first letter, sent four weeks after her arrival, contained the reassuring news that Gertrude Nettleship was much stronger than when she left England to return to Ceylon and that she herself had received a very warm welcome. While Sister Gertrude had been on furlough the 'house' of the Biblewomen had been ruined by the north-east monsoon, so one of the first things she did on her return was discuss the matter with the Chairman of the District, the Rev. G. J. Trimmer, with the result that she made an appeal for £150 to build a Biblewomen's Home and Training Institution. She received a promise of £50 and, on 9th January 1911, she wrote asking Bradfield if he would publicise her need in *Flying Leaves* in the hope that some other friends would respond.[23]

When the Foreign Missions General Secretary, the Rev. J. Milton Brown (1905-12) and his wife visited Puttur they were amazed at the effect the work of the Wesley Deaconesses had had, because when they had been missionaries in the Jaffna District (1866-83) 'Puttoor (sic) was known as a very difficult and almost fruitless field of labour'. After visiting the Dispensary the local people gave the Browns their own exuberant welcome, with music, presentation of gifts and ceremonial addresses in both English and Tamil.

---

21. *FL* (February 1910) p.26, (December 1911) p.174
22. *FL* (January 1911) p.5
23. *FL* (November 1910) pp.129, 130, 155, (March 1911) pp.37-38, (June 1911) p.85, (December 1911) p.168, (February 1912) p.20

Foreign Missions General Secretary's Visit to Puttur, 1911

. . . Mr. Brown said that he thought the name of the village Puttoor ought to be changed to 'Puth-oor', meaning 'new village', so great were the changes since he had last visited it.

and in a letter to the Warden:

You are doing a beautiful bit of work there, for which I devoutly thank God. When I knew the village thirty or forty years ago it was a wilderness, and regarded as the most barren soil of our district; to-day, it looks like a fruitful garden.

Source: Flying Leaves (April 1911) p.53; (May 1911) p.78

At the end of January 1912 the deaconesses in Puttur wrote describing the chaotic conditions under which they worked when called to the home of a seriously ill woman only to find the very dirty cluttered room crowded with sympathisers. The poor patient was writhing in agony from the 'dreadful Tamil medicine she had been having for two days, and which we feared would kill her'. Looking back afterwards they recalled with amusement the fee for their medical services – 'fowls'!

Fee for medical services rendered   **Puttur, 1912**

. . . we had to go through the usual discussion about the fee . . . These people seemed very poor, and so we told them if they could get fowls, we would buy them, and give the money to the hospital as a fee. They agreed and we started off . . . [description of home and patient]. . . All this time the men outside were racing about shouting and chasing fowls for the fee! Presently one poor bird flew into the room, and flew madly about, the men shrieking to the women 'catch it, catch it'. We could not see the humour of it all at the time, but we are very thankful there is a very humorous side to our experiences – it helps us through with them.

Source: Flying Leaves (March 1912) pp.37-38

Money for the Tamil Deaconesses Hostel had been forthcoming so excavations for the foundations and preparations for the stone-laying were underway when the rains and floods came, and everything had to stop until it all dried out and work could restart. Another urgent problem was the shortage of stores and the Sisters sent a list of their requirements to the Warden who published it in

Flying Leaves with the comment that the Rev. and Mrs. John Eagles would be returning to Ceylon in April and had agreed to take out the items donated. Easter Hayden acknowledged their arrival.[24]

Elizabeth Spence wrote of her year – 1911 – in Batticaloa, which had been 'an exceptional one for many digressions from the usual routine'. Several workers had been ill and she had had to take patients 'to the hills', which meant an extra 800 miles travelling in addition to the 34 she had to travel each week. She was much encouraged at being consulted by 'a quack doctor' and also by having patients sent to her for medicine by native doctors. So a little 'evangelistic' work was done. While Gertrude Nettleship wrote to Convocation as usual, saying that they hoped the building of the Biblewomen's Home would eventually become a Tamil Wesley Deaconess College, as, purposely, the foundations laid had been substantial enough to allow a second storey to be added when the money was available.[25]

Meanwhile Gertrude and Easter had organised a Sale of Work, which had required a great deal of thought and planning. It was a big venture for a little village sewing meeting: the Sisters had written to firms in England asking for samples and Easter had contacted *The Nursing Mirror* telling nurses about the work in Ceylon and asking for donations. The response had been wonderful. The Sale was held in the boarding school, which was beautifully decorated for the occasion. Although, at the time of writing, Easter did not know the financial result she felt it had been a great success and that now they would be able to afford half the cost of 'our new church window shutters' which would at least ensure a dry church during the monsoon season.

Sale of Work at Puttur, 1912   Sister Easter Hayden

The response [from the firms to which they wrote] was really wonderful – Nestle's Milk Co. sent us a large box of their various preparations, milks, foods, chocolates etc., carriage paid to Jaffna. Cadbury's wrote to their Colombo agents giving them instructions to send us a case of chocolates, cocoa, etc. Fry's sent two large parcels per parcels post; Horlick's, Allen and Hanbury and several others sent parcels pre-paid to the Mission House, which Mr. Hoyle packed in a

---

24. *FL* (March 1912) pp.37-38, (April 1912) p.55, (September 1912) pp.125-26, (October 1912) p.141, (December 1912) p.173
25. *FL* (April 1912) p.53, (June 1912) pp.88-89

> box and sent out to us, and several other parcels we received by post. Several firms said they did not usually send goods to bazaars, but would make an exception in this case. I don't think Sister Gertrude or I had faith enough to expect anything like such a response when we wrote – don't you think it was splendid?
>
> *Source: Flying Leaves* (December 1912) p.176

Easter Hayden explained, in April 1913, that unfortunately the 'Tamil Deaconess Hostel' was not quite ready, but they hoped that Sister Ethel Westlake, who in September 1912 had taken up an appointment at 'The Friends' Mission,' in Clodagh, Matale, would be the first deaconess to stay there, which would be marvellous as there was not enough room in their bungalow for visitors. However, progress must have been made because soon they could write that now money was needed to furnish it and the Hostel was officially opened on 6th October 1913.[26]

Wanted at Puttur **Sisters Gertrude and Easter**

First of all we want some money for the simple furnishing of our Tamil Deaconess Hostel, also some coloured Scripture pictures for the walls, and good maps of Palestine, Asia, Travels of St. Paul.

Then our cupboards are quite bare of toys, slates, pencils, exercise books, etc., for village school prizes for memorising Scripture. Any pieces of print, muslin and cotton stuffs are most valuable. We are most grateful to the Mothers' Meeting which has a yearly 'print collection' for us.

Contributions of drugs or appliances, old linen or cotton sheets are always welcome, and we badly need Quinine. We use *pounds* in a year!

Source: Flying Leaves (September 1913) p.132

---

26. *FL* (July/August 1913) pp.99-100, (September 1913) p.132, (December 1913) p.174

Training Home, Puttur (staff in the doorway), 1914

Sister Elizabeth Spence's 1912 report from Batticaloa was one of mixed fortunes, giving some indication of the problems facing the missionaries:

> Thalenkudah and Arrapatai are no longer being visited owing to the opposition of the Hindus. They have objected to the teaching of the Scriptures to the children and patients. Last June I was stormed out of the village of Thalenkudah by a Hindu priest and one of his adherents. This village has been visited weekly for the past six years and we have never before had any trouble.

However, on the plus side she had been engaged by the Local Board Committee as District Midwife and had two Tamil married women to train as midwives and nurses whom she felt promised to be very useful. Tuesdays were Elizabeth's 'Village Day' when she and her nurse colleague visited several villages in the area, treating patients and visiting schools before driving home tired, but happy. In June 1915 Sister Elizabeth reported that, having returned on 8th January from her furlough, she was delighted that the use of the 'little hospital ward' was being much appreciated and seemed to be breaking down prejudice. However, the sad news was that the Provincial Engineer had carried out an inspection and declared it structurally unsound. As there were no funds for rebuilding she was afraid that she might have to close it.[27]

From this point there is little information as *Flying Leaves* ceased because of World War I. However, in January 1922 the new magazine, *The Agenda,* came into being. It was very different from

---

27. *FL* (May 1914) p.79, (June 1915) p.44

Flying Leaves, being much smaller with fewer actual reports of deaconess work. It also appeared rather intermittently. The first communication from Puttur, a letter from 'Emily', the first Tamil Deaconess student trained at the Puttur Training Home appeared in February 1922. Students at Ilkley had written to her and she replied describing her work and further training since leaving the Home. She had returned to Vembadi Girls' High School as the teacher of Domestic Science and Nursing, but took some needlework, 'Dictation and Recitation' and Scripture classes, plus a Junior class meeting and Bible class meetings for Christian and Hindu girls. She was also in charge of the School Dispensary. Emily added that her fellow student at the Training Home had gone to Columbo for a six month course at 'the Lying-in-Home' where she had obtained the Government certificate in midwifery.[28] This letter pays tribute to the success of the deaconesses' work in Puttur and the far-sightedness which set up the Training Home so that local girls could be trained to help their own people.

Tamil Training Home at Puttur　　　　　　　　**'Emily'**

Before leaving Puttur, I had given to me a badge on which is the Training Home motto, 'Others'. My earnest wish is that I may live for the good of 'Others'.

Source: The Agenda (February 1922) p.7

The Women's Local Committee of the North Ceylon District wrote to the Warden, Dr. Maltby expressing appreciation of the work of the two deaconesses in Puttur and the support given by the Order. They were also grateful for the services of Sister Flemoms who was working at Trincomalie under the auspices of the Women's Auxiliary. They added their plea to Sister Easter's for a third deaconess at Puttur, especially to cover furloughs. They reported that there were now six residents in training at the Tamil Training Home, where the curriculum included 'Bible Study, Hygiene, Home Nursing, Domestic Science and Infant and Maternal Welfare' as well as practical work.[29]

On 24th November 1922 Gertrude Nettleship returned from her furlough. While she had been away Sister Easter had been assisted by Mrs. Ester J. James, a Tamil worker who was a trained teacher.

---

28. *The Agenda* (February 1922) pp.7-8
29. *The Agenda* (May 1922) p.13

Mrs. James wrote a very revealing letter telling how, in spite of family opposition, she had gone to Puttur and now felt it was where God wanted her to be. She described the Training Home – 'a real home' – the course of study undertaken and also the practical work, both in the Dispensary and the villages.[30] Gertrude and Easter sent a heartening progress report which reinforced Mrs. James' account. They explained how the students had prepared and given a 'Lyrical Lantern Service' on *The Pilgrim's Progress* to both Christian and Hindu audiences in the villages. When the lantern service was over they had been amused to hear the men on the other side of the sheet discussing it and especially when one man said, 'The Brahmins read to us in April, but why don't they teach us that life is a battle between good and evil and how to meet it – and *women* can tell us!'

Lyrical Lantern Addresses   **Puttur Tamil Students**

They have practised and arranged several lyrical addresses, and these always rivet the attention of hearers, and through the year's work we have noted again and again how Ear Gate (this lyrical preaching) and Eye Gate (the Lantern Meetings) have carried home great truths in a very impressive way. As a result, we expect to see more intelligent baptisms in this village Circuit than we have ever experienced.

Source: The Agenda (December 1923) p.12

The plea for a third deaconess did not go unheeded for the Warden reported that 'a generous friend has made it possible for a worker to be sent out to Puttur to relieve Sister Easter Hayden, and allow her to return home for furlough in the autumn. Sister Evelyn Lowe, who is a fully trained nurse and has had a wide and varied experience, is preparing to sail in September.' She sailed on 4th October 1923. Sister Lydia Smith received an appointment under the Women's Auxiliary and took a short course at Kingsmead College, Birmingham before going out to Welimadi, being consecrated at Tadcaster on 16th December 1923 and sailing on the 28th. That month Maltby remarked that the Order's relations with the Women's Auxiliary and the Missionary Society 'are closer and more fruitful' as more deaconesses were feeling the call to missionary work.[31] Much more co-operation between the Wesley

---

30. *The Agenda* (October 1922) p.7, (December 1922) pp.10-12
31. *The Agenda* (July 1923) p.12, (November 1923) p.9, (December 1923) pp.6, 7, (January 1924) p.8

Deaconess Order and the Women's Auxiliary occurred from then onwards, but the Order continued to support the two deaconesses at Puttur as its special missionary contribution. The position at Puttur, as reported to the General Committee in December 1924, was that 'The Women Auxiliary has now taken over the administration of the work there, the Wesley Deaconess Order agreeing to be responsible for the allowances of two workers at £140 a year for the present and £280 altogether – also for £15 per year to be sent by the W. Deaconess Order to each Sister direct as long as the present workers remain there.'[32] Apart from recording the appointments, sailings and arrivals of the deaconesses who were working under the auspices of the Women's Auxiliary there is very little else about their work in Ceylon, so we will leave them and concentrate on the work at Puttur. Each year the students held a Missionary Anniversary to raise money for the Ceylon Fund to support *their* deaconesses.

In November 1924 Sister Easter Hayden sailed back to Puttur, but before her departure she pleaded for gifts in money or kind for the Dispensary and village work as they were hoping to open some new Infant Welfare Centres. They needed 'Baby weighing scales, enamel jugs, basins' and baby toiletries, medicines, first aid items, scraps of material and anything which could be used as prizes in the village schools.[33]

Ceylon Day at Ilkley College 1950: Play: 'Two Modern Moralities' (Chas. Williams) Ceylon Days were held each Year to raise money to support the Wesley Deaconesses in Puttur

May 1925 brought the news that Gertrude Nettleship had been unwell for a while, so Sister Easter had taken her to hospital in Colombo where she had had an appendix operation and made an excellent recovery. The sad thing was that because of this she had missed the Warden's visit to Puttur during his trip to India and Ceylon. Gertrude wrote cheerfully from hospital in Colombo that

---

32. WDIMins II p.212
33. *The Agenda* (September 1924) pp.9-10, (November 1924) p.12, (December 1924) p.16

she was 'still very much "on strike" so far as work and duty are concerned'. However, she had so much enjoyed the chance of catching up on her reading that it had seemed like a holiday and she really wondered if she might be able 'to grow another appendix (or somethings (sic) perhaps a little less painful in removal) that will secure me another free time. I must say I think "Hospital" spells the quietest, most restful and irresponsible vacation obtainable.'[34]

In 1927 Gertrude Nettleship celebrated over 30 years' work in Ceylon by a trip home, but rather than 'retiring' she intended to go back. On her safe return Easter set off for her furlough returning on 27th December. Gertrude Nettleship retired in 1930 and the General Committee agreed that she should receive a pension of £100 a year, part of which would come from the Retiring Fund and the rest from the contribution made to the Women's Department for the work in Ceylon. There is a mention of a Miss Jean Sharp, 'training deaconesses in Puttur', who brought greetings to Convocation and was asked to take 'love and thoughts' back to them. It is presumed she was a lay missionary teaching at the Tamil Training Home. Circumstances had changed over the years and Sister Hettie Addy, reporting to the 1930 Convocation that £150 was still needed to support the two deaconesses in Puttur, suggested 'the time may have come to reconsider . . . [the Wesley Deaconess Order's] responsibility to the Women's Department for the support of two Deaconesses in Ceylon'.[35]

In July 1932 Gladys Stephenson, travelling home from China, broke her journey in Ceylon and took the opportunity to visit Puttur. Immediately on her arrival in Colombo she went to the 'oldest Methodist Church' in Asia and met the Tamil deaconess who had been trained at Puttur. Remembering the 1915 Convocation when Gertrude Nettleship had spoken of her desire to establish the Training Centre Gladys was delighted 'to see a qualified deaconess at her work in a City Mission'. She travelled to Puttur, where Sister Easter Hayden was waiting for her. Together they went to a village where the deaconess students were holding Child Welfare Clinics and Easter told her that in the early days the work had been very hard, but 'the villages had now become Christian' and indeed many of the children had been brought into the world by the Sisters. In the afternoon they visited the English and Tamil High Schools and the

---

34. *The Agenda* (May 1925) p.14, (June 1925) p.6
35. *The Agenda*, (Christmas 1928) p.4, (April 1929) p.5, (March 1930) p.3; WDIMins II p.256; *The Agenda* (June 1930) pp.8, 10

Women's Missionary Society in Jaffna and attended a meeting of the Tamil Ladies Auxiliary who wanted to hear about China. Gladys also saw the Dispensary and Training Home, meeting the staff and students to tell them of her work in China. She commented:

> What splendid work those deaconesses are doing – they are breaking down age-long barriers of prejudice, blazing trails for an emancipated Christian womanhood, and showing to their own countrymen that God has a work for His daughters to do with honour and success. These Tamil deaconesses are now sometimes asked to preach at a general service, an entirely new departure, one that even the Pastors have been slow to allow but quick to appreciate.
>
> Puttur looks to the Deaconess Order in a very special way to uphold them in prayer. Do not let us fail them, or cease to remember that this work is peculiarly the bit of missionary service begun and maintained by our sisterhood.

From Ceylon Gladys crossed to India to visit Sister Gertrude who had been very ill and had retired to a cottage on a South Indian Hill Station to live with her sister, Mrs. Ross. In spite of her illness she was cheerful and happy and, for the first time in 18 months, had been able to go to church and 'take one or two gentle walks'. Sister Gladys found it 'good to hear Sister tell me of those early days, thirty-three years ago, when she was the first deaconesses sent out to Ceylon supported by the Order to begin work for the depressed people of North Ceylon'.[36]

Deaconess Training Centre, Puttur

Sister Gladys Stephenson

The Deaconess Training Centre at Puttur is Ilkley's own daughter. They give us always a full measure of daughter's love and gratitude, and look to us for the strengthening help that our love and prayers can give from the Mother House.

Source: The Agenda (Christmas 1932) p.9

---

36. *The Agenda* (Christmas 1932) pp.7-9

Easter Hayden wrote a little pamphlet containing an appreciation of Gertrude Nettleship 'our Periammah' and all the work she had done. Elizabeth Baker, the other deaconess, wrote of her first impressions of Puttur. The pamphlet ended with an appeal:

> All these developments bring responsibility, and the call for funds, staff and equipment and . . . *Retrenchment* – is the cry of the day! Should we halt? Should we say we have reached the limit? For thirty-five years Sister Gertrude has laboured and established this work. For thirty-five years the members of the Wesley Deaconess Order and their friends have loyally supported her labours with love, prayer and gifts. We appeal to all Old friends and New friends to help the women of this land to meet the new opportunities and challenge to service that open today.[37]

Elizabeth Baker, during her 1937 furlough, was able to attend Convocation and give a first-hand account of the work at Puttur which made the assembled Sisters feel involved with it. Christine Cox, on behalf of the ex-United Methodist sisters, expressed their willingness to help with the Ceylon Fund.[38]

It was pleasing to record that, in 1936, Kate Chelliah, a student from Puttur, went to Ilkley for a year so that she could do deaconess work on her return. This gives some indication of the value of the work in Puttur, especially bearing in mind the high entry standards set by the Order.[39] In June 1938 Puttur held its own Convocation of Deaconesses and Social Service Workers and sent a greeting, signed by everyone, including Kate Chelliah, to the British Convocation. The Warden was delighted to learn that Kate had been 'dedicated' at the Puttur Convocation. Miss M. Dore, who had spent the last term at the College, sailed to Ceylon on 19th May 1939 to join Easter at Puttur. She was presumably a lay missionary, possibly a teacher. Easter Hayden had been the only deaconess at Puttur since 1938, being listed as doing 'Medical, Training, and Evang. Work', so another pair of hands must have been very welcome.[40]

---

37. *The Agenda* (October 1933) p.4
38. Mins. of Conv. (1937) p.17
39. *The Agenda* (October 1936) and see chapters 6 & 8 for entry standards
40. *The Agenda* (December 1938) pp.8-9, 14 (June 1939) p.6 cf. *WDO Stations* 1938-39

Sister Easter Hayden and the Puttur Ceylonese Deaconess

In 1939 Sister Easter described the problems encountered when the old building at Puttur was demolished to make way for a new one: she was having to spend a great deal of time supervising the builders, in addition to doing her usual work.

Work at Puttur 1939　　　　　**Sister Easter Hayden**

The school clinic grows in interest and value. Every morning the children from the non-caste villages come to the room where we provide soap liquid, combs, mirror and little baskets each labelled with the name of its owner, in which is the school garment. Here at 9 a.m. they come, wash, comb, oil their hair. Any small ailments are attended to. The dirty bit of rag that covers them is removed, and, dressed in the little clean garments, what a transformation has taken place as they trot off two and two to the school on the other side of the road. In the afternoons back they come again. There is more time to spend now, so seated in a circle they listen to a Bible story and learn some lyrics.

Source: The Agenda (June 1939) pp.6-7

During World War II contact with the deaconesses was rather spasmodic, but in August 1942 'an airgraph letter' told the Warden that Elizabeth Baker at Batticaloa was safe and well. Easter Hayden came home at the end of March 1944, but had to go straight to Belfast, from where she retired. After the return of Sister Easter no more appointments for Puttur are listed. Other deaconesses, who worked in Ceylon were at other stations, and, presumably, worked under the auspices of the Women's Auxiliary. Glory N. Swamisthos wrote a letter, signed by all the deaconesses and other friends, giving details of the 1944 Ceylon Convocation held at Jaffna. It was attended by the Chairman of the District and representatives from the Anglican, Methodist, Baptist and Congregational churches.[41]

Miss C. Hamilton wrote about the deaconess work and training in Ceylon in *The Agenda* of January 1946 emphasising that the work had three aspects – the evangelistic work in the villages, the medical work in the Dispensary and the Training Centre with three year courses for students wishing to become deaconesses and other shorter courses. She noted that there were 20 deaconesses altogether working in the Tamil speaking areas of North and East Ceylon and in the Colombo City Mission. Other denominations had taken advantage of the training offered. The 1946 British Convocation sent greetings to the deaconesses in Ceylon for their Convocation.[42]

This seems a convenient place to leave the specifically funded Wesley Deaconess Order work in Puttur. Obviously the Training Home, which started so humbly and with such faith had now grown to be of inestimable value in training Tamil women to work among their own people. The relationship with the Methodist Missionary Society and the Women's Auxiliary had changed and many Wesley Deaconesses were now working under their auspices. In 1951 Convocation sent £350 to the Mission House for Puttur which left the Ceylon Fund with a balance of £230. The possibility of some of the fund's money being sent to help the new growing West Indies Deaconess Order was discussed and it was agreed that the Convocation Committee should consult the Mission House. The following Convocation decided that, after reference to the Ceylon Synod, the Order's support should be transferred to the West Indies. This was the end of an era, as for 55 years the Order had supported the work in Puttur. The 1953 Convocation agreed that it would now be more appropriate to change the fund's name to the Overseas Deaconess Fund.[43]

Wesley Deaconess Order Work in Ceylon

Fifty-five years ago, in response to an appeal in Convocation, the Wesley Deaconess Order undertook to send two of its number to Puttur in North Ceylon and to raise the funds for their support. The

---

41. *The Agenda* (August 1942) p.6, (July 1944) pp.11-12, (Christmas 1944) pp.7-8
42. *The Agenda* (January 1946) pp.9-10; Mins. of Conv. (1946) p.72
43. Mins. of Conv. (1951) p.129, (1952) p.139, (1953) p.148; *WDMag.* (July 1953) p.11

medical and evangelistic work centred in Puttur, and particularly the training of Tamil women as Deaconesses, has during all those years been the special responsibility of the Order. But 'the old order changeth': the work in Ceylon is well established; on the other hand there is a newer and growing work in the West Indies and, largely through the vision and labour of our own Sisters, a small West Indian Order has come into being. So while the link with Puttur remains, and that work in Ceylon will ever have its place in the hearts and prayers of members of the Order, the financial support is to be transferred to the developing Deaconess work in the West Indies.

Source: Wesley Deaconess Magazine (July 1953) p.11

Burma and Indonesia

Although there had been informal contact with Burma and Indonesia through the deaconess work in other parts of Asia no deaconesses had actually been stationed there until the 1930s. In 1932 Elizabeth Bush went out to Mandalay and served in Burma until 1944 doing evangelistic and educational work. She also worked with lepers. Lilian Topping had just a short while there in 1932-33, but had to return home through illness.[44] In 1951 we learn from the *Wesley Deaconess Magazine* that two Burmese students, Ma Mi and Ma Hnin Yin, had spent two years studying at Ilkley and had now returned to Burma where they were working among their own people.[45] Then in 1968 Eileen Mason went out to Sumatra, Indonesia, to serve alongside American Methodist colleagues continuing to do pioneer mission work as a pastor and teacher until 1978.[46]

India

In March 1900 Stephenson reported to the General Council meeting that he had had a letter from the Rev. R. W. Allen requesting the appointment of a deaconess as Lady Superintendent of the Soldiers' Home in Secunderabad. The request was received sympathetically and the Council resolved that a deaconess should be sent 'if suitable arrangements can be made with the Army and Navy

---

44. *The Agenda* (Christmas 1932) p.5, (October 1933) pp.3-4; *WDO Stations* 1932-44
45. *WDMag.* (December 1951) p.13
46. *Doers of the Word* (Autumn 1959) pp.16-18; *A Way of Serving* (Autumn (1975) pp.18-22

Committee'. However, nothing further is recorded, so presumably no one was appointed. The important thing is that obviously the Order's work had become so highly esteemed in the 10 years of its existence that requests were coming from overseas for the deaconesses.[47]

The first reference to any actual deaconess work in India is to be found in *Flying Leaves* in the July/August 1906 issue when a letter from Helen Ingram, a Methodist Episcopal Church deaconess, who described herself and a colleague by writing 'There are only two of us deaconesses here. We have a small Rescue Home for native women, and besides, have charge of the Zenanas work and visiting amongst the Indian Christians. I give nearly all my time to the visiting amongst the Eurasians in connection with our English Church. . . . We have four Missionaries in Lucknow belonging to four societies. The Wesleyan Church has four workers. We meet for a United Missionary Conference in different houses once a month, and we have a weekly prayer meeting for the revival. We do so need it and long for it.' However, as can be seen, this letter from

the 'Deaconess' Home, Lucknow, 2nd May, 1906' gives an insight into the work being done there and indicates that it was well established.[48] Presumably it provided a basis on which the Wesley Deaconess Order could build. On 28th September 1907 Sister Adela Moss sailed to Medak. She had spent three years at the Edinburgh Training Hospital and then some time at Dr. McCoy's Home in Clapham in order to gain special knowledge and training which would, as the Warden put it, 'better fit her to grapple with the needs in Medak'. Initially she was expecting to do hospital work, but then 'evangelistic and medical touring'.[49]

Sister Adela Moss, India, 1907

The Women's Auxiliary, one of the oldest of the Women's Missionary societies, was celebrating its Jubilee in 1908. Annie M. Hellier, writing in the December 1907 issue of *Flying Leaves*,

---

47. WDIMins I p.71
48. Helen Ingram, a British citizen, was born in India. Her family came into contact with the American Methodist Mission there and she became one of their deaconesses. She worked for several years 'at her own charge'. She visited the 1905 Convocation. *FL* (June 1905) pp.265-66, (July 1905) p.278, (July/August 1906) p.111
49. *FL* (October 1907) p.140, (May 1910) p.72

pointed out that the first call for women missionaries came from India to do work, especially teaching, with young girls before they entered the Zenanas. The Zenanas were described as 'prisons' in which Indian women were incarcerated, excluded from contact with the outside world. However, by 'teaching the little girls' the doors of the Zenanas were beginning to open as the missionary workers tried to keep in contact with their old pupils. The work developed with the establishment of Boarding Schools, hospitals, converts' homes and rescue homes. Native Biblewomen had been trained and the workers had a special concern for the widows and deserted wives and were training them as teachers or nurses or for other work.[50]

Sister Adela Moss wrote on 3rd November 1907 to tell the Warden and Mrs. Bradfield of her safe arrival in Medak, via Madras and Secunderabad. Soon after arriving she had her first lesson in Telegu, which proved to be a difficult language to master, but she felt that until 'the language is gripped' she would be of little use. Later she described a very different Christmas Day with 'blazing sun', a feast, early morning carol singers and receiving a gift of a live fowl. An assiduous letter-writer, others tell of her visits, often with a Miss Wigfield, probably a Women's Auxiliary missionary, to outlying dispensaries and schools. Having visited Bolarum they travelled on to Ellareddypett where they dispensed medicines and made tentative plans for the building of a dispensary.[51]

Medak and the surrounding villages were hit by a cholera epidemic in 1908 and hundreds died while the local priests and priestesses played on the people's fear by offering sacrifices and demanding gifts to placate 'the cholera devil'. The ceremonies shocked and upset the missionaries who asked for the prayers of their friends at home to combat such evils. On 2nd October Adela wrote of yet another disaster – this time floods, which cut communications, leaving 50,000 dead in the Hyderabad area, only to be followed by pestilence, famine and great destitution. In her hospital work Adela found that 'Mohammedan' families were now coming for treatment and this seemed likely to open hitherto closed doors. However, having Muslims in the hospital brought its own problems and so she sought the help of friends back home to enable her to give them the necessary privacy their religion required.[52]

---

50. *FL* (December 1907) pp.171-73
51. *FL* (January 1908) p.191, (March 1908) pp.216-17, (June 1908) pp.267-69
52. *FL* (October 1908) pp.322-23, (December 1908) pp.256-57, 351, 357

Privacy Plea, Medak   **Sister Adela Moss**

I want some screens for our big wards. Mohammedans are strictly 'purdah', and must either have a room to themselves, or part made private. I cannot spare a whole ward for one or even two patients, and if I could gather about £3, I could get wooden divisions made, which would be of very great advantage to us. Our small wards are always overflowing, and if we could divide our big medical and surgical ward in two or three, we could easily get all full. What would it mean? All attend prayers night and morning, and it is their only chance of hearing about the great and loving Physician.

Source: Flying Leaves (December 1908) p.357

In January 1909 Adela was on her travels again to the villages around Medak, visiting schools and treating patients. Welcome to the missionaries varied from polite interest, considerable curiosity, discourtesy and great kindness and respect. The matter-of-fact descriptions in her 'Tour Journal' of the dangers of travelling through the countryside, over swollen rivers, through floods, never being sure of the welcome they might receive, pitching tents overnight in all sorts of places, meeting eager enquirers and fearful, secret, persecuted Christians is a story in itself and shows the intrepidness and faith of the early pioneers in India.[53]

A letter, dated 31st August 1909, sent from Ellareddypett, Indur Zillah, remarks that she had now settled in her new quarters where she was 'very happy and much too busy to feel more than passing pangs of loneliness'. She was delighted to report that in the three weeks since her arrival she had been into 'at least one hundred and twenty-two zenanas' and that 'the antagonism is very quickly breaking down, although it is deemed necessary that I should have two armed policemen and an armed chepassie. I feel rather as a criminal must feel – always followed, always in sight. Nevertheless even those who made the policemen necessary – the Arabs – are gradually yielding.' She remarked casually, almost in passing, that 'just behind a rock in front of my verandah (sic), was a great hole dug by jackals, and close by, leading round my house the spoor of a panther. It was a trifle startling, for I always sleep on the verandah (sic).' So it was rather a relief when, two days later, the local magistrate issued an order enabling her to move to a house in the village. During these three weeks she had treated more than 800 patients and received nearly nine shillings in her collection box.

---

53. *FL* (May 1909) pp.74-76, (September 1909) pp.125-26

Each patient, unless too poor, put two pice (one third of a penny (d)) in the box.[54] This incident shows Adela's practical common sense and a realistic understanding of the people with whom she was dealing.

Collection (Sanda) Box	**Sister Adela Moss**
I instituted the 'Sanda' (collection) here from the very beginning, because I have found the richer people come from curiosity, and, although really needing medicine, throw it away from very fear. If they pay a couple of pice, and *all* can afford that, they do not ask for it unless they mean to drink it.	
	Source: Flying Leaves (December 1909) p.171

Adela hoped that the new dispensary would be built at Ellareddypett, but although the site had been chosen nothing could be done until the Nizam gave his permission and signed the permit and this was proving difficult to obtain. Her journal, printed in *Flying Leaves,* paints vivid pictures of the very different world in which she found herself – the weather, the customs, the prejudices, the different religions and much illness and suffering. In a covering letter sent with her journal she wrote:

> We *must* have a hospital, however small, and with a doctor we shall dare anything. You need not fear for me, but if you *can* influence anyone to lend a helping hand to put stones in the walls of my hospital, I shall be a very happy woman indeed – it is the only way to do the work properly – so many *cannot* get better without daily personal treatment.[55]

When it came to Christmas Day 1909 Adela was 'very lonely', but very touched because the villagers had discovered that it was 'my great feast day', so, in the afternoon, the village lawyer visited her and hung garlands of flowers round her neck while 'the village band squatted in front of my chair on the verandah (sic) and played! tom-toms and pipes with all the strength their arms and lungs were capable of – Harmonious? Anything but that! It was a hideous row! But my thoughts went back to the beginning when I dare not go unprotected in the village; when I had to move off into the dirty Eastern gutter to make room for passers by, and be roughly jostled and remarked about, and now the difference!'[56]

---

54. *FL* (December 1909) pp.170-71
55. *FL* (January 1910) pp.5-8
56. *FL* (March 1910) pp.38-39

A letter, dated 14th March 1910, contains a hint of the physical cost entailed by working in India.

Medak   **Sister Adela Moss**

Have just arrived home after five days roughing it in the jungle, and am very tired; mother earth has dealt badly with my bones these past nights, and my bed will be a rest of luxury to-night . . .

The weather is terribly hot, and most of the tanks of the villages absolutely dry. My bandy went through the beds; everything is dry and burnt up, and crops are a failure round here.

Source: Flying Leaves (June 1910) p.93

In October 1910 Adela Moss was encountering many difficulties as a local influential Mohammedan was trying to block the purchase of the land chosen for the dispensary at Ellareddypett, so she wrote asking for special prayers. Apparently the land had been bought in the name of one of the native evangelists, but was very rocky and only with great difficulty had they managed to build a house and dig a well. No more land was available as the man had ordered that none should be let or leased to the missionaries and it seemed that if none could be obtained the work at Ellareddypett would have to close. Fortunately the Rev. Charles W. Posnett intervened and met 'the big men of the place' who were anxious to keep them and have a hospital built. Hence a petition was sent to the Nizam, who, it was hoped, would allow them '*to purchase in our own name* the land we need'. The difficulty, in fact, had turned out to be a blessing in disguise as now the land would be theirs and not held in the native man's name. So building commenced and 'I am rapidly turning into a contractor and builder, and I've already served an apprenticeship in carpentering.'[57] It was planned that Ellareddypett would become the head of a new circuit, so Adela was very enthusiastic and full of hope for the future.

Vision for Ellareddypett   **Sister Adela Moss**

We need a bungalow, for a married padrie (sic) and his wife, and by degrees a school for boys and another for girls, as well as a hospital. There is room in my bungalow for another lady worker – a lady doctor, I hope – then we shall have to enlarge to take in a head for

---

57. *FL* (December 1910) pp.174-75, (February 1911) p.22

> schools and a Zenana worker. Don't smile! I feel sure I am not
> looking more than nine or ten years ahead. There is a great future in
> this hitherto untouched part of the Nizam's Dominions.
>
> *Source: Flying Leaves* (February 1911) p.22

After 15 months Adela could only look back in wonder at the
change in the village – from being cursed as 'the white devil' to
being welcomed on all sides. Even the Mohammedan 'enemy' was
nursed through a dangerous bout of septic poisoning and, while in
her care, came to change his opinions and acknowledge that 'we are
indeed doing God's work, and that the work is a work of love'.
Tribute to Adela's work and influence was paid when the Rev. H.
Guard Price wrote:

> I have lately returned from a visit to Ellareddypett, the
> centre of Sister Adela Moss's sphere of influence. I
> should like to say how delighted I was with all I learnt
> and saw, even during a three days' stay, of the
> character and extent of her work. She is a true heroine,
> and devoted to her work, and by her tact, energy,
> sympathy and love, has changed the whole attitude of
> the people of the district from open hostility to
> affectionate and enthusiastic admiration.[58]

After all the problems Adela got great joy from 'watching my
hospital walls go up', but even so she could not neglect her touring
duties to the neighbouring villages where from 7.00 a.m. to sunset
she treated the sick and then showed 'wonderful pictures' and told 'a
wonderful story' after darkness fell. She herself was a wonderful
storyteller, bringing her experiences to life for her readers. The
Sisters in England must have been enthralled and amazed by some
of her adventures.

> **Sick Visiting, Indian style**   **Sister Adela Moss**
>
> . . . a camel solemnly stalked up and knelt down in front of the tent.
> The driver explained that he had been to Ellareddy for me, and had
> followed me from village to village. A palanquin was coming to meet
> me, and would I, as father and mother, show love, and lay healing on
> his master, who was indeed very sick, and like to die.
>
> When at last I deciphered the note, it was indeed, a piteous, urgent

---

58. *FL* (May 1911) pp.78-79

appeal for help, and one I did not feel ought to be refused. So hastily packing some medicines, and telling my nurse to see that the medicines, a rug and a cushion were strapped on to the camel, I changed into my astride skirt, and mounted the long-legged steed, hoping to meet the palanquin 'ere long. I had never been on a camel in my life – it could only be ridden astride, and the bumps and shakes were quite indescribable. May it never fall to my lot to mount again!

It was a little after seven a.m. when we started. No palanquin appeared, and it was eighteen *Irish* miles in a broiling sun, and past noon when we arrived. Nevertheless it was worth it all, even though, on dismounting, my legs refused to hold me up! The patient's life was saved, and today I hear (a week later) that all is well.

Source: Flying Leaves (July/August 1911) pp.112-13

Although Adela had used her new magic lantern and slides in the surrounding villages she was rather wary of using it in Ellareddypett, bearing in mind the early opposition she had encountered. Then one Sunday afternoon, having been to talk to the women in the outcast Mala quarter, she said, 'If you care to come to the bungalow after eating your food tonight, I will show you the pictures of what you have been hearing this afternoon, through a wonderful lamp.' She expected little response, so was greatly surprised and encouraged when 300 turned up – 'Brahmins, Komaties, Silversmiths, Weavers, Agriculturalists, Mohommedans, Arabs and outcastes sat together, or stood crowded without thought of caste or creed!' There was such a crowd that many had to be sent away with the promise of a showing another evening. Thereafter there was a slide show every evening somewhere. Then one day Adela and her colleague went on an overnight visit to the Rajah and his household in Bolarum and when everyone else had left, 'the Rajah talked until midnight about Christianity. The Rani told me next morning he had discussed it for another two hours with her, and acknowledged it was all true, and that they as Hindoos, need no longer look for the "Saviour of the World" to come – he had already come.' The problem was that neither the Rajah nor the Brahmins, who taught his sons, dared come out into the open about their Christianity. The difficulties, courage and steadfast faith of converts is graphically illustrated by the story of Ejenkama, the first person to be baptized in Ellareddypett. 'An ordinary cooley' he had worked on the hospital building and eventually became Adela's 'handy boy'. For about two years he had wanted to be baptized, but had waited trying to persuade his family to join him, but to no avail. He was persecuted in all manner of ways and when he finally asked for baptism was tricked into going to his home village where he was subjected to much intimidation, but he stood fast and was baptized on 27th December being named Jasu Ratnam (Jewel of Jesus). Adela took him with her when she left, but his relatives created 'most trying scenes'. The relatives on both sides tried to persuade him to return to them and when he refused they disowned him and gave his wife back to her own mother. However, Adela was hopeful that in time they would get the wife back because 'if she refuses to return, we can make them pay the marriage debt of 90s. (contracted by the elders), and eight years interest, amounting to 96s., in all 186s. This is quite an impossibility, so there is every hope that the wife will be restored and then they will both live here in the Compound. She will then be taught, and we are looking forward to the time when she will be baptized too. I believe that 'ere long all his relatives will yield – there is evidence of it, and if that quarter comes, there will be a mass movement in the other quarter where our evangelist lives and where there are at least 300 people. Pray for the lad and for his relatives. There is a great future before him.'[59]

In spring 1912 Sister Adela left Medak for a well-earned furlough. Obviously there was a financial problem as we learn that everyone, both at home and in Ellareddypett, had been praying that she would be able to return, so the Warden was delighted to report that a lady had generously offered to pay for her support and expenses. Returning to a very warm welcome and just before the rains, which 'spell food', arrived, Adela soon found herself feeling, 'I have never been away.'[60]

On 20th September 1910 the General Committee learned that Sister Nellie Atkins had been accepted by the Women's Auxiliary for work at Hassan, Mysore and was due to sail on 8th October. In charge of the Girls' Orphanage at the Wesley Mission in Hassan, Nellie Atkins was delighted to report, in 1913, a great sense of freedom from having passed her Kanarese examination and feeling able to make plans for future work. In order to help girls who were not suitable to be trained as teachers, but who had to stay at the Mission School until they married, the staff experimented with teaching them to make woollen caps so that they could be partially

---

59. *FL* (November 1911) pp.156-57, (April 1912) pp.56-58
60. *FL* (March 1912) p.37, (May 1912) p.68, (January 1913) pp.4, 8, (September 1913) p.129

self-supporting.[61]   Sister Nellie also managed to organise a very successful Women's Convention for about 110 women.

Sister Annie Braithwaite sailed for Hassan on 26th April 1912 to join Nellie Atkins and sent back a fascinating account of the Orphanage girls' trip to Bangalore for special thanksgiving services in October 1913.   Some set off to walk, while Sisters Annie and Nellie eventually left in 'a tonga'.   Both groups met for a lunch of 'curry and rice, served on a leaf plate and eaten with our fingers'. The night was spent at Aisikere – Annie and Nellie in the Travellers' Bungalow and the girls in the little church.   Having bought train tickets for all the girls and for more than a hundred other people, they left at 7.30 a.m. and arrived in Bangalore at 6.00 p.m.   The thanksgiving services, meetings and other celebrations were good and well attended, one of the chief benefits being the bringing together of small scattered groups of Christians and thus enabling them to feel part of a much bigger church.   A procession, walking four abreast, stretched for nearly a quarter of a mile and provided a great act of witness.   A major problem was the catering for over 2,000, but it was undertaken by the native ministers and evangelists who distributed 'the rice and curry etc. each day'.[62]

Feeding the Multitude, Bangalore   Sister Annie Braithwaite

One [native minister] was heard to remark that he began to have doubts about the accuracy of our Gospel narrative; he had no difficulty in believing that our Lord multiplied the loaves and fishes to the satisfaction of 5,000 people, but he couldn't see how the disciples succeeded in making them sit down in orderly groups, for he found it impossible, with less than half that number. The order went forth in the meetings that women and children were to be served first. A new thing for India!

Source: Flying Leaves (January 1914) p.10

Apparently Convocation 1914 voted that a gift be sent to Sister Adela at Ellareddypett and she expressed her delight and thanks, writing that the building would be completed as soon as the rains ceased and any money remaining would be used to start a fund to put an iron fence round the compound to 'keep out wild beasts at

---

61. WDIMins I p.268; *FL* (October 1910) pp.139-40, (November 1910) p.155, (October 1913) p.142, (May 1914) p.83
62. *FL* (January 1914) pp.9-10

Cliff being rude to anyone, though he must have been sorely tempted at times as he struggled to give sensible answers to silly questions.

This was a wasted opportunity. Apart from his Christian faith, there are many topics on which viewers would have been glad to hear Cliff Richard's views.

Mention was made of his friendship with Tony and Ch-

In **Dispatches – MPs, Planes and Gravy Trains** (Channel 4), Alex Thomson tried to discover how our legislators filled the 82 days between the end of one session of Parliament and the beginning of the next.

This was no easy task because the Freedom of Information Act does not cover such matters.

However, it was possible to about the ways unsuspecting passengers can be ripped off at airports – even more than by the no-frills airlines where the gap between the advertised fare and the actual fare begins to resemble a banker's bonus.

The feeling left by **MPs, Planes and Gravy Trains**, however, was that it is we the public who are being cheated most of all.

Christian art scheme launched

A PILOT scheme leading to the establishment of a nationwide Christian Arts Academy was launched in Cheltenham earlier this month. Among subjects to be taught are dance, drama, fine arts, technical skills, worship leading and writing. The courses are part time so that students can learn new skills alongside their regular employment.

Information

Further information is obtainable from Arts Ecclesia and Mission, e-mail (artseccles@googlemail.com); from the internet (www.artsecclesia.org.uk); or by sending a stamped addressed envelope to 19 Thessaly Road, Cirencester, Gloucestershire, GL7 2NG.

Ugandan choir visit

A CHOIR made up of Ugandan children living with HIV is visiting the UK to celebrate the 21st birthday of Europe's first dedicated HIV/AIDS hospice – Mildmay Mission Hospital in East London.

Mildmay, now an international Christian NGO, is committed to giving people with HIV a voice and the children's choir represents one of the ways this is being achieved.

Anniversary

The group's 11 young singers will perform at Mildmay's thanksgiving anniversary service, due to be held at Southwark Cathedral on Monday, October 12, from 3 pm.

The Bishop of Southwark will lead the service, which will also include reflections from figures from Mildmay's history, as well as from leading figures in the HIV and charity sector.

by Dorothy O'Neill

LONG before I presented myself as a candidate for the Wesley Deaconess Order, one of the roguish girls in our church youth group would rile me by occasionally calling me "Sister". Me a deaconess? No thanks! I just wasn't that type. So it was with a sense of shock that I finally realised that God was calling me to this work. Eventually, one bright September day in the early 1950s, I entered the doors of the Wesley Deaconess College at Ilkley, Yorkshire, to begin two years' training as a probationer deaconess.

Our Warden was the Rev Thomas Morrow, married to Connie, and they lived in a house near the college. Tom Morrow was well suited to his work. He was wise and had a great sense of humour and was in the line of succession to the Rev Dr Thomas B Stephenson who founded the Order. Phoebe, a woman in the Early Church, described by St Paul as "a servant of the church at Cenchrea" was chosen as a model for deaconesses. So, in keeping with their vocation, the first Wesley deaconesses wore large white aprons as part of their uniform.

In city slums, where messes had to be cleaned up, an apron was essential. The story is told of one deaconess, working in the London slums, who was called on to visit a woman who had been beaten up by her husband.

Sister's sympathy was cut short by the victim saying: "It might 'ave been worse, Sister. I could 'ave been without an 'usband like you!" Aprons had long since vanished by the time I reached Ilkley. My uniform as a probationer deaconess was a grey dress with a stiff white collar, grey stockings and black shoes.

Awe

Sister Dorothy Farrer was vice-president of the order. I was much in awe of her. I remember that one term I had to dust her study – all students were given daily chores. I found this an ordeal. What if I swept something precious from a shelf? I'm sure that Sister Dorothy didn't want this veneration, for she was a kindly woman, though with a penetrating gaze.

She was often away from college for she was greatly in demand as a conference speaker.

It would be hard to find a more diverse group of stu-

dents under one roof. The varied in temperament, edu cation and background.

There were nurses an teachers, girls from farı backgrounds, clerical officer social workers.

We came from differer parts of Britain although Be yl came from South Africa an Susanna from Ireland. Susar na was a lovely woman, prol ably in her late 20s, with gentle manner and engagin Irish brogue. Susanna and became friends at once an remained so throughout ou college days.

Jo and Dixie were traine teachers in their mid-20 Dixie was tall and good-look ing, with shining brown ey and crisp dark hair.

Jo was small and dark, wit cropped curly hair. Jo was great one for hugging. I wasn always sure whether the hug were expressing friendship saying: "Cheer up, worse th ngs happen at sea!" Merle w another friend.

Rosy-cheeked and blond with an infectious laugh and broad country accent, Merl had left her life and work o the family farm to join th order. She missed farmin very much.

"Farming had never seeme so sweet as when I left it," sh

night and prowling cattle during the day'. She added, 'We are well-nigh desperate, and at our wits' end' because many villages longed for an evangelist to care for the Christian community, and although suitably qualified people were available funds were lacking to support them. She asked for the Order's prayers.[63]

Sister Adela continued her work in India until 1923, then, returning home, she did a year's deputation work for the Women's Auxiliary before becoming Matron of the Mildmay Maternity Nursing Home. From 1926-28 she was at Welwyn Nursing Home, after which she spent 1929 'nursing' and then returned to Mildmay, where she was Matron of the Nurses' Home until her retirement in 1938. She died on 2nd July 1966.[64]

By 1914 Sister Ethel Tompkinson had completed her nursing course, plus some special training, and was appointed by the Women's Auxiliary to the Holdsworth Memorial Hospital in Mysore where she would train native nurses. The outbreak of World War I was obviously going to make it difficult for deaconesses in India, especially in the matter of furloughs, but Nellie Atkins hoped to sail home on 12th December 1915.[65] After this, as noted before, news became scarce when *Flying Leaves* ceased publication.

In November 1922 Ethel Wilson sailed for Hyderabad and at the end of 1923 Bessie Heard went to work in Hyderabad for the Women's Auxiliary, having completed a short course at Kingsmead, the Methodist Missionary College, Selly Oak, Birmingham. As already observed, the relationship between the Order, the Women's Auxiliary and the Missionary Society was becoming closer with more sisters going to serve overseas under their auspices. Sister Ethel Slaytor went out to Nagapatam on 29th December and on her arrival spent a week at the girls' boarding school in Trichinopoly before going on a 10 month language course in Kodai.[66]

Dr. Maltby, the Warden, left Birkenhead on 16th September 1924 for a visit of several months to India and Ceylon at the invitation of the Student Christian Movement and with the blessing

63. *FL* (October 1914) p.144
64. *The Agenda* (June 1923) p.16; *WDO Stations* 1922-66
65. *FL* (January 1914) p.5 (February 1914) p.21, (May 1914) p.78, (November 1915) p.87, (December 1915) p.94
66. *The Agenda* (January 1922) p.11, (November 1923) p.9, (December 1923) p.7, (May 1924) pp.23-24

of the various missionary societies. He was hoping to visit many colleges and meet the students in North and South India and Ceylon. In fact, although he sent back lengthy and interesting letters, which were printed in *The Agenda,* he said surprisingly little about the Wesley Deaconesses and their work. This must have been a little disappointing to the Sisters at home who would doubtless have been longing to have news of their colleagues in India.[67]

Sister Bessie Heard felt that Nizamabad was 'a real missionary station' which just fitted her dreams:

> There is nothing of civilisation; a stone's-throw in one direction is a Hindu Temple, and a stone's-throw in another is a Mohammedan one. Far into the night we can see and hear the people worshipping. We do practically everything to the sound of tom-toms.
>
> In our Compound there is a church (a fine one, too), a school, a hospital and dispensary, and two bungalows.
>
> During the last two years the medical work has been carried on by an Indian nurse. She has done the work most faithfully – but she has been handicapped by the lack of another medical worker.
>
> There is no doctor here; I have to diagnose, and prescribe, and nurse, and a few other things all rolled into one.[68]

In August 1925, Sister Gladys Crump and Adela Moss set off on their seven month tour of India and Ceylon – it would no doubt be a nostalgic trip for Adela. At this time there were seven Wesley Deaconesses serving in the four Districts in India and the Order continued to send deaconesses to India, often in appointments for different missionary organisations. For example, on 27th September 1927 Maud Millican went to take up an appointment in charge of the Women's Department in Kalna under the auspices of the United Free Church of Scotland.[69]

There were two extracts from letters from India in the April 1929 issue of *The Agenda* – one was from Ethel Tomkinson in Mysore saying that her life was very busy, and the other was from

67. *The Agenda* (September 1924) pp.7-8, (November 1924) pp.11-12, (December 1924) pp.15-16, (February 1925) pp.10-11, (March 1925) pp.11-14, (April 1925) pp.9-11, (May 1925) pp.3-9
68. *The Agenda* (September 1924) p.11
69. *The Agenda* (October 1927) p.7, (April) p.6, (June 1928) p.15

Elsie Kitchener in Akbarpur explaining how they had 'invited purdah ladies to a formal opening of the extension of the Hospital'. However, the thing which most delighted her was completely unexpected – a high caste Hindu lady gave a lift in her carriage to 'one of the humblest Moslem women'. As Elsie commented, 'Only those who have seen and grieved over the great gulf fixed between Hindu and Moslem can fully appreciate this incident, perhaps. This act, so like His Own in the days of His flesh, was surely inspired by Him in Whose name we were met.'[70]

Hospital Extension Opening	**Sister Elsie Kitchener**
Ladies who never leave their homes for any more public function than the wedding of a relative or a family reunion came in carriages, made purdah for the occasion with sheets draped round them. The gathering followed the Hindu 'Feast of Lights', and the central act was the lighting of a new lamp in the courtyard by a Hindu caste lady who had never done anything in public in her life! Children from our school – Hindus – led in the Lord's Prayer, and the singing of Christian Bhajans. Hindus, Mussalmans and Christians were seated together, a small but surely significant gathering.	
Source: The Agenda (April 1929) p.10	

Ethel Tomkinson wrote from Mangala, South India in the summer of 1939 describing the difficulties the people were experiencing because the failure of the rains meant the crops died. The missionaries were trying to alleviate the suffering as best as they could.

Famine	**Sister Ethel Tomkinson**
We are therefore arranging for each evangelist to have a little store of grain which he can distribute daily to our people until they can obtain cooly work that will provide them with the equivalent of a few pence per day. Also after our twenty-six babies have had their daily morning bath in Premalaya, we give the older ones and the mothers and other hungry members of their families a big cup of conjee (porridge). How I wish you could see the eagerness with which they drink this – and never stop until the last drop has disappeared! Yet this is only supplying the need of *one* out of our seventeen baby clinics.	
Source: The Agenda (June 1939) p.7	

---

70. *The Agenda* (April 1929) p.10

After Ethel Wilson returned to Hyderabad in 1939 she sent an 'open letter' which was printed in *The Agenda* thanking everyone for the wonderful furlough she had enjoyed and the privilege of meeting old friends when she was on deputation work. She ended by saying that the rest and renewal she had experienced had prepared her 'for the next term of service, which will not be easy, for I am proposed as Miss Green's successor. To follow such a worker who, for thirty years, has built up the work like that in Ramayanpett, where during May last fifty babies first saw the light, will take all the strength and energy I have been enabled to secure here this year.'[71]

Bessie Heard's ill-health during her furlough had meant a delay in her return to India, but when she recovered she had been able to do some nursing at home and then set off on her journey to the sub-continent in 1943. Eventually Bessie wrote from the hospital at Doodgaon, Nizamabad to tell of her safe arrival after a three and a half month trip – because of the war she had had to go via New York, through the Panama Canal, to the Pitcairn Islands to New Zealand, where they had had to wait for a fortnight because of engine trouble. They were entertained royally and as the Methodist Conference was just ending the President stayed on an extra day to meet them. Both she and the Rev. H. Evans spoke at a public meeting and in the audience were two deaonesses and four deaconess students who were thrilled to meet her. One of them had been a missionary in the Bolona Islands and had escaped in a submarine from under the very noses of the Japanese.[72]

Wartime Travel to India **Sister Bessie Heard**

After 3 ½ months on the ship I have reached my destination . . .

Before we reached New York we were chased by submarines for three days and nights – 40 depth charges were dropped and we stayed up all night, dressed complete with life jackets, passports and valuables. There was no panic – all were joking.

Source: The Agenda (December 1943) pp.5-6

Sister Bessie returned home after her years of service in India and worked in a Moral Welfare appointment for five years before retiring in 1954.[73]

---

71. *The Agenda* (December 1938) p.10, (March 1939) p.11
72. *The Agenda* (December 1943) pp.5, 6
73. *WDMag.* (December 1954) p.15

In 1944 Ethel Wilson arrived home in time for Convocation and returned immediately after the 1945 one. It is interesting to get an independent inside view of the feeling engendered by the establishment of the Church of South India so the letter from Ethel saying that, although she was still a Wesley Deaconess, she was now a member of the Church of South India was very welcome. Ethel Wilson retired in 1954, after serving as a medical missionary in South India for 37 years.[74]

Church of South India   **Sister Ethel Wilson**

Tomorrow I go to our first Diocesan Council. We had our last meeting as a part of the Methodist Church just before Christmas, and although we are very glad and feel we have lived to see a great step forward in the Church Universal, yet we could not but be a little sad that we were meeting no more with all our fellow workers of the Hyderabad District. Over Christmas I spent a few days in the Dornakal Diocese. We had real Union then, for one of our former Church of England fellow missionaries of Dornakal gave us Communion in the little Chapel at our Karim Nagar Hospital . . . I was privileged to attend the inauguration of the Church Union in Madras. It was a great joy and one felt very humble to partake in the Communion that was celebrated at that time, when so many who have worked unsparingly for this were unable to be present in the flesh. But the Invisible Company of Believers were there, rejoicing with us in the great lead the Church is giving in this land where divisions are causing so much sorrow.

Source: The Agenda (July 1948) p.13

In 1951 Sister Annie Chapman retired after 32 years in the Lucknow and Benares District as a nurse-evangelist and her Chairman of the District paid her a glowing tribute:

> She has been a frequent visitor to the Palace of the local Indian Prince in Benares, and has been equally ready to enter the house of the humblest street sweeper. Before people of all kinds she has set an example of Christian love and service which many of us find difficult to follow.[75]

---

74. *WDMag.* (December 1954) p.15
75. *WDMag.* (July 1951) pp.17-18

Sister Ethel Tomkinson wrote a personal letter from Chamarajanagar in South India indicating that although there were great difficulties in that region there were some 'signs of [Christian] penetrating influence' with converts being made.[76] Even though retired for a number of years, Ethel was still deeply involved in work in India and in 1951 she described how the old mission hospital at Mandagadde in Mysore State, which had been derelict, had once again become 'a place of Christian worship, prayer and healing'. It was only a small hospital of three wards, but space was provided for family and friends as 'our desire is to receive each patient (whether Christian or non-Christian) into the fellowship of the ashram family so that unselfish service may be rendered to each sufferer'.[77]

Although work was still continuing in India at the closure of recruitment to the Order in 1978 an article by Ethel Tomkinson, written in 1949, in which she reflects on her time in India, provides a fitting conclusion to this section:

> From January, 1914, when I first sailed for India until March, 1948, when I returned to this country for my last furlough, there has grown upon me an ever-increasing desire that the scope of our Deaconess fellowship might extend to our Church in South India . . .

> After spending twenty years in the Holdsworth Memorial Hospital at Mysore I was appointed to village work . . .

> Advancing years have made it necessary for me now to retire, but God in His great love is still giving me strength for a good day's work in India. The Women's Work Committee are therefore willing for me to retire and live in Premalaya . . . It will fall to my happy lot to guide the Baby Clinic and Nursery School work and to organise regular courses of training for women.

> One of the biggest needs today in the new United Church of South India is for a great army of devoted nationals, men and women, who witness through word and deed to all they meet that Jesus Christ alone is the Saviour of the world and that in His sight there is neither high-caste nor out-caste, Hindu nor Muslim nor British, for the one God is the Universal Father of all mankind.[78]

---

76. *The Agenda* (January 1946) p.10
77. *WDMag.* (December 1951) p.16
78. *The Agenda* (April 1949) p.9

China

The missionaries in China had long wished for a Nurse-Deaconess to go out to take charge of the Hankow Men's Missionary Hospital, Wuchang District, but the Wesley Deaconess Order had not had anyone suitable. Eventually, as the Order had grown and developed, the possibility of being able to respond to the call seemed more likely. Then, in early 1905, the Warden reported that he had received a request from the Rev. Dr. Hodge 'for the appointment of a Nurse-Deaconess to the Hankow Missionary Hospital' and although a number of deaconesses were ready to go none was suitably qualified. However, a young woman, who was a nurse, but unable for personal reasons, to become a deaconess had offered to 'hold the fort' and this offer had been accepted for a limited period. Under these special circumstances Sister Mabel Roscorla was ranked 'as a companion of the Order' and sailed for China in March to become the Sister-in-Charge in the Hankow Men's Hospital.[79]

Companion of the Order	**Sister Mabel Roscorla**

Until a suitable appointment of a trained Wesley Deaconess could be made, Nurse Mabel Roscorla had volunteered to fill the gap for two years. The Committee, in the very special circumstances authorised the employment of Nurse Mabel Roscorla on the terms stated in the correspondence between the Warden and Dr. Hodge; but with the understanding that the terms are inclusive, and that no claim will arise upon the Superannuation Fund of the W. D. Institute. During her term of service at Hankow, Sister Mabel Roscorla shall be attached as a 'Companion of the Order' for special service.

Source: Wesley Deaconess Institute Minutes (1895-1910) p.232

During her time in China Mabel suffered from a severe bout of dysentery while having a well-deserved few weeks' break in Central China, but made a good recovery. She reported in 1906 that things were going well at the hospital and that she was 'so interested and happy in my work and everything looks so smart

*Sister Mabel Roscola,
China, 1905 made
'a companion of the Order'*

---

79. WDIMins I p.232; *FL* (March 1905) p.212, (April 1905) pp.229-30

and nice'. On a later occasion she gave an account of the Christmas festivities in Hankow.[80]

At the Executive Committee Meeting on 28th November 1905 Sister Bessie Mountford, a Nurse-Deaconess from Leicester was appointed to the hospital 'in place of Sister Mabel Roscorla, whose term of special service before marriage will be completed'. After a special consecration service held at the College Bessie left on 16th March. Bessie had become a deaconess candidate at a very young age and this plus her four year nursing course, which had resulted in first class certificates, meant that she had actually been in the Order for nearly eight years before she went to China.[81]

In the January 1907 *Flying Leaves* Sister Bessie wrote that she was living happily with Dr. and Mrs. Hodge in Hankow and although she had found the work very different from at home she was sure that when she had a better command of the language and customs things would be easier. An indication of the trauma experienced by working so far from familiar surroundings can be appreciated when Bessie wrote to the Warden expressing thanks for letters from home which helped to combat the feelings of loneliness and distance.

Sister Bessie Mountford, China, 1906

She remarked that the Men's Hospital was very busy and always full because people who would not go to the Mission House would quite happily go to the hospital and were receptive to the Evangelists as they read in the wards, so there was much work to be done and 'workers of every description are wanted; I am hoping the time will soon come when I shall not be the only Wesley Deaconess here'.[82]

Mrs. E. C. Cooper (formerly Sister Elise Searle, entered 1892, left on marriage 1903-04), who had gone out as the wife of a missionary, the Rev. E. C. Cooper, to Yung Chou Fu, Hunan, wrote to the Order expressing her delight that the Women's Auxiliary had appointed Miss Derham to do women's work there. She described the new Hospital and the boarding schools for both boys and girls connected with the Mission. So, obviously, although technically no

---

80. *FL* (December 1905) p.355, (January 1906) p.24, (March 1906) p.45
81. WDIMins I pp.255, 259, 261; *FL* (April 1906) p.59
82. *FL* (January 1907) p.10, (July 1907) pp.106-07

longer a Wesley Deaconess, Sister Elise's work continued and she kept in touch, writing later to tell her friends at Ilkley about the work of the missionaries in China, and in particular on 5th May 1910 she referred to the difficulties encountered because riots in Chang Sha had destroyed their home.[83]

The Rev. W. Arthur Tatchell wrote home just after Christmas 1908 from the Wesleyan Mission House, Hankow, and described the festive celebrations for which Sister Bessie, along with the doctors' wives had worked hard, so that everyone – staff and patients – in the hospital had received a little present. All the rooms in the church were colourfully decorated (with a note that red was not used because the nation was still in mourning for the Emperor and Empress Dowager) and on Christmas Eve the gates were flung wide open for anyone to enter. Many did and the 'native Christians' took the opportunity to explain that the celebrations were for the birth of Christ. Christmas Day started with carol singing and 400 people packed into the church for the 11.00 a.m. service, which was followed by a meal. Then came a party in the Men's Hospital and a meal for the men patients and staff while the missionaries went on to the Jubilee Women's Hospital where a short service was held and presents given out, then it was back to the Men's Hospital for the distribution of yet more presents. Finally all went home tired, but happy.[84]

Sister Alice Shackleton, China, 1910

Sister Alice Shackleton went out to Canton on 26th August 1910, having previously taken a dispensary course to fit her for her work there. She went to relieve Bessie Mountford, who in fact married the Rev. R. Hutchinson of Skelins, Kirby Stephen on 1st October in Hankow.[85]

An agreement drawn up between Hankow Hospital and the Wesley Deaconess Institute was approved by the Committee in December 1910 with regard to the service of Alice Shackleton. It is likely that this agreement formed the basis for further arrangements

83. *FL* (November 1907) p.152, (December 1907) p.175, (July/August 1910) p.115
84. *FL* (March 1909) pp.43-44
85. WDIMins I pp.354, 359, 367; *FL* (September 1910) p.125, (December 1910) p.173

and it shows the care taken by the Institute to safeguard the welfare of the deaconesses working in China.

1. Term of service to be five years.
2. Passage 2nd class to Shanghai, and 1st class up river to Hankow, to be paid by the Hospital.
3. Outfit £20 to be paid by the Hospital.
4. Extra freight to be paid, half by the Hospital, and half by Wesley Deaconess Institute.
5. a. A minimum holiday of six weeks during the hot season, extra board allowance during her stay at Kuling, return steamer fare to Kuiang, and £1 towards the expenses of the land journey from Kuiang to Kuling.
   b. Allowances to begin the day she leaves England.
6. Furnished quarters to be provided, and £30 a year for board, or whatever beyond it may cost. This, however, does not include sheets, blankets, pillow cases, towels etc.
7. Personal allowance at the rate of £25 a year, apart from the above named board.
8. A further sum of £5 to be paid to her for travelling.
9. Payment to the Superannuation Fund of the Wesley Deaconess Institute of £5 yearly.
10. A furlough of fifteen months from the time of leaving to date of return in China, once in six years. Passage home to be paid, and outward passage also, should she return. If returning, furlough allowance to be at the rate of £40 per year, and also £10 for renewal of outfit.
11. The Superintendent of Hospital Department to be the responsible person with whom the Deaconess and the Institute deal.
12. Six months' notice on either side to be given before terminating the Agreement.
13. The financial arrangements to be reconsidered at the end of two years, if not found to work satisfactorily.[86]

Sister Alice sent her first letter home, dated 11th November 1910, saying that she was 'very, very happy here. The hospital is a fine place, far above my highest expectations'. When she wrote on 31st October 1911 it was to reassure the Warden that she was safe in

---

86. WDIMins I pp.372-73

spite of the war conditions caused by the revolution in China. Unfortunately, this letter was followed the very next day by another saying that the native quarter of Hankow was on fire and they were afraid the houses, schools and hospital compound would be burned down. Writing again on 3rd November she said some of the buildings had been destroyed, but everyone had got away safely and she had sent copies of the local newspapers which contained more details. Few of these got through. Tributes to her work were paid at the General Committee Meeting on 14th April 1912.[87]

Danger, Hankow, November 1911   **Sister Shackleton**

I have a very, very heavy heart as I sit to write this letter. Hankow native city is one mass of smoke, on fire. Never in my life have I seen such a sight. Our hospital has one hundred and fifty patients in. There is a blind school full of boys, and the women's hospital – all the servants and nurses are there too.

There is no attempt to stop the fire, caused by the explosive shells the Imperials are using. Dr. Booth got a big steamer, or rather an old gun-boat, with a big red cross on it, fifty Red Cross men, besides doctors and our men, and a few volunteers to assist in getting patients and assistants away. They had not gone far before they were fired on – so much the Chinese take notice of the Red Cross – ever so many times they were fired on, one shot just missing Dr. Booth's head. The mast nearly caught fire. After going a good way, they had to retreat, else they would probably all have lost their lives.

You can just imagine the state we are all in here. We feel sure that our hospital, houses and schools are burnt to the ground. We have very few goods here. I have no summer clothes at all, and all my personal belongings are there. We all had to leave in such a hurry, and only took what was absolutely necessary. But that is a detail; one can always get new clothes, but some things can never be replaced. The thing we are most anxious about are our patients and nurses – where are they?

Source: Flying Leaves (December 1911) p.171

Alice and her fellow workers were allowed back on 20th January and found that trying to replace the hospital items lost during the unrest and cope with patients meant life was extremely busy. Although she had extra help in the form of eight new nurses

---

87. *FL* (December 1911) pp.170-72, (January 1912) p.7; WDIMins II p.24

that was a mixed blessing as they were 'boys, only sixteen and seventeen years of age' whom she had to teach and train, so that she had very little leisure time. As well as the nursing, prayers and Bible Study classes were part of her life.[88] One result of the revolution had been an easing of prejudice against foreign hospitals because of the work done by the Red Cross, so in addition to civilian patients the hospital treated soldiers and was also trying to help opium addicts. On 22nd June, once again, the hospital was threatened when a nearby shop caught fire. Days without rain, temperatures into the 90s and a breeze blowing towards the compound made it a very anxious time, but fortunately the wind changed and disaster was averted.[89]

Disaster averted, Hankow, June 1912

Sister Alice Shackleton

The fire brigade here consists of a box on big wheels which is pulled along the street by coolies, who never hurry, even though the fire is raging. They have hosepipes, but are not properly trained to use them. It is a wonder they manage to put out a fire at all . . .

The coolies (of the hospital) and nurses formed a chain, and handed up buckets of water. We saturated everything possible, so that as the sparks fell, they went out again . . .

Oh, how we prayed God to save us . . .

Suddenly the wind changed, and in an hour's time, the fire was out. It seemed too good to be true. We could hardly believe it. Even the people on the street said, 'The wind has changed; we are saved. These foreign buildings can never be burnt.' . . .

A curious coincidence happened on Monday. The electric wires were broken, and, as the man was mending them, he noticed what seemed like a shell hole in the wall, near the roof. He put in his hand and pulled out a big shell, with just the top broken off, but not exploded – a reminder of the revolution. If a spark had fallen on the shell, a lot of damage might have been done.

Source: Flying Leaves (September 1912) p.131

Dr. Tatchell wrote a letter, printed in the May 1913 issue of the magazine, which told of the work done at the Hodge Memorial Hospital (as it was now named) in Hankow where Alice was Matron. He said that at times the hospital had been overwhelmed by

---

88. *FL* (April 1912) p.55
89. *FL* (September 1911) pp.130-31

the numbers seeking admission, proving that the people were now willing to be treated by the medical missionaries.[90]

Profile of Sister Alice Shackleton and her Work in China

Sister Alice Shackleton, who has been Matron of the Hodge Memorial Hospital, Hankow, China for the last four years, has the somewhat unusual task of training and working with men nurses. It is against Chinese rules for women to nurse men, so it falls to Sister Alice's lot to train Chinese youths in medical and surgical nursing. And her work for them is not confined to a professional aspect only. Every Sunday afternoon Sister Alice and her assistants meet together to talk of Christ and the Christian religion, and lives are being won for the Master through the influence of that Bible Class in the hospital.

And the people who come into the wards, too, see the reflection of the Christ-life in the ministry of the Matron and her nurses, as they accompany Dr. Tatchell on his rounds, and busy themselves in a hundred services to suffering people.

During the recent rebellion in China, Sister Alice remained at her post, and rendered such efficient service in Red Cross work that, when peace was restored, the newly-formed Government of China presented her with two medals in acknowledgement of her courage and work.

Source: Flying Leaves (May 1914) pp.71-72

After all her traumatic experiences Alice arrived home for a well-deserved furlough on 12th December 1915.[91]

Gladys Stephenson, having successfully completed her three year hospital course, plus a year's special training, went to Ilkley for one year before going overseas to a nursing appointment. Convocation in 1915 made 'an offer to the Missionary Committee of the money to support a nurse in China for one year'. The offer was accepted and Sister Gladys Stephenson, after being consecrated at her home church of Southall on 1st September, sailed with a missionary party on the *SS Medina* on the 4th for the Wuchang District. The Order now set about raising the £100 promised for her support. Following a special consecration service held at Ilkley Wesleyan Methodist Church Sister Mary McCord left for Anlu to join her on 24th December 1915.[92]

---

90. *FL* (May 1913) pp.73-4
91. WDIMins II p.90; *FL* (December 1915) p.94
92. *FL* (November 1914) p.152, (July/August 1915) p.53, (September 1915) p.70,

The December 1915 issue saw the cessation of *Flying Leaves,* as noted earlier in the chapter, and so further information is slight until the start of *The Agenda* in 1922. However, Sister Gladys arrived home in March 1920 and in December 1924 Sister Elsie Cuthbertson and Maud Millican were appointed to China under the auspices of the Women's Auxiliary. Meanwhile Alice Shackleton had spent her 1922 furlough 'with her own people' in Australia before returning to her post in Hankow. Her resignation upon her marriage to Dr. Pell was reported in December 1925.[93]

The first issue of the new magazine in January 1922 contains a lengthy and informative letter from Sister Gladys in which she describes her work in the Men's Hospital, Anlu, where she was particularly involved in training young men as nurses. The progress of some was impressive both in the public examinations and in obtaining responsible posts in various hospitals. All had become Christians and one a Local Preacher who hoped to become a minister.   This encouraging report was counterbalanced by an account of the plight of the ordinary people. They had suffered from civil unrest and also from a great natural disaster when the embankments on the River Han collapsed, resulting in terrible flooding.   The tragedy was that it was all unnecessary; if only money had been used to build proper embankments.[94]

Deaconesses in Central China 1924/5 (taken in Mrs Cooper's garden at Kuling)

Left to right:	*Top Row:*	*Sisters Mary McCord, Rene Wayne, Maud Millican*
	Centre Row:	*Sisters Alice Shackleton, Mrs Cooper, Gladys Stephenson*
	Front Row:	*Sisters Hilda Darch, Elsie Cook*

(October 1915) pp.80, 81; WDIMins II p.85, *FL* (December 1915) pp.94, 96
93. WDIMins II pp.156, 221; *The Agenda* (December 1922) p.12
94. *The Agenda* (January 1922) pp.10-11

The Warden passed on an interesting, but unexpected piece of news in *The Agenda* of November 1923, that he had just learned that Sister Hilda Darch, who had been working in the Hankow Hospital and learning Chinese, had gone to Japan to help with the rescue work in the earthquake area, while Gladys Stephenson, stationed at Anlu, got permission to go with an American missionary nurse to visit the northern hospitals which she found very rewarding as so many of the missionaries were working on their own and 'were overjoyed to welcome two travelling nurses'.[95]

The services of the Wesley Deaconesses in China were obviously greatly appreciated for in 1924 Gladys Stephenson was elected President of the Nurses Association of China and Alice Shackleton as Chairman of the Curriculum Committee.[96] Hilda Darch pleaded for help to train more nurses.

Wesleyan Mission, Teian, Hupeh, China

Sister Hilda Darch

The nurses are very keen on working the curriculum of the Nurses' Association of China, and want me to start classes this autumn. Some of the lads have been here for years, and are working into a sort of blind alley. I feel something must be done for these lads and for China by giving them the best training possible. The curriculum is difficult, and unless I can get a qualified nurse for teaching, etc., it will be impossible to open a Training School. It would mean that I should have to give up the Women's work, and I must carry on with that at all costs. There is a great opportunity to get in personal touch with these women in our little ward across the road.

Do you know of any enthusiastic souls who would be willing to help support a trained nurse, *i.e.*, a teacher? The cost would be a pound a month. I am not asking for the whole, but for help towards it. H. D.

Source: The Agenda (April 1925) p.12

The work in China was growing and Irene Bartleet sailed for Hankow on 26th October 1923 to be followed by three more deaconesses – Sister Elsie Cuthertson (Han Yang), Eva Lyth (Canton) and Maud Millican, (previously in India) (Yiyang), who went out under the auspices of the Women's Auxiliary in January 1925. In 1926 Elsie went to Piang Kiang in the Hunan District to

---

95. *The Agenda* (November 1923) p.10, (February 1924) p.14
96. *The Agenda* (September 1924) p.9, (April 1925) p.12

take charge of a small boarding school and look after the women's work in that area.[97] Unfortunately Mary McCord had had to leave her work in Anlu because work in the country and much travelling had affected her eyes, so she moved to take charge of the evangelistic work at the Hankow Women's Hospital and at the Bible School where it was hoped her condition would ease. She had a serious operation in 1926, but was able to travel home in 1927. However, the illness recurred and she died in 1929.

Obituary of Sister Mary McCord 1929
[born: 5th January 1883; entered: September 1912;
sailed for China: December 1915; died: 14th April 1929]

After five years of strenuous and ungrudging service (in China) she came home for furlough in 1921, and returned again to Anlu in 1922. But after nearly three more years she underwent a serious operation and was obliged to return home – as she hoped to recover her strength and to return again to China where all her thoughts still were. When the malady returned she fought it with courage and hope, and when at last she knew it to be incurable – with still rarer courage and more beautiful faith she accepted the new situation and looked death steadily in the face.

Source: The Agenda (May 1929) p.11

There is a rather cryptic reference in the April 1926 issue of *The Agenda* following Sister Eva Lyth's return from Canton in the South China District in December 1925. Apparently she had suffered some 'nerve-racking experiences' which had resulted in 'the closing of the work there on account of the present troubles'.[98] It presumably refers to the impending China Civil War.

The General Strike in 1926 forced the abandonment of Convocation so many missed the opportunity to meet Gladys Stephenson while she was on furlough. The plan was for her to return to China via America where she was to take a special course of study at the Cleveland School of Nursing, then after her arrival in Shanghai she would go on to Anlu to take charge of both hospitals there. However, there seems to have been some alteration, maybe because of 'the troubles' because apparently on 25th August 1927

---

97. *The Agenda* (November 1923) p.9, (July 1924) pp.7-8, (December 1924) p.16, (June 1926) p.4
98. *The Agenda* (October 1925) p.13, (April 1926) pp.8-9

she sailed for Hankow.[99] Nonetheless the report she sent in 1929 about her training work for nurses in central China was very encouraging:

> . . . we have had a wonderful year from the evangelistic and medical points of view. Finance is our one serious worry.[100]

In 1938-39 Sister Muriel Webb was in the Hunan District doing 'Language Study' and she sent her greetings to the Order. She explained that as Maud Millican was on furlough she had had the difficult job of taking charge of the women's work just 11 months after arriving in Hong Kong, but nevertheless she felt that not only was she 'in the *place* where the Lord wants me to be, but He has brought me here at this special *time*'. She was also delighted to report that when she had a meeting with the Biblewoman to plan new work she had actually '*made myself understood*'.[101]

With the coming of Methodist Union in 1932 the work in China increased as the United Methodist Church had long had many missionary workers there. So we find that Sister Ethel Simpson had been disappointed not to go to East Africa, but was then offered an appointment in China where she trained and directed the work of Biblewomen in the Wenchow District. A candidate, Miss Marchant, was accepted for Foreign Work in June 1924 and expected to go to China. However, her medical report precluded this appointment, so she was accepted for 'home work'. Sister Amelia was working in China and was allowed to wear the United Methodist deaconess uniform. Sister Lily (Armitt) was accepted 'as a missionary among women in China' in September 1913, but the Institute was anxious to know 'what work [she] was to undertake . . . and what her status would be there' and were reassured that not only would she be doing deaconess work but also training 'Chinese native women for that work'. Lily Armitt provided training for both voluntary and paid Biblewomen at Wuting in the North China District. While on deputation work in this country in 1922 Sister Lily wore the cloak and bonnet of the sisterhood.[102] In June 1926 the Institute received a letter from the Secretary of the Women's Missionary Auxiliary asking if there were 'any sisters who would be likely to respond to the call for service in China as evangelists'. The Warden, the Rev.

---

99. *The Agenda* (October 1926) p.13, (October 1927) pp.7, 15
100. *The Agenda* (April 1929) p.10
101. *The Agenda* (June 1929) p.7
102. UMDIMins II pp.162-63, 166, 172, 179, 184, 194, 197-98, 206 cf. Smith, Swallow and Treffry pp.131, 133, 397; UMDIMins II p.125

R. Gair, was asked to bring the request to the attention of the Sisters, but no indication of the response is recorded. There were four deaconesses, three nurses and three 'educationists' still serving in China in the 1930s.[103]

Little information is available from China in this period, the 1930s, for two reasons – one, the spasmodic issue of *The Agenda* and two, the difficulties and unrest in China itself. What news there was tells of remarkable courage. Maud Millican was 'once more a refugee in Changha' where the situation had become too perilous for the missionaries to remain. However, one piece of good news came when Gladys Stephenson was able to send a letter to Convocation in 1936 in which she described the consecration service of a Chinese deaconess, the second to be consecrated in recent months. Convocation was delighted to send a letter of good wishes to these Sisters.[104]

Sister Glady Stephenson outside the Nurses' Chapel, December 1936

Gladys Stephenson sent her greetings to the 1938 Convocation and her letter refers to the war which was raging. Reports of conditions for the missionaries who were in enemy-occupied areas 'were too horrible to contemplate and has made us decide that if Hankow falls we must get all our girls and young people, nurses too, away into the country and hills around while we ourselves do what we can for sick and refugees without our staff. We hope that Hankow will not be taken; in my heart I don't believe that it will, but the British Consul feels that it is so uncertain, that we must be prepared with full plans in case the city should fall.'[105]

War in China, 1938   **Sister Gladys Stephenson**

The plight of the refugees is heartbreaking; we have the sick ones in our wards here, four have died in the last few days, worn out with exposure, starvation, anxiety and grief. Children have died in terrible numbers; yet the undaunted faith and endurance of the people

---

103. *The Agenda* (October 1933) pp.5, 12; Smith, Swallow and Treffry pp.307-8
104. *The Agenda* (October 1936) pp.7-8, Mins. of Conv. (27th April 1936) p.5
105. *The Agenda* (April 1938) p.17

> continues unabated, and for all they know of the unspeakable atrocities committed against their own people, they continue to pray for Japan, her people, and even her soldiers and militarists.
>
> I am due for leave in September, but have asked permission to stay until the war is over as I cannot possibly leave the hospital at this time.
>
> *Source: The Agenda* (April 1938) p.17

Writing again on 30th July Gladys stressed how important letters from home were 'in these unhappy days' and described the joy of being reunited with a Chinese deaconess, Sister Olive, with whom she had once worked in Anlu. The whereabouts of Sister Olive had been causing anxiety to her friends as the city in which she was working had been invaded by the enemy in the spring, but after an incredible journey she had arrived in Hankow with a group of women and children just a week or so before.[106]

> ## Sister Olive's Escape   Sister Gladys Stephenson
>
> With a group of women refugees, she left the city that is some days' journey from here, in the time of snow, and all these months has been on the road.
>
> Their city fell rather suddenly and so many people had to escape on foot. Sister Olive with her group of women and children had to make for the hills, where they were obliged to hide in caves for some weeks. Food was very scarce indeed, if they managed one meal a day of some plain bean curd, they felt very fortunate.
>
> After a time, they started on their long trek over unknown roads, frequently losing their way and having to make wide detours to avoid meeting enemy soldiers. Twice they fell in with some of their own soldiers who hurried them over bridges 'ere they destroyed them.
>
> More than once they fell into swamps . . . One of the children fell desperately ill and Sister Olive carried her . . . Sister Olive used to have some slight heart attacks . . . on this exhausting journey, she fell by the roadside one hot day gasping and longing for water . . .
>
> At the village, they found all the people had fled and no food was to be obtained and there was only the open road on which to sleep. Finally she arrived at a country station where the Chinese minister (her one-time colleague) could not at first recognise her . . .
>
> We gathered that [they] . . . would not have accomplished that

---

106. *The Agenda* (October 1938) pp.13-15

> journey without Sister Olive and her steadfast courage and faith in God. Everyone is amazed at her abounding joy and her song of praise and her simple talks on God's grace during that journey has greatly encouraged many fainting souls.
>
> *Source: The Agenda* (October 1938) pp.13-14

Gladys' account of the raids on Hankow were graphic and shocking. Death and destruction were all around and devastating air-raids were so common an occurrence that the doctors and nurses were only able to help those with a chance of survival. Some idea of the traumatic conditions with which she and her colleagues had to deal can be gathered from her report that: 'While the doctors started work at once in the operating rooms, I went along, sorting out those on the stretchers who had a chance of life and sending them in next for treatment and care. Relatives kept imploring me to let their particular patient go in first, loath to accept the sorrowful fact I had to tell them, that they were beyond human aid. Our four doctors worked at high pressure, but forty could have been kept busy all the hours of that sorrowful day.' In her final paragraph she notes that Kinkiang (Joe-Yang) had fallen, that the war was very near them and that people were leaving Hankow in droves, fearful that the city itself would soon be occupied.[107]

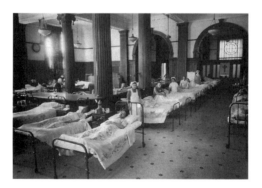

Methodist General Hospital (Hospital of Universal Love), Hankow, Central China. The hospital was temporarily housed in the Bank of China building during the Japanese invasion (September-November 1938). Sister Gladys Stephenson is near the arch.

---

107. *The Agenda* (October 1938) pp.13-15

News from China was sparse so a visit to the College from the Rev. and Mrs. Constantine (née Sister Dorothy Furniss) was greatly welcomed. It seemed likely that Hankow would have fallen and so the hospital had been 'transferred to within the Foreign Concession', but all the missionaries were reported to be safe.[108]

There was hope in early March 1939 that Gladys Stephenson might be able to travel home; however, on 15th February she wrote that 'The unpleasant truth is forcing itself upon me that I cannot be home for Convocation this year as I had hoped. The Japanese promised travelling facilities for third-power nationals wanting to leave, but so far they have put us off and put us off, always "military necessity", etc. Now it is 15th February and still no facilities afforded and no British steamers allowed to leave.' Things improved somewhat and she was due home on 22nd or 23rd April, but then, on returning to China, she was interned, along with Edith Anstey. The 1942 Convocation remembered those deaconesses who were isolated overseas through the war conditions and was glad to welcome Maud Millican, working at a hospital in Nantwich, and Hilda Stephens, doing caravan work, until they could return to China. Occasionally Gladys was able to send letters, but apparently none from home were getting through as by a message received by her family from the internment camp at Shanghai in 1944 which they passed on to the Order shows: 'No news for two years. Hope all is well. Strenuous – but keep well.' The Order continued to send letters in the hope that some might arrive. Edith Anstey, interned in Canton, was able to send a message through the Red Cross to the Mission House, which likewise was passed on: 'Still well, happy. Class Minor Prophets. Study Old Testament, Wheeler Robinson, Fosdick. Preach once ten weeks. Restarted Chinese after year's rest.'[109] After these brief contacts there was a long silence until at last in 1946 came a lengthy letter describing the celebrations when the gates were opened on the second day of peace, after the surrender.

---

108. *The Agenda* (December 1938) pp.10-11

109. *The Agenda* (March 1939) p.7, (April 1939) p.9, (June 1939) p.6, (June 1943) p.3, (July 1944) p.12, (Christmas 1944) p.7, Mins. of Conv. (1942) p.35

Thanksgiving Service　　　　**Sister Gladys Stephenson**

Since 1917, when the Japanese presented their twenty-one demands, the Chinese had lived under the terror of Japan and endured eight years of frightful war, devastation and oppression, so one does not wonder at the delirious joy in the freedom we are witnessing. The Community Church here held a special Thanksgiving Service last Sunday, with a welcome to all missionaries from the camps. Oh, what a welcome we had!. I just choked and couldn't sing, it was so lovely to be back with all those dear Christians once more . . . we heard of days of fasting and prayer the Church leaders had held again and again, and how the last time when the situation in Shanghai was very critical, after two days of fasting and prayer together, such a wonderful spirit of peace and acceptance prevaded them all that they knew an answer had come, and shortly, to their surprise, came the unexpected surrender of Japan.

Source: The Agenda (January 1946) p.9

Gladys gave a picture of life in the camp and emphasised that in spite of her first ever attack of malaria she had recovered and in fact all the internees were really very fit, chiefly due to the fact that the camp was in the country and they 'were obliged, fortunately, to spend much time in the open.' The main deprivation had been the lack of news from home, family and friends, but, she commented that 'Looking back now, many of us say we would not have missed all the inner spiritual communion that came to us in these circumstances for any time of freedom.' Edith Anstey had been ill, but wrote cheerfully from the American Presbyterian Hospital in Canton to which she had been sent when she was liberated.[110]

Internment Camp, Shanghai　　　**Sister Gladys Stephenson**

Apart from all the duties we each had of cleaning, fetching food and water, taking hours each day as it often involved long intervals standing in queues, we each had our camp work, cooking, cleaning, nursing, teaching, building paths, stoves for boiling water, stoking etc., etc. We ran a school for 400 children and a small hospital of twenty beds where I worked. Only 33 per cent. of us were full Britishers, the rest were Eurasians, Russians, Jews, Portugese, Dutch, even a few negroes and one or two of the "tough guy" element. All

---

110. *The Agenda* (January 1946) pp.8-9, 11, (September 1945) p.11

> alike we shared our quarters, our meals, our quota of drinking water,
> etc., etc. and so we had a unique opportunity of studying the human
> family. We ran Sunday School as well as services, and an evening
> intercession period which became very precious to a small group of
> us and was really and truly our "power house."
>
> *Source: The Agenda* (January 1946) p.8

Much as everyone was longing to see Gladys Stephenson when
at last she came home, after her three year internment, the Warden
warned, in no uncertain terms, that she needed several months
complete rest. The Convocation of 1946 unanimously nominated
her as Vice President of the Order that year, but she wrote
expressing her disappointment at not arriving in time for
Convocation and explaining that she would be back in China before
the next one – as this meant she could not become Vice President
she was unanimously elected in 1951 and presided at the 1952
Convocation. Gladys thanked everyone for their letters and
prayerful support, which meant so much to the deaconesses
overseas. About China she said she felt that the Church there had
emerged stronger from its ordeal and she had been overjoyed
recently to receive news of the successful conference of nurses, the
first to be held for ten years, and to learn that the Nursing
Association was now entirely in the hands of 'our Chinese nurses'
which was what the missionary nurses had been praying for and
working towards.[111]

Gladys returned to China via America in February 1947.[112] She
wrote to give an account of the progress she found had been made in
the hospital and School of Nursing in Hankow. Fifty-seven young
women out of about a hundred applicants for the Nurses' Training
School had been selected. As well as taking the usual nursing and
allied subjects they studied Chinese, English and the Bible and all
were 'enrolled into Bible classes and several have already asked for
baptism, but the rule of the Church here is a year on trial as an
Enquirer first. We have special preparatory classes for baptism, and
to me these classes have always been one of the rich and satisfying
parts of our work.'

---

111. *The Agenda* (September 1946) p.7, (Christmas 1946) pp.7-8, 11, Mins. of
     Conv.(1951) pp.124-25, (1952) pp.135, 140
112. *The Agenda* (July 1947) p.13

Life in Hankow, 1947   Sister Gladys Stephenson

In spite of the Communist refusal to co-operate with the government, thus keeping the country in disorder and constantly rising prices, China is making great progress in many domestic concerns. Last week a most attractive and competent young woman came to ask permission to address the Nurses. I found she was the ex-Head Mistress of a large Girls School, and was a candidate to the People's Assembly to be held at the end of this year. All Chinese over the age of twenty may vote, and the women of each area may vote for their own woman candidate. This young woman was a candidate to represent the women of Hankow. I took the chair at the meeting and greatly enjoyed her excellent speech. The election takes place this very week, and this candidate has obtained three or four trucks to take the nurses to the voting booth.

Source: The Agenda (Christmas 1947) p.13

In a letter from Hankow in 1949 Gladys Stephenson hinted at the difficult time the Church in China was facing under the Communist regime, saying, 'The Church is having a time of fresh testing, different in character to that which took place during the Japanese invasion, but penetrating and difficult to face. As ever in such times, there is a falling away of adherents but a deeper hold upon God for those who boldly come out to witness for Him. The Church is being purified and strengthened.'[113]

Gladys Stephenson was the last remaining Wesley Deaconess in China and when she retired in 1953 this brought to an end over 50 years' work. *The Wesley Deaconess Magazine* in December 1953 commented that although she, after 41 years' service, had officially retired she was still very active and 'doing a fine work among the Chinese in London'.[114] However, she still kept in close touch with her friends in China and from time to time gave news both of the Chinese Church there and in London.

The Wesley Deaconess Magazine of December 1959 was largely devoted to articles about the early or pioneer days of the Order and the article by Gladys Stephenson provides a fitting conclusion to this section on China. She started by recalling her 'Consecration and Valedictory Service' and how it had left 'an

---

113. *WDMag.* (1949) p.17
114. *WDMag.* (December 1953) p.14

indelible impression on my mind of the seal the church sets upon those called of God to go forth in His and their name'. Arriving in China in October 1915 she went to the Men's Hospital as the supply during Alice Shackleton's furlough and found that 'Everyone in the Hospital, patients, nurses, doctors, cooks and laundry-men were all men and I, the only woman amongst them. Walking along the dimly-lit corridors at night, suddenly meeting a man I had not seen approaching, it was reassuring to hear a warm voice saying, "Gooder-niter Sis-si-ter" and realise it was one of the nurses speaking to me in my own language. Then, working at their own wonderful language, loving it and absorbing it, feeling more at home with them each day.' Gladys remembered vividly her first Sunday there. In the church the women and girls sat on one side with the men and boys on the other and there was a choir consisting of 60 boys from the David Hill Blind School with their blind organist. When Sister Alice returned Gladys went to her own station three hundred miles inland to establish a Training School for Nurses in a new hospital. Gladys' new work was very rewarding as the 'keen young teenage lads' were eager to learn and several became local preachers delighting to go out with missionaries to preach the Gospel. Now, over 40 years later, many of these early converts had grown-up children of their own who were facing 'death and imprisonment for their faith'.[115]

Journeying into Inland China   Sister Gladys Stephenson

The journey took some days by river junk and then more days by sedan chair, overland. Finding the narrow lath-like seat anything but comfortable, I got out to walk whenever possible. Walking briskly on paths between the fields, here and there, a man looked up startled from his work to see a woman with large feet striding along in a manner unknown to Chinese women. "Horses feet", one would hear the exclamation. It was soon after that time that the fiat went forth from the Chinese Government that small girls' feet were no longer to be bound.

Source: The Wesley Deaconess Magazine (December 1959) p.10

As a last postscript to deaconess work connected with China we note that in 1956-57 Sister Mary Mellows was 'seconded to the China Inland Mission' and stationed in Singapore for eight years. She then spent a further two years in Formosa.[116]

---

115. *WDMag.* (December 1959) pp.9-11
116. *WDO Stations* 1956/7-1967/8

Chapter 5

Wesley Deaconesses Work Overseas – The Rest of the World

New Zealand

The New Zealand Advocate, quoted in *Highways and Hedges* in June 1899, reported that 'Some two years ago, the "Fathers" of our Church in New Zealand thought the time was ripe for similar work (to that of the Wesley Deaconess Institute in England) in our own land. It was deemed advisable to confer . . . *re* the feasibility of sending out one of their number to begin such work in our midst. Several gentlemen of Christchurch undertook to guarantee a Deaconess's salary for five years . . . Accordingly, . . . word was received that "Sister Christian Hughes" had been appointed, to be attached to the Durham Street Circuit, and to inaugurate a Deaconess' Order, affiliated to the Home Society . . . it is hoped . . . to begin a Deaconess' Home, where girls of our own land may be trained for this work.'[1] So began deaconess work in New Zealand.

Sister Christian Hughes (New Zealand), 1903

In December 1896 Dr. Stephenson reported to the Deaconess committee that he had received a letter from the Rev. W. Morley[2] asking for the immediate appointment of a Wesley Deaconess to New Zealand. Unfortunately a regretful telegram had to be sent as no one was available immediately, but this was followed by a letter asking for further details about any financial arrangements and also about 'the relation of the proposed Deaconess Institute in New Zealand to the Wesley Deaconess Institute'. After further correspondence between Stephenson and Morley it was agreed that a deaconess should be sent to New Zealand. So this urgent request for an experienced Wesley Deaconess to become the Sister-in-Charge of a Deaconess House,

---

1. *HH* (June 1899) pp.141-42
2. The Rev. Dr. William Morley was the father of Sister Muriel Morley – see pp.5-6

which would 'train a Branch Order of Colonial women', was answered and, in September 1897, Sister Christian Hughes, who had been working in Ipswich for three and a half years, was appointed. A valedictory service was held and she sailed for New Zealand on Thursday 16th September.[3] The Warden commented:

> Her departure marks an important step in the Deaconess movement. At the request of the Rev. William Morley and friends at Christchurch, a branch of the Wesley Deaconess Institute is to be formed in New Zealand, preserving the essential features of our Order, but having perfect freedom to adapt itself to local needs.[4]

The March *Highways and Hedges* contains Christian's first letter telling of her arrival in Christchurch, where she received a warm welcome. The formal reception service was addressed by the President of Conference and in reply Christian gave an account of the Wesley Deaconess Institute. She felt that there was plenty of work to be done in Christchurch, that Methodism there was fairly strong and that the people were very sympathetic to the Deaconess movement.[5] She wrote a lengthy letter from 26 Durham Street, Christchurch in the spring of 1898, hoping it would arrive in time for Convocation, in which she said that much of the work in New Zealand consisted of home visiting, in addition to starting classes and Mothers' Meetings. Many of the same social problems as she had encountered at home seemed to be present too.[6]

Sister Christian Hughes   Rev. Wesley Chambers

She arrived in Christchurch in November 1897; worked in association with Durham Street and St. Asaph Street Churches, observed carefully what the human needs were; and kept a diary of her work. This record so convinced her sponsors of the value of the work, that it was decided to employ a second sister and hopefully rent a house to commence training Deaconesses in this country. Subscriptions were

---

3. WDIMins I pp.37, 43, 50
4. *HH* (April 1897) p.87; (September 1897) pp.210-11, 212, (October 1897) pp.232-3, (November 1897) p.256, (December 1897) p.277, (January 1898) p.19
5. *HH* (March 1898) p.67, (May 1898) p.114
6. *HH* (May 1898) pp.115-16, (November 1898) pp.259-60

> invited and Mr George Bowron,[7] one of the initiating laymen, was appointed treasurer.
>
> *Source:* Chambers, Wesley A., *Not Self – But Others: The Story of the New Zealand Methodist Deaconess Order* (Wesley Historical Society (New Zealand) Proceedings No.48, August 1987) p.23

The July 1900 issue of the magazine contains an article from *The Advocate and New Zealand Methodist* which reports that Christian Hughes had travelled to Dunedin to join in the first anniversary celebrations of the Central Mission Sisterhood at the end of January.[8] Sister Christian sent news in 1900 that 'after steady preparation, a Deaconess House has at last been opened, and there is a fair prospect that we shall have an affiliated Branch of the Order in this important Colony.' The Warden remarked that

> so highly is the value and importance of the work estimated, that steps are now being taken for the establishment of the New Zealand Branch. It is sanctioned by the Conference of the colony: and will be upon the lines of our Order in England. It will, moreover, be a recognised Branch of the Order in England. But financially it will be quite independent: and whilst the members of the New Zealand Order will be Associates of the English Order, they will not be members of it. There are many practical and prudential reasons for this. Sister Christian Hughes is, of course, one of our own Sisters, and will retain her full membership here. We are thankful for this development of our work.[9]

The report from New Zealand in 1901 told of the establishment of the Deaconess House:

> The Deaconess House in Barbadoes Street has been secured for a term of five years, at a very moderate rental, and is found admirably adapted and situated for the carrying on of the work. Through the kindness of a lady friend, in furnishing one of the rooms, thereby

---

7. The Bowron family, who were instrumental in setting up the United Methodist Deaconess Institute, had both family and business connections with New Zealand.
8. *HH* (July 1900) pp.166-67
9. *HH* (November 1900) p.259, (December 1900) p.279, *FL* (November 1901) p.5

affording increased accommodation, an arrangement was made with a lady to live at the house; and further arrangements have just been concluded with Miss Elsie Lilly, who has undergone a course of training in Dunedin, to enter almost immediately into the work. The Committee have also under consideration an application from another young lady who is desirous of working under Sister Christian's directions, and if this needed help can be secured, a very much larger result will follow, as up to the present, it has been found impossible to cope with the numerous cases that are met with.

Sister Christian Hughes writes in a recent communication:- The work is steadily growing in interest, . . . The work of 'Sisters' has so far recommended itself . . . that quite a number are now at work in three of our large centres, and our Presbyterian friends have also secured one 'Sister,' and will, probably, have others before long. This convinces us more than ever of the need of Training Homes in our midst, so that our young people may serve in their own colony, without have to send to England or Australia for trained workers.[10]

Writing to the Order for the 1902 Convocation from the 'Methodist Deaconess House, 128 Barbadoes Street, Christchurch,' Christian reported that 'it is nearly eighteen months since our bright, pretty little Deaconess House was opened, and since then all sorts and conditions of people have come to us with their woes and their joys.' She went on to tell how 'only last Sunday' four sailors from *HMS Royal Arthur* had waited for her outside the Church and she took them home with her where they exchanged stories of home and sang 'all the old favourite hymns'. Referring to the Deaconess House she said 'Sister Elsie' had been there for a year's training before going out to India and was doing good practical work in two small suburban churches, while, at least six others had 'offered for the work', but the chief problem was lack of funds. However, Synod had decided that the work ought to be extended and had sent a recommendation to the Conference which was meeting in Dunedin. As a result Conference had appointed a committee to examine the situation fully.[11]

---

10. *FL* (February 1902) p.11
11. *FL* (June/July 1902) pp.92-94

In early 1903 Christian Hughes was on her way home via Australia, where she planned to visit relations, before continuing her journey in the *SS Britannia*. She arrived at Ilkley on 24th March to an enthusiastic welcome and, after her 'five years of faithful and successful service' in New Zealand, her next appointment was as 'oversister' at the College. Her efforts in New Zealand had resulted in Sisters Isabel Sinclair and Frances Cannon becoming Wesley Deaconesses.[12] An article in *Flying Leaves* remarked that four years previously Isabel Sinclair, a New Zealander, had journeyed to England to become a Wesley Deaconess, so that 'after due training and experience she might return to do the like in her own sunny land' and a year later she was joined by Frances Cannon. On 22nd August 1900 Isabel entered Mewburn House as a probationer from Dunedin, where she had served for four years in the Sisters Mission at Trinity Church. When she finished her training Isabel was appointed to London, Blackheath (Sunfields) in September 1901 and worked there until 1904. She was consecrated at Ilkley on 24th April 1903. Frances Elizabeth Cannon trained at Mewburn House from September 1901-July 1902 and in September 1902 worked in London, Hammersmith (Rivercourt Church) for one year, after which she went to London, Great Queen's Street (Prince of Wales Road).

While in London Frances Cannon spent a week of her first summer holiday working with the Salvation Army in Whitechapel. Her account of this time throws an interesting light on the social and ethnic conditions in that part of London, which was predominately Jewish and antagonistic to Christianity, and on the evangelistic work of the Salvation Army. Another 'noteworthy' experience for Frances was '*War Cry* selling' in the local public houses.

Sister Frances Cannon (New Zealand), 1904

---

12. *FL* (March 1903) p.36, (April 1903) p.54, (May 1903) pp.69-70, (September 1903) p.122; WDIMins I p.131

War Cry Selling   **Sister Frances Cannon**

A new experience to me was *War Cry* selling' – 'Pub. Booming' the Salvationists call it. 'This is our work on Saturday afternoons,' the Lassies explained: so armed with a bundle of *War Cries* and *Social Gazettes* we sallied forth one afternoon, I, with my heart in my mouth very nearly. We visited some thirty of the largest public-houses in London - meeting with all grades of society and types of humanity. I was surprised at the numbers of papers that were sold and at the number of 'regular customers' in the various saloon bars.

Source: Flying Leaves (July/August 1903) pp.117-8

She was consecrated at Hull in April 1904. The *Stations* for 1904-05 list both Sisters Isabel and Frances for New Zealand and the Warden commented that Isabel would go to Wellington and Frances to 'Canterbury or some other important centre. They retain their connection with our Order. Possibly they will be able to establish an affiliated Order in New Zealand.'[13]

Special Cases of Deaconesses returning to New Zealand, 1904

The Executive Committee recommended that these deaconesses (Isabel Sinclair and Frances Cannon) be allowed to retain their connection with the Order on condition:

(1) that they write a report of their work to the Warden twice a year;

(2) That a yearly report be received from the Superintendent minister of the circuit in which they reside.

(3) That they neither pay into nor receive benefit from the Superannuation Fund.

Source: Minutes of Meeting of Executive Committee held at Oxford Place Chapel Vestry, Leeds, on Tuesday 24th March, 1904 p.204

Frances Cannon appears to have served in New Zealand for only a short time because she is not listed in the 1906-07 *Stations*. Although these records are among the Wesley Deaconess Order papers, despite enquiries, there seems to be no record in New

---

13. 'Wesley Deaconess Order: J Elsworth's own MS Notes & Register'; *FL* (September 1904) p.126, (October 1904) pp.129, 142, (November 1904) p.148; (March 1905) pp.221-22

Zealand itself of her being a Deaconess. She obviously left the Order as her name is not on the Convocation Membership Roll of 1907 and Isabel Sinclair was described as 'the only Wesley Deaconess in New Zealand' in 1907 when she gave an account of her visit to Rotorua:

> The whole district underneath the surface is one mass of boiling sulphuric springs for a radius of about fifty miles or more.
>
> Clouds of steam are continually rising from huge ponds, and this is the case over the whole of our locality.[14]

Isabel wrote that she was having considerable success in Wellington, having made six new converts in the last two months, congregations had increased, perhaps chiefly because of the attraction of small orchestra which played for Sunday evening services. Her life was full with visiting and meetings, but she added, 'I shall never forget dear old England and the many friends who were kind to me there.' In 1911 Isabel Sinclair was listed at Brisbane, in the Australian Conference and the New Zealand stations disappeared altogether for four years.[15]

Sister Isabel Sinclair (New Zealand), 1905

Another 'New Zealander' who had been studying at Ilkley and gaining experience in England was Annie Anderson. Just before returning home she wrote a 'goodbye' letter to her friends in the Order with whom she had spent four happy years. She explained she was sailing in the *SS India* and would arrive just before Christmas, then, after a fortnight with her family, she was expecting to go to Trinity Church in Dunedin.[16] Settled, Annie wrote, in 1909, describing her work, which was involved with meetings and classes, both, in 'one of the best' churches in New Zealand and also at the Mission Hall. She remarked that the Prayer meeting at the Mission Hall was composed entirely of young folk who were often full of noisy high spirits.

---

14. *FL* (April 1907) p.54
15. *FL* (October 1906) p.157, (September 1911) p.112; (September 1914) p.136; *WDO Stations* 1904-18
16. *FL* (November 1907) p.153

Prayer Meeting, Mission Hall, Dunedin

Sister Annie Anderson

. . . last Sunday evening, as I was praying, there was a burst of laughter, and I had to stop in my prayer and reprimand them, and then try to take up the thread of the prayer again. On enquiry afterwards as to the cause of the outburst, I heard the following story:- 'Punch' Pine, a real hooligan, had brought a little rabbit to the meeting with him. He had the creature safely up his sleeve, and during prayer, seeing a man in front with a bald patch on the top of his head . . . he could not resist the temptation of putting this animal on the smooth part. The outburst of laughter was easily accounted for, but I sincerely hope it will never happen again while I am trying to pray.

Source: Flying Leaves (February 1909) p.22

In addition to her strictly church work Annie also ran St. John's Ambulance Classes at the local biscuit factories and followed this up by starting nursing classes. As the Mission Hall was situated just off the main street and next to 'one of the worst public houses in the city' many drunks found their way into her Men's Club, so she was delighted to report that at the recent election 'in Dunedin we have carried 'Reduction by the Local Option' vote, which means we shall close nine public-houses, and then at next Election probably we shall wipe the whole lot out'. In a letter to Mrs. Stephenson, later in 1909, Annie expressed her delight at having received news from England and described a visit to her home church where, at the request of her father, a circuit steward for 35 years, she had taken three services and given a lecture – 'quite sufficient on holiday'! She then toured the West Coast

*Sister Annie Anderson
(New Zealand), 1905*

with its beautiful scenery and experienced a breathtaking ride down steep hills in a coach pulled by five or six horses, before returning by boat and suffering terrible sea-sickness in the coastal waters. Annie wrote that she had had a good year at Dunedin and was pleased that 'Reduction' had now meant the closure of fifteen public-houses during the year.[17] Sister Annie influenced a number

---

17. *FL* (February 1909) pp.22-23; (June 1909) pp.89-90

of New Zealand deaconesses to go to Ilkley for training. Her name disappears from the *Stations* list and Convocation Roll in September 1910 when she resigned to marry the Rev. E. O. Blamires.[18]

Flying Leaves of October 1910 contains news of a Sister Mabel Morley, a New Zealand Deaconess, the eldest daughter of the Rev. Dr. William and Mrs Morley. Mabel had been appointed to the Durham Street Church, Christchurch in 1907 and when 74 Asaph Street West, Christchurch was bought to be the Deaconess Training House she became the first Lady Superintendent, also continuing to work at Durham Street Church. In 1909 her health failed and she travelled to England where she visited Ilkley and served in the West London Mission. Returning to New Zealand she resumed her duties as Lady Superintendent of the Deaconess House.[19] Sister Mabel sent back a photograph of the House to her friends in Ilkley and mentioned that she had been to Dunedin to attend the Girls' Bible Class Convention where she had renewed her acquaintance with Sister Annie Anderson (now Mrs E. O. Blamires). She was also delighted to report that the first 'fledgling' of the New Zealand Deaconess House was doing well in her circuit and added that:

> Following your lead, we are adopting the grey uniform for the Probationers, and I am glad to say their first year in circuit work will still be considered probation – two years in the Deaconess House and one year in circuit before their Consecration.[20]

In 1913 Sister Mabel left her post as the Lady Superintendent and in 1914 became the Sister-in-Charge of the newly established South Island Orphanage and Children's Home at Papanui until 1920 when she was forced to retire through ill-health. The Methodist Church in New Zealand applied to Bradfield, the Warden of the Order, for a Deaconess to take Sister Mabel's place as Lady Superintendent. Hence on 7th January Sister Grace Crump left on the *SS Otranto* to take charge of the Training Home for Deaconesses in Christchurch and she was publicly welcomed in the Durham Street Methodist Church on 20th February.[21] One of the last references to New Zealand before the cessation of *Flying Leaves* was that 'Sister Grace

---

18. WDIMins I p.358; Chambers, Wesley A., *Not Self – But Others: The Story of the New Zealand Methodist Deaconess Order* (Wesley Historical Society (New Zealand) Proceedings No.48, August 1987) (hereafter Chambers) p.59
19. Chambers pp.25, 50
20. *FL* (October 1910) p.142
21. WDIMins II p.53; *FL* (February 1914) pp.21, 28; (June 1914) p.91, Chambers pp.102-03

Crump . . . proposes to leave New Zealand about 24th January 1916' Wesley Chambers notes that while in New Zealand she was the 'Methodist Deaconess for Christchurch Hospitals', that she 'instituted the first Deaconess Convocation in New Zealand' and pressed for the enlargement of the Deaconess House to offer more facilities to the women of Christchurch, including hostel accommodation for women students.[22]

Sister Gladys Crump   **Rev. Wesley A Chambers**

During the two years of Sister Grace's leadership, she also imparted a vision of what the Deaconess House could be in the life of the church. She saw it not only as a centre for training Deaconesses, but also as a hostel for women students in the city, a meeting place for women's groups in and around Christchurch, and a base for missionary related activities. Not even the long years of World War I and Sister Grace's return to the United Kingdom, put out the fires of that vision. It glowed in the hearts of Mr and Mrs George Bowron who brought it to fruitition.

Source: Chambers, Wesley A., *Not Self – But Others: The Story of the New Zealand Methodist Deaconess Order* (Wesley Historical Society (New Zealand) Proceedings No.48, August 1987) p.59

When Sister Grace returned to England she went to the Bradford Mission for a year (1917-18) before being seconded to the Women's Auxiliary, later Women's Work, from 1918-36, when she retired. She died in 1959.[23]

Sister Isabel Sinclair returned to Christchurch from Australia in 1914. The New Zealand station is not listed in 1918, but Sister Isabel is recorded as 'travelling' and in 1919 she is listed as at Portsville, Pennsylvania in the United States of America, where she remained until 1921. Wesley Chambers says that in 1922 she went to the Young Women's Christian Association in Sydney, and the Convocation Roll records her death in August 1922, though Chambers gives it as 8th May 1922 in Sydney.[24]

---

22. Chambers, op cit. pp.23, 73-74
23. *WDO Stations* (September 1917 onwards)
24. *WDO Stations* (September 1918-22); Chambers, op.cit. p.111-12; Convocation Membership Roll 1903-23

This seems to be the end of the New Zealand (and slight Australian) direct connection with the Wesley Deaconess Order in England, presumably because their own Deaconess Order was now sufficiently well-established to stand on its own. However it is worth noting that there had been local deaconesses associated with various missions in Australia over the years, but the official Deaconess Order was started in 1945 and Convocation sent greetings to its members.[25]

West Indies

There was no deaconess work in the West Indies until the Hayti (sic) and Santo Domingo District (America) appears for the first time on the Wesley Deaconess Order *Stations.* Sister Edith Le Masurier had been out in the Sierra Leone and Gambia District in 1906/7 before returning on furlough in 1910 and was then described as 'resting either on account of health or home claims.' However, the problem must have been resolved as on 7th January she sailed for Haiti to become Principal of Bird College, Port-au-Prince. The history of Haiti and of Methodism there is a turbulent story, however for our purposes we need only note that the Rev. Mark B. Bird (1807-1880) served for nearly forty years in Haiti and was a distinguished Chairman of the District. His long cherished dream of starting a girls' boarding school eventually came to fruition in 1893 and it was named Bird's College. As the first Protestant Girls' High School it enjoyed considerable success. However, Sister Edith's appointment was short-lived as the Institute Minutes, with no explanation, reported, in October 1912 'the appointment at Haiti has been given up.'[26] It is likely that there were so many problems in Haiti, where the District seems to have been lurching from one crisis to another, that the final disaster of a terrible fire, which destroyed the Methodist premises in Port-au-Prince in 1911-12, caused the closure of the school and with it Edith's appointment came to an untimely end. Edith resigned from the Order in June 1913.[27]

---

25. Mins. of Conv. (1946) p.72, (1952) p.135
26. *FL* (January 1911) p.12, (February 1911) p.20
27. *WMMins. of Conf.* (1881) pp.13-15; G. G. Findlay & W.W. Holdworth, *The History of the Wesleyan Methodist Missionary Society* (1921) vol.2 espec. pp.515, 518; WDIMins II p.39

> **Appointment in Haiti, 1911** **The Warden**
>
> We are glad to report the arrival of Sister Edith Le Masurier in Haiti. It was hardly as peaceful as we should have liked, as there seem to have been some political disturbances in the town of Port-au-Prince, and bullets were flying. We thankfully note that Sister Edith reports that the School buildings of the College are bullet proof, and we are glad to think that nobody will desire to do any injury to the College or its inhabitants; but the political methods seem to be somewhat unusual!
>
> *Source: Flying Leaves* (April 1911) p.51

In 1927-28 the Methodist Synod in Jamaica asked for Wesley Deaconesses to go there. At the Joint Candidates Committee of the Missionary Society on 9th January 1928 Sister Muriel Ellis was accepted for work in Jamaica and was due to sail in March and Sister Jessie Kerridge also was appointed to Kingston in the Jamaica District. So the real work in the Caribbean began. In 1929 first hand news was brought to the Order by the Rev. and Mrs A. G. Burnham, missionaries in Jamaica, together with greetings from Sisters Muriel and Jessie. Miss Greenwood, who, as related in chapter 8, with her sister provided a holiday house, 'Restawhile', for the deaconesses, went to see Muriel Ellis and Jessie Kerridge and wrote to tell the Order about her visit. She said they were comfortably settled and busy with rescue work in addition to all their normal activities. The usual pattern for furloughs was put into place, and Sister Mary Morton, accepted by the Missionary Committee for work in Jamaica, went out in 1933 to join Sister Jessie in Kingston. Sister Muriel resigned on her marriage to the Rev. Wilfred Easton, a missionary in Jamaica.[28] In December 1938, writing from Bermuda *en route* for the Bahamas, Sister Jessie sent an interesting account of some of her journey around the Caribbean.

> **Travels in the West Indies** **Sister Jessie Kerridge**
>
> 'I shall never forget the day I spent on the Pomeroon River. We set out at 6.00 a.m. to drive 20 miles along a terrible road (no 60 miles an hour there!). Then we had 50 miles to go on the mighty

---

28. *The Agenda* (February 1928) p.6; *WDO Stations* 1928; *The Agenda* (June 1929) p.13, (June 1929) p.13, (May 1930) p.13, (Christmas 1932) p.5, (October 1933) p.4

> Pomeroon River in a small three-horse power engine launch. The wind and tide were against us most of the way, so we were an hour late for the first service and three hours late for the other two. There are no roads or paths over the Pomeroon - folk travel by boat. They paddle with one hand and hold up an umbrella with the other! So they came to Church on that wet, dull day, and they waited the three hours, and waited cheerfully, and we had three wonderfully warm-hearted and happy services.'
>
> *Source: The Agenda* (December 1938) p.11

There is very little information about the deaconesses in the West Indies until the 1943 Report to the Synod is reproduced in *The Agenda*. Entitled 'Deaconess Work in The West Indies' it reports that Sister Gladys Cook had spent much time 'in adventurous and uncomfortable voyages among the tiny and remote islands of the Leewards group'. She had run a number of courses to prepare people to work in the local churches and also training days for day school teachers She commented that some of her voyages were quite eventful as, although there were usually a number of passengers, 'the sailing sloops' had no accommodation for them and 'we travel in company with a varied collection of donkeys, cattle, pigs, goats, hens, and turtles, to say nothing of the rest of the cargo.' Her journeys could take from between 16 hours to a week, but 'the welcome on the far shore is always so warm that one forgets the difficulties of getting there.' Sister Jessie Kerridge was in charge of the Deaconess House in Kingston, Jamaica. Sisters Gladys and Jessie were joined by Sister Marjorie Watson and then, to great rejoicing, the first West Indian Deaconess, Sister Elsie Bemand, was ordained, while two more candidates had started their training at the Deaconess House, which had been enlarged so that many training courses for voluntary workers were offered as well as domestic science classes to enable trainees to obtain good employment. In addition to this the Sisters and students took part in many youth and social activities in the town churches and visited hospitals, the prison and the local internment camp. They were also involved with the 84 Girls' League branches which had 1,280 members. M. V. H, (Sister Mary V. Hunter) the writer of the report, concluded:

> It is hard to estimate the immense value of all this work among women and girls both now and even more in the days to come, in the higher standards of home life, social life, and the life of the Church. We are thankful that so few have, by God's grace, been able to do so much, and

in so short a time, for it is only 15 years since the first Deaconess was appointed to Jamaica.[29]

The Warden noted that on 11th March 1944 Jessie Kerridge arrived home after 'a peaceful voyage', presumably a reference to the perils of wartime travel. She spoke to the 1945 Convocation about the work in the West Indies, describing the vastness of the area covered by the various islands, the background of slavery and the development of the deaconess work in Jamaica in particular.[30]

A red-letter day was the Deaconess Ordination Service which took place at Wesley Church in Kingston on Wednesday 5th November 1947, when Sister Olga Brookes-Smith was ordained by the Chairman of the District, the Rev. E. Armon Jones. Everyone was filled with 'wonder and praise for the growth and development of the past twenty years and thanksgiving for the women of the West Indies who, having heard God's call, are offering their lives for His service'.[31]

Sister Marjorie Watson, now stationed in Trinidad, wrote telling how 20 young women had travelled by a variety of means from the islands to their first District Girls' League Conference at Easter 1949. Her special news was about the official opening of the Deaconess House there, which was 'not very big - has two good sized bedrooms and a small one, my study and a drawing room and dining room, but it is OUR DEACONESS HOUSE and my home ... It will be used not only as the home of the Trinidad Deaconess but as a training centre for women and girls who are giving voluntary service to the Church.'[32]

On 25th May 1951 Elsie Bemand, who, as noted earlier, was the first West Indian deaconess to be ordained, visited Ilkley and took part in that year's 'Ceylon Day'.[33] 1951 also saw, after Synod, 'the little Order of West Indian Deaconesses, plus the five Wesley Deaconesses, meeting together 'in their first Convocation', with Elsie Bemand as one of the speakers. Then Kingston was hit by a hurricane and the Deaconess House and garden sustained a great deal of damage. The Sisters volunteered to help the Red Cross deal with the local communities which had 'suffered very grievously.'

29. *The Agenda* (July 1944) pp.9-11
30. *The Agenda* (Christmas 1944) p.7; Mins. of Conv. (1945) p.59
31. *The Agenda* (July 1948) pp.13-14
32. *WDMag.* (1949) p.17
33. *WDMag.* (July 1951) p.17

Their help was gladly received and they helped to ferry relief workers back and forth wherever they were needed.

Hurricane, Kingston Jamaica   **Sister Vera Gridley**

At Deaconess House Sister Jessie and Sister Olga had a rough night. Sister Jessie's new study got the worst of the storm and very early its windows were smashed by flying shingles and pieces of trees. They then retreated into her bedroom, but again the force of the storm was too great, Eventually they barricaded themselves in the spare bedroom by nailing a wardrobe to one window and a mattress to the other, and there they spent the remainder of the night. . . .

His Excellency the Governor said that the hurricane had blown down the trees around Kings House and given him a better view of the mountains. A foreign Consul said the hurricane had blown down his walls and revealed neighbours he never knew he had. There is symbolism lying behind both statements – the hurricane has made us more aware of the everlasting strength and unfailing mercies of our God, and it has drawn us nearer to our fellow men.

Source: The Wesley Deaconess Magazine (December 1951) pp.14-16)

In 1953 (as noted in the section on Ceylon, in chapter 4), the Ceylon Fund was transferred to support the young West Indian Order and the name changed to the Overseas Fund. The Silver Jubilee of Deaconess Work in the West Indies was celebrated on 30th September 1953 by an early morning prayer meeting and a public thanksgiving service at which the Chairman of the District presided. Lady Foot was present and 'that she should read the greetings from the deaconesses stationed in other parts of the Western area was a happy choice, for each one was known to Lady Foot . . .'. Sister Jessie Kerridge took part in a broadcast of 'Women's Diary' in which she described the training of the deaconesses, their probation and ordination for the work of a Wesley Deaconess. She went on explain that six had already been trained, two were still training and that there were also seven who had been trained in England. Deaconesses were working in Eleuthera, St. Kitts, Antigua, St. Vincent, Trinidad and Jamaica and during the next year centres would be established in Honduras and probably Nassau, while Haiti and Panama and other islands were also anxious to have deaconesses. So she ended with an appeal for more young women to answer the call 'to dedicate their lives in service to others'.[34]

---

34. *WDMag.* (December 1953) pp.11-12

After this there is little detailed information about the West Indian work for almost twenty years, apart from the note that a special ordination service was held in Kingston on 8th November 1954 for Sister Dora Dixon, because she had sailed to Jamaica before the ordination service at Convocation, and an account of the deaconesses from the West Indies' visit to the 1963 Convocation. On the latter occasion Sister Jessie Kerridge

Deaconesses in Jamaica with Mr J. A. Stead, Vice-President of the Conference 1949-50

described the beginning of the work there, while Sisters Gladys Cooke (Leewards Islands and British Guiana), Mary Morton (Bahamas) and Vera Gridley (Haiti) told of their experiences. Sister Gladys Holmes (Caribbean) sang a Spiritual and Sister Cynthia Clare represented the West Indian Deaconess Order, founded 21 years earlier. At the conclusion they all sang the new Jamaican National Anthem, the words of which had been composed by the Chairman of the District, the Rev. Hugh B. Sherlock, OBE. 1963 also saw the retirement of Sister Jessie after 35 years' service in the West Indies.[35] An offical letter of greeting from 1968 Convocation was sent to the Convocation of the West Indian Deaconess Order.[36]

The silence was broken in 1973 when Joyce McCaffer wrote about the work she was doing in the Caribbean. Having given an evocative geographical description of Jamaica, she went on to talk of the different races to be found in the population and the struggle the 'young idealistic government' was having in trying 'to provide an adequate and fair way of life for everyone through education, medical services and employment. There was much unemployment and poverty which led to 'a sense of hopelessness' and a tendency to crime. So this was the background against which the Church was working. She said that when she came on furlough in September there were ten Deaconesses serving in Jamaica in six different spheres of work:

> – one as Deaconess-tutor at the United Theological College of the West Indies; another as Warden at Deaconess House; three in rural ministerial appointments; four on the staffs of Kingston Circuits

---

35. *WDMag.* (December 1954) p.16; Mins. of Conv.1963 pp.5, 7
36. Mins. of Conv. 1968 p.4

and one in a rural circuit. One was working with the Caribbean Council of Churches and one, though officially retired, served wherever a need arose.[37]

Sister Joyce, herself, along with her ministerial colleagues, was engaged in looking after three churches and a house church, with a membership of almost 2,000, plus many young people. The work comprised all the usual Church and allied activities. She also helped with the women and children's work in a smaller circuit, and co-ordinated children's groups throughout Jamaica, including planning Summer Camps. She felt 'thankful to God for what we were able to do – but I am even more conscious of the task ahead of the Church in that country'.[38] British Wesley Deaconesses ceased to be stationed in the Methodist Church of the Caribbean and the Americas from 1974.[39]

Sister Jessie Kerridge, who as we saw earlier, with Sister Muriel Ellis, really started deaconess work in the West Indies, wrote, in 1977, to celebrate the opening and dedication of the new Deaconess House for the Deaconess Order of the Caribbean and the Americas. The Methodist Church owned a large site five miles out of the city on which there already was a Church and other buildings, so, as the original House had served its purpose the new Deaconess House was built there. Then, after renovation, part of the old House was to be used as classrooms. The new House was commodious, providing each deaconess working in Kingston with a small flat, accommodation for 12 student boarders, guest rooms and a cafeteria. A classroom, sitting room and dining room were also included in the new building. The official opening was timed to coincide with both the Conference and Convocation and Sister Jessie was the honoured guest. Great preparations were made for an outdoor service of thanksgiving, but the weather intervened and it had to be held in the Church. Nevertheless, it was still a joyous occasion. Sister Jessie attended Convocation and listened with great interest to the discussions and commented that 'several appointments in Kingston cannot be filled. It was in Convocation that, as well as the opportunities, the problems and difficulties of the Order were faced. There is great similarity between the Caribbean problems and ours.'

---

37. *A Way of Serving* (Autumn 1974) pp.12-14; as only two and a 'without appointment, marriage' deaconesses are named in the *WDO Stations* of 1973 the other must have been from the West Indian Order.
38. *A Way of Serving* (Autumn 1974) pp.12-14
39. *WDO Stations* 1973, 1974

The Next Step Forward   **Sister Jessie Kerridge**

Many stations remain vacant, new opportunities are opening up. There is desire for change that will provide more varied forms of service to meet present needs. I was asked if I thought it would be possible to get deaconesses from Britain to help. My reply could only be that I was sure help would be given if possible, while reminding them that we also have too few workers to fill appointments. Thankfully I recognised that once again the day might come when the two Orders would work together on the same field.

The Next Step Forward? . . .

Training to meet the present needs, yes

Vision and faith to find God's way for to-day and to follow it with courage. This the West Indian deaconesses are set to do. We can support them in our prayers . . .

Source: A Way of Serving (Autumn 1977) pp.15,16

Finally an article by Gladys Holmes about the Golden Jubilee of deaconess work in the Caribbean, which was celebrated in 1978, provides a fitting conclusion. Sister Gladys joined the celebrations in the Bahamas District, renewed old friendships and was delighted to see that 'the overall picture was one of hope, under Sister Olga Brooks Smith's able leadership . . .' She then went on to the Jamaica District, where, again, she met people she had known during her service in the West Indies. Everyone was thrilled to have Sister Jessie Kerridge[40] there with them to join the Retreat in the Blue Mountains, the Sunday thanksgiving service, which was broadcast, and to go on the Monday to Government House to be received by the Governor General – a Methodist, who 'was a young boy in the Sunday School when Sister Jessie first arrived in Jamaica, and (who) now seeks to serve his country well in a very difficult period of its history.' One of the items in the Jubilee meeting was a pageant, entitled *These Fifty Years,* which had been written by one of Sister Jessie's first Guides. Then, on the Tuesday, the Deaconess House held an Open Day, with displays from all the Districts, regional food was provided and there was much chatting and many reminiscences. The week ended with the Golden Jubilee Banquet, described by the Chairman of the District rather as a 'love-feast', the proceeds from which went towards the future rehabilitation work planned for the Deaconess House.

---

40. Sister Jessie died on 15th July 2001, aged 99

The Golden Jubilee 'Love-feast'   **Sister Gladys Holmes**

This was the atmosphere of the whole evening during which the Governor General thanked God for bringing Sister Jessie to Jamaica; and presentations were made to Sister Jessie and Sister Elsie Bemand, the first West Indian deaconess, now retired but still very active. We were a diverse crowd with one great thing in common - a deep sense of thanksgiving to God for what He had done, and still is doing, through and with the West Indian Deaconess Order.

It was a tremendous privilege to share in that thanksgiving, and worth changing beds thirteen times in twenty nights in order to be there!'

Source: A Way of Serving (Autumn 1979) p.9

Memorial Service for Sister Jessie Kerridge MBE, July 2001

Canada

The Methodist Church in Canada had a well-established Deaconess work, which followed the American Methodist Episcopal Church pattern, and which was based in Toronto, but from time to time the Wesley Deaconess Order had connections with it. The first mention came in October 1913 when the Deaconess Institute Committee 'gave its approval to Miss Laura Dickinson doing Deaconess work in Canada.' At that time Laura Edith Dickinson was a student in the College, having been accepted as a candidate in March 1913. On 8th December the Warden reported that he had received satisfactory reports from Toronto about her,[41] but there is no record of her being consecrated as a Wesley Deaconess and her name does not appear in the *Stations*. It is possible that this was an unofficial arrangement and she decided not to become a Wesley Deaconess or she married and left before being consecrated.

The next time Canada is listed is in 1924 when Sisters Elsie Ward and Margaret Saunders were appointed. However, Elsie was apparently only there for the one year as in 1925 she was 'resting', while Margaret is recorded as being at 'Toronto – Board of Evangelism and Social Services'. The station disappeared in 1926, presumably when Sister Margaret resigned and married the Rev. J. W. Schofield in Toronto on 2nd June that year.[42]

From 1950-56 Sister Isabel Squires BA was seconded to the United Church of Canada 'by special arrangement'. In 1975 Mrs. Isabel Clark (formerly Sister Isabel Squires) applied for re-instatement as a Wesley Deaconess, but, because of the difficulties of receiving back someone of retiring age who was domiciled abroad, after correspondence it was agreed that she could not be re-instated.[43] Sister Sarah Jackson was also in Canada, but just for the one year of 1951-52, after which she was stationed at Birmingham (Rocky Lane).[44] In the summer of 1952 Sarah wrote from Canada:

> Work in such a cosmopolitan area is both interesting and educating. Enrolling ten scholars one Sunday morning I found they represented six nationalities, French, German, Russian, Polish, Ukranian, Japanese, and others have come since then. The majority are Ukrainian. Hence we have a Ukrainian Minister on the

41. WDIMins II pp.37, 48, 52
42. *WDO Stations* 1924-1926; *The Agenda* (June 1926) p.4
43. WDIMins IV 9 June 1975, 9th January 1976
44. *WDO Stations* 1950-56

staff, and he conducts a Communion service at this mission once per quarter . . . The reception given to me has been really wonderful, and I have been bombarded with invitations to address meetings. I have already been to eighteen churches in the city . . . I have started a junior choir of girls. They look perfectly angelic in their surplices, but they are lovely singers and so quick to learn tunes. I am thoroughly enjoying this piece of my work.[45]

Over the years Wesley Deaconesses were involved in work in different parts of the world, often for short periods of time. It is important to note these in order to give as complete a picture as possible of the scope of the overseas work of the Order.

Peru and Spain

The General Committee on 17th June 1913 was informed that 'Sister Isabel Adams desires to work in South America'.[46] Sister Isabel entered the Order in 1910 and was consecrated in May 1913. On 22nd January 1914 she sailed on the *SS Orcoma* from Liverpool to Lima, Peru, where she was going to work under the auspices of the Evangelical Union of South America, which was a missionary society with the Revs. J. Stuart Holde, G. Campbell Morgan and Dr. Len Broughton on its Committee.[47]

Voyage to Peru of Sister Isabel Adam	**The Warden**

Sister Isabel will have a most interesting voyage. Her ship, after calling at some Spanish and Portuguese ports, and Las Palmas in the Canary Islands, goes to St. Vincent and down to the eastern coasts of South America, through the Straits of Magellan to the Western coast of South America, calling at Pernambuco, Bahia, Rio, Santos, Monte Video, Punto Arenas, Coronel Talcahuano, Valparaiso, Coquimbo, Antofagasta, Iquique, Arica, Mollendo, Callao.

Source: Flying Leaves (February 1914) p.21

Isabel had learned Spanish for this appointment and had also taken a nursing course. While on her journey she wrote from Valparaiso on

---

45. *WDMag.* (July 1952) p.16
46. WDIMins II p.40
47. *FL* (February 1914) p.21

4th March about her voyage. Most of the other passengers had disembarked there leaving her as the only English-speaking passenger. She wrote:

> Most of the time I have been studying Spanish, and I have begun to feel that I know a little. I have enjoyed the voyage very much, and have been very conscious of the prayers of friends at home. I am, however, very glad to be so near to my destination, and am looking forward eagerly to my work. I see by the papers that last week Lima was the scene of riots and bloodshed. I know not how we shall find it on arrival, but I am not afraid. I know all of you at Ilkley will be praying specially for me, and this new work at this time. I pray that you all there may be given great joy in your ministry of intercession for needy South America.[48]

The first World War, declared on 4th August 1914, disrupted communications with deaconesses working abroad and in December the Warden reported that, although he had had no direct news of Isabel, the Evangelical Union of South America had told him that despite being unable to send out money to its missionaries since the outbreak of war they knew that they had sufficient funds to meet their needs.[49] However, definite news came from Isabel herself in early 1915 when she wrote that she was well, very busy and that

> the effect of the war in Peru is disastrous. Hundreds of people here are out of work. The cotton trade is, I believe, absolutely at a standstill. Paper money has been introduced, and the trouble is that it is not worth the paper on which it is printed, and it becomes increasingly difficult to do any shopping. As a Mission, too, we are feeling the effect. We are trying to economise in every possible way and yet keep the work in full swing.[50]

Later she wrote contrasting the 'animated fashion plates' of Lima, who had nothing 'to live for' with the terrible living conditions of the poor. Further news of Isabel Adams and her experiences in Peru was given in the October issue. It is obvious that she was encountering many difficulties with the different culture,

---

48. *FL* (May 1914) pp.73-74
49. *FL* (December 1914) p.159
50. *FL* (January 1915) p.4

predominate (Roman Catholic) religion and lack of nursing and hospital facilities. There seemed to be a great fear of sickness and so many ill people were left unattended. She commented that she had started a Girls' Club for the over 14s, but it had to meet on a Saturday afternoon as it was not safe for young people to be out at night. The library which she had opened for the girls had been a great success as 'the literature placed before the public here is disgraceful'. As Sister Isabel was hoping to start a drill class and to form a 'Purity League' she appealed for suggestions on running a Girls' Club and for 'information on crafts for girls'.[51]

Isabel Adams stayed in Lima until late 1923 and then Warden reported that 'after a rest she is hoping to go abroad again, to some Spanish speaking country'. The rest seems to have referred not only to her stressful time in Peru, but also to her recovering from an operation and so in the *Stations* for September 1923 she is listed as

'waiting appointment'.[52] In 1924 Sister Isabel's wish was granted as she went to Barcelona, Spain where she remained until her death in 1953.

The first news of her Spanish appointment was given in the March issue of *The Agenda* saying that she had settled in Barcelona and the Warden commented that 'it is pioneer work and difficult, but Sister Isabel is used difficulties and we are confident that she will prevail'.[53] After this very little is heard of Sister Isabel until a note in *The Agenda* of June 1928 stated that she was sailing to Barcelona, so, presumably she had been home on furlough.[54] News from Spain was very sparse, because of the unrest, coups and rebellion which culminated in the Spanish Civil War (1936-39), and was followed by the second World War (1939-45). However, in 1936, Sister Edith Bolton who was travelling 'in those parts' must have been a very welcome visitor for Isabel. When she was able to send a letter home Isabel described the first few days of the Civil War and its effect on the people. Apparently, she was told that the British Consul had

*Sister Isabel Adams
(Peru and Spain), 1914*

---

51. *FL* (February 1915) p.12, (October 1915) p.81
52. *The Agenda* (December 1922) p.11, (February 1923) p.11; cf. *WDO Stations* 1914-23
53. *The Agenda* (March 1924) p.3
54. *The Agenda* (June 1928) p.15

advised all the women and children to leave to which Isabel replied, rather characteristically, 'I know nothing about it; I'm not going.' So, although thousands of foreigners left, Isabel felt she was needed and refused to go. She was convinced that '. . . in the new Spain there will really be a place not for religion but for God'.[55]

During 1938 *The Agenda* printed three letters from Sister Isabel, which had been received either by the Order or the Mission House, and they paint graphic pictures of the conditions under which she was living and working. She urged everyone not to worry if they did not hear from her and that the principle that 'no news was good news' should be accepted as, if anything happened to her, someone would be left to let them know. She had been busy distributing food from the consignments she had received and mentioned, almost in passing, that there was constant bombing, but that all 'our folk' seemed to be all right – 'The condition of the city is terrible; glass everywhere. People are living in the underground railway . . . Please pray on and pray through.' Isabel's courage and faith shone through a letter she sent on 14th July telling of her delight that 27 women 'wished to confess their faith in Jesus Christ as their Saviour', that she had translated the Covenant Service and used part of it at her meetings to good effect. So, although 'recent heavy bombardments have rendered hundreds homeless' she felt that these 'signs of spiritual awakening confirm my faith in the triumph of the Republic.' The last letter emphazises the tragic events occurring in Barcelona, with almost non-existent transport, little electricity, constant bombardments, homes and businesses destroyed and people driven to suicide.[56]

Naturally, Sister Isabel was very much in the thoughts and prayers of the Order and the 1938 Convocation received a letter acknowledging a gift sent from the previous Convocation to help provide food for the destitute and in it she spoke of 'peace of heart amid distressing surroundings'. A further retiring collection for the Fund for Spanish Relief raised over £11.[57] Then the Mission House received a postcard on 13th February 1939 and the Warden commented cryptically that the surrender of Barcelona had 'spared it the customary horrors' and Convocation decided to send Isabel £5 from the proceeds of the Ceylon Fund Missionary Anniversary.[58]

55. *The Agenda* (October 1936) p.3
56. *The Agenda* (April 1938) pp.16-17, (October 1938) p.15, (December 1938) pp.11-12
57. Mins. of Conv. (1937) p.15, (1938) pp.19, 24; *The Agenda* (June 1938) pp.16, 19
58. *The Agenda* (March 1939) pp.6-7, 12; Mins. of Conv. (1939) p.30

Postcard from Barcelona, February 1939

Sister Isabel Adams

No news to give you save I am carrying on as before. I hope you received cablegram sent last Sunday. Please do not send money until I ask for it. Just heard from one of the boys who was reported dead in January, 1937. We never believed it. How great are the Lord's mercies!

Source: The Agenda (March 1939) p.7

Isabel's sister passed on a letter, dated 15th March, which said that the mail was very erratic, but hopefully things would get back to normal in due course and, while the food situation was reasonable, what the money there was had little value and so the people were unable to purchase the goods they needed. She, herself, was financially all right – the chief thing she was missing was 'lard', so she had not been able to do 'any baking for several weeks'.[59] Convocation each year remembered Sister Isabel and sent its greetings by letter and with gifts. Even after the end of the Civil War conditions did not improve and the new regime was only able to maintain its authority with harshness, but Isabel struggled on with determined courage.

Barcelona, 1943   **Sister Isabel Adams**

Last week we did not have a single ration of bread. To-day, just before dinner, we got a double ration, so we had very special reason to give thanks . . . So far as the work is concerned there is no change. Legally only twelve persons may meet together for any purpose – party, dance, conference, etc., without special permission. Any number over 12 is considered a clandestine meeting. So we go on praying and praising. He understands. He undertakes. That is my strong consolation.

Source: The Agenda (December 1943) p.6

By 1946 Sister Isabel was able to have a short furlough, but soon returned to Barcelona, then she paid a short visit home in 1949.[60] Nothing further is to be gleaned about Isabel Adams until

---

59. *The Agenda* (April 1939) pp.9-10
60. *The Agenda* (Christmas 1946) p.11; Mins. of Conv. (1945) p.62, (1946) p.71, (1949) p.100

the announcement of her death on 9th September 1953 with the comment that 'hers was a wonderful and devoted ministry, and in time of war, privation and persecution she remained at her post and cared for people'.[61] The Chairman of the Spain District and General Superintendent, the Rev. George Bell, paid a glowing tribute to her in the obituary printed in *The Wesley Deaconess Magazine*.

Obituary of Sister Isabel Adams, died 9th September, 1953

The work of Sister Isabel, Deaconess and Missionary, extended over forty-two years and was done in three spheres:

1911-1914, as a Deaconess at the Queen's Hall Mission, Hull;
1914-1923, as a Missionary with the Evangelical Union of South
          America at Lima, Peru;
1924-1953, as a Deaconess in our work in Barcelona, Spain.
... [account of her work] ...

When the war [Spanish Civil War] ended everything was in a chaotic state. Every department of life presented first-class problems, under a new Regime which had to treat everybody as an enemy until they were either dead or in abject submission. All meetings were banned. The Roman Church found itself possessed of its old power and lost no time in using it against all "heretics". Therefore, our work had to face hostility ...

During some four years Sister Isabel had to handle these things singlehanded (sic) ... This stouthearted (sic) servant of God held on and gave her all in the service of God and of our people in Barcelona.

It was a great joy to her to see our new Church taking shape, and it gave us all deep pleasure to see her "Open" the door for the Dedication Service on 17th January, 1953. Her strength had been failing for more than a year, and she quietly answered the Call to Higher Service on 9th September, 1953. We are confident that the seed she was privileged to sow will continue to bear harvest for many years.

George Bell

Source: The Wesley Deaconess Magazine (December 1953) pp.20-22

Sister Isabel's appointments from 1914, both in Peru and Spain, were unusual and demanded a great degree of dedication, courage and fortitude, which was typical of the deaconesses, who served both abroad and at home.

---

61. *WDMag.* (December 1953) p.14

France

Sister Elise Mahy (France), 1914

In June 1913 the General Committee was informed that Sister Elise Mahy was offering for work in France and subsequently she was appointed to Le Havre in September. In May 1914 *Flying Leaves* published profiles of a number of deaconesses and their work, often by the sisters themselves and Sister Elise described the little Methodist Church in Le Havre, which had a membership of 94 with 60 adherents. The Sunday School of 120 scholars met before the morning service. The church itself, with a seating capacity of 250, was in the centre of the town, then there was a hall, hidden in the working class area, which could hold 200 people, and another small rented hall in the factory district. Sunday morning services were held in the chapel and large hall and evening ones in all three places, as well as weekly lantern lectures. Open-air meetings were forbidden by law and 'long working hours, late dinners and no early closing day' made it difficult to organize meetings. In the church the Sunday morning service (presumably in French) was followed by an English service and during the winter Sunday afternoons the Schoolroom had been open and many nationalities had met together there. An average of eight attended the Women's Meeting, but Sister Elise had been well-received in people's homes and was 'often asked to pray and read something out of my "book"; sometimes by those indifferent to "religious" meetings. Most of those among whom I work have been brought up in the Church of Rome.'[62] However, by September 1915 she was listed as 'not at present available for appointment' and in 1917 as 'temporarily resting'. It was reported to the General Committee in October 1919 that Sister Elise Mahy had resigned from September 1st on the grounds of 'health and home claims'.[63] Finally, it is interesting to note that the *Stations* for 1915-19 have Sister Annie Clymo doing Red Cross Nursing in France, where she was joined by Sister Mary Gossling.[64] Unfortunately there are no records of the work done at this time by either of these sisters.

---

62. *FL* (May 1914) pp.74-5
63. WDIMins II p.40; *WDO Stations* 1914-17; WDIMins II p.147
64. *WDO Stations* 1915-19

The Falklands

Just as a point of interest, to show how far and also how early, news of the work and effectiveness the work of the Wesley Deaconess had spread we learn that in 1910 a request for a deaconess was received from the Falkland Islands. The Warden conveyed this request to the Order, explaining that the Islands were about as far away as one could get, describing its geographical position and climate and asking for volunteers. Apparently the Governor of the Islands was visiting Britain and so any deaconess who responded to the call would be able to travel back with him in November. It seems that the Free Church there had a former Cliff College student as Pastor, who reported that the small population was English speaking and that the life would be lonely, but the work rewarding. However, either no one volunteered or no one suitable was available as on 12th June 1911 Robert Johnson, presumably the Pastor, wrote to Bradfield, giving him an account his work in the Falklands and regretting that no deaconess had joined him.[65]

---

65. *FL* (November 1910) p.156, (September 1911) pp.121-22; WDIMins I p.374

Chapter 6

From the Beginning –
A Brief Historical Overview

The Rev. Dr. Thomas Bowman Stephenson, well-known as the founder of the National Children's Home, was also the initiator of the Wesley Deaconess Order. He had long recognised that there was a rôle for dedicated women to play in the Wesleyan Methodist Church. In fact, as early as September 1868, when he was minister at Fletcher Street Wesleyan Methodist Church, Bolton, he wrote in the church magazine of 'Miss Entwistle, our deaconess'.

He started The Children's Home (the original name) in 1869 and as it developed he quickly realised that it would be necessary to have a group of women to help care for and teach the children: such women would need to be well-trained and, after a probationary period, would be 'set apart' specifically for this work. So here were the two important elements which, right from the beginning and down the years, formed the backbone of deaconess work – the deaconess must be efficient, with her training recognised by the Church, and she must be called of God and set apart by the Church for this work.

From the beginning the physical care of the children in The Children's Home went hand in hand with concern for their spiritual welfare. Many of the Sisters were able to engage in evangelistic mission work, not only to the children themselves, but also to the women of the neighbourhood, particularly harassed mothers and elderly women. Obviously there was great opportunity for such work within the Church as the success of Hugh Price Hughes' 'Sisters of the People' and other similar organisations evidenced. So we find bands of 'deaconesses' being established, for example, in the London East End, Leeds, and Manchester Missions, as well as in Halifax and Rugby. In fact, many churches and missions which were becoming involved with 'The Forward Movement',[1] attracted by its informality and spontaneity, were anxious to set up such

---

1. 'The Forward Movement' was an evangelistic and social movement involving the setting up of the City Missions/Central Halls and attempting to make contact with the unchurched masses. cf. Rupp, Davies, George, eds., *The History of the Methodist Church in Great Britain*, (1983) Vol. 3 pp.136-37, 139, 311-12

groups. The scene was set for an explosion of unco-ordinated groups up and down the Connexion, but fortunately Thomas Bowman Stephenson managed to create order out of potential chaos by starting the Wesley Deaconess Institute, because he realised that the work was so important that it needed to be authorised by the Church and recognised as an official 'order of ministry'.

Unfortunately Stephenson's idea of starting an institution for training both men and women for work in The Children's Home was not received with great enthusiasm. In fact, a Minute for 17th November 1872 reads:

> While the Committee approved generally of the scheme, it should not seek immediately to carry it into effect, but wait for the indications of Divine Providence respecting it: that when any suitable candidates offered themselves their cases might be considered.[2]

However, on 21st March 1873 two men and one woman were accepted for training. That year Stephenson also had contact with the 'Metropolitan Methodist Lay Mission', which used deaconesses in house-to-house visiting, Bible classes, women's meetings and sick visiting and, becoming even more convinced of the value of deaconess work, wrote a series of articles in *The Methodist Family* on women's work in the Church. In 1890 Stephenson published *Concerning Sisterhoods* in which he traced the development of, and commented on, deaconess work right from the time of the Early Church to his own day and put forward his 'essential ideas'.

Principles for Deaconess Work
Rev. Dr. Thomas B. Stephenson

1. There must be vocation though no vow . . .
2. There must be discipline without servility . . .
3. There must be association, not excluding freedom . . .

Source: *Concerning Sisterhoods* (T. B. Stephenson, 1890) pp.62-70

On the question of uniform Stephenson explained that he had been against a specific dress until he had observed for himself the benefit of it during the Franco-Prussian War when the Kaiserswerth

---

2. Quoted in William Bradfield, *The Life of Thomas Bowman Stephenson* (1913) (hereafter Bradfield) p.172 – not in WDO records, probably in The Children's Home ones.

Sisters were recognised and respected wherever they went. He felt that a distinctive uniform would not only open up more opportunities for service, but would also form a protection for his deaconesses against unwelcome attentions.

With great insight and vision Stephenson outlined the areas of work where deaconesses might be used within the Church. Firstly, as it was then extremely difficult for any non-conformist girls to become trained nurses, he felt this matter needed to be addressed and that trained Christian deaconess-nurses could render great service both to the patient and the church. Secondly, trained workers could provide staff for places such as 'orphanages, asylums, homes for the aged poor' and other such institutions. Thirdly, deaconesses would be ideally suited to be very effective visitors, thus relieving 'the minister'. Fourthly, deaconess-nurses could be usefully engaged in helping with the social concerns of large city churches. However, Stephenson was not only concerned with large city churches, but also appreciated the needs of rural Methodism and so, fifthly, he suggested that a deaconess could be employed in a village or group of villages, unable to sustain a minister. Here she would live and work in the church and community, as 'a sort of pastor of the little flock', perhaps even being allowed to preach 'if necessity did occur'. Forestalling criticism on the grounds of cost Stephenson was at pains to emphasise that in many cases the volunteers would give their services, though some might need financial support. Even so he insisted 'the cost of maintenance of such women should be very small'.

Stephenson initially felt that any Deaconess Institute which was established should not be under the direct control of the Conference. While the office of deaconess should be recognised by and have a place in church life the actual 'management and maintenance of the Deaconess Institutions should be in the hands of individuals, sustained and guaranteed by small sympathetic committees'. The 'stationing' of deaconesses should be arranged between the deaconess, the local circuit or church and the Deaconess House. Thus, in these early days, deaconess work would be recognised and respected by the Church, but the whole Church would not be committed to the experiment.

Mewburn House

On 19th June 1890 Stephenson was able to write to the Editor of *The Methodist Times* to report: 'I am thankful to be able to announce that this project has now taken practical form . . .' The same month a preliminary prospectus was issued indicating the purpose of the Institute, qualifications for entry, details of training and courses, domestic arrangements – board and lodging, finance, uniform – commitment to the work and stationing. The first Deaconess House at 7 St. Agnes Terrace, London opened in July 1890, with Sister Rita Hawkings as Sister-in-Charge and one probationer. It was named after Mr. Mewburn who gave a gift of £500 which enabled Stephenson to buy the property. On 28th August 1890 he wrote to the paper again saying that the Institute was now operational and he would

> be happy to hear from any ladies who may desire to give themselves to this work. Letters of inquiry respecting terms and conditions will be duly answered. But let me say we do not desire to hear from persons who simply are on the look-out for a situation. We desire women of good education, who feel themselves called by the grace of God, to devote themselves to His service.[3]

In particular he needed 'a godly lady' who was a trained nurse with, or was willing to obtain, the midwifery certificate. The work developed rapidly and by January 1891 there were six deaconesses resident in Mewburn House. Then in the spring of 1893 the Institute, keeping the name of Mewburn House, moved from 7 St. Agnes Terrace to 84 Bonner Road. This had originally been the home of Dr. Stephenson, but when he found it necessary to move further from the headquarters of The Children's Home, it became the base for the Wesley Deaconess Institute giving more facilities for the work and having accommodation for 12 Sisters as well as the Sister-in-Charge. By 1894 the Institute was so firmly established that the 1895 Wesleyan Methodist Conference agreed to a constitution being drawn up, but it did not achieve Connexional status until 1901-02. Thereafter many more applications for the services of deaconesses were received from circuits, and these were all approved when an agreed amount was paid to the Institute.

---

3. *Methodist Times* (28th August 1890) p.889

Dr. Stephenson tendered his resignation as Principal of The Children's Home to the 1900 Conference, but remained in the active ministry and accepted an invitation to become the Superintendent Minister of the Ilkley Circuit, in the Halifax and Bradford District, Yorkshire, from September 1900. However, he continued his work with the Wesley Deaconess Institute, assisted by Dr. Gregory, who had been appointed his successor as Principal of The Children's Home.

November 1901 saw the first proposals for a separate magazine for the Wesley Deaconess Institute. Up till now the Institute had had a small section in The Children's Home magazine, *Highways and Hedgeways: The Children's Advocate*, but it was now decided to issue quarterly *Flying Leaves from the Wesley Deaconess Institute* with the Warden as Editor. The name was borrowed from a German organization which helped care for children in need. The magazine was a great success and quickly became a monthly publication when it was realized that it fulfilled a need of keeping the deaconesses in touch with the Institute and each other, as well as spreading information about the Institute and its work far and wide.

Yet another sign that the Institute was an established institution was the desire for a distinctive badge. The small committee, set up in November 1901, reported and the General Committee adopted a Maltese Cross as the Badge of the Order.

The Deaconess College, Ilkley

A very early picture of Ilkley College: the tower was removed by 1903

In 1902 the headquarters of the Institute moved to Ilkley. There seem to have been two main reasons for this: one, Stephenson was now based in the Ilkley Circuit, and two, as the Institute had become a Connexional Institution, extra accommodation was required so that more deaconesses could be trained and the work developed to meet the needs of the circuits at home and requests from abroad. Realizing how the deaconess work was developing and the calls upon his time, Stephenson felt that he should devote all his energies to the Order by committing himself to it full-time. However, the Order was not in a position to afford to maintain a full-time Warden and the Conference had not been asked to provide a minister devoted to this work. Moreover, as it was equally obvious that the headquarters of the Institute could not be expected to move around with Stephenson every three years or so, he was of the opinion that if he were to continue as Warden it would be necessary for the Order's base to be firmly established nearby. A large building, formerly a boys' school, was purchased for £4,500 with the help of donations, a bank advance and later, in 1903, a grant of £3,000 from the Twentieth Century Fund. After some necessary alterations the 'Wesley Deaconess College' was established. It was emphasised by the Warden at Convocation in 1902 that the Conference and Church's recognition of the Order meant an increased responsibility and as 'their ministry to Christ & souls could only be justified by its fruits' he urged all present 'to a fuller dedication of themselves to their holy service'.[4] From this it is obvious that great hopes were placed on the Order having a permanent home and being able to develop its training programme, so that the Sisters would be as well-equipped as possible to serve the Church.

Wesley Deaconess College, Queen's Road, Ilkley

It would provide accommodation for the Offices of the Institute, the residence of a Warden, & the Training of 27 (twenty-seven) Students. In addition to which, it was designed to be the Mother House of the Order & to provide a Home for the Deaconess-Evangelists, & for other members of the Order who might need rest. It was hoped also that ultimately in connection with this property some special provision might be made for retired Deaconesses.

It was expected that the new building would be available for occupation in September next. This would involve the removal of the Training work from London to Ilkley . . .'

Source: Records of Convocation (1892-1935) (Thursday 25th April 1902)

---

4. RConv. (25th April 1902)

Clearly the Conference must have appreciated Stephenson's work with the Wesley Deaconesses as the Rev. T. H. Mallinson was appointed to the Ilkley Circuit as his pre-collegiate assistant in 1902, thus enabling Stephenson to move from the circuit manse into the College. Stephenson intimated that he wished to pay for the accommodation of himself and his family, but the Sub-Committee insisted that as they all gave such valuable service to the Institute 'no such payment ought to be made'.[5] By now Stephenson had realized it would not be practicable for him to move to another circuit from Ilkley and so he gave up any idea of accepting another appointment in order to concentrate on his work with the Order. However, the fact that he was still regarded by the Conference as a minister in the full work and in 1905 was appointed as Chairman of the Halifax and Bradford District, surely indicates that the Connexion appreciated both the man and his work.

Arrangements for the opening of the College were put in the hands of the Leeds and Bradford members of the General Committee. Although it had been hoped to take in the first students on 1st September 1902 their admission was postponed till 30th September, when, in spite of workmen still putting the finishing touches to the building, 17 students started their studies. The official opening had to be delayed, but Thursday 30th October at 3.00 p.m. was finally set for the dedication. Many people, especially those associated with the Institute, were present and the President of Conference, the Rev. John Shaw Banks, in dedicating the building declared:

> Hitherto the work of Wesley Deaconesses has been, to
> a very large extent, experimental; it now passes out of
> the experimental stage, and acquires a local habitation
> and a name.

He went on to praise the enthusiasm and foresight of Dr. Stephenson in establishing the Deaconess Institute, saying that 'there is an enormous amount of good work which if it is not done by women will not be done at all, and there is a great deal more work that can better be done by women than by men'. He agreed with Stephenson's judgement that training was important so that the work could be most effective. Many more speakers, some from other denominations, added their good wishes for the success of the enterprise. An evening meeting followed the official dedication

---

5. WDIMins I pp.115-16, 117

service in which affectionate tribute was paid to Sister Dorothy Coy, Sister-in-Charge of Calvert House, the branch house in Leicester, who had recently died.[6]

The 1902-03 accounts showed a deficit of £1201.1s.3d. but, in view of the recent establishment of the College at Ilkley and the inevitable uncertainty of costs during that first year of operation, this was not considered unsatisfactory and Stephenson pledged himself to try to raise income in the coming year, so that the Institute could be run economically and be settled on a sound financial basis. Most of the Minutes from this time onwards deal with domestic arrangements in relation to the smooth running of Ilkley College, for example, the identification of Stephenson's private furniture and books, some of which were bought for £75.6s. for the use of the students. Various appointments, general financial matters and the examination and acceptance of candidates are also covered.

When it became generally known in 1907 that Dr. Stephenson had been advised by his doctors to retire, he wrote a rather apologetic personal note in the July 1907 issue of *Flying Leaves* in which he admitted that it would be 'a terrible wrench . . . to retire from all responsibility for a great Christian enterprise which he [had] been permitted to establish'.[7] In the Wesleyan Methodist Conference Agenda of 1907 the Institute expressed its gratitude to him on the occasion of his 'resignation (under imperative medical orders) . . . as Warden . . .' and resolved that a fitting tribute should be printed in the *Minutes of Conference*. Three names were submitted to the Conference as his successor – the Revs. William Bradfield, BA, W. Hodson Smith, and William E. Sellers. It was felt appropriate to include a brief history of the Deaconess work and it was noted that the Order now consisted of 98 consecrated or fully accredited Deaconesses and 56 Probationer Deaconesses at work and 19 accepted for training, making a total of 173. A detailed breakdown is given which showed how the Order had grown numerically and in scope since Dr. Stephenson first opened Mewburn House in July 1890.

---

6. *FL* (December 1902) pp.180-89 cf. (January 1903) pp.4-7; WDIMins I pp.123-24
7. *FL* (July 1907) p.100

Growth of the Institute (1890-1907)

5 are Officers of the Institute.

2 maintain and manage the Doddington Home of Rest.

80 are employed in circuits; 20 in London and 60 in the provinces.

37 are engaged in Central Missions; 8 in London and 29 elsewhere.

15 are engaged in Foreign Missionary work.

2 are Deaconess-Evangelists.

3 are at home for health or family claims.

10 are either Qualified or Probationer Nurses.

19 are Student-Probationers for College Training during the coming year.

Source: Wesley Deaconess Institute Minutes (1895-1910) pp.303, 292-93

The Second Warden – The Rev. William Bradfield, BA, (1907-20)

The resignation of Stephenson meant that various financial affairs and also the furnishing of the Warden's House had to be settled for the incoming Warden, the Rev. William Bradfield. A sub-committee decided that he should be entitled to the same allowances, around £200, as a minister in circuit with the actual details to be finalised by the Warden and the Treasurer. Estimates of £129 were approved for the refurbishment of the House and a further £129 for furnishings, because much of the existing furniture belonged to the Stephensons. It was agreed that in addition to the two sitting rooms already in the College a third one, with a fireplace, mantel-shelf and tiled hearth at a cost of £6.6s.0d. should be provided for visiting and sick members of the Order.

The Rev. and Mrs. William Bradfield attended meetings on 8th August and 24th September 1907 when they were welcomed as the new Warden and Lady Superintendent. In October Bradfield wrote in his first issue as Editor of *Flying Leaves* that he was still finding his feet, but was impressed by what he had learned so far; that he was delighted the Conference had 'definitely accorded to the Wesley Deaconess Institute the position which, in fact, it had already won for itself, of a separate and important department of our Connexional organisation' and that he was sure the Order would justify the confidence thus placed in it and 'develop into an absolutely essential and indispensible part of our Church life'. In this open letter he also hinted at his own special interests for

248

deaconess work which he hoped to pursue. The first opportunity that the whole body of deaconesses had to welcome Mr. and Mrs. Bradfield was at the 1908 Convocation when they were assured of their loyalty and love.

One of Bradfield's first actions was to review the finances of the Institute to see where savings could be made and additional income raised. In February 1908 he presented a detailed statement of the 'financial position and prospects' which, in brief, showed that there would be a deficit of £634.15s.6d. However, gifts totalling £226 had already been promised towards its reduction and his aim was to clear the debt by Convocation. Bradfield suggested economies aimed at making the running of the Institute more efficient and proposed that a request from the Wesley Guild Holidays to use the College for four holiday parties at a charge of £1 each per week should be granted. In the event not only did the College finances benefit from this arrangement, but £30 was raised for the Ceylon Deaconess Work Fund. Bradfield also arranged a tour of South West England by Sister Jeanie Banks, one of the Deaconess-Evangelists. This undoubtedly had a double purpose – an evangelistic one, but also a financial one as apparently deaconess work was little known in that part of the country and it was hoped if more interest could be aroused then some monetary contributions would follow and more Lady Associates, an important source for fund-raising, would be recruited. Even so for many years the finances of the Institute were in a parlous state and the Warden was forced to make many pleas for financial assistance to try to clear the debts as well as provide money for the on-going work and expenses of the Institute. One example of Bradfield's determination to improve the Institute's finances came with the application to the West Riding County Council Education Committee for a course of lectures on sanitation and hygiene to which, for a small charge, the public could be admitted.

A proposal was put forward in September 1909 for alterations to the College buildings, at a cost of £1,500-£1,800, to provide extra bedrooms. These could then be used to accommodate more fee-paying visiting students, who wished to have Christian training, but not necessarily become deaconesses. Not only would this give such women the benefits of attending lectures, but it would also generate income. Very optimistically it was pointed out that if the alterations were completed in time the opening could take place during the 1910 Wesleyan Methodist Conference in Bradford. However, although gifts of £700 were available, further support was not forthcoming and so the main scheme had to be shelved, but the heating system was overhauled and the gymnasium adapted for use as a lecture room. It is evident that Bradfield was bitterly disappointed about this set-back for he comments in the December issue of *Flying Leaves,* 'The special proposals . . . will have to be withdrawn for the present, though it is most desirable . . . that they should be carried out as soon as possible. I confidently believe that they would save the Committee from £100 to £200 a year . . .'[8] However, in spite of this the College hosted a Conference Garden Party on Saturday 16th July 1910.

The Order was saddened by the death of the Rev. Dr. Thomas Bowman Stephenson, the founder of the Institute, on 16th July 1912. A tribute to him was included in the October issue of *Flying Leaves.* At the 1913 Convocation, held most appropriately in Bradford, Sister Ruth Northcroft presented a portrait of Dr. Stephenson on behalf of the Order to the Committee. Then, many years later, in 1951, the Order received a £800 legacy from Dr. Stephenson's estate.[9]

The 1913 Conference reappointed Bradfield as Warden and, once again, that September the General Committee tried to tackle the need for extra accommodation at the College. A proposal for an extra 13 bedrooms and other facilities at a cost of £2,000, which would be provided by erecting another storey above the College Hall, was received sympathetically. The Hall was built right up to the kitchen garden of the Wells House Hydropathic Co. Ltd. on its southern boundary so there was no light from that side, only from the other side and the roof. However, after approaching the Company it offered 'to sell permanent rights of light on the south side of the College Hall (for four windows in the present building, and seven windows in the proposed upper-storey) for £150', which offer was accepted.[10] It was agreed to launch an appeal for the building work and that if two-thirds of the cost was promised it would go ahead. Although a Building Committee was appointed in June 1914 there is no indication that work started, presumably because of the outbreak of the First World War. Indeed the following June it was judged that, in the present circumstances, it was not expedient to launch a public appeal for any financial help

---

8. *FL* (December 1909) p.173; cf. (July/August 1910) pp.104-05
9. WDIMins II pp.28, 75; *Flying Leaves* (October 1912) pp.127-30; cf. WDO Finance Com. Mins, 28th May, 19th July 1951
10. WDIMins II pp.44, 49, 53-54; *FL* (November 1913) pp.156-58, (March 1914) p.36, (July/August 1914) p.102

and the Warden undertook to approach interested friends. Two other items of interest on the property front were the proposal from Ilkley Urban District Council that the College should have electricity. The Council offered to give advice and tender estimates and the matter was left to the Warden's discretion. Then there was a decision, in 1916, to 'purchase a quantity of dark green casement cloth from Burley Mills, from which curtains could be made for many of the windows; and the rest to be fitted with dark paper blinds' in order to comply with the requirements of the Lighting Restrictions in Ilkley, but nothing more is heard about the installation of electricity till 1921-22. In the 1915-16 Report a reference was made to the war and Zeppelin raids, which may have been the reason for Ilkley's 'black-out', and in September 1916 the College property was insured against aircraft damage.

The Warden indicated in 1917 that he intended, yet again, to press the forthcoming Conference for 'connexional financial recognition of the claims of the Institute'. Up to this time most of the money for the funding of the Institute had come from the circuits where the deaconesses were stationed, from subscriptions and donations raised by the Lady Associates, from private gifts and loans from sympathetic friends and collections at public meetings. Bradfield felt that not only should the church as a whole 'own' this valuable resource, but that the very fact of its receiving funding from the Connexion would enhance its status among the Methodist people and hopefully ease the ever-present financial pressures. It seems that the Warden's pleas to the Conference did not go unheard as in October he was able to report the Resolutions of Conference which recommended a grant to the Institute from the Home Mission Committee or from the Education Fund. He could be pleased with the ultimate result as the Education Committee gave the Institute £250 per annum and the Finance Committee of the Home Mission Fund was understood to be recommending to the Conference a grant of £200 per annum.[11]

Having been Warden since 1907 Bradfield felt that the time had come for him to retire from the Wardenship at the 1920 Conference. The Committee regretfully accepted his decision, paid tribute to his work and set up a nomination sub-committee. This sub-committee in February 1920, later confirmed by the General Committee,

---

11. WDIMins II pp.117, 123 cf. Report of General Committee 1917-18 (1st June 1917 to 28th February 1918) (between pp.130-31) where amounts granted are reversed.

submitted the name of the Rev. Dr. Charles Ryder Smith to the Conference as the next Warden. In fact Ryder Smith was appointed to Richmond Theological College as Systematic Theology Tutor and the Rev. William Russell Maltby became Warden with his stipend being set on the same scale as the tutors in the theological institutions. This surely indicates the growing status and acceptance of the Institute and the training given to the deaconesses and of the value that they were to the Church.

The Third Warden – The Rev. Dr. W. Russell Maltby, DD, (1920-40)

Conference, having appointed W. Russell Maltby as Warden, welcomed him and his wife at the October meeting of the General Committee when Maltby spoke of his impressions of the work, paying tribute to its founders, emphasising the great responsibilities the Order faced in the present changing times and of the new ventures he envisaged taking place. After three months in office Maltby presented his ideas on the development of the work. The financial situation, in the country, the Church and the Institute, had caused him to take stock, to talk to various people and to make the following observations:

> At present we bear the cost of [the Women's Auxiliary] candidates who afterwards offer for missionary work. If we were to meet the needs of Methodism we ought to provide for a two year period of training for our Deaconesses. This would mean accommodation for a larger number of students and some increase in the teaching staff. It would be wise also . . . to encourage the admission of paying students who came for training in the Christian faith and Christian service, though not necessarily pledging themselves for deaconess work.[12]

Having heard the Warden's statement the Committee gave him its backing and authorised an appeal to the Methodist people for support.

Considering that it had just appointed Maltby as Warden it seems a little strange to find that the same 1920 Conference should direct that

---

12. WDIMins II p.162

the Committee of the Wesley Deaconess Institute . . .
consider during this year the desirability of the
appointment of a suitable woman as Warden of the
Institute . . .[13]

What was the thinking behind this? Was it because it seems
right to have a woman in charge of a women's organisation? Was it
the beginning of feminism in Methodism? Was it the start of the
movement for 'women in the ministry'? Were women now feeling
that they had the right to take a more prominent rôle and place in the
Church? It would be interesting to know whether the proposal
emanated from men or women, from ministers or lay people. The
special committee set up to deal with this Conference resolution met
on 8th June 1921 and after much conversation

the following Resolution was unanimously passed, viz:-
The Committee having given consideration to the
question referred to it by the Conference, of the
desirability of a woman Warden of the Institute finds:

1. That the present constitution of the Wesley
   Deaconess Institute, as established by the
   Conference of 1907, provided that the Warden shall
   be a minister in full connexion with the Conference.

2. That, in the opinion of the Committee, the
   Conference arrangement is working well, and ought
   not for the present to be disturbed.

3. That, in the present situation, there are many duties
   falling to the Warden which can only be discharged
   by someone in such close touch with Methodism
   throughout the country as is only possible to a
   minister.

4. That, in the judgement (sic)of the Committee, the
   Conference ought to be free to select a woman for
   the office, when occasion arises, and that the
   necessary changes of the Constitution might then be
   made, so as to secure for the Woman Warden the
   opportunities and powers needful for the office.[14]

It seems that honour was satisfied – the matter had been discussed
and successfully sidelined – so Conference approved of the
resolution and there the matter rested until 1980 when Sister Yvonne

---

13. *WMMins. of Conf.* (1920) p.86
14. WDIMins II pp. 167-68; *WMMins. of Conf.* (1921) pp.53-54

Hunkin was appointed as 'Deaconess Warden' (1980-84), followed by Sister Sheila Parnell (1984-89) and then by Sister Christine Walters, who, in 1992, was named officially as Warden of the re-opened mixed Methodist Diaconal Order, without the *Minutes of Conference* listing a 'Ministerial Secretary'.[15]

Following the new Warden's proposal for the extension of training and enlargement of the College and his assessment of the financial position, the whole matter had been laid before the Home Mission Committee which had set up a sub-committee to consult with the Institute to consider whether an additional grant might be made. The Wesley Deaconess Committee suggested it would be beneficial for the Warden to be a member of the Home Mission Committee. The deliberations of the sub-committee and the Institute resulted in the Home Mission Committee recommending an extra grant of £250 on condition that the Education Committee increased its grant as well. Later the Home Mission Fund promised to continue this grant 'if the Institute showed promise of extension and wider service'. The Rt. Hon. T. R. Ferens MP proposed that there should be more advertising of deaconess work and backed this up by promising £100 towards it. Ideas of the best way to do this included postal appeals, advertisements in the Methodist Press, asking the Associate members to double their subscriptions, more public meetings and enlisting the help of the Women's Auxiliary. Maltby commented that the cessation of *Flying Leaves* in October 1915, for financial reasons during the war, had meant the loss of considerable publicity and he wondered if Mr. Ferens' offer might be modified – presumably he had in mind using it to launch and underwrite, certainly in its initial stages, another magazine. The idea of a monthly magazine was welcomed and *The Agenda* came into being in January 1922. A further idea floated, presumably by the Home Mission Committee representatives, was that the College might amalgamate with Cliff College. This was firmly rejected.

At long last the very necessary alterations to the College were put in hand and the money, which Bradfield worked so hard to raise before the onset of the war to finance his proposed extension and alterations, was put to good use. During the Christmas vacation of 1921-22 the work started. The old Library was divided into four bedrooms, a study and bathroom, while the old Committee Room was turned into a new library and the original prayer room or chapel restored to its proper use. Electric light, later extended to provide

---

15. *Mins. of Conf.* (1980-92)

more comfort and save expense, was installed. One can imagine how delighted Bradfield must have been to see at least part of his dream realised. In 1931 the College Prayer Room was refurbished and redecorated with most of the cost being defrayed by a gift of £50 from Dr. Peter Thomas of West Africa and, after considerable discussion in Convocation of how best deaconesses who 'had died in the work' should be commemorated, it was agreed that the names should be painted on a panel in the Prayer Room and also inscribed in a book. The names of the Revs. Drs. Thomas Bowman Stephenson and William Bradfield, who had died on 4th January, 1923, following a short, but serious, illness, were to be included.[16] It was decided that a fitting memorial to Bradfield would be the purchase of 'the bulk of his books and the presentation of them to the College Library with a suitable inscription' – apparently there were many on psychology and these were in great demand by the students. A portrait of Bradfield was presented to the College and placed in the library.

At the end of 1929 the General Committee was a little disturbed when it was reported that recent developments at Cliff College, with the suggestion that women might be admitted for special courses of study, had taken place. It was decided that the Warden should monitor the situation and, if anything was proposed which might be against the interests of the Wesley Deaconess Order, he was authorized to express the Committee's concern to those responsible. As noted earlier, in more recent years Ilkley College had been opening its doors to women who wished to have Christian training without necessarily having the vocation to join the Order, so it is little wonder that the prospect of a rival college competing for such students would set alarm bells ringing. It also had a financial dimension as the Institute had always had money problems and the loss of income from visiting students would have serious repercussions.

For a number of years Maltby had been concerned that the Trust for the College property ought to be renewed, but nothing further was heard about it. However, in December 1930 it was done and the new Trust consisted of 14 members. Of these, seven were Wesleyan Methodist ministers, the others being an insurance broker, a manufacturer, two accountants, a solicitor and two 'spinsters'.

---

16. RConv. (20th April 1931)

Methodist Union

With Methodist Union drawing ever closer, Sister Bessie (Roe), a group of deaconesses representing the United Methodist Deaconess Institute, and the Warden, the Rev. R. W. Gair, visited the 1930 Convocation held in London. Mr. Gair 'expressed his belief that our union will be a living Fellowship' and Sister Bessie struck a note echoed by all when she said, 'All I must have is the fullest opportunity to fulfil my calling, to reveal Jesus Christ.' Then apparently Convocation 'discovered a Primitive Methodist Deaconess whom we were entertaining unawares.' So deaconesses of the three branches of Methodism were well ahead with their plans for co-operation when Union happened. The General Committee decided in July 1930 that the Rev. R. W. Gair should be invited to attend its meetings and in December a sub-committee was appointed to meet with representatives of the United Methodist and Primitive Methodist deaconesses to discuss matters of mutual concern. Having talked to the United Methodist Warden, Mr. Gair, about the Retiring Funds of both organisations, it seemed that combining them would cause little problem. Negotiations between the Wesley Deaconess Order, the United Methodist Deaconess Institute and the Primitive Methodist authorities were very amicable and no difficulty was anticipated after Union took place.

Since the property at Ilkley had been purchased in 1902 various building, extension and alteration schemes had been proposed and a number had materialized. It was perhaps the prospect of the coming Methodist Union and a possible increase in numbers that caused the Warden, in December 1931, to report that accommodation at the College was still inadequate, especially with regard to the library and bedrooms. However, the lease of the house next door with an option to buy was offered to the College. After discussion a sub-committee with power to act was set up to explore the feasibility of this offer. The Warden was delighted to announce the following July that the house in question, 5 Queen's Road, had now been given to the College by an anonymous donor and a committee was deputed to oversee any alterations and its furnishings. The Warden and his family moved there, and so, after some refurbishment, the whole of the College premises was available for use by the staff and students. In total these improvements cost £475.

Naturally with Union came some reorganization. The full Deaconess Committee now consisted of 50 members of whom 30 were ex-Wesleyan, but for convenience it had been divided into two

– the London (Wandsworth House) Committee, consisting of ex-United Methodist members plus the Rev. R. W. Gair, [UM] the Rev. G. Wiles, [PM] the Rev. J. Gilbert [PM] and the Treasurers, which would be mainly concerned with Bowron House, the ex-United Methodist Training House, and the Ilkley House Committee consisting of the serving ex-Wesleyan Methodist members plus the Rev. R. W. Gair, [UM] the Rev. G. Wiles, [PM] the Rev. J. Gilbert [PM] and the Rev. Dr. T. J. Cope [UM] and the Treasurers, which would initially be chiefly concerned with Ilkley College.

Methodist Union meant that various administrative and organisational issues had to be settled. Since Union there had been two Wardens, but by 1935 only one was required, so it was agreed to recommend to the Conference that Dr. Maltby be appointed for a further three years from 1935, with Mr. Gair and the Rev. G. W. Thorn as joint secretaries. Mr. Gair had been the United Methodist Warden since 1922 and the committee was anxious that his expertise, especially his knowledge of his own deaconesses and their appointments, should not be lost. Equally the committee was of the opinion that Maltby's appointment as Warden should be extended to 1938, presumably until the problems associated with unifying the Orders were resolved and the Secretary was requested to prepare a 'reasoned statement' to submit to the Conference to this effect.

The Primitive Methodist Sisters had been based in the Sisters' Settlement at St. George's Hall, Bermondsey and it was decided to explore the possibilities of this East London Settlement being used in connection with the united Order. As noted earlier, in October 1933 23 ex-Primitive Methodist Sisters were recommended for acceptance and received the following year into the fellowship of the Order, which thus truly became the Wesley Deaconess Order of the Methodist Church.[17]

When the matter of nominating a Warden for appointment in 1938 arose reference was made to the 1921 Conference suggestion that the Committee should consider whether the appointment of a Woman Warden would be appropriate. Convocation was asked for its opinion, but decided that it was important to continue having a minister as Warden of the Order. As it turned out the matter could be shelved for the moment for, although Maltby had intended to retire in 1938, he had been persuaded to reconsider and agreed to continue. Therefore, the General Committee in December 1936

---

17. WDOMins III p.10; RConv. (April 1934)

asked that his Wardenship be extended for a further period from 1938 and this was granted for another three years. Hence in July 1939 a sub-committee was convened to recommend a name to the 1940 Conference for appointment in 1941 and decided upon the Rev. W. Harold Beales. However, because of ill-health Maltby felt obliged to retire in 1940, but he settled locally and maintained his contact with the Order. In consequence Beale's appointment was brought forward with effect from 1940. Arrangements about decoration and furnishings for the Warden's house were made and as Mr. Beales wished to have central heating because of his wife's health, and had offered to pay half the cost, this was installed.

The Fourth Warden – The Rev. W. Harold Beales, MA, (1940-52)

At the same time as the Order lost Dr. Maltby as Warden, the long-serving Rev. G. W. Thorn, a Committee member for 20 years and Ministerial Secretary for the last 13, decided to retire. He suggested that as Maltby would be on hand to assist the new Warden there was no real need to appoint another Ministerial Secretary and that Sister Margaret Statham's post as Secretary be made a Connexional appointment. The Executive Committee agreed; however, the General Committee, while concurring for 1940, emphasised that the appointment of a Ministerial Secretary was desirable. The post of Ministerial Secretary remained until 1992.

In 1928 it had been decided that the time spent by students in College should be extended from three to five terms and then supervised practical training was added in 1930. Maltby was convinced that this extra training was invaluable in the development of the students. In December 1937 he expressed concern that in the past six months 16 deaconesses had left the Order through retirement or resignation, leaving no one on the Reserve List – in fact, he had had to send out four students to fill emergency appointments before they had completed their training. Therefore he insisted that it would be necessary to accept more candidates, always being careful to select those of the right calibre. The result was that on 6th April 1938 he put forward a proposal for the extension of the College premises, together with an appeal to Synods to look for suitable candidates for the Order. After careful consideration it was felt that Maltby's suggestion of an extra 10 study bedrooms at a cost of £1,800 was too modest and that a larger building was required. A building sub-committee was formed and a mere fortnight later an architect had submitted provisional plans for a two-storey building:

> The plans provided 14 study bedrooms and a large lecture room together with additional baths and lavatories. He estimated the cost at £2895, without architect's fees, but including built-in wardrobes, study tables, and wash basins in each room.[18]

The outline scheme was accepted and complete plans requested for 3rd May. However, at that meeting the Warden reported he had received an offer of Ranmoor College (formerly the Methodist New Connexion Theological College, now the property of Sheffield Council) at a rental of £150 on a 99-year lease. However, although it had the advantage of being a purpose-built College, it provided less accommodation than Ilkley and offered little opportunity for building, so the committee reluctantly rejected the offer and accepted the architect's plan for the extension at Ilkley. Tenders were received and accepted and by the autumn of 1938 building work costing around £4000, including furnishing, had started with a completion date of 30th April. Eventually the opening ceremony, to be followed by a public tea and meeting, was scheduled for 20th September at 4.00 p.m. However, national events overtook these plans when war was declared and, understandably, the Warden cancelled the official ceremony. Appropriately the new building was called after the man who had been its prime mover, becoming known as 'The Maltby Wing'.

The Manchester Convocation in 1938 was given a civic reception at the Town Hall. This was the first time such an honour had been extended to the Order and indicates recognition of the increasing importance placed on the rôle of the Sisters in both church and community.

As 1940 would mark 50 years since Thomas Bowman Stephenson had separated the training of the Mission Sisters from the Children's Home Sisters, and as the ex-United Methodist Institute had started about the same time, it was felt that there should be some Jubilee celebrations. An added bonus would be that such celebrations would bring the Order to the attention of the Church and people and, hopefully, result in more candidates coming forward as well as an increased number of Associate members to

---

18. WDOMins III p.61

help with fund-raising. Ideas for the celebration included:

> . . . (1) a central Thanksgiving Service in connection with Convocation, (2) other thanksgiving services at suitable centres, (3) publication of a popular History of the Order, Sister Mary Hunter to be asked to edit.

The July meeting of the General Committee agreed that arrangements should be made, but deferred detailed discussion until the December. However, the outbreak of war intervened and nothing more is recorded of the project, though Mary Hunter did produce a 19-page booklet which she described thus: 'The following pages are not a history of the Order but a summary of facts relating to the origin, growth and work of the Order, especially for the use of Sisters. M. V. H.'

Sister Mary Hunter:
Tutor

The outbreak of the Second World War saw deaconesses serving in many different capacities. However, the war had an immediate effect on College life as part of Hunmanby Hall Methodist Girls' School, Filey, was relocated to Wheatley Lawn and High Clere, Ilkley, when the school's own premises were requisitioned by the army. The Warden, Beales, and ex-Warden, Maltby, acted as chaplains and some of the College staff assisted with lessons. As forces were billeted and many evacuees housed in the Ilkley area the students undertook visiting and also held services for the many elderly people who had been transferred to the Middleton Hospital. These experiences would serve the students well when they went from College into circuit and the wider world.

War meant a rise in the cost of living for deaconesses, as for the rest of the population, so it was decided that, instead of raising the deaconesses' allowances, to ask circuits and Missions, if possible, to make a 'one-off' gift to their own Sisters. Difficulties of a different nature occurred because of clothes rationing and the consequent shortage of some items of uniform. Then, as happened with the First World War, Convocation had to be abandoned in favour of regional meetings, with the ordinations in 1940-43 taking place in London, Reading and Nottingham. Inevitably the war in Europe and, later in the Far East, had repercussions on the Order, as recorded in chapters 3-5, in that Sisters serving overseas could not easily get home on furlough and a number were interned in China, while Isabel Adams found life in Barcelona very difficult.[19]

As the war meant that women had been engaged in jobs which would not have been available in earlier years and had to deal with very different social conditions, so more opportunities presented themselves in new areas of work, such as youth work and moral welfare. The consequence of this was that, in spite of the Maltby Wing extension in 1939, more accommodation was needed at Ilkley and when 'Linnburn', a property very close to the College, came on the market in 1945 it was purchased for £2,650, plus the cost of alterations, decoration and furnishings, for use as a hostel for 15 extra students and to provide a caretaker's flat.

Linneburn Hostel, Ilkley

In 1948 it was felt that the name of the Magazine should be changed from *The Agenda* and made more attractive. This resulted in a general review of publicity in order to raise awareness of the Order with a view to recruiting more candidates and gaining more financial support. Several suggestions for the new name were made, but finally *The Wesley Deaconess Magazine of the Methodist Church* was selected and so it remained until 1964, when it was changed to *Doers of the Word* and then in 1973 it became *A Way of Serving*.

In 1949 it was realised that the Warden was due to retire in 1952 and the wheels were set in motion to find a successor. It was also necessary to obtain a new Ministerial Secretary, following the retirement of the Rev. W. Lorne Cornish. This latter proved relatively easy and the Rev. A. Simpson Leck was nominated for immediate appointment. Unfortunately Mr. Leck was in the post for barely two years before ill-health forced his resignation in 1952 and he died on 24th July of that year. However, a replacement for Beales was more difficult, but eventually from nine possible names the sub-

---

19. WDIMins II p.138 (February 1942); Mins. of Conv. (June 1940) pp.33, 34, (April 1941) p.35, (April 1942) p.35, 37, (June 1943) p.44, (April 1945) p.62; *The Agenda* (April 1939) pp.9-10; Wesley Deaconess Order Minutes (1948-78) (hereafter WDOMins IV) 11th December 1953 cf. chapters 3, 4, 5

committee charged with the task drew up a short list. The names changed over the months, but finally the choice was between the Revs. George R. Osborn and Thomas M. Morrow. Then the former was ruled out because he was being considered for 'other Departments' (Education Department). So it was agreed that Mr. Morrow be asked to allow his name to go forward for nomination. The sub-committee had a contingency list in case he refused, but fortunately he accepted and his name was submitted to the Conference as first choice with that of the Rev. Wilfred Wade as second. The Conference duly appointed Morrow to serve from 1952. While all these negotiations were proceeding the Order was deeply saddened by the death of Dr. Maltby, the third Warden, on 9th January 1951.[20]

Death of the Rev. Dr. W. Russell Maltby
9th January 1951

. . . many Sisters paid tribute to his memory, and told how he had made Christ real in their lives. All spoke of him with very deep gratitude and affection, and even those who had not had the privilege of knowing him well could tell of his tremendous influence on their lives, and the life and work of the Order.

Source: Minutes of Convocation (1936-69) (April 1951) p.124

50th Jubilee Group 1952

The Executive Committee realised in March 1952 that it would be 50 years since the College at Ilkley opened in October 1902, having been preceded a few months earlier by the first Convocation of the Wesley Deaconess Order in Leeds, so that some celebrations would be appropriate. A Jubilee fund was opened and special meetings were held on 24th October at the College and in different parts of the country. It was hoped that the celebratory events would both raise the profile of the Order and bring in extra income. The Jubilee was deemed a success as not only was £2,170 raised, but perhaps, more important, 351 new Associate members and subscribers were recruited. It was felt that

---

20. WDOMins IV 19th April 1951; Mins. of Conv.(April 1951) p.124

the publicity had been valuable and should be built on, so the following suggestions were made – that there should be a Deaconess Meeting at Conference; that certain Deaconesses should be set aside to go on deputation as ministers did; and that girls in Methodist Schools should be made aware of the Order. Sister Dorothy Farrar, who was Vice-President of the Conference (1952-53), visited several schools during her Vice-Presidential year.

So Beales, having seen the Order through the troubled times of the War and the difficulties of the post-war years, retired in 1952. The General Committee paid him, both in its meeting and in the Conference Report, a glowing tribute and Convocation presented him with a book and a cheque. In April the Finance Committee was informed that £150 worth of Burnley Building Society shares had been purchased with the cheque and it was Beales' intention to hand them over to the Committee:

> . . . on the understanding that the income received on them shall be paid to him during his lifetime, and to his wife if she outlives him. Upon the death of the survivor, the shares shall become the absolute property of the Wesley Deaconess Order . . . the capital shall be held permanently intact . . . the income received being used for the benefit of the College Chapel, whether for additions to the Chapel Library or for the purchase of any other equipment.[21]

In 1968 Mrs. Beales relinquished her interest in the bequest and the money was reinvested. In 1974 it was agreed to use the money to purchase devotional books.[22] Tribute was paid to Beales when, in 1954, alterations, consisting of nine study bedrooms on the West and Middle Corridors and improvements to the Library, were made and the refurbished wing was named after him.

The Fifth Warden – The Rev. Thomas Manser Morrow, MA, (1952-64)

The Rev. Thomas M. Morrow became the new Warden of the Order at the beginning of the next Connexional year and prior to his arrival the Warden's house was refurbished. It is interesting to note that at last the need for some sort of parity was recognised when it was stated that in future the Warden's stipend should be the same as

---

21. WDO Finance Com. Mins. 28th May 1952
22. WDO Finance Com. Mins. 11th March 1968; 18th September 1974

that of Ministers in other Methodist Departments, namely £550 per annum. Another instance of the same thing had come earlier that year when Convocation was informed that the Ministers' Missionary Union would welcome deaconesses as members.

Sister Margaret Statham (Tutor)

Since the resignation of the Rev. A. Simpson Leck in 1952 the Order had been without a Ministerial Secretary but this was rectified in 1954 with the appointment of the Rev. Oliver Phillipson, MA. Just as a new face appeared the Order bade farewell to a long serving member of staff, for Sister Margaret Statham, who had been associated with the College at Ilkley in various capacities since 1931, left in January 1955 to become Secretary of the Women's Fellowship. Then in December 1960 Sister Dorothy Farrar gave notice that she intended to retire from the active work in September 1962 and so it would be necessary to find a new Vice Principal of the College. The Executive Committee convened a sub-committee which recommended Sister Lilian Topping as Vice Principal for three years from September 1962, with Sister Jean Miller being asked to join the tutorial staff at the same time with a view to becoming Vice Principal. A new Secretary of the Order was also needed and it was felt 'desirable that the Secretary should be resident in the College, and so be in close touch with the affairs of the Order'. The name of Sister Helen Smales was suggested for appointment from the Conference in 1961.

Recruitment had fallen so much that in September 1960 it was decided that 'Linnburn', acquired as a hostel in 1945 when more room was needed for student accommodation, should be closed temporarily and put on a 'care and maintenance' basis for 12 months. Then in October 1960 it was proposed to let the 15 study bedrooms and the Common Room to the Ilkley College of Housecraft from September 1965 to June 1966. However, in the spring another offer was made and 'Linnburn' was let as a hostel for Ilkley College of Education on a three-year lease at £250 per annum from 1st January 1966. By the autumn the College of Education thought it would probably require more teaching space and was offered the Maltby Class Room. Six of its students were accommodated in the Wesley Deaconess College. When, in the spring of 1967, the Order decided to sell the Ilkley property the

West Riding County Council was offered first refusal, but was only interested in purchasing 'Linnburn'. The Finance Committee was against the separate sale of 'Linnburn' and duly gave notice to the County Council of termination of the lease as from 31st March 1968. This was later extended until the end of July 1968.

Concern was expressed in 1961 about the effect that the Stewardship Campaigns, which were being run in many circuits and churches, might have on the finances of the Order. It was decided to write to the Circuits involved. The Finance Committee obviously felt that the Stewardship Campaigns were having an adverse effect on the Order's income as subscriptions had dropped by 1963 and this doubtless led to a publicity drive.

In December 1962 the Rev. Thomas Morrow had intimated that after 12 years he would be retiring as Warden in 1964. A sub-committee was appointed to consider names for nomination to the Conference. Seventeen names were submitted and a short list of seven was drawn up, but by February no clear favourite had emerged. Then the Warden suggested that the Rev. Geoffrey Litherland MA. who was serving in the Bahamas be approached. Mr. Litherland replied positively and so three names with reasoned statements were submitted to the Conference. Mr. Litherland was appointed as the Sixth Warden by the 1963 Conference.

The Sixth Warden – The Rev. Geoffrey Litherland, MA, BD, (1964-72) – Winds of Change

The Rev. Geoffrey Litherland could hardly have expected when he took over from the Rev. Thomas Morrow that he would be involved in such a great upheaval as occurred over the next few years. The decline in numbers of candidates, the closing of a number of appointments as well as the introduction of a third year of specialised training, all meant that fundamental changes were going to affect the Order.

In 1961 it had become obvious that the College course would need to be extended with a third year of specialised training. A sub-committee had produced a curriculum for training, which was accepted in general. So from September 1965 the deaconesses shared lectures with the Wesley College, Headingley, Leeds ministerial students. When it was learned that the Ministerial Training Department was considering the future of its theological colleges, including Headingley, it became urgent to address the question of where future deaconess students should be trained if Headingley closed. When the Conference of 1966 did decide on the closure of Headingley the Order felt impelled, after conversations with the Ministerial Training Committee, to face the likelihood of selling the Ilkley property. At first a move to Bristol, with its Methodist Theological College and the University, seemed to be a suitable proposition. Exploration was also being made about the Order being linked with Handsworth Theological College and the University of Birmingham. By the end of 1967 the die was cast and the Order decided that a move to Birmingham and co-operation with Handsworth College was the best option. So approval of the following scheme, together with a request that the Order be invited to share in any discussions, was solicited from the Ministerial Training Committee and the Conference:

> (a) that student candidates for the Deaconess Order be accommodated for training at Handsworth College from September 1968;
> (b) that the administrative centre and home for the Order be moved to the vicinity of Handsworth at the same time;
> (c) that the cost of the mutually agreed alterations to the Handsworth premises necessary for the accommodation provided in (a) and (b) be borne by the Deaconess Order;
> d) that the oversight of Deaconess students be maintained by the Order. Nothing in this scheme is to affect the separate disciplines of the Ministry and the Deaconess Order.

On 9th April 1968 an emergency meeting of the General Committee was called because 'of recent developments concerning the future of Ministerial Training'. The Warden gave a résumé of events whereby the Working Party on the Future of Ministerial Training, on which the Deaconess Order was represented, 'after following a strange procedure recommended on a majority vote "That Handsworth College be closed in 1969" '. However, the Ministerial Training Committee had refused to accept this and had tabled the following resolution to go to the Conference:

> (1) that the enlargement and improving of Hartley Victoria College be further considered;
> (2) that the enlargement of Wesley College Bristol goes ahead as planned;

(3) that Wesley House alterations go ahead as planned;

(4) that we aim to merge Handsworth College with another college by 1970;

(5) that Richmond College continues as at present.

The Warden reported that, as a consequence of all this, Hartley Victoria had been visited and it was a possibility as a base for training members of the Order. So it seemed that certain avenues were open, namely, '1. to stay where we are for another year. 2. to go to Manchester and throw in our lot there. 3. to go to Birmingham as already planned'. Conversations were being held between Handsworth and The Queen's College (Anglican) about setting up an ecumenical college in Birmingham and if this became a reality it was thought that the Order could most likely be associated with it 'either integrally or federally'. During the ensuing discussion Mr. Spensley, the Treasurer, said it was his opinion that it would be impossible for the Order to remain at Ilkley even for one more year. In due course the Committee confirmed its earlier decision to move to Birmingham. The decision having been taken appreciation was expressed to the Ilkley Circuit and other local friends for their co-operation over the past 66 years. Ilkley College closed on 14th June 1968 and the sale of it and the other property associated with it for £24,000 was finally completed in October 1968. The furniture from the College Chapel went on loan to Eastbrook Hall, Bradford where it was dedicated on Wednesday, 30th April 1969 and eventually in 1985 it was transferred to Christchurch, Ilkley.

In view of the Ministerial Training Committee's decision to participate in an ecumenical college the Order realised that it might only be connected with the old Handsworth College for two years and then could be involved with the new partnership formed by the amalgamation of Handsworth and The Queen's College in 1970. In the meantime it was proposed to adapt the North Wing of Handsworth for the deaconess students' use and to buy property for tutors' houses and the deaconess centre. The arrangement was that the deaconess training with the ministerial students at Handsworth should be in operation from September 1968. Certain financial matters regarding payment for the alterations to the North Wing, fees and the house purchases had to be settled, but eventually three properties were bought – 81 College Road (£4,850) for a tutor; 27 North Drive (£6,250) for the Warden, and 97 Devonshire Road (£6,000) for the Rev. H. J. Cook. 144 Friary Road was adapted to provide the Deaconess headquarters where the Sisters met together on Mondays.

Within a year the Order was having to prepare itself for yet another move as the proposed amalgamation of Handsworth and The Queen's College went ahead. The Queen's College buildings at the corner of Somerset Road and Farquhar Road, Edgbaston were to be used, so in October 1969 property for use as the deaconess centre was being sought in that area. One of the houses viewed was 7 Pritchatts Road and, despite internal vandalism, it was thought worthy of serious consideration. Then 24 Somerset Road seemed ideal and the Finance Committee recommended its acquisition, but that purchase fell through and eventually a scheme for the purchase and adaptation of 7 Pritchatts Road was accepted in face of considerable opposition from some members of the Committee, resulting in the resignation of one of the Treasurers and two other members. It seems that the cost of the alterations and the fact that the leasehold of the property ran out in 2001 were the main objections. However, on 15th May 1970 the Warden signed the contract with A. M. Griffiths and Sons and work started on the 18th with a promised completion date of 26 weeks. In the event Griffiths claimed an extra month because of 'unforeseeable delays' and student accommodation was expected to be ready by the end of October with the remaining buildings just before Christmas. In the meantime 81 College Road was sold for £4,900 (net £4,652) and 97 Devonshire Road was on the market for £6,600. While waiting for 7 Pritchatts Road to be ready the Order had the use of the house next door to 144 Friary Road as a student hostel. The final cost of Ilkley House, 7 Pritchatts Road was £34,945 plus £321 for curtains and carpets. It was hoped that the Ministerial Training Committee would give the Order a grant in respect of the money paid to Handsworth for the adaptation of the North Wing and in due course £5,000 was received. The official opening of Ilkley House by the President of Conference, the Rev. Rupert E. Davies, was held on 9th March 1971 at 3.30 p.m.

Ilkley House, 7 Pritchatts Road, Edgbaston, Birmingham

In May 1972 it was decided to sell the Warden's house, 27 North Drive and buy one nearer to Ilkley House, preferably in Northfield, where housing was cheaper than in Edgbaston. North Drive was sold for £10,000 and 1 Wirral Road, Northfield, bought for £9,200 to which a fourth bedroom costing £1,500 was added in the autumn of 1973.

Litherland was nominated in 1968 to continue as Warden for another three years from 1970 and the Rev. Kenneth L. Waights, who had become the Ministerial Secretary in 1969 on the death of the Rev. J. M. Neilson, was renominated in 1971. In June 1970 following all the upheaval of the move from Ilkley to Handsworth and again to Edgbaston and the different circumstances of new patterns of training with ministerial students a working party was set up 'to make recommendations about the future staffing of the Deaconess Centre, both as regards function and personnel, including nominations for Warden in 1972'. After much deliberation the working party drew up job descriptions for the Ministerial Secretary, Warden, Associate Warden, Director of Deaconess Studies, Vice President, Administrative Secretary and Treasurers and presented its resolutions, which were adopted, to the General Committee in January 1971.

Staffing of the Deaconess Centre Recommendations – 1971

1.   . . . accepts the job-descriptions presented, and approves the changed titles and appointment procedures involved.

2.   . . . nominates the following ministers to Conference in connexion with the designation of Warden for 1972
a)................. b)....................c)................. ....

3.   . . . nominates Sister Jean Baillie for appointment as Associate Warden for three years from 1971.

4.   . . . nominates Sister Margaret Budd for appointment as Director of Deaconess Studies forthwith, and invites her to serve in this capacity for a fourth year, namely 1972-73.

5.   . . . requests the following change in a Standing Order so that the newly designated officers may take their places ex-officio in the committees of the Order: . . .

Source: Wesley Deaconess Order Minutes (1948-78),
15th January 1971 (plus loose papers)

With regard to the appointment of a new Warden, Litherland was at pains to emphasise that this appointment was in no way 'to be considered as a holding operation pending the admission of women to the Ministry of the Word and Sacraments, but that belief in the Diakonate (sic) and its real place in the Church was a necessary qualification for the post'. Eventually three names emerged: Rev. Brian J. N. Galliers, MA, MTh, Rev. James B. Bates, BA, Rev. Donald G. Knighton, MA, BA and it fell to Mr. Galliers to take the Order forward into its new phase.

Methodist Restructuring

As Methodism worked towards modernising its structures, inevitably the Wesley Deaconess Order became involved and the problem was how to integrate the Order into the proposed Division of Ministries without infringing the Order's own special ethos and its integrity, but Litherland felt that, by June 1971, a satisfactory understanding had been reached. Resolutions from the Conference regarding the future of the Order came before the General Committee in January 1972 where it was agreed that the entire report should be submitted to Convocation for 'their thought and judgement' (sic). It was emphasized that above all else 'with the consideration of the broader scope of the Order care should be taken not to lose the vital link which members of the Order had with the Order itself'.[23] This restructuring in Methodism obviously affected the organization of the Wesley Deaconess Order and so the committees of the Order were reviewed with the following suggestion that in future Convocation would continue with a small Convocation Committee and a Pastoral Committee to advise the Warden. Otherwise, whereas the former General Committee had appointed four sub-committees – finance, selection, oversight and executive – there would now be the finance committee with the other three combined to form the Oversight or Training Committee. The Warden reported that at first about a third of the work of the Order, but eventually all of it, would come under the Division of Ministries – selection and training of candidates, and the oversight of probationers.

In anticipation that a number of deaconesses would wish to candidate for the presbyteral ministry the 1972 Convocation asked the General Committee to accept the following resolution:

> That ordained Deaconesses who are accepted for the ministry and wish to retain links with the Order be called, 'Associates of the Order'. The Associates would be non-voting members of Convocation attending at their own expense. They should receive the magazines and monthly letter, and be members of the local Deaconess group.
>
> That the present Associates be renamed, 'Friends' and could then in future include both men and women.[24]

---

23. WDOMins IV 14th January 1972
24. WDOMins IV 12th June 1972; WDO Finance Com. Mins. 15th May 1972

The last Ministerial Warden – The Rev. Brian J. N. Galliers, MA, BD, MTh, (1972-80)

Along with continuing this restructuring which he had inherited, the Rev. Brian Galliers, the seventh Warden, had to deal with the changing thinking on the nature of the diaconate which had occurred with the opening of the presbyteral ministry to women and in due course the Division of Ministries produced a study paper on the Order and the diaconate. So when Sister Margaret Budd, the Director of Deaconess Studies, expressed a wish to return to circuit work in 1973 it was proposed that the Associate Warden and the Administrative Secretary should take over some of the Warden's work, thus releasing him to have oversight of the training. It was felt that this would be an advantage both on economic and other grounds.

In January 1976 it was reported that a Memorandum on Training and Ordination recommended that a working party be set up 'to consider the nature of the Order, recruitment, training and ordination of deaconesses'. The working party presented its findings to the October Committee where some amendments were made, then the second draft, after being discussed in January, was passed to the Board of the Division of Ministries. The paper dealt with 1) the reason for the setting up of the working party, an analysis of the numbers of deaconesses in the active work and an 'educated guess' at future numbers, an observation about how deaconesses had been used in the past, 2) how, by deaconesses working alongside the local presbyteral minister, there might be a 'releasing (of) the spirit of diakonia (sic) in local churches', 3) how the church might be encouraged to reassess the work of the Wesley Deaconess Order, 4) the possibility of a wider diaconate, 5) the problems raised by marriage of a deaconess and her stationing, 6) the suggestion of a moratorium on recruitment was discussed, but not felt to be necessary, 7) that training could be better assessed 'when the Methodist Church and the W.D.O. are clearer than they are now about what is wanted from members of the diaconate', 8) more finance would be needed to train a wider diaconate. The working party recommended:

1. That the report be accepted.
2. That the work of the existing members of the W.D.O. be developed in accordance with section 3.
3. That a Methodist order of deacons, the nucleus of which would be the existing members of the W.D.O., be formed, open to men and women.

Deaconesses at Convocation, April 1976

The Deaconess Order Committee, on accepting this report, gave the Warden discretion to convene a small committee after the Conference 'to prepare a paper, on the wider Order, in the light of the decision of the Conference on the sector and auxiliary ministries' for consideration at the January committee.[25]
So, in January 1978, there was a lengthy discussion on the idea of a wider diaconate and the opinion of Convocation sought. In the meantime the Warden was asked to convey the Order's concerns to the Board of Division of Ministries. In the event the Board decided to recommend:

> (a) that the Church cease recruitment for the Wesley Deaconess Order from 1978, (b) that a committee of the Division consider the present rôle of the Order and redefine its rôle for the future, (c) that the same Committee consider the possibility of a new Order of lay service within the Church.

The Warden reported that these decisions had been conveyed 'to Convocation, discussed fully and accepted – nem.con. and the Division's Executive had already appointed a working party to deal with (b) and (c)'.[26]

In 1977 Sister Jean Baillie, the Associate Warden for the past six years, retired and Sister Yvonne Hunkin was appointed. To Sister Yvonne fell the task of taking the Wesley Deaconess Order forward into the wider Methodist Church Diaconal Order.

---

25. WDO Finance Com. Mins. 9th January 1976, 15th October 1976, and report of the Working Party (October 1976) [stapled into WDOMins IV], 7th January 1977
26. WDOMins IV 6th January 1978, 22nd May 1978

*The last Convocation before the Wesley Deaconess Order
ceased recruiting, Swanick, 1978*

*Sister Vera Vandersteen,
Vice President of the Wesley Deaconess Order March 1978-79*

Chapter 7

The Branch Deaconess Houses

Very quickly after Stephenson had organised his Sisters into a separate Deaconess Institute others in the Wesleyan Methodist Church began to see the advantages such an important resource could provide. It soon became obvious that many more deaconesses were required than could be accommodated and trained in Mewburn House. So several branch houses were set up, often by local initiative, in different parts of the country: for the most part they were effective, but short-lived. Often they were expensive to run and staff and eventually they were incorporated into the Wesley Deaconess Institute. The first two branch houses, at Norwich and Leicester, as well as providing a home for the Sisters, also gave some training, particularly of a practical nature. Both had a Sub-Warden and a Sister-in-Charge, who dealt with the running of the house at a local level. Other houses provided comfortable community living quarters for deaconesses working in the same area and the Convalescent Home at Doddington was a special initiative to meet an urgent need.

Bowman House, Norwich Branch Training House, Southwell House, Norwich

The Chairman of the East Anglia District, the Rev. John Gould, was very anxious that a Deaconess House should be established in his District and he was able to procure sufficient funding and even provided the money to furnish it so that Bowman House in Southfield Road, Norwich was opened shortly after the first public recognition service in September 1891 with two resident deaconesses, Sister Hilda Rich, who had been very successful in the Leysian Mission, as the Sister-in-Charge[1] and Sister Nellie Gosling. The house had accommodation for three deaconesses besides the Sister-in-Charge. Then Sister Sarah Freer joined the House as a roving evangelist working in the villages of Norfolk and Suffolk for several months.

---

1. *HH* (October 1891) pp.182, 200, (December 1891) p.234

Deaconess Work, 1892   **Sister Sarah Freer**

This is my seventh Mission, and I have given at least one hundred addresses since leaving London . . .

I have found my medical knowledge very useful . . . Only the other day an old man spoke to me as being 'half a doctor', while others have termed me a 'doctoress of divinity'. . . .

Source: Highways and Hedges (May 1892) p.98

From 1st September 1893 Sister Elise Searle was in charge of Bowman House and in 1895 she was elected as a Guardian of the Poor in Norwich by a very large vote, which indicated the esteem in which she and the deaconesses' work was held. In particular she was appointed to serve on the relief committee which dealt with cases receiving 'outdoor parish help' and she used this work as an opportunity to talk to and sing old familiar hymns with the waiting applicants.[2] Although Stephenson was Warden of the Institute each branch house had its own sub-Warden and in October 1895 the Rev. R. W. Little was appointed at Norwich when the financial statement showed that the estimated cost for the year was £166.[3] However, by December 1895 it seems that the work of the Norwich Branch House could not be sustained and so the Council regretfully resolved that:

Sister Elise Searle, in charge of Bowman House, Norwich

> we would agree to close the house at Norwich and would help in maintaining two Sisters if the Norwich friends would pay some reasonable quota.

The Chairman of the District reported that he had raised or contributed the money for the furniture for the house, but now agreed that it should be transferred to another Wesley Deaconess House.[4]

---

2. *HH* (February 1895) p.38, (July 1895) p.136
3. WDIMins I p.10
4. WDIMins I pp.17, 21

The Rev. R. W. Little sent a letter of protest to the Executive Committee of the Institute from the Deaconess Committee in Norwich pointing out that contributions promised for the coming year, especially one from Mr. J. J. Coleman, who in promising it remarked that his wife had furnished one of the rooms, would not be honoured if the house was closed and the Sisters sent into lodgings. The local Committee apparently agreed to there only being two instead of three Sisters and offered to contribute '£80 to the Deaconess Executive Council on condition that Bowman House with two Sisters shall be continued until March 1897'. The protest was successful and the Norwich House was reprieved, but asked to raise as much as possible towards the estimated £130 cost of maintaining the branch. The Rev. W. L. Tasker was appointed sub-Warden in September 1896. In March 1897 the Norwich Circuit requested that two deaconesses continue to be appointed and offered to pay £70 towards their upkeep, but the Council insisted that the contribution should be £50 for one deaconess or £100 for two. Obviously this was not acceptable as in May the Warden reported that 'Bowman House would close in June and the services of the deaconesses would not be required after that date'.[5]

Leicester Branch Training House, 4 St. Stephen's Road, Leicester (1892-97/98); Highfield St. 1897-98/1906-07

Calvert House, the Branch House, Leicester

Some idea of the impact made by the Wesley Deaconess movement and its rapid progress can be seen by the fact that in November 1892 a second branch house was opened in Leicester. It seems that there had been a revival of religion in the city, led by the Rev. Joseph Posnett, who felt that there was considerable scope for 'women's work' and was very enthusiastic about the possibilities opening up for deaconess involvement in the Leicester area. Mr. Posnett wrote to Stephenson requesting two deaconesses be sent, but Stephenson replied that he would rather establish a Deaconess House there where women could be trained and if Miss Mary Coy (later Sister Dorothy) would agree to take

---

5. WDIMins I pp.23-24, 42, 43

charge of it and the local Methodists pay for two deaconesses, then he would open a house in Leicester.

Calvert House, Leicester   The Rev. William Bradfield

I should like to tell you what difference there is between having one or two women workers and having a Deaconess House like ours in Leicester. *One* difference is this: that if there is a house, people in the town soon get to know it as a house to which they can go, all sorts of people with all sorts of troubles, and a house which they can remember with gratitude.

Source: *Flying Leaves* (December 1902) pp.187-88

Initially it was planned that the house should be called 'Carey House' after the great Baptist Missionary, but it was eventually realised that this might be confusing so it was named 'Calvert House'. Sister Dorothy Coy, a trained nurse, was the Sister-in-Charge with Sister Ruth Northcroft and Sister Sylvia Pryce-Jones in residence. Sister Louie, known as the Singing Evangelist, had been connected with the North Birmingham Mission, which had yet another group of independent Sisters, but from 1892 she was attached to the Wesley Deaconess Institute as a Probationer Deaconess and based at the Leicester House when she was not engaged in her missions. Sister Louie had been trained at the Royal Academy of Music and was using her talent to sing 'the Gospel' and 'would be available for work as a Song Evangelist in various parts of the country'.[6] Sister Louie never seems to have been consecrated.

Calvert House was described as 'commodious and comfortable', with accommodation for seven deaconesses. It was originally furnished by John Coy, Sister Dorothy's father, at no cost to the Institute, but when the Institute was recognised as a Connexional movement the General Committee decided, in 1902, to reimburse Mr. Coy to the tune of £320.[7]

Sister Dorothy reported on the work done in Leicester during the first year of Calvert House: Sister Ruth worked with the 'Wesleyan People's Mission' and Sister Sylvia was attached to the Bishop Street Circuit. The training given was very similar to that at

---

6. *HH* (July 1892) p.138, (November 1892) p.216; (January 1893) p.16, (September 1893) p.180
7. WDIMins I p.120; *HH* (September 1893) p.180; *FL* (August 1902) pp.118-19

Mewburn House involving Biblical, Theological and Medical lectures and necessary study, while practical experience was gained by visiting in the local circuits.[8]

Time-table at Calvert House, Leicester

7 a.m. Rise; 7.45 House duties; 8.00 Breakfast; 8.30 Prayers; 9.00 Private devotion; 9.30 Singing Practice; 10.00 Study; 10.30 Minister's Hour; 12.00 Study; 12.30 Singing Class; 1.00 Dinner; 2.30 District engagements; 5.00 Tea; 5.30 Prayers; 6.00 Reading aloud; 7.00 District engagements; 9.30 Supper; 10.15 Retire to rest.

Source: Highways and Hedges (January 1894) p.20

Ruth Northcroft made a point of recording her work at Leicester which gives some idea of both scope and development of her own endeavours and of deaconess work in general. So in the 1894 April issue of *Highways and Hedges* she wrote:

> . . . since the beginning of the Conference Year . . . [I have] undertaken . . . Soup Kitchen, seven times. Visits, 350. Meetings attended, 111. Addresses given, 14.
>
> I should like to tell you that I have increasing joy in the work, and especially in the purely evangelistic speaking.[9]

The Treasurer of the Leicester Branch, Mr. R. S. Mantle, died in the winter of 1895-96 and warm tribute was paid to him for all his endeavours in connection with the deaconess work. The new Treasurer was Mr. John Coy. The Deaconess Committee, in March 1897, gave permission for a larger house to be sought so some time in 1898 Calvert House moved from its original home in St. Stephens Road to Highfield Street and a local committee was formed to look after its affairs.[10] The Institute always seemed to carry a deficit for Calvert House, but struggled to maintain it either directly or through local support because of the valuable work it was doing in the area.

Sister Dorothy became seriously ill in 1902, probably through overwork, (she died in October), so Sister Lucy Hawken was appointed as temporary Sister-in-Charge. The report that year shows that four student probationers had been transferred there from Mewburn House to complete their practical training. Lucy Hawken

---

8. *HH* (January 1894) pp.19-20
9. *HH* (April 1894) p.79 cf. (October 1894) p.198
10. WDIMins I pp.19, 41, 46, 65

contributed some 'Notes on the Past Year' showing how the work in the Leicester, Bishop Street and Humberston Road Circuits was progressing. The Deaconess-Nurse had been kept busy, with several patients actually having to be nursed in Calvert House, while there had been much sick visiting to do.[11] Belgrave Hall was one of the churches in Leicester which benefited from the services of the Wesley Deaconesses and reported that

> one of the mightiest instrumentalities for good is to be found in the ministrations of the Deaconess. Of the ceaseless activity and devotion of our Deaconess we cannot speak too highly. She has won her way into many hearts, and her visits to the sick and poor have been greatly blessed. Her devotional and spiritual talks in the homes have been much appreciated.[12]

When the College at Ilkley was established training work at Leicester ceased, but Calvert House continued as a Deaconess House with its own Sub-Warden until May 1905, when, apparently, Leicester Methodism felt able to accept responsibility for maintaining it, so the last accounts appear in the 1905 financial statement. However, the Institute gave a 'special grant' of £90 to Leicester in 1906. The House is not listed in the 1907-08 *Stations*, although the same five Wesley Deaconesses were still attached to the same three Leicester circuits so it can only be assumed that the house closed and the circuits made their own arrangements.[13]

The Manchester/Salford Deaconess House, New Gravel Lane

The *Stations of the Wesley Deaconesses* for September 1894, as well as listing Mewburn House and the branch houses at Norwich and Leicester, includes one in Manchester (Gravel Lane) with Sister Ruth Northcroft as Sister-in-Charge. In 1894 the house had one other deaconess and a probationer. Mr. H. B. Harrison had had a great deal to do with the erection of this new house in Gravel Lane, Salford which was purpose-built and regarded an ideal blue-print for any future plans. The block of property in which it was situated also included the chapel, the Working Men's Club, the Girls' Parlour and a Home for a Lay Missionary.

11. *FL* (November 1902) pp.168-71, 179
12. *FL* (February 1905) pp.201-02
13. *HH* (September 1898) p.208 cf. (December 1898) p.278 (January 1899) pp.16-18; *FL* (June 1905) p.260, (September 1905) p.309, (September 1906) p.131; *WDO Stations* 1906, 1907

It is well placed; in the midst of the population for whose benefit it is intended; yet it is in a wide and open street. Two lines of railway are within five minutes' walk, and the centre of the tram system for all Manchester is only three minutes distant. The rooms are well arranged; large enough but not too large. There are eight bedrooms, accommodating the three resident Deaconesses, as well as visitors and helpers who, coming from the suburbs, can give two or three days a week to work for the masses. The financial responsibility is undertaken by a Local Committee: but the house is associated with the Wesley Deaconess Institute, three of our Sisters being resident there.[14]

Sister Ruth gave an inside view of the house at Salford and of the work done from there. She was delighted to have charge of a purpose-built home and felt that the 'finishings and furnishings have been most carefully selected, and combined to give . . . the greatest result of serviceableness, brightness, and comfort'. She explained how two rooms were used by ladies who came in to help the poor in Salford, while three were occupied by the Sisters and two remained to be furnished. As the house was situated in the midst of the population people were readily able to turn to the Sisters for help in times of need. The work at Gravel Lane Chapel was very varied because it also had the services of a Bible-woman and a lay-missionary as well as an enthusiastic group of voluntary workers. Even so there was much for the deaconesses to do.

'Flat-iron market' Salford   **Sister Ruth Northcroft**

. . . the flat-iron market spreads in full view every Saturday and Monday . . .

Spread on the ground you may see a motley collection of wares, the vendor surrounded by his collection. Old iron goods, old boots, old pictures, second-hand clothes; and once the scene was dignified by the appearance of an ancient four-post bedstead, and some family portraits in oils! Around these the purchaser saunters, bargaining, selecting, refusing, and comparing prices, but taking his time and combining the business in hand with the luxury of gossip.

Source: Highways and Hedges (February 1895) p.39

---

14.   *HH* (November 1895) p.218, (September 1894) p.179, (October 1894) p.198

In 1895 Sister Florence Thornton succeeded Ruth Northcroft as Sister-in-Charge and special celebrations were held on the first anniversary of its opening. The Salford Deaconess House was not a training house, but rather a home where the deaconesses lived together and could use it for a base for their work in the locality. For example, for several months during the winter Sister Erica conducted a weekly dinner-hour service in a cigar factory and a number of the girl workers joined her Girls' Club at Gravel Lane.[15] Much of their work was typical social or welfare work as there was a great deal of poverty and drunkenness in the area.

Comment by Minister   **Rev. C. W. Martin**

The Sisters do their work with a cheerfulness and Christian devotion that renders it at once encouraging and effective. The good results of their service are sometimes apparent, but are often out of sight – none the less good and valuable on that account, however. For their ministry, many have good reason to thank and praise God, in which feeling and exercise I myself heartily participate.

Source: Highways and Hedges (May 1900) p.119

Other Deaconess Houses

A further development occurred when arrangements were made for a group of deaconesses to live together in a Deaconess House rather than in separate lodgings. This had considerable advantages on economic grounds and in providing opportunities for much support and fellowship missing when deaconesses lived in isolation. The Annual Report of the Wesley Deaconess Institute for 1904-05 remarked that

> In some places Deaconess Houses have been established, in which lodge the deaconesses who are at work within a considerable area around: but for the upkeep of such houses the Institute is not responsible.

---

15. *HH* (February 1895) pp.38-39, (April 1895) pp.78-79, (November 1895) p.218, (December 1898) pp.278-88

Bow Deaconess House, London

The first mention of Bow as a Deaconess House is given in the advertisement at the beginning of *Flying Leaves*.[16] It seems that the minister, the Rev. Arthur Wood, felt that a group of Wesley Deaconesses working together could do much in the Poplar and Bow Mission and surrounding area. So a house, 14 Mornington Road, Bow was obtained in which they could live together. This had economic advantages, but more important it meant that the deaconesses could live in comfort and provide mutual support and fellowship for each other.[17] Ruth Northcroft had trained at Mewburn House for a year (1890-91). After one year in Truro she went to Calvert House (1892-94), then in 1894-95 became Sister-in-Charge at the new Salford Deaconess House. Following a break of six months, when she was suffering from typhoid fever, she was appointed to Lady Margaret Road Church in the Kentish Town, London Circuit where she served for three years. Then the Children's Home decided to open a Training School for Home Workers to be named Willard House, after Frances Willard, the American advocate of the Temperance Movement, who was also deeply interested in deaconess work among women and children.[18] Sister Ruth Northcroft, with all her experience, was the ideal person to take charge of this new venture when it opened on 1st September 1898. So for two years Ruth trained students at Willard House, but from November 1900-September 1901 she was away from work in Plymouth. Returning to active service she was appointed to the Poplar and Bow Mission and when the Bow Deaconess House came into being she became its first Sister-in-Charge in 1902.[19] In November she reported that her work was anything but typical, as in addition to normal mission work, she had to run the Deaconess House and look after 'our family of six Deaconesses, with all that concerns their physical needs, and the household arrangements'. Although this meant that she could not get out to do much visiting in the district there was still plenty of work in the Mission itself.[20] Christmas 1902 looked like being a very bleak one for the people of Poplar and Bow, so the Mission Sisters determined to try to bring a little happiness into the lives of 'the little ones' on Christmas Day. Fortunately generous 'friends in the city' offered to cover the expenses. Two hundred and fifty tickets were issued to children

16. *FL* (1902) frontispiece
17. *FL* (January 1904) pp.10-11
18. *HH* (January 1893) p.16
19. 'Wesley Deaconess Order: J. Elsworth's Own MS notes & Register'; *HH* (October 1898) p.230, (June 1899) p.125; *FL* (September 1902) p.138
20. *FL* (November 1902) p.165

who were fatherless or whose fathers were out of work. Great discussions were held about the food, but eventually it was decided to provide hot saveloys with plenty of 'really good bread and butter and jam or marmalade for the tinies'. Christmas Eve evening was spent in preparing great mounds of bread and butter and one friend provided 'a huge clothes basket' filled with oranges, while another gave 250 'dainty bags of sweets'. Then just as the workers were leaving at 11.00 p.m. for a well-earned rest another gift arrived – 'a joint of beef. "You will know what to do with it, Sister!" and so we did!' Christmas Day dawned and at 9.00 a.m. the guests arrived to enjoy a hearty breakfast. Within an hour it was all over and the two Sisters who had helped at the breakfast went, 'weary but very happy', into St. Paul's Cathedral to rejoice in the birth of Christ and 'listened to the Christmas psalms, taking in as, perhaps, never before the wonderful breadth of the message of love, but smitten with the sharpness of the contrast. Linked together, yet so far apart; the pain and the struggle in the east, little pinched faces and hungry eyes – while here all that wealth and art and culture could bring, and costly-robed worshippers coming in softly to hear the message of peace.'

Christmas 1902, Bow   Sister Ruth Northcroft

At the door they were drafted off to their right tables, and soon the room was quite full. Oh, what a sight! The bigger ones leading little toddlers; could they be five years? Better not ask too closely! Boys keen and businesslike, making sure they were provided, each with his tempting, smoking saveloy.

At a word they stand and sing grace, and then fall to – wonderfully quiet, it is a serious business, and must not be made light of. But after half an hour or so tongues are loosened, and mirth begins; the cheery helpers have to persuade and cajole, 'Just one piece more,' says one, after the fifteenth has disappeared, and that being accepted the recipient with it surely beats the record for a good breakfast!

When grace is sung, at the word of command out they go, in single file – no rush, no disorder, and as happy as children can well be, receiving as they go each a bag of sweets and an orange.

Have they learnt, these little robins, that Christmas means kindliness and love, even from people who know nothing about you, but that you are poor and hungry?

Source: Flying Leaves (March 1903) pp.45-46

Mrs. Lucy Rider Meyer, one of the chief 'inspirers' of deaconess work in America and superintendent of the Methodist Episcopal Church Deaconess Training House in Chicago, was a frequent visitor to the Wesley Deaconess Order. In 1906 she wrote of a visit she and others paid to Bow. They were delighted to be invited by Sister Christian, one of the deaconesses working there, actually to stay in the Deaconess House. Mrs. Meyer described the House and the work the deaconesses were doing in the locality: the slum areas shocked the American visitors, but they realized what a great service was being rendered to the women and children and came to appreciate all the effort expended. So the planned visit of one or two days stretched into five and words could not express the 'true and sweet fellowship with our fellow workers there'.

'As Others See Us'　　　　　**Mrs. Lucy Rider Meyer**

At Bow four splendid women were living together, everyone having full work in the field. There was no 'superintendent' at all. Sister Christian was only head-sister. The house is provided by the Church, and so is the housekeeper, for that matter; the Deaconesses simply live in the house and go out from it to do their work . . .

Dinner (supper – Ed.) at the little Deaconess House was a social affair, not very formal. The Deaconesses all came in from their evening work, and we ate and talked from nine o'clock until bedtime . . . We discussed many things, comparing especially English and American methods of Deaconess work. It was delightful to hear the same expressions of joy in the work and of confidence in the future that greet our ears in America.

Source: Flying Leaves (December 1905) pp.362-63

Although the house at Mornington Road may have been kept for use by the Poplar and Bow Mission it ceased to be listed as 'Deaconess House' in the 1907-08 *Wesley Deaconess Order Stations.*[21]

Other possible Houses

Although not listed separately on the *Wesley Deaconess Order Stations* it is possible that other large centres, especially Missions, also had houses where several deaconesses were able to live together. For example, *Flying Leaves* in April 1906 mentioned such

---

21. *WDO Stations* 1907-08

a house at Bradford. Indeed, that year there were four Wesley Deaconesses stationed at Eastbrook, Bradford Mission and Sister Edith Booth was described as *'in charge'*, so this reinforces this supposition.[22]

Doddington Convalescent Home, Faversham

When, in 1890, the Rev. Samuel Wickes had been appointed to the Hackney Road Mission, Stephenson had promised him 'the help of two deaconesses from Mewburn House'. In an article in the following February he gives a glowing report of their work.[23] The conditions in this part of East London most probably provided the inspiration for a very interesting and enterprising venture: the establishment of a Convalescent Home at Doddington. The first mention of this is to be found in the *Wesley Deaconess Order Stations* of September 1900, printed in *Highways and Hedges,* when Sister Mary Broad and Julia Langdon were stationed there.[24] Doddington was a small village near Faversham in Kent and the sisters helped with the local Methodist Church and in the village community as well as running the Convalescent Home.

Doddington Deaconess House, Faversham, Kent

Sister Julia Langdon had become a Probationer Wesley Deaconess in 1891 and undertook a year's training at Mewburn House before being stationed at Hackney Wick Mission in North East London in 1892. She was consecrated in July 1893. Sister Mary Broad was already at Hackney Wick when Julia went there. Mary Agar Broad was the elder daughter of Charles Morris and Mary Anne Broad and a cousin of the Rev. Dr. Agar Beet. She entered the Wesley Deaconess Order in July 1893 and was consecrated the following year. Officially at Hackney Wick Mission as a Wesley Deaconess from 1893, she had already served there as a Sister from October 1878 when the Mission started. Mary commented that 'my previous many years' service at Hackney Wick

---

22. *WDO Stations* 1906-07, 1907-08; *FL* (April 1906) p.50
23. *HH* (February 1891) p.60 cf. (March 1891) p.100
24. *HH* (September 1900) p.214

Mission was taken instead of Probation and I did not enter any Training House'.[25] In an article in the 1894 *Highways and Hedges* she wrote of her delight in having Sister Julia as a colleague and 'a friend to share the work and the responsibility' in a situation in which there was 'much to depress and sadden'. It is obvious that Mary was especially involved with, and concerned about, the children of the area, where poverty was rife. She had started a branch of the 'Children's and Young People's Scripture Union' which was attended by an increasing number of children, some of whom then went on to join her or Sister Julia's Junior Society Class. These children's groups influenced the adults, so that by 1901 not only were there about 300 children on the register, but over 300 adults attached to Hackney Wick.[26]

Hackney Wick Mission	**Sister Mary Broad**
The general visiting is one of the saddest parts of our work. The people are so poor. Their homes (if the one room, or two rooms, that have to shelter a whole family can be called *home*) are often bare of bedstead or bedding, or anything that can be called furniture. We cannot do even an hour's visiting without finding people lacking even bread or fire, often some member of the family ill, and no money to pay for doctor or medicine. Some are chronic cases, others out of work for a time, and if we can give them temporary help to keep the wolf from the door, will be able to get on again.	

Source: Highways and Hedges (November 1894) pp.217-18

It seems fairly evident that this work of Sister Mary and Julia at Hackney Wick Mission was the motivating force behind the setting up of the Convalescent Home at Doddington. When *Flying Leaves* started in 1901 the frontispiece had an advertisement which listed Doddington, Kent, among the Deaconess Houses, with a note that the Training Houses were Mewburn House, London and Calvert House, Leicester.[27] This was followed by a report in the November issue which stated that 'two are devoting themselves to the establishment and management of a Convalescent Home for poor women and children'.[28]

---

25. 'Wesley Deaconess Order: J. Elsworth's Own MS notes & Register'
26. *HH* (November 1894) pp.217-18
27. *FL* (September 1901) frontispiece
28. *FL* (November 1901) p.5

The first real report came in April 1902 when Julia Langdon explained the work done at Doddington, where Sister Mary did the 'teaching, superintending cooking, keeping accounts, writing letters, business, etc.'; and Miss W--- did the mending, while she herself did much dressmaking and housekeeping.

Convalescent Home, Doddington   Sister Julia Langdon

We lead very busy lives here in this lovely spot. I rise at 6.30 during the cold weather, at 6 in the summer, and am busy until I retire to my room at night. Sister Mary and myself are kept at it – Sister Mary at teaching, superintending cooking, keeping accounts, writing letters, business, etc.;' and Miss W--- at mending, and I at making dresses and round cloaks and underclothing for the children and studying the problem how to make boots and shoes last. I have not solved the latter yet, for they will wear out. Then I fill and trim the lamps, and this large house has to be kept in order. Sometimes I have found myself asking – "Am I a Deaconess?" and I have come to the conclusion that I really am if Deaconess means 'to serve', or to 'minister' to the needs of others. That is what I live for.

Source: Flying Leaves (April 1902) pp.52-53

When Julia became seriously ill in 1902 Mary was under considerable pressure to maintain the work in the Home and the village, as well as nursing her colleague. However, Sister Frances Sugden, who had had to retire temporarily (February 1901-August 1902) to nurse her dying sister, now was free to go to the rescue and she helped out at Doddington for a year. The Wesley Deaconess connection with the village was highlighted when Dr. Stephenson passed on the news that Sister Mary had been appointed as Society Steward and Sister Julia as Poor Steward at the Wesleyan Chapel.[29]

The Warden's comment in 1903 about the Deaconess House at Doddington helps to throw some light on the special deaconess work done there. Stephenson remarked that the work was 'proving its usefulness'. Then he went on:

> Established and supported by the generosity of Sister Mary Broad, it is welcoming to rest and refreshment a number of ailing people from the London slums, to whom it gives something like new life. It benefits in the same

---

29. *FL* (November 1902) p.165; (January 1903) p.8

way needy children, who go from the courts and alleys to enjoy for a while the open country and the fresh sweet air.

An added bonus had been that the arrival of the Sisters had revitalised the local Methodist church and community, where both services and classes had recovered, so much so that a new chapel was in course of erection. A further opportunity for evangelism had presented itself with the coming of the hop pickers during the summer. The deaconesses visited the hop pickers' camps at Kingsdown to take services and there they had felt it was 'like old times to be surrounded by London East-end men, women and children once more. They were so pleased to see us. Some said they remembered the services from last year. They listened most attentively to the singing and addresses.' When the hop pickers had left, many filled with new hope, Mary and Julia began to give lessons to the children in the Home. However, that was not all, for the local people were encouraged too and came to the evening services at Doddington, which were being held in the Board School while the new chapel was being built.[30]

At the London Anniversary of the Wesley Deaconess Institute, held on 27th November 1907, Sister Julia spoke about her work in the village of Doddington. She commented that when she went to the chapel on Sunday mornings she was always conscious that she must be prepared to take the service in case the preacher did not turn up, remarking that quite often on the Sunday morning just before the service she would receive a telegram or postcard saying 'So sorry, unable to come.' As there was no one else – 'I *must* preach . . . Village work *is* important. The people, who live in the lonely cottages, must not be neglected. At some lonely farmhouses they do not get a visit once in twelve months from anyone but the Sister.' Julia also told of open-air meetings and her work with Sister Mary Broad among the children in the Convalescent Home.

Travelling by Donkey Carriage   **Sister Julia Langdon**

Unless I say *the donkey takes me,* I must say, 'I drive out', and that sounds much too grand for a Deaconess; for if I say *I take the donkey,* that does not sound right either, so I will say *we go together!*

Source: *Flying Leaves* (January 1908) p.187

---

30. *FL* (November 1903) pp.166-67

A note was inserted in the magazine in 1909 indicating that 'The Sisters at Doddington "Home of Rest" have a Furnished Cottage *"To Let"*, standing in their own grounds, containing, two bedrooms, sitting room, kitchen and scullery. Rent per week in July and August, 15/-; in September or October 10/-.'[31] This implies that the Home stood in considerable grounds, that Mary Broad and her family had resources they were willing to put to good use for the benefit of those in need and that the cottage was being made available, at a reasonable cost, to those wanting a holiday.

Over the years Doddington is variously named in the *Wesley Deaconess Order Stations* as 'Doddington', 'Doddington Convalescent Home' (1906) and 'Doddington Home of Rest' (1906-10).' It ceased to be listed in September 1911, although it had appeared in January. No indication is given as to what happened to it. However, it seems as if the breaking of the connection with the Order was triggered off by the marriage of Sister Mary Broad. Sister Mary was married in the Wesleyan Chapel at Doddington on 26th April 1911 to William Moxon of Pontefract.[32] This presumably left a vacancy at Doddington Home of Rest and in the 1911 September *Stations* Sister Julia had moved to Grantham to do 'evangelistic work'. It would be interesting to know whether responsibility for it was taken over by another Methodist organisation, the local authority or some other body. It is worth remembering that, especially in the early years, many of the deaconesses came from fairly well-to-do homes and were largely supported by their families. So it could be that Mary Broad had private means which enabled her to establish and support the Home at Doddington, most possibly to provide a break from their dreary, poverty-stricken lives for the women and children she had encountered in Hackney Wick Mission. Hackney Wick Mission only appeared in the *Minutes of the Wesleyan Methodist Conference* for the years 1878, 1879, 1880, where it is listed, with William Booth as minister, under the London (Hackney) Circuit. Did the Hackney Mission or its successor(s) take over responsibility for Doddington House when Mary married and Julia moved on to Grantham?

---

31. *FL* (July/August 1909) p.98
32. *FL* (July/August 1911) p.98

Other deaconess groups which joined the Wesley Deaconess Order at different times

Yarmouth Circuit

It seems that the Yarmouth Circuit was one of those which had had a group of independent deaconesses, working under the direction of the Rev. T. F. Hulme, BA. They lived at Worford House and in July 1896 the Rev. John Gould intimated that the 'circuit desired to affiliate the work of the Sisters there with the Wesley Deaconess Institute'. The Executive Committee was willing to accept Sister Alice Coe, who had commenced deaconess work at Yarmouth in February 1895, as a Wesley Deaconess if the Yarmouth Circuit agreed to meet all her expenses, which was confirmed in December.[33]

Leeds Mission, Oxford Place – Deaconess House, Vernon Road

In January 1896 an approach was made to the Council by the Rev. Samuel Chadwick for a deaconess to be appointed to Leeds (Oxford Place), but the request could not be acceded to at that time.[34] However, Chadwick must have started a group of Sisters connected with mission, known as the Leeds Mission Sisterhood, because in 1904 he again entered into discussions with Stephenson for his Sisters to join the Wesley Deaconess Order. Following correspondence with Stephenson, Chadwick was invited to attend the Annual Meeting of the Wesley Deaconess Institute General Committee on 27th June 1904 to present the case for the amalgamation of his Sisterhood with the Wesley Deaconess Institute. As he was unable to attend the meeting in person, he submitted a letter reporting that the Leeds Mission had agreed to the amalgamation and would undertake the cost and management of the Sisters' Home and pay the personal cost of each deaconess. However, he wished to clarify several points – the appointment of a Matron; that the Sisters who had given faithful service would be given special consideration as, although it was felt that several would benefit from residence at the College, there were two or three who would find this impossible and, in view of their long service, it was hoped it might be counted as their probation and that those deaconesses who were engaged in local circuits might live in the Leeds Sisters' House, with the financial arrangements being

---

33. WDIMins I. pp.34, 35, 37 cf. 'Wesley Deaconess Order: J. Elsworth's Own MS notes & Register'
34. WDIMins I p.21

made between the circuits and the Institute, which would then pay the House a maintenance allowance. The amalgamation was agreed with three provisos – that the Wesley Deaconess Institute should not incur any additional expense; that Sisters who were not connected with the Leeds Mission should not be required to live in the Leeds Deaconess House and that, while the Institute was sympathetic to the position of the Leeds Sisters, they must each be accepted on their own merits.[35] This last point reiterates yet again the way in which the Committee jealously guarded the high standards of the Order. So the special committee set up to deal with the amalgamation passed the following resolutions which were endorsed by the General Committee:

Leeds Mission Sisterhood

1.   That the Leeds Mission Sisterhood by this arrangement ceases to exist as such.

2.   That the Deaconess House in Vernon Road be kept by the Leeds Mission without any Financial Responsibility resting on the Wesley Deaconess Institute.

3.   That the payment by the Leeds Mission for each Wesley Deaconess employed be £21.10.0 (including payment to the Superannuation Fund).

4.   That it be understood that Residence at the Deaconess Home is desirable for all Wesley Deaconesses employed in Leeds, if there be room, unless distance or other special circumstances should cause the Officers of the Order to decide otherwise.

Source: MSS Wesley Deaconess Institute Minute Book (1895-1910) pp.213-15

Of the Leeds Sisters – Annie Tomlinson (38), who had served as a member of the Leeds Sisterhood for 14 years, was accepted and would be consecrated at the next Convocation; Frances Mann (24), who had similarly served for five years, was accepted as a probationer as she was engaged to be married to a minister; one was required to be trained; one withdrew and the others together with any other Sisters employed in any other Leeds circuits were asked to offer as candidates in the usual way. It was resolved that if possible three other Wesley Deaconesses should be appointed to the Leeds Mission to work with Annie Tomlinson and Frances Mann.[36] Mr. Chadwick and Mr. William Middlebrook joined the deaconess committee.

---

35.   WDIMins I pp.209-11
36.   WDIMins I pp.213-5 cf.226; RConv. 1905 (Saturday 20th May) 4, 3

Manchester Mission

It is likely that the Sisters of the People at Manchester Mission started around 1890 as the first officially appointed deaconess was recorded in September 1891. As the work of the Mission extended the numbers grew, so that there was quite a large group of Sisters attached to the Mission. However, even though the Wesley Deaconess Order had become well-established, the Manchester and Salford 'Visiting Sisters of the People' remained an independent organisation until 1936.[37] It seems that when the deaconesses of the Wesleyan, United and Primitive Methodist Churches discussed closer co-operation in 1930, in view of the impending Union, the Manchester Mission committee felt unable to undertake the extra financial obligation entailed, so the proposal that they might join the Wesley Deaconess Order was shelved for the time being. However, in the autumn of 1934 there were discussions between Dr. Maltby, the Rev. Herbert Cooper and the Treasurer of the Manchester and Salford Mission to see if the Mission's Sisters could be taken into the Order. A draft scheme, particularly relating to allowances, was produced as a basis for further negotiations. Two years later Mr. Cooper had managed to raise £2,000 to improve the Mission Sisters' allowances in order 'to make it possible so far as financial arrangements were concerned for them to join the Wesley Deaconess Order . . .'. These arrangements were confirmed in

March 1937 and on 10th April 12 Sisters were received into the full fellowship of the Order, but with 11 continuing to work in the Mission as the responsibility of the Mission, while another would spend some time at Ilkley College and then be received into full membership of the Order.[38]

Sisters of the People,
with the Rev. Herbert Cooper and staff,
Manchester and Salford Mission, 1930s

---

37. see J. Banks, *The Story So Far: The first 100 years of the Manchester and Salford Methodist Mission* (1986) espec. ch.6 pp.79-93 for account of these sisters.
38. WDOMins III pp.24, 42-43, 45 (14th December 1934; 11th December 1936; 10th March 1937); Mins. of Conv. p.11; Local Arrangements & Executive Arrangements for planning Convocation Minutes 1937-52 p.1

Chapter 8

Training and Development

Once Mewburn House was established as a training house for the Wesley Deaconess Institute the numbers grew and soon deaconesses were working very effectively in various districts. So many requests for their services were being received that Stephenson was anxious to enrol another seven or eight suitable women; however, he notes, that although many applications were being made, most of the candidates were not acceptable. Sister Rita seems to have realized that there were many women who were interested in deaconess work, but were unable to undertake it themselves and so she suggested that they might be prepared to help by contributing donations and fund raising. This was the forerunner of the Lady Associates, which played such an important rôle in providing the means for sustaining deaconess training and work, especially in poorer circuits.

Response to appeal

Dear Dr. Stephenson, – I have just finished reading the June number of *Highways and Hedges*, and was so touched by Sister Rita's appeal, that I at once obtained a Postal Order for 10s., which I enclose thereto.

Yours faithfully,
W. L.

P.S. I have received an appeal from a Lady Abbess in Devon, offering 2,125 days' indulgence for each 'Hail Mary' said on beads offered at 5s. I thought it best, however, to invest double that amount in *Lady Abbess Rita's* work!

Source: Highways and Hedges (July 1891) p.140

As in the beginning The Children's Home and the Wesley Deaconess Institute were so closely associated, and indeed the latter grew out of the former, it is important to keep in mind Stephenson's constant insistence that they were two different organisations, with their own areas of work, needs and outlook and that their funds were kept quite separate. So that friends of either could be sure that their support was channelled as they wished. This obviously became even more important as the work of each developed and the two institutions went their separate ways and found their own identity.

The first report of the Mewburn House Deaconess Institute was issued in July-August 1891 and the founders of the enterprise were much encouraged by its success and arranged a series of meetings in Nottingham during the Wesleyan Methodist Conference to publicize the venture. By 1894 the numbers and work of the Deaconess Institute had increased so much that the time seemed ripe for there to be a more official organisation: active steps were taken to appoint a Committee which would become responsible for running the Institute. The Wesleyan Methodist Conference of 1894 resolved that:

> The following committee is appointed to consider whether the Wesley Deaconess Institute may be brought under the sanction or direction of the Conference, and if so, in what manner this may best be done: ...[1]

This Committee met in London on Tuesday 29th November, 1894 when Dr. Stephenson presented a statement on the history and aims of the Institute. After considerable conversation the following resolution, proposed by Dr. Waller and seconded by Mr. James E. Vanner, was passed:

> The Committee is of the opinion that the work of the Deaconesses and other women workers is of great value to the Church, and deserves to be encouraged. That whilst not prepared, at present, to recommend that the Wesley Deaconess Institute should be brought under the direction of the Conference, the Committee learns with satisfaction that a responsible Committee of Management is being formed, consisting of members of our Church, and suggests that the Conference should cordially recommend the work to the confidence and sympathy of the Connexion.[2]

The Wesleyan Methodist Conference of 1895 endorsed the Committee's Report.

---

1. *HH* (July 1895) pp.135-36; *WMMins. of Conf.* (1894) p.322
2. WDIMins I pp.1-4; *HH* (July 1895) pp.135-36

The first meeting of the Council was held at the Centenary Hall, Bishopsgate Street, London on Wednesday 19th June 1895 when a draft constitution for the Institute was presented and carefully considered. After some necessary emendations had been made the amended Constitution was formally presented and accepted by the next meeting on 29th October. Also at that meeting the Executive Committee and Officers were appointed, various administrative decisions taken, the financial statement presented and an appeal for monetary support made. Arrangements were put in hand for an annual public meeting and it was reported that, at the present time, there were 24 deaconesses and 18 probationers associated with the Institute, beside the Sisters connected with The Children's Home. The Council Meeting in December received applications from various circuits for the services of a deaconess. However, of great significance was a request from Johannesburg for another Sister to take the place of Sister Evelyn Oats who had moved to Durban and negotiations were under way to agree terms. Sister Evelyn Oats became a probationer in 1892 and, having served in London and the Isle of Wight, a special service of consecration was held on Tuesday 13th March 1894 so that she could sail for Durban on Saturday 17th March to extend the work of the Wesley Deaconess Institute overseas, as related in chapter 3.

In April 1896 the Candidates' sub-committee took an important decision when it admitted Miss Jeanie Banks as a Wesley Deaconess. Jeanie Banks, the daughter of Wesleyan Methodist missionary parents, had already worked for eight years with the Rev. Peter Thompson in the East London Mission. She expressed a wish 'to be employed chiefly in specialist evangelistic work, in which she had already been greatly blessed, but would take ordinary Deaconess work whenever required to do so'. Her previous years of service were taken into account and she was excused the usual period of probation, being consecrated in April 1896. Jeanie Banks worked assiduously and most effectively as a Deaconess Evangelist for 16 years before retiring in 1912 when she again achieved a 'first' by being the first deaconess to superannuate. A glowing tribute to her life and work was inserted in the General Committee Minutes and *Flying Leaves*. Sister Jeanie was granted an annuity of £12.00.[3]

September 1896 saw the first report of a legacy when Mr. Rothwell of Colwyn Bay bequeathed £1,350 to the Institute. It was decided to invest £1,000 and use the balance to reduce the Institute's

---

3. WDIMins I p.27; see chapter 2 for work of the Deaconess Evangelists

debt. An interesting feature of the legacy was that the Institute officers had to undertake that no part of it should 'be used in any way for the promotion of the drink traffic'. Over the years other legacies were received from well-wishers and often these gifts enabled the Order to develop its work or ward off financial embarrassment.

It was a sign that the Wesley Deaconess Institute was evolving from an ad hoc movement to an organisation when the questions of '(a) allowances to deaconesses, (b) uniform, (c) removal expenses, (d) the cases of Sisters laid aside by temporary sickness, (e) the provision of a sick and retiring fund' needed to be addressed. So in 1897 it was agreed:

> 1. That the allowances to a Deaconess should be of the value of at least £20 per ann.
>
> 2. That the allowance in cash be £16 with material for two dresses, a cloak or jacket and two bonnets . . .
>
> 4. That the travelling expenses of a Deaconess removing from one appointment to another should in no case be borne by herself and that it is desirable to include a reasonable sum to cover the cost of removals in the amount charged to Circuits.
>
> 5. That for the present cases of sickness should be considered individually . . . but that it is very desirable, as soon as it is practicable, to form a Sick & Retiring Fund.

A formal agreement for use between circuits which wished to engage a deaconess and the Institute was prepared. By 1899 the deaconesses' allowance was £52 plus uniform.

Obviously as the work of the deaconesses had become widely known and appreciated the Institute received more requests for their services than could be met. It is also noticeable that the work put considerable strain on the women as a number of them had to take sick leave or retire altogether, so experienced Sisters such as Sarah Freer, one of the first to be consecrated in July 1890, had to retire because of ill-health in 1898. Filling these vacancies further reduced the number of deaconesses available for new appointments. In spite of this, many women who offered for the work were rejected as the Institute's officers remained faithful to the standards for potential probationers which had been set by Stephenson right at the beginning. Another complication was that by the very nature of their work Deaconess Nurses often had to deal with infectious illnesses to which some succumbed, thus Lucy Hawken, working in Maidstone, Kent during an epidemic in 1898 fell victim to the fever herself. Similarly two others contracted scarlet fever and diphtheria.

After nine years as the first Sister-in-Charge at Mewburn House Rita Hawkins resigned in 1899 in order to marry the Rev. William C. Williams and was succeeded by Sister Elizabeth Barraclough. At the same time the female members of the Council and the officers formed a House Committee for Mewburn House.

In 1898 Conference had judged that the forthcoming 20th century would provide a 'suitable occasion for the Wesleyan Methodist Church and its adherents to gratefully acknowledge the way in which God has led them . . .' So it resolved that:

> (1) A Special Connexional fund, to be called the Wesleyan Methodist Twentieth Century Fund, shall be raised and applied to the Evangelistic, Educational, and Philanthropic purposes of our Church at home and abroad.
>
> (2) The amount . . . to endeavour to raise shall be not less than One Million Guineas.
>
> (3) . . . the proposed Century Fund shall be raised by at least one million Methodists, who shall between 1st January 1899, and 1st January 1901, give or collect a sum of at least One Million Guineas.

The objects of the Fund and its allocation were:

> (i) To assist in the purchase of sites and the erection of Wesleyan Methodist places of worship . . . and Soldiers' and Sailors' Homes, and to help the completion of extension schemes already begun, £300,000.
>
> (ii) For educational work in connexion with the Higher, Secondary, Elementary, or other Educational Institutions associated with the Wesleyan Methodist Church, and for the mental improvement and training of Local Preachers, £200,000 . . .
>
> (iii) For Foreign Missionary work, £100,000.

(iv) For Home Missionary work, including Temperance work, £100,000.

(v) For the purchase of a suitable site in London . . . and the erection thereon of a monumental Connexional Building, £250,000.

(v) For the development of the work of the Children's Home . . . £50,000 . . .[4]

It seems that, as early as September, the Institute was informed that it was proposed that the Fund would give it a grant of £2,000 and so a sub-committee was set up to decide how best to use the money. The financing of the Institute had always been a concern as there was often a substantial overdraft and efforts were constantly being made to reduce it by appealing for an increase in the subscription list. It was pointed out that at least an extra £700 was needed if the admission of candidates and their training was not to be curtailed.

As already indicated in chapter 6, at this time the official records deal chiefly with domestic matters, general financial questions and the examination and acceptance of candidates; however, several important issues arose which had considerable impact on the development of the Order.

January 1905 saw a widening of the Order when it was decided that some eminent women who had given special service in the Christian Church should be admitted into Honorary Membership. The first two names put forward were Mrs. Lucy Rider Meyer, founder of the American Methodist Episcopal Church Deaconess Order, and one of its own members, Marjorie Sheard. Marjorie Sheard had been appointed as Sister-in-Charge at Calvert House, Leicester, but, for family reasons, had had to go to Huntingdon, where she had still been able to do considerable work and it was felt that this membership would keep her in contact with the Order.

---

4. *WMMins. of Conf.* (1898) pp.342-47; (1899) pp.337-41, Appendix XIV pp.512-33; (1900) pp.328-32, Appendix XIV pp.493-501; (1901) pp.98-102, Appendix XIII pp.502-06; (1902) pp.97-101, Appendix XIII pp.505-09; (1903) pp.103-07, Appendix XII pp.508-11, Appendix XIII pp.511-18; (1904) pp.92-96, 112-14, Appendix XII pp.511-15

Candidates and Probationers

A sub-committee of the Council was set up in 1896 to deal with the examination and selection of candidates and the appointment of deaconesses. Dr. Stephenson was given discretion to offer advice and admonition to deaconesses and probationers when he judged it necessary. March 1897 saw the first recorded entrance of a probationer from another denomination when Miss Alice C. Fishe 'lately an officer in the Salvation Army' was accepted. Others were received over the years from Baptist and Primitive Methodist backgrounds, but their applications to enter the Order were always carefully scrutinised and, if they were not found suitable, they were rejected. In some cases flexibility was allowed in the matter of residential training with Alice Stokes being resident, but permitted to continue to work in the Bow Circuit as long as the circuit contributed £25 to the Wesley Deaconess Institute and she attended all the classes, while Miss Shrimpton, who was training at Bow Infirmary, was allowed to reside in the neighbourhood, rather than in Mewburn House.

In November 1903 the question of student-probationers was tackled when the importance of a preliminary period of probation was emphasised so that the high standard required of candidates could be maintained. In consequence it was agreed that a potential candidate

> before appearing before the Committee of Examination, should be tested by a paper upon General and Biblical Knowledge, to be written in the presence of her minister.[5]

Following the acceptance of this practice it was decided in June 1904 to adopt a system of marking for candidates which would determine their selection or otherwise for training as deaconesses:

Mark 1   – Unanimously recommended.
Mark 2   – Also recommended, if there be room.
Mark 3   – Recommended, but less desirable.
Mark 4   – Declined.[6]

This system was adjusted slightly in the following June, so that candidates in category 2, especially those receiving 2+, were accepted and those in 3 could be admitted if there was room.

---

5. WDIMins I pp.185-86
6. WDIMins I p.206

A step toward conformity with Methodist theological colleges can be seen in early November 1906 when it was decided that, in order to examine and assess the potential and suitability of candidates for the Order, they should be invited to meet at the College for several days. Previously selection had been done by simple examination and interview. The experiment proved so successful that the practice was adopted. Regular lists of candidates and their acceptance or rejection show how the Order maintained its standards, taking into account examination results and suitability for deaconess work, both as regards health and stamina, family and marital commitments and also noting when candidates from other denominations offered themselves. For example, in 1906 Esther Louise Taylor, who had served as the College accountant for several years, was accepted, Edith Fanny Jay was declined because of 'her strict Baptist views', five were declined on health grounds and eight others did not reach the required grade. Certain candidates such as Annie Elizabeth Passmore, rejected 'solely on health grounds', Fraulein Hoffman, Miss Fenton, Miss Melling and Winifred Horrell, who had been a member of the Leeds Sisterhood, were accepted as Bible Students, with their families meeting the cost of their fees, set in 1907 at £40. The January 1908 issue of *Flying Leaves* has an article on 'Examination of Candidates' which gives some idea of the thinking behind the process of candidature and selection and emphasises that a candidate who was not selected should not feel 'condemned' or 'rejected' and certainly not 'that God didn't want her', rather that her willingness to offer as a deaconess was 'a test of character necessary before He can open the door to some other and far more appropriate place of service'. Following queries about the type of written papers set in the examination the papers are reproduced with the warning that each year the papers might be very different so it would not be possible to prepare answers! The object of the candidates' examination was to 'give an opportunity to each one to shew her range of knowledge, her powers of observation, and her ability to write down what she knows in a methodical and intelligent way'. The rest of the time spent at the College was taken up by a medical examination, a testimony meeting, oral examinations and interviews, then the Committee met to consider each applicant and the decision was mailed the same evening. After the following year's examinations the comment was made that general knowledge of the Bible was very poor and that obviously the churches and Sunday Schools were not teaching their people well.

Some of the examination questions – 1908

PAPER I

1. Tell the story of the Temptation in the Garden of Eden as correctly as you can.

7. What do you know of either the Apostle Thomas or Andrew?

9. Give the meaning of two of the following:- Repentance, Justification, Regeneration, Salvation.

10. What blessings may we hope for at the Lord's Supper?

PAPER II

2. Name three of the Great Railway Companies of England, and in each case mention six towns they serve.

5. Write down the names of either twenty English wild plants, ten English freshwater fish, ten English wild birds, or six English wild animals.

6. What are the duties of three of the following:- a Policeman, Guardian of the Poor, Member of the Town Council, Magistrate, Sanitary Inspector, or School Attendance Officer.

9. Give a brief account of either Henry VIII, Queen Elizabeth, Charles I, or William III.

10. Give the titles of four of the works of the following:- Charles Dickens, Thackerary, Ruskin, George Eliot.

11. If 3 guineas had to be divided between six women and six boys, the women to get twice as much as the boys, how much would each get?

Source: Flying Leaves (January 1908) p.186

Flying Leaves, in its July-August 1913 number, contains a copy of Bradfield's 'Letter to intending Candidates' in which he defines the nature of the Order and sets out the requirements for prospective candidates – age, education, health, talents, Christian experience – and explains the procedure for candidature and the cost of training.

The Order had always been concerned for its image and had maintained a high standard for the acceptance of candidates and for regulating their behaviour and work. However, by September 1915 Bradfield felt that the existing constitution of the Discipline Committee needed overhauling. He reported that recently he had instituted a system whereby a small meeting, chaired by an ex-President of Conference, was convened so that all sides of a case could be heard privately. This procedure had worked well and he now wished it to be regularised. The Committee, therefore, agreed that in matters which could be easily resolved this procedure should be used, but in more serious cases a formal disciplinary committee should be convened. This committee would consist of the Chairman, preferably an ex-President or other senior minister, Mr. and Mrs. Bradfield, four members of the Deaconess Committee – ideally one chosen by the deaconess and one by the person bringing the charge, otherwise the Warden was empowered to make the selection. In cases without a definite charge the deaconess concerned would choose three members of the committee and the Warden one. Furthermore the Committee authorised the Warden in urgent cases to suspend the deaconess, but recognised she had the right of appeal to the Disciplinary Committee.

In December 1923 it was decided that candidates for the Order should be invited to the College at the beginning of the January term, having first provided a medical report and satisfied the Warden of their suitability for training for the work of a deaconess. The expenses of that term's residence would be borne by the candidate or her friends, except in special cases, and her acceptance would be decided at the end of the term. It seems that not only was this a financial measure exacerbated by war conditions, but it also enabled the Warden and College tutors better to assess the candidate's potential, which again could save wasting precious resources.

It is interesting to learn that the Institute accepted four candidates in May 1920 from the Primitive Methodist Church as paying students. This indicates two things: first, that there were Primitive Methodist Deaconesses, second, that although most of that church's deaconess training was basically practical in nature – they learned 'on the job' at St. George's Hall, Bermondsey – some of them did receive more 'academic' training by attending lectures either at Ilkley or at the United Methodist Deaconess Institute, in London. It is worth noting that of the 22 accepted in 1932, 16 Sisters 'trained at St. George's Hall' and many became permanent members of staff at the Mission; five had 'no institutional training' and one, Frances Flint, 'trained at the Bible Training Institute, Glasgow'. Mary Annie Davies, born 1868 in Walsall, served for 42 years and is described as 'Evangelist'.

For a while there had been a feeling that it would be good to have a Retired Deaconess Fellowship and the Warden had given his backing to it, so on 27th April 1938 at the Manchester Convocation 24 deaconesses met together to consider the suggestion. It was hoped that such a fellowship 'would strengthen the bond of sympathy and love'; help the transition from 'active service to the passive side; and provide more 'interest at Convocation'. The suggestion was accepted unanimously and The Retired Deaconess Circle came into being.

The acute shortage of deaconesses in 1938, and throughout the war years led to some easing of the hitherto strict admission regulations, for example, Greta Temple and Irene Brown, Visiting Students at the College who were engaged to ministers, served until their marriages and several unattached deaconesses were used, while Doris Parsons (neé Crook) was allowed to remain as a Probationer-Deaconess after her marriage and Sister Frances Jones, serving at Piggott St., but shortly to be married to a soldier, was permitted to continue in her appointment as a member of the Order.

Some concern was expressed in 1951 that, because of the large number of candidates coming forward, there was not adequate time at the July Committee to interview each one properly, so it was decided that a sub-committee should review the procedure and suggest ways of improving the situation. It made two recommendations, namely that for the present year 'obviously fully acceptable' candidates should be accepted without their references needing to be scrutinised, but that for the future a Candidates' sub-committee should be set up to meet, interview and report on candidates prior to the General Committee.

There is a significant sentence in the Warden's Report to the General Committee on 16th December 1955, when he commented 'that in many new appointments deaconesses were being called upon to do the kind of work complementary to that of a minister'.[7] So it looks as if the status of deaconesses was now being recognised and this may also have had an influence on the future as regards training and appointments.

The 1957 Convocation was concerned about the decrease in the number of candidates and the increase in resignations from the Order. It was stated 'that since 1947, 134 candidates had been

---

7. WDOMins IV 15th December 1955

accepted and that 33 had resigned after leaving College, 18 on account of marriage'. After discussion the following resolutions were passed:

> 1. That definite studies should be set for probationers and that Superintendent Ministers should be notified that these studies are compulsory.
> 2. That probationers should return to College at least once during their time of probation – this visit to be at the expense of the College.
> 3. That the Finance Committee should be asked to consider the financial situation as regards candidates offering for the Order at an age above the average age for candidating, in view of the heavy commitment to the Retirement Fund required of such older candidates.[8]

For a number of years, during the 1950s, there were so few candidates that all the requests for appointments could not be met, in spite of various publicity schemes. However, it was strongly emphasised that standards should not be lowered to attract applicants. In order to address the situation it was suggested that Synods should be approached and asked to bring the Wesley Deaconess Order to the attention of their churches' members. The Publicity Committee made a number of recommendations which were implemented including a series of articles in the *Methodist Recorder* followed by an interview with the Warden. One Chairman of the District had arranged a meeting to highlight the Order and a contribution had been put in the Youth Magazine. As a totally new approach, in conjunction with the Home Mission Department, the members of the Order attended Butlin's Camp Conference. A request was received from local circuits for illustrative material to display at the Keighley Show. Pembury Local Preachers' Summer School and Easter Schools, Sixth Formers' Conferences and Career Fairs were all suggested as venues where the Order might be publicized. The Publicity Committee further suggested that the Methodist Training Colleges and Synods, via the Chairmen of the Districts, should be targeted and also that there should be a stand at Conference and, following the success of the display at Harrogate Careers Exhibition, further such ventures should be explored.

---

8. Mins. of Conv. (May 1957) pp.186, 190

In spite of a decrease in the membership of the Order in June 1958 the Warden was able to report that he had managed to fill all the appointments requested because some long-standing appointments had been closed for financial reasons. He stressed that 'there was a great need for the right type of candidate, but . . . we must guard against sacrificing quality for numbers as the appointments which were opening up brought with them fuller opportunity and fuller responsibility.[9]

Training and Studies

Highways and Hedges in 1891 gave details of the training the deaconesses received. On the theoretical side Biblical Lectures were given by the Rev. A. E. Gregory, and Dr. A. C. Tunstall provided Medical Instruction based on the St. John's Ambulance Association courses: all the Sisters of the Children and the Wesley Deaconesses participated in these. Practical experience in church work was gained by the attachment of two of the Sisters to the Hackney Road Mission under the oversight of the Rev. Samuel Wilkes, as noted in chapter 7, who was so impressed with the work of Sisters Ruth and Annette that he soon agreed to assist Stephenson by becoming Honorary Secretary. Deaconesses also worked in the Bethnal Green Circuit with the Rev. Josiah E. Whydale. A manuscript diary (1900-01) of Elizabeth Ann Pitts (Sister Annie) survives, but says little about the training at Mewburn House and her practical experiences are similar to those recounted in chapter 1. She left the Order before she completed her probation to be married.

With the move to Ilkley urgent consideration had to be given to the staff required and it was decided that Dr. Stephenson, as Warden, Mrs. Stephenson as the 'Lady Superintendent', and Sister Dora Stephenson, as 'Honorary Corresponding Secretary' should live in the College, plus a 'Tutress in General Studies'. In addition there should be a non-resident tutor in Theology and special arrangements made for tuition in medical nursing, 'artisan and invalid' cookery and physical education. This programme indicates both the scope and practicality of the training offered to prepare the deaconesses for their work. Then, when William Bradfield took over as Warden in 1907, he broadened the educational base by arranging for lectures to be given on the licensing laws, local government, sanitation and hygiene, so that the deaconesses would

---

9. WDOMins IV 30th June 1958

be better fitted to work in a changing world. He also instituted an elocution course to help them with public speaking and the conduct of meetings.

For the first time, in 1908, there were deaconesses without appointment. This is perhaps some measure of the success of the venture in that more suitable candidates were coming forward and being trained and perhaps fewer were leaving the Order or having to rest through ill-health. Or could it be that one of Bradfield's financial measures had backfired? He had sent a letter asking circuits employing a deaconess for an extra three pounds a year and some circuits, therefore, found they could no longer afford a deaconess. However, the surplus meant that some of the older Sisters were offered a three-month rest at the College with the opportunity of attending lectures. This sabbatical period had several advantages in that it eased the appointments situation, gave some deaconesses a much needed rest and also allowed them time for some more study, which most would have little chance of doing while they were working. Reports were received from both the American and Canadian Deaconess organisations and in 1908 two items were highlighted for consideration. The American report pointed out that there had been such a growth in demand for their Sisters that there was a shortage, upon which Bradfield commented that the same could well happen in this country or that, if the Wesley Deaconess Order had a surplus of Sisters, some could go to work in America. On the Canadian report he remarked that their system of allowing deaconesses who had served for a continuous term of three years to take a three month break for further study was an admirable one which the Wesley Deaconess Order might copy.

From January 1904 *Flying Leaves* contained a 'Table of Bible Readings' each month so that the deaconesses could have directed Bible Study and this was supplemented when almost every month, from January 1908, *Flying Leaves* contained a series of studies under the title 'The Warden's Bible Class' in which Bradfield sought to ensure the continuing education of the deaconesses by making sure that they became thoroughly familiar with the Biblical texts. He also provided ideas for their own devotional reading and discussions, as well as offering useful advice on how they might 'evangelise' in various situations. In 1911 Bradfield gave a practical address to Convocation on 'a course of reading suitable for a deaconess' and commended helpful works so that they could maintain their studies.

Recommended reading 1911

Illingworth,	*Personality: Human & Divine,*
	Reason and Revelation,
	The Divine Immanence,
Orr,	*Christian View of God & the World,*
Stalker,	*The Trial and Death of Jesus Christ,*
Denney,	*The Death of Christ,*
Dale,	*The Atonement,*
G. A. Smith,	*Isaiah,*
Skinner,	*Ezekiel*

Source: Record of Convocation (May 1911)

The Rev. Dr. William Russell Maltby, who became Warden in 1920, suggested that some of the students would benefit from practical experience before taking up their first appointments. In order to achieve this a furnished flat was rented on favourable terms and the experiment put in hand at Leeds Mission. Such experience would be very valuable to the students who would learn different aspects of deaconess work before being placed, often on their own, in a strange circuit. They would be able to share and discuss their experiences with others and with the tutors at Ilkley. The experiment would also enable the College staff to see how the students coped with life in the church and in the community and with all the pressures of the job to which they had dedicated themselves and finally the Leeds Mission would benefit from having extra staff to help in their work.

Ilkley College Staff (1914-17):
Esther Taylor (Secretary);
Emily Orr (Tutor);
Gwladys Phillips (Home Sister);
Muriel Murphy (Uniform);
Helena Rattenbury (Office);
Elsie Ward (Office)

When, in 1922, Maltby restarted the deaconess magazine as *The Agenda* (*Flying Leaves* had been discontinued during World War I), in the very first issue he stated he intended that there would be some very practical 'helps' for the work of the Order. Thereafter, 'Studies in the Character of Christ (for a Bible Class or a Junior Class)'; 'For a Guild or Reading Circle (Agenda for two Evenings)'; and 'The Practice of Prayer' and similar studies appeared in almost every issue.

Obviously the training given at Ilkley was highly esteemed because the Women's Auxiliary in 1923 offered £100 per annum 'in acknowledgement of the help given in training and providing (sic) their candidates' and there was growing co-operation between the two with four deaconesses being accepted by the Women's Auxiliary for work overseas in 1924. In September that same year Miss Florence Polkinhorne, Secretary of the Home Preparation Work of the Women's Auxiliary, came to live and work at the College to affiliate the work of the Deaconess Order with that organisation in the hope that there would be an expansion among those who wished to equip themselves for work in the Church, but did not necessarily intend to become missionaries. In some cases the Women's Auxiliary students who were receiving training at Ilkley found their vocation and offered for the Order. Other visiting students, who took part in the life of the College and paid their own fees or were sponsored by another organization, but who were not necessarily intending to become Wesley Deaconesses, had always been part of the College community. A number of these came from other denominations and quite a few from overseas. For example, in the late 1940s there were students from South Africa and Burma. It is perhaps an indication of the high esteem in which the training given at Ilkley was held that this occurred, but it also meant that those in College gained a wider knowledge of, and deeper insight into, the Church overseas.

For some time the General Committee had entertained the hope that one day the period of training could be extended to two years and in 1928 the opportunity arose. There was a special meeting to discuss a proposal for closing the College for a term and extending the training period over five terms instead of three, when it was decided that 'in view of the need for a more extended training, and of the fact that not more than eight or ten additional deaconesses are required per year, it was resolved:- That the next College year shall begin in January 1929 . . .'. Later in the year it was agreed that no candidates over thirty should be accepted except in very special circumstances. A further development in training occurred in 1930 when it was agreed to close the College for the autumn term so that the first-year students might gain practical experience by being placed in circuits and Missions under special arrangements. When the College re-opened in January 1931 Miss Hunter and Miss Dorothy Farrar were the tutors and the College was delighted in July 1931 to learn that Dorothy Farrar, BA had obtained a PhD. She eventually entered the Order in March 1936 and became Vice

Principal in 1942 and was, in 1952, only the second woman to be Vice President of the Methodist Conference.

Maltby followed in the footsteps of his predecessor by facing up to the ever changing nature of deaconess work when he accepted a renewed request from Convocation, endorsed by the General Committee, in 1929 to try to engage a lecturer or lecturers

Ilkley College Staff (July 1939):
Dr. Maltby (Warden); Dorothy Farrar;
Mary McCord, Mary Hunter,
Margaret Statham; Mrs. Maltby (seated)

with expert knowledge and practical experience of social work . . . to give a short course or courses of Lectures on Sex Ethics, Social Purity, and other aspects of social work.[10]

Miss Higson, who had previously given addresses on Rescue work and other aspects of social work to Convocation, visited the College for three days in April 1930 to give lectures on Social Hygiene, presumably in response to this request. Does this mean that the social work side of deaconess work, which had always been important, was now becoming even more so? Did it mean that in the freer atmosphere of the late 1920s the deaconesses felt that their training was not keeping pace with the rate of change in society? It surely indicates that the deaconesses wished to be as fully equipped as possible for their work.

No difficulty was anticipated after Methodist Union took place about amalgamating the Wesley Deaconess order, the United Methodist Deaconess order and the Primitive Methodist Deaconess Orders as relations between the three organisations were very friendly. The Warden reported to the 1931 Convocation, that preliminary conversations having taken place, it was probable that all students would take the first year of their training at Ilkley and that the second year might be spent in practical work. Sister Annie Chapman, a Primitive Methodist Deaconess visited the 1932 Convocation and 'spoke of the value of such a fellowship of ours, and of the good work done by the Sisters of her own church at St. George's Hall, London'.

---

10. WDIMins II p.256; *The Agenda* (June 1929) p.9

It seemed only right when, in 1931, there were 11 unemployed deaconesses, to formulate a policy for unemployed Sisters as the Order realised that in times of financial stringency circuits tended to dispense with the services of their deaconess. It was also considered advisable to have one or two deaconesses without appointment so that unexpected vacancies could be filled quickly, but more important issues needed to be addressed. Unemployed Sisters received £5.00 a month: this was about one third of their allowance when in work and doubtless meant difficulties for them personally, but it was also a drain on the slender financial resources of the Order as it tried to find this money, as well as, presumably, 'keeping' them at the College, where they would also occupy much needed accommodation. So, at the 1932 Convocation and in the General Committee the following November, the question was raised as to whether any candidates at all should be accepted for 1933-34. Maltby emphasised to both that the crisis was at the present time and to accept no candidates would not help. He stressed the value of a second year's training, pointing out that the longer college course had practically halved the number of candidates accepted. Finally, he insisted on the importance and necessity of maintaining continuity in college life. By March 1933, as the situation had altered drastically because of Methodist Union and all the re-organisation that that had necessitated in circuits and churches throughout the Connexion, it was decided that no more than six should be accepted.[11]

Results of Union

In view of the changed position, including a large number of withdrawals and resignations, also some fresh appointments, with the result that there is no longer a waiting list, we think it advisable that some candidates should be taken this year, though the number should be small.

Source: Wesley Deaconess Institute Minutes (1911-33) p.279

Once Methodist Union had taken place and the deaconess organisations were working together to produce a coherent whole, it was extremely important to define future policy so that the Orders could be united in all aspects of deaconess work. Therefore it was important to standardise the conditions of entry as the Wesley Deaconess Order, as we have seen previously, had been extremely

---

11. WDIMins II pp.272, 274, 279; WDOMins III p.2

jealous of the high standards it demanded. So a small committee consisting of the Wardens, the Revs. G. E Wiles, J. E. Gilbert, in consultation with the staffs of both the Wesley Deaconess Order College and the United Methodist Deaconess Institute, met to draw up a 'common Form of Application and Standard of Examination' and a single selection committee for candidates was established. Obviously it was not necessary for both training houses to be retained and this was recognised by the United Methodist members on the Deaconess Committee in 1933, when the Rev. J. Boden and R. W. Gair proposed that Ilkley should be the Training College and the administration of their Order was transferred to Ilkley in September 1935. The corollary of this was that Bowron House in Wandsworth was to be sold, but the ex-United Methodist Deaconesses were anxious to hold a reunion there on 4th and 5th July 1935 before this happened. Bowron House was eventually sold in the autumn and, after the deduction of costs, realised £2,328.7s.0. The ex-United Methodist Deaconesses presented a Bible and vase for the chapel at Ilkley as a tribute to Mr. Gair, who remained a valued advisor and joint secretary until his death in the autumn of 1938.

The 1947 Convocation asked the General Committee to consider providing a Retreat during the summer of 1948 and also that deaconesses with more than 10 years' service might have refresher courses. The Committee thoroughly approved of both requests and readily acceded to the first, but in view of the shortage of Sisters felt unable to agree to the second at that time.

Lecture Room at Ilkley College with Dorothy Farrar

In March 1961 Dorothy Farrar pointed out to the General Committee that the time would come when training would need to be increased either by:

1.   Possibility of a third year at Ilkley.

2.   Possibility of a third year in some specialised training, say in youth work, moral welfare, or further academic courses.

3.   Whether it ought to be immediately after the two years at Ilkley, or whether it would be better after Ordination . . .[12]

In June the Warden took up this and reiterated the importance of having a third year of specialized training 'in view of the Albemarle Report with its stress on the need for qualified Youth Leaders, the growing need for Moral Work, and the increasing opportunities for Industrial Chaplaincies'. The College staff were asked to work out a definite plan for future studies in time for the next meeting. So at the December meeting an outline of the further year of study was presented:

1.   Before Candidating: . . . G.C.E. standard of education . . . (or) at least one or two subjects in 'O' level including English.

2.   Before College: . . . some candidates . . . might be directed . . . (to improve) their general education . . . graduates . . . might be directed into work which would bring them into contact with other types of people, prepare them for College, and help them to mature.

3.   In College: Those whose educational standard permits should be encouraged to take subjects which could play a part in the BD or Diploma in Theology, e.g. Greek and Hebrew . . .

4.   After College: Those . . . preparing for BD or Diploma in theology should continue their preparation through their probationer studies . . .

Special courses could be arranged in Youth work, Industrial chaplaincy, to Moral Welfare . . .

---

12.   WDOMins IV 27th March 1961, 26th June 1961

5. <u>Finance</u>: . . . charge on our Funds, and a Bursary might be made available. Grants by Local Authorities especially for Youth Leadership Courses.

6. <u>Selection</u>: . . . by a Committee . . .[13]

This was accepted as an interim scheme and passed on to the Executive Committee for confirmation. The Warden referred to the plans for the third year of study and pointed out much would depend on an increase both in the number of candidates and appointments. The third year was quickly put into effect and in December 1962 it was reported 'that as a result of the introduction of the third year we now had one deaconess who is taking further course of Social Study at Southampton. In addition to this the Methodist Youth Department is arranging a course on Youth Work for the London deaconesses.' This matter of specialized training continued to be debated in the Order and in 1963 Convocation sent a resolution to the General Committee:

> In view of the demand and opportunities presented by our society today, we are convinced that it is now a matter of urgency that the whole method of training . . . be reviewed and we urge the staff with a Committee appointed by the General Committee to consider schemes and report to Convocation.

The Special Training Committee which had been set up on 24th June 1963 by the General Committee met three or four times and produced an interim paper on the purpose, the standard, the length, the place of training and the curriculum. At its meeting in January 1964, when the place where deaconesses should be trained was discussed, it was pointed out by the Warden that if the recommendation that they should be trained along with ministerial students was agreed it would be better if all the deaconess students were in one College. It was also noted that deaconesses needed a headquarters to which they could return and that it was essential that the ethos of the Order be maintained. It was suggested that consultations should be held with the Ministerial Training Department. At the General Committee on 22nd June 1964 Sister Dorothy Farrar presented a Memorandum representing her thoughts on the interim report of the Training Committee. The report was then discussed in light of her observations. As a result the following resolutions were agreed:

---

13. WDOMins IV 15th December 1961, 14th December 1962

1. That we should receive the Memorandum prepared by Sister Dorothy and in order that its true potential for the future of the Order might be understood two working parties should be set up by the Warden in consultation with Sister Dorothy, the College staff, and the Vice President of the Order.

2. That we welcome the Training Committee Report.

3. That the Training Committee – which has worked well within the limits of its recommendation – be re-appointed and that it should be with addition of the Vice President, the ex-Vice President, and the Vice President designate, and with power to co-opt the Treasurers of the Order when necessary.[14]

So the future of training was a very important problem facing not only the new Warden, Rev. Geoffrey Litherland, but also the various committees and the Order itself.

A new curriculum including a specialized third year of study was introduced and the principle accepted that the deaconesses should be trained alongside ministerial students. A first step was taken when, from September 1965, the students from Ilkley attended lectures at Wesley College, Headingley, Leeds and vice versa. These lectures included Systematic Theology, Church History, Sociology and Psychology. Then the fact that the Church was reviewing its whole ministerial training strategy meant that a serious situation had to be faced. Over recent years the number of candidates offering for the Order had fallen in spite of increased publicity. Much of this was due to the prevailing social conditions which had opened many other avenues of work to women, the feeling that deaconesses were not being afforded the status their work merited and the fact that the climate in the Methodist Church was moving, at last, towards the likelihood of admitting women into the Ministry of the Word and Sacraments. Were the Ministerial Training Department to decide to close Headingley College, the General Committee noted that there were three possible courses of action:

---

14. Mins. of Conv. (April 1963) p.4 (April/May 1965) pp.7, 9 (April 1966) p.2; WDOMins IV 24th June 1963, 12th November 1963, 6th January 1964, 2nd March 1964, 22nd June 1964, 11th December 1964

1. To reduce the period of training again to two years.

2. To appoint additional staff at Ilkley so as to be able to sustain the three-year course.

3. To move to some other site where we can share in facilities which will enable us to sustain our training course.

It was agreed that the Order's plight should be brought to the attention of Conference and that the following Notice of Motion should be submitted:

> In view of the Conference decision of recent years extending the training of students for the Deaconess Order and linking it with that of candidates for the ministry, the Conference directs that in all discussion concerning new buildings for training and particularly concerning the timing of changes affecting Wesley College, Headingley, the Deaconess Order be fully represented.

As noted in chapter 6 when Headingley College closed the Order moved to Birmingham so that the deaconesses could receive adequate training at Handsworth Theological College and the University.[15]

After having seen the Order settled in Edgbaston, Birmingham, and having begun the integration of the Order into the new Division of Ministries, the Rev. Geoffrey Litherland retired in 1972. The new Warden, the Rev. Brian Galliers, inherited this integration, which evolved as Methodism worked towards modernising its structures. He also had to deal with the changing thinking on the nature of the diaconate, which had occurred with the opening of the presbyteral ministry to women and in due course the Division of Ministries produced a study paper on the Order and the diaconate. The result was that the Board of the Division of Ministries recommended that the Wesley Deaconess Order cease recruiting from 1978.

---

15. WDOMins IV 20th June 1966, 15th December 1966, 19th June 1967; Mins. of Conv. (April 1967) p.3, (April 1968) p.5 WDOExec. Com. Mins. 13th February 1968

Convocation

From 1881 The Children's Home was accustomed to have an Annual Conference of Workers and the one on 8th July 1891 was attended by the deaconesses from Mewburn House. Then, the first public recognition service of three Sisters from Mewburn House, who had completed their training, was held on the evening of 17th September in the Chapel of The Children's Home. They were Sisters Rita, in charge of Mewburn House, Hilda Rich, to become Sister-in-Charge at the new Bowman Branch House, Norwich, and Sarah Freer, who was to go to Truro. The service was conducted by the President of Conference, who that year, most appropriately, was the Rev. Dr. Thomas Bowman Stephenson, assisted by the Rev. Samuel Wilkes. Dr. Stephenson handed each Sister a Bible with the words: 'Take this Holy Book; make it your constant companion; and find in it comfort, guidance, and help for yourself, and your work.' They then received Holy Communion. This service eventually developed into the Consecration Service, which was normally held during Convocation – an annual event which lasted up to a week. Stephenson who was very musical and he wrote a number of hymns and songs for the Children's Home Choirs and also 'Our Own Deaconess Hymn', with a tune by T. E. Perkins. This came to be called the 'Convocation Hymn', being used regularly at Convocation and Consecration Services until the mid-1960s. A new tune was composed by Sir John Frederick Bridge, musical editor of the 1904 hymn book, and Stephenson remarked it would be entitled 'Convocation' in the new Hymn Book as a reminder of the Order.[16] Convocation still plays an important part in the calendar of the Wesley Deaconess Order and the Methodist Diaconal Order.

---

16. In fact the tune was entitled 'Lothian' (hymn 765 *The Methodist Hymn Book with Tunes,* 1904), (hymn 786 *The Methodist Hymn Book with Tunes,* 1933). In 1960 after a committee had looked at alternative tunes Convocation decided on 'Kingston' by W. Hayes. The hymn was omitted from *Hymns & Psalms* (1983) cf, *FL* (October 1901) p.16, (April 1904) pp.52-53

> ## Convocation Hymn   Rev. Dr. T. B. Stephenson
>
> Lord, grant us, like the watching five,
> To wait Thy coming, and to strive
> Each one her lamp to trim;
> And, since the oil Thou dost impart,
> Pour daily grace into each heart,
> Lest any lamp grow dim.
>
> May we not wait in selfish sloth,
> But mingle prayer and work, that both
> May trim the shining light;
> So, from the midnight of their sin
> May many, with us, enter in,
> To banquet in Thy sight.
>
> We would not come alone, dear Lord,
> To Thy great feast, and at Thy board
> In rapture sit and gaze;
> But bring the lost, the sick, the lone,
> The little ones to be Thine own,
> And look into Thy face.
>
> *Source: Flying Leaves* (April 1904) p.53

The yearly Convocation of the Wesley Deaconess Order had previously been held in connection with The Children's Home, but from April 1902 the Order met in its own Convocation in different towns, with the first one being held at Oxford Place, Leeds. A very appropriate venue as Stephenson was now stationed in the Ilkley Circuit and negotiations were underway for the establishment of a training house in the area. Very soon Convocation evolved a basic pattern for its meetings, starting with a service of Holy Communion, followed by addresses of welcome and letters of greeting. Then the record of the previous year's Convocation was read, the Roll of Deaconesses called, a report of the state of the Order presented, business sessions dealt with the following questions:

1. Who has died during the year?

2. Who have ceased to be acknowledged/recognised as Wesley Deaconesses?

3. Who are still recognised as belonging to the Order, although not actively employed?

4. Who has been received during the year?

and other matters relating to the smooth running of the Order, such as correspondence, including reports from deaconesses working overseas, uniform, finance and appointments. In later years resolutions and notices of motion to be submitted to the General Committee were passed. During Convocation addresses of devotional, inspirational and practical nature were given and testimony services held. The most moving service, usually conducted by the President of the Conference, was the Consecration Service of the Deaconesses who had completed their probation.

One of the first things which had to be settled when Methodist Union took place was the name by which the unified Order should be known. The General Committee, believing that this was a matter for the deaconesses themselves, referred it to the 1933 Convocation. A number of suggestions were made, such as 'Methodist Deaconess Order', or the name of a saint as it was thought that using 'Wesley' might seem to be too Wesleyan, though some of the ex-United Methodist Sisters were very willing for it to be used. After some discussion it was decided the different sections should look at the matter in their separate sessions with the result that the ex-Wesleyans decided to wait to see what the ex-United Methodist Sisters preferred. They opted

> to have the name 'Methodist' in if possible, but if that was not in harmony with the wishes of the majority, and the name of a saint should be preferred, it was unanimously resolved to agree to the name of 'Wesley'.

The final debate in Convocation resulted in the following unanimous resolution being forwarded to the General Committee for submission to the Conference:

> The Convocation, having been requested by the Committee to consider the question of the name to be given to the Order into which the Deaconesses of the Methodist Church are now united, expresses its judgement that it is desirable that the custom of calling such an Order by the name of some revered personality in the history of the Church should be followed. And seeing that Methodism in all its branches traces its origin and inspiration to the life and labours of John Wesley & that the name 'Wesley' cannot be regarded as sectional or as belonging to our old divisions, but

rather as symbolising our common heritage, the Convocation recommends to the Committee that the Order now united be called 'The Wesley Deaconess Order of the Methodist Church'.[17]

In 1921, as discussed in chapter 6, a suggestion had been made in Conference that perhaps the Order should have a Woman Warden and reference was made to this when the nomination for Warden needed to be made in 1928. The General Committee was anxious to have the opinion of Convocation, which felt that it was important that the Warden should be a minister and drew up a reasoned statement to that effect.

Warden – Woman or Minister?

This Convocation considers that the next Warden to be appointed should be an ordained minister. In all the administrative work of the Order, in Conference, Synods and Circuits, it is invaluable to have a Warden who is also a Minister. Further, this Convocation welcomes the presence on the College Staff of a Warden who is a Minister, and of the Warden along with other men on the Deaconess Committee, being convinced that such co-operation between men and women is an enrichment to all the work of the Order.

Source: Minutes of Convocation (1936-69) (April 1936) p.6

Holiday Homes

The 1922 Convocation passed on to the General Committee a desire, first raised in 1920, from many of the sisters for a small Rest Home, as distinct from the College, adding that several were so keen on the idea that they were willing to take small shares of about £5 in any such venture. While the Committee was broadly in sympathy with the idea it felt unable to proceed solely on financial grounds at that particular moment. However, several months later Maltby indicated that progress was being made in the matter and by the December meeting he was able to report that

the Misses Greenwood had built, furnished and endowed a Cottage at Hampsthwaite nr. Harrogate, to be used as a Holiday Home for educated women, governesses, deaconesses, and others of limited means,

---

17. WDOMins III p.1 (14th November 1932); RConv. 1933 (24th, 25th, 26th April)

> who are sometimes unable to obtain the change and rest which their work or their health demand. The management of the House had been offered to the Wesley Deaconess Committee and provisionally accepted on their behalf by the Warden.
>
> The endowment fund of £6,000 was invested with the Board of Trustees in Manchester to be administered by our Committee, and the property which at present was copyhold would shortly become freehold under the new Act and would be conveyed to Trustees named by the Committee.

Needless to say the Committee gratefully accepted and sent a letter of appreciation to the Misses Greenwood. Hampsthwaite was about four miles outside Harrogate towards Pateley Bridge. 'Restawhile' opened on 5th December with Sister Esther Taylor as Sister-in-Charge and room for three visitors. The normal length of stay was to be between two and three weeks, with initially no charge apart from laundry. That 'Restawhile' was well used is indicated by the report of its first year which then showed

> . . . that the House had been occupied throughout the year and that there was a continuous demand for the benefit of it. The income received for the year was £227.9.0 and the expenditure up to date £202.15.8. On the first year's working the accounts show that after everything is included, the dividends from the invested money given by the Misses Greenwood will cover the expenses and leave a small margin as a Reserve for Furnishing & Repairs or any emergency.[18]

Obviously the house, as well as paying its way, fulfilled a need and provided a place of rest and relaxation for those who stayed there. Indeed *The Agenda* reported that in nine months 49 guests had been accommodated. Congratulations were also offered to Miss Nellie Greenwood on her marriage, while her sister joined the Wesley Deaconess Committee. In July 1929 the Warden informed the Committee that Miss Mabel Greenwood and her sister, Mrs. Mumme, had bought a house in Ilkley with the intention of

---

18. RConv. 1920 (20th May), 1922 (29th May); WDIMins II pp.182, 186, 189, 197, 211, 222 (loose agenda sheet says 'redecorated and repapered'), 255, 259 cf. *The Agenda* (July 1922) p.10, (December 1922) pp.5, 10 (January 1923) pp.8, 14 (November 1923) p.11

transferring 'Restawhile' there to serve the same purpose and in December the Committee members were given the opportunity to visit the new house.

By 1951 'Restawhile' Holiday Home in Hangingstone Road, which had served the Order so well since 1929, was not being fully used and was running at a loss. The deficiency had been masked because Miss Mabel Greenwood had met the short-fall for several years. Now she suggested that it might be better to sell the property and buy a house in a more central position. This seemed a wise thing to do and so the old 'Restawhile' was sold for £2,500 and 'Moorland', renamed 'Restawhile', Ben Rhydding Road, was purchased for £4,500 with Miss Greenwood making up the difference. It opened in August 1952 and continued in use for around 10 years, but by December 1959 it had become apparent that it was no longer 'serving its purpose and that there had been very few guests'. So, after consultation with Miss Greenwood and the Trustees for Methodist Church Purposes, the actual owners of the property, it was agreed that the Order's responsibility for 'Restawhile' should cease from the end of February 1960. When 'Restawhile' was sold permission was given by the Charity Commissioners to 'apply the clear yearly income to defraying the cost of recuperative holidays for such educated women or other female persons of limited means . . . in Holiday Homes selected by the Managing Trustees'. Hence the Trustees for Methodist Church Purposes offered the Order 12 yearly bursaries of £25 each. In 1958 Miss Greenwood retired from the General Committee and the Committee paid tribute to her 'gracious and generous giving which has placed the whole Order in her debt'.[19]

A property which came into the ownership of the Wesley Deaconess Order was 13 St. George's Road, Worthing. This was left, fully furnished and endowed, to the Order by Sister Mabel Robinson. It opened as a Holiday Home on 1st July 1946 with Sister Doris Nicholson in charge to complement the long established 'Restawhile' in Ilkley. This Holiday Home fulfilled its purpose well until the shortage of staff made it difficult to keep open so it closed on 31st August 1980 and was sold the following May.

Yet another practical caring matter came to the fore when the question of deaconesses who had had to retire from active work through ill-health or family commitments, but wished to keep in

19. WDOExec. Com. Mins. 27th February 1958

contact with the Order was raised. It was decided that possibilities for implementing such a contact should be explored. In connection with this it is interesting to note what happened to deaconesses who did have to retire. For example, Martha Ellis, forced through deafness to leave the active work, opened a boarding house with a friend at St. Anne's on Sea with the £18 she could withdraw from the Annuitant Fund and a grant of £100 from the Retiring Fund. Adela Moss, a trained nurse and a missionary in India from 1907-23, (as noted in chapter 4), when she returned home worked for a year on deputation for the Women Auxiliary before becoming Matron of the Mildmay Maternity Nursing Home for two years after which she 'by special arrangement' ran a Nursing Home at Welwyn Garden City. Two of the senior deaconesses, Ruth Northcroft, one of the earliest deaconesses, who entered in 1890 and Phillis Pryce-Jones, entered 1892, retired in 1923 to a little house, Fron-galed in Corris Merioneth, where they kept open house, on reasonable terms, for any Sisters who might need a break, as did Marjorie Sheard near Hunstanton when she had to retire. Isabelle Volckman, entered 1916, resigned in 1924 through ill-health and opened a Hostel for University women and Students in London. It seems that deaconesses who retired or engaged in suitable 'private work' were often allowed to retain their connection with the Order.

Retirement Homes

Over the years there had been concern about provision of a home for the 'Aged and Infirm' deaconesses and in 1948 it was reported that £3,370 was in hand for such a project. Then a Miss Furneaux offered a very suitable house in Woking 'by Deed of Gift' for the purpose. The Rank Trust was prepared to grant some money and a gift from Miss Florence Rowbotham was received so that all seemed settled for the house to come into operation. This was in December 1950, but unfortunately the Finance Committee came across a problem in 'The Statute of Mortmain' (definition – 'the state or condition of lands etc. held inalienably, as by an ecclesiastical or other corporation') which precluded acceptance of this generous gift. However, in September 1952 a house in Cleethorpes was offered and accepted:

> . . . The house had been acquired . . . through the generosity of Mr. and Mrs. Osborne, whose parents owned the house. The accommodation available . . . would be for 12 Sisters and four resident staff . . . A gardener was already at work and the home would be opened in September . . .

Mr. and Mrs. Osborne had offered the house at £2,000 with £1,000 being paid on completion and the remainder, free of interest, over five years. A local committee was appointed to have general oversight of the house, called Albemarle, which opened officially on 24th October 1953. The house served a very useful purpose for many years as providing a safe haven for 'aged', changed later to 'retired', deaconesses. In the 1960s it was decided to offer temporary respite care and then to admit Sisters' relations. Increased costs, staffing difficulties and lack of fire precautions forced the closure of Albemarle in 1978. Some of the residents were moved into Methodist Homes for the Aged. The Finance Committee accepted an offer of £40,000 for the property from Mr. and Mrs. J. D. Roberts who were willing to take over responsibility for any residents who could not go into Methodist Homes for the Aged.

Albemarle, Cleethorpes:
the Retirement Home

Sister Frances Ayles, who died on 30th April 1946, along with many other deaconesses, had been very concerned about the older retired sisters and so she made arrangements in her will for a row of houses to be left especially for their benefit.[20] These houses, probably eight, in Upper Brassey Street, Birkenhead were valued at around £2,450. It was decided not to sell them immediately as they brought in a rent of £293.16s.0d. gross. However, it seems likely that by 1950 the Order was considering selling off the houses as that year one was sold to the sitting tenant for £750 and the agents were instructed not to relet any of the property without consulting the Warden and the General Committee. Then in 1953 No. 50 was sold for around £600. In 1958 after repairs had been done to conform with the 1957 Rent Act the Order decided that the time had come to dispose of the houses. No. 56 was accordingly sold for £610.13s.4d. An enquiry was made about No. 48 in 1963 and the Order was prepared to sell at around £700, but a further offer of £1,400 for the four remaining houses was rejected. In April 1973 a letter was received from the agents in Birkenhead regarding a request from the

---

20. Mins. of Conv. (April 1944) p.52, (May 1946) p.72 cf. (April 1948) pp.92-93 [Nos. 48, 50, 52, 54, 56, 58, 60 and possibly 46 or 62 can be identified]

Social Services for alterations to be made to one of the houses for the installation of an inside toilet. Social Services was willing to pay for the structural alterations if the Order would provide the 'new pedestal'. Having agreed to this the Warden was asked to investigate the possibility of selling any house which became vacant. It was reported in June that the estate agents thought that £1,500, subject to a charge for dilapidations, would be realised by the sale. However, when the property was put up for auction with a reserve price of £1,800, an offer of £2,000 was received, but in the end the property fetched £3,774 net.

It seems to have been recognised by the Church that not all deaconesses wished to go into a Home like Albemarle and just as ministers were enabled to find houses when they retired, so some provision should be made for deaconesses. To this end the London (Wanstead and Woodford) Circuit sent a Memorial to the 1961 Conference asking that the needs of retired deaconesses be considered.[21] The General Committee referred it to the Finance Committee which decided it should be reported to the Conference that the Order was 'seeking to build up a Fund which after a period of three or four years will make it possible to give Retirement Grants, as this was considered to be a better way of meeting the needs of deaconesses on their retirement'. The Order obviously made an effort to fulfil this promise as in November 1963: 'It was agreed that as from 31st August 1964 a furnishing grant of £50 should be paid to each deaconess retiring from the active work.' However, over the next few years opinions must have changed as by 1964 the Order was actively seeking suitable property and co-operating with the Methodist Ministers' Housing Association. Sister Celia Cotton submitted a proposal relating to 'a £250,000 Church Community Scheme' by the Methodists of Lowestoft which included a 10 storey block of flats, and she had hopes that two of the flats might be made available to the Order however, the project proved too costly. After a conversation with the Ministers' Housing Association it was suggested that if any house offered to it was too small or too large for a minister and his wife it might be made available to the Order. Then apparently little progress was made about getting housing for retired deaconesses for around 10 years. However, in June 1973 the Warden reported that the Joseph Rank Benevolent Trust might be willing to help the Order buy five

---

21. *Mins. of Conf.* (1961) p.86; WDOMins IV 15th December 1961, (cf Finance Com. Mins. 13th February 1962, WDO Exec. Com. Mins. 20th February 1962)

bungalows over the next three years by providing £6,000 per annum, with the possibility of renewal after the three years, but the Order would have to raise an equivalent sum of money. Five thousand pounds had also been received for the project from the Methodist Missionary Society. The first retirement bungalow, 26 Forest Road, Broseley, near Bridgnorth was purchased in 1974 and the following year a flat at 160 Kingsway, Sunniside, Gateshead, was acquired. In due course, after the presbyteral ministry was opened to women, the retirement arrangements were subsumed into the Methodist Ministers' Housing Association.

Chapter 9

The United Methodist Institute and the Primitive Methodist Sisters

The United Methodist Free Churches Deaconess Order (1891-1907)

The Beginnings

Another branch of Methodism, the United Methodist Free Churches, also felt the need for some kind of female work at about the same time that Thomas Bowman Stephenson and others were starting their organisations.   So the Connexional Evangelistic Secretary, the Rev. Alfred Jones, began to take steps in that direction.   In June 1890 he and the Rev. Henry T. Chapman, superintendent minister of the Lady Lane Mission, Leeds, visited Mr. George Clegg's Home for Female Evangelists in Halifax.[1] It is obvious from the article Chapman wrote in *The Free Methodist* that he and Jones were much impressed by the Home and its organisation and hoped to be able to set up something similar for the United Methodist Free Churches. Apparently in response to their questions Clegg replied that women who offered themselves as female evangelists were 'intelligent, well-brought up, capable and godly', and after some initial reservations they were generally accepted and appreciated by the circuits and that it cost around £250 a year, mainly paid by Clegg himself, to train the Sisters. It seems that following an appeal by Chapman in the newspaper a young lady responded and was working with him at Lady Lane and he was convinced that there must be others 'who if not for life, for a few years' would do the same. He acknowledged that those who offered their services would need training, but believed that some of the more affluent members of the Church would help with 'the funding and maintaining, at first in a small way, a Home for the training of female Evangelists'.

---

1. George Clegg was a Wesleyan Methodist industrialist, who, in 1887, established a female evangelists' home in Halifax as a branch of the Joyful News Mission cf. John A. Hargreaves in *A Dictionary of Methodism in Britain and Ireland* (ed. J. A. Vickers, 2000) pp.70-71

Appeal for help

Surely the time has come for us as Churches to rise to the exigencies of the hour . . . We may not have anyone willing or even able to give £250 a year for the working of such a Home as we visited. But I am sure of one thing, that such an institution would be of incalculable good to our Churches . . . We have scores of Churches languishing, if not dying, for lack of such service as lady evangelists could give. . . . We want not only evangelists, but those able and willing to combine the functions of the evangelist and those of the *sister*.

Source: The Free Methodist (26th June 1890) p.7; cf. Henry Smith, *Ministering Women: The Story of the Work of the Sisters connected with the United Methodist Deaconess Institute . . .'* (n.d. 1912-13) pp.21-22

In November 1890 Mr. Jones engaged a young woman to do evangelistic and visiting work. Obviously the impact was considerable as, by January, he reported that he could find work for four or five others and stated categorically, 'We need a female evangelist agency and we must have one', following up these words by producing a plan to have 'a Home, with a department for female evangelists, and a department for sick nursing'. Inevitably he met some resistance, but with the help of others was able to recruit two more young women in April 1891, but he became so discouraged by 'the indifference and conservatism' of most of the church that he was tempted to abandon the scheme altogether. However, a virtually unknown minister, the Rev. T. J. Cope, was feeling his way in the same direction. In 1890 Cope moved from the Farsley and Yeadon Circuit in Yorkshire to the superintendency of the London VII Circuit, with its main church in Westmoreland Street, Pimlico. The Pimlico Chapel had been established around 1860 and was then a thriving society, but over the years the district had changed and many influential members had either died or moved away, so membership had declined with consequent financial difficulties. Cope was well aware of the problems he would face in an area which had deteriorated and where there were many social problems. He realized that if he were to have any sort of impact on the neighbourhood an intensive programme of visitation was needed. His interest in the work that women could do in the church was sparked off by the sisterhood work of the West London Mission and he quickly became convinced that he had to find suitable women to help him with visiting and attending to the poor and needy and the young people. He appealed unsuccessfully to various wealthy and influential people for support. Refusing to give up hope, at length he turned to the Bowron brothers for help. J. A. and S. Bowron had at one time had connections with the Pimlico church, chiefly through their father William (1810-90). Between 1880 and 1890 William Bowron had travelled to and from New Zealand on business, but on the voyage home in 1889 he fell dangerously ill and was nursed devotedly by a Sister of Mercy. Knowing of this, and thinking the sons might be grateful for the care given to their father and interested in his proposal, Cope visited them on 1st January 1891 to explain his ideas. They agreed not only to support two women, but also to furnish and pay the rent of suitable apartments for them.[2]

To make sure that he secured the most suitably trained women Cope visited various deaconess institutions and talked to many people. He found Dr. Stephenson and the Rev. and Mrs. Hugh Price Hughes to be extremely helpful. Unfortunately he was unable to find any suitable women immediately available to work with him in Pimlico. His vision broadened and he began to think in terms of Free Methodism having its own Deaconess Institute and he talked over his enlarged scheme with the Bowron brothers who gave him their wholehearted approval. The three, therefore, determined to 'establish a House in which godly women should be trained to serve the churches in the threefold capacity of evangelist, district visitor, and nurse'.[3]

Bowron House:
the first United Methodist
Deaconess Institute House

The Bowrons promised that if Cope could establish an institution in Pimlico similar to the Wesley Deaconess Institute they would bear the initial cost and underwrite the project against any financial loss. Cope, having consulted the Rev. Andrew Crombie, the United Methodist Free Churches Book Steward and Editor of the *Free Methodist*, accepted their offer and so the United Methodist Free Churches Deaconess Institute came into being.[4] The first step was to obtain a suitable house, so 165 Lupus Street, Pimlico, London SW was acquired and named Bowron House in memory of William Bowron. It was described as being

---

2. Smith pp.22, 29-32;. Cope, pp.7-10
3. Smith, p.25
4. Smith, p.35; Cope p.10; *UMFC Mins. of Conf.* (1888-91) p.187

in a central position, easily reached by bus, by train, or by boat to the New Exhibition Pier. It is the midst of a large population, very near the big blocks of Peabody buildings, and a short distance from Westmoreland Street chapel. The situation is a healthy one . . . Outside . . . is a large well-engraved plate, bearing the inscription: BOWRON HOUSE. METHODIST DEACONESSES' HOME AND TRAINING INSTITUTION.' The house is home-like and comfortable; it contains nine rooms and a scullery; the drawing and sitting rooms are well carpeted, and the other rooms are covered with linoleum of a pleasant pattern with rugs here and there. Papers and painting are in good taste. The rooms are light and lofty; kitchen and scullery accommodation all that is necessary. To the right of the hall on entering is a room that will be used as a waiting-room, library and office. The bedrooms are of fair size; the furniture is substantial and suitable in all parts of the house . . .[5]

The Deaconess Institute Report to the 1892 United Methodist Free Churches Conference remarked that, despite the initial problems of setting up a new institution, much was encouraging. There had been many several successful missions and much visiting so that 'help [has been] . . . given to poor and needy, temperance pledges have been secured, desertion of children prevented, situations secured for servants, children gathered into schools, men and women won to the house of prayer and induced to surrender themselves to the Lord'. It was noted that the cost of the venture was £293.6s.4d., excluding the deaconesses 'costumes' which had been donated by the Bowron brothers, and that £77.13s.8d. had been received towards the cost. It seems fairly obvious that the Bowrons met the shortfall in the accounts for a number of years.[6]

The Deaconess Institute gave particular emphasis to evangelism and nursing and Mrs. William Mallinson offered to pay the College fees for a Sister to take a two-year medical course at Zenana Medical College if the Missionary Committee would undertake to send out a lady missionary and in 1895 Sister May was reported as taking the 'certificate of the obstetric Society'.[7]

---

5. Smith, pp.39-40
6. *UMFC Mins. of Conf.* (1892) p.187, (1893) pp.200-01; (1894) p.196; (1895) p.210; (1896) p.15; (1897) p.231
7. *UMFC Mins. of Conf.* (1893) p.199

The contacts which Cope had made while researching for the establishing of the Institute were continued as the deaconesses met with Hugh Price Hughes, Thomas Bowman Stephenson and Peter Thompson and visited their organizations to learn about their work and to get practical experience.[8]

Another step in the development of the Institute was when the *Free Methodist* newspaper, which had been very involved and helpful from the outset, agreed to allow the Institute to have a permanent column in its publication as 'the official organ of the work'.[9] This arrangement continued after the 1907 Union with the United Methodist newspaper. These columns, along with the monthly letter from the Warden, acted instead of a magazine for the United Methodist Sisters.

The Organization

As Stephenson before him, Cope now had to find someone to take charge of the newly established Deaconess Home and Training Institute. It proved difficult to find a suitable Methodist lady, however, Cope had had contact previously with the Tottenham Deaconess Institute Hospital which had been established in 1856 and two deaconesses were kindly seconded to him – one to act as superintendent and the other Sister to take charge of the district work. The course of study with the appropriate teachers was arranged.[10] So Sister Lily (Miss Briscoe), who was already experienced in district visiting in the East End of London, became the first probationer student. Bowron House was formally opened on 21st April 1891 with a service of prayer and praise in the afternoon and a public meeting in the evening. Speakers included 'Messrs. J. A. and Sydney Bowron, the Rev. Andrew Crombie, Sisters Marjorie, Alice and Lily of Bowron House, two Sisters from the Wesley Deaconess Institute, Sister Christian, the lady superintendent of the Tottenham Deaconess Institute and the Rev. T. J. Cope'.[11] As the Connexional Committee of the Church was meeting in London during the following week it was decided to have a second inaugural meeting in Westmoreland Street Chapel on 29th April, so that status of the new Institute could be affirmed by the whole Church. Its establishment was endorsed by a large and enthusiastic congregation.

---

8. *UMFC Mins. of Conf.* (1893) p.200
9. *UMFC Mins. of Conf.* (1893) p.200 (cf. *Free Methodist* March 1893)
10. Smith, pp.195-96
11. Smith, p.41; Cope pp.10-11

Almost inevitably there were some teething problems. First, both the Sisters from the Tottenham Institute, who were trained nurses, were not Methodists, one being Church of England and the other Baptist and naturally they wished to attend their own places of worship as well as Westmoreland Street United Free Methodist Church. Eventually it was felt that it would be in the best interests of all concerned if a Methodist lady superintendent could be appointed. This was easier said than done, but Stephenson came to the rescue by offering to lend Sister Annette to Cope until he was able to make a more permanent appointment. Then second, the original idea had been for the Institute to be run for a while by a select committee before becoming a connexional organisation, but misunderstandings developed as some local churches refused both to support or to accept help from Bowron House. The Deaconess Institute had been established in April 1891 at Pimlico in order to help that church and 'to supply the Denomination with godly women, trained to serve in the threefold capacity of evangelist, district visitor, and nurse' so in the early days there had been a close association with the Pimlico Mission to which Cope had been appointed. When the church leaders at Pimlico raised objections because the Institute was not under their control it was decided to make an earlier approach to the Annual Assembly for recognition. Hence 'Messrs Bowron, acting on the advice of Mr. Crombie and Mr. Cope, wrote a letter asking the United Methodist Free Church (sic) Assembly to accept Bowron House as a training institution for deaconesses and to appoint a Committee to arrange for the curriculum and for the selection of the Sisters to be trained, to select a lady superintendent, and to place the management in the hands of a committee of its own appointing.'[12] The Annual Assembly, in July 1891, accepted it 'believing that the training of women for special work would supply a long felt need in our Churches'[13] and appointed a small committee of six, later enlarged to 22, to oversee the running of the Deaconess Institute. This committee made the following appointments – the Rev. T. B. Saul to oversee Biblical and Theological studies; the Rev. T. J. Cope's eldest son, Dr. A. E. Cope, would prepare the students for the St. John's Ambulance Examination in First Aid and Nursing.

12. Smith, p.44
13. UMDIMins pp.46-49, 54-55

Miss Bushnell,
Lady Superintendent
of the United Deaconess
Institute, 1894-1912

Miss Wilkes was appointed as lady superintendent, an office she held for three months before being succeeded by Miss Brown of Darlington, who, after three years, on 10th December 1894 was followed by Miss Bushnell. Miss Bushnell served in that capacity for the next 17 years, retiring when the Institute came of age in 1912, though she remained on the committee for several months. She died on 1st December 1926.[14]

The enlarged committee convened on 8th December 1891 for its first meeting and adopted the following:

CONSTITUTION OF THE DEACONESS INSTITUTE

The object of the Free Methodist Deaconess Institute is to prepare Christian Women for the service of Christ: (i) As Evangelists, to labour in Churches, Circuits, Mission Centres, and Villages. (ii) As Bible Women and Nurses, to visit the people in their homes, and to minister to the sick and to the poor. (iii) As Missionaries, to serve on Foreign Stations. (iv) As Special Agents, to organise Societies of Women and Workers throughout our Churches.

CANDIDATES

Candidates must be members of some Evangelical Christian Church, recommended to the Committee by those who have had opportunities of judging of their suitability for the work. They must be women of good mental capacity, education, and address, of high Christian character, and spiritual force.

PROBATION

After passing a suitable examination, accepted candidates shall enter the House as probationers, and continue as such until the Committee is satisfied as to their suitability for the work; they shall then be received as full students, and continue in training for a period to be determined by the Committee.

---

14. Smith, p.45; Cope, pp.12-15; *UMFC Mins. of Conf.* (1888-91) p.187; UMDIMins II pp.254-55

TERMS

Board and lodging will be provided during the whole time of training, but during probation no financial allowance will be made, except in very special cases; after the probation cloaks and bonnets will be provided, and a small allowance will be made to cover incidental expenses. It is expected, however, that those who are able will contribute towards their own support.

COURSE OF TRAINING

During the period of training all candidates will be required to take (i) A course of Biblical and Theological Teaching; (ii) A course of Medical Instruction; (iii) A suitable course of General Reading; (iv) To spend some hours daily in Practical Christian Work.

OBLIGATIONS

No vows will be taken by any Sister, but those who enter upon the work must be prepared to devote to it a considerable term of years. Yet, Sisters will be at liberty to retire, and are liable to dismissal if found unsuitable. Each Sister will be expected to accept any post of duty to which she may be appointed; to wear the Bowron House dress when provided; to conform to the religious services recognised in the Home; and to obey such subordinate regulations affecting the daily life of the Sisters as may from time to time be made.

DEDICATION AND SERVICE

At the close of their training, if the Sisters satisfy the Committee as to their suitability for permanent engagement, they shall be set apart to their work at an appropriate religious service. They shall retain their connection with Bowron House; all arrangements for their services shall be made by the Committee; and all future changes shall be entirely under the Committee's control.

When fully set apart, the Sisters shall receive an additional allowance from the funds of the Institution to meet their enlarged requirements; but all moneys received by them, from the persons to whom they minister, shall be handed to the Treasurer towards the support of the Institution.[15]

---

15. Smith, pp.49-52

When Smith wrote *Ministering Women,* around 1912-13, he commented that, apart from minor changes, this constitution was still in operation and he also acknowledged the debt owed to the ideals of Stephenson and Hugh Price Hughes.

In July 1895 the Institute Committee recommended that the Secretary of the Institute should be 'set apart' to work for the Institute and the 1896 Annual Assembly agreed so the original ties with the Pimlico Mission were weakened. In 1900 it was decided that the Connexional Officers should be ex-officio members of the Institute Committee. Then the Uniting Conference of 1907 'showed its appreciation of the Institute by resolving that one of the objects of the "Thanksgiving Fund" should be "The development of the Deaconess Institute" the Conference of 1908 further recommended the Home Mission Committee to make a grant of £150 to the Deaconess Institute, it being greatly in need of funds'.

By 1908 it was obvious that the Rev. T. J. Cope, who had been superintendent of the Pimlico Mission as well as Warden of the Deaconess Institute, was finding it too much of a strain. Also Mr. J. A. Bowron wished to give up the post as treasurer. So at its meeting on 22nd June 1908 the Institute's Committee agreed to send the following resolution to Conference:

> That the Deaconess Institute Committee and the Home Mission Committee be requested to consider the relationship of the Deaconess Institute to the Connexional Home Mission organisation and to report to the Connexional Committee which shall report to the next Conference.[16]

The Conference received the resolution and so a joint meeting was held on 23rd April 1909 which accepted that the usefulness of the Institute would be greatly increased if it was brought into closer touch with the Home Missions Committee and that there should be close co-operation between the two committees.[17]

During this period, from the Institute's foundation up to the 1907 Union, there are several other points to be noted about its development. In 1899 came the start of the Helpers' League whose members promised 'to pray for blessing on the work and when convenient send an offering to its funds'. In 1902 members were

---

16. UMDIMins I pp.6, 25, 30, 31, 47
17. UMDIMins I pp.54-55

asked to contribute 4d (less than 2p) a year. Then the Lady Superintendent, Miss Bushnell, visited the Sisters in their appointments. This enabled her not only to keep in closer touch with them, but also to see their work at first hand and learn about the situations in which they found themselves. Such information would be invaluable for organizing their training and stationing. In order to help in the training field it became desirable to have a library at Bowron House and so an appeal was made which resulted in the Institute soon having a well-stocked Library.[18]

Finance was always a problem and without the generosity of the Bowron brothers, who by 1903 had given £1,400, and various gifts from other well-wishers it is possible, especially when the Simultaneous Mission[19] hit the Institute's income, that the enterprise might have foundered. The annual Anniversary was usually reckoned a great success in many ways, not least financially! The 1903 one was outstanding as it was 'helped to the extent of £59. 2s. raised by an autograph quilt arranged and carried out by Miss Bushnell and the sisters and kindly put together by Mrs. Monkhouse . . . .'.[20] So it seems that the Institute members were inventive and enterprising!

In 1903 Bowron House moved to 25 Bolingbroke Grove, Wandsworth Common, London SW and the 1904 Report states:

Second United Methodist Deaconess Institute

> The great event of the year has been the purchase of a new house as a training house for the sisters. For years the old house in Pimlico was inconveniently small for the students, and there was no room for any of the Sisters working in circuits if they needed a brief rest and change to avoid a breakdown in health. The freehold of a suitable house in Bolingbroke Grove, Wandsworth Common, SW was offered for £2,300. Liberal

---

18. *UMFC Mins. of Conf.* (1899) p.223, (1900) p.234, (1902) p.259
19. In 1907 the Joint Committee of the three denominations, which came together to form the United Methodist Church, recommended to the Conference that a Simultaneous Mission be held in every church throughout the denominations in January and February 1908 cf. UMDIMins I pp.14-16
20. *UMFC Mins. of Conf.* (1903) p.257

promises of help were received, and the Committee purchased and took possession of the premises on December 2nd. On January 18th the house was formally dedicated by the President of the Annual Assembly. A strong and representative Trust Board has been formed, and the property will be settled on the Connexional Reference Deed. The Committee estimated the cost involved in the purchase of the house, the alterations, furnishing, legal expenses, and deficiency in ordinary funds through special appeal for the house at £3,000.[21]

The outstanding debt of £600 was cleared during 1904-05 and the house settled on the Connexional Reference Deed. The surplus furniture from the 129 Warwick Street house was sold with the proceeds going to the New House and Furnishing Fund. Money was still needed to complete the furnishing, but eventually everything was ready for the Uniting Conference in September 1907 and the Fund closed in September 1910, with the balance of £14.18s.5d. being transferred into the General Account.

The deaconesses held a Public Meeting at the 1907 Annual Meeting and Bowron House was not only open to visitors during the Conference, but was also ready to entertain representatives. As the Uniting Conference was imminent it seemed only right that representatives from the Methodist New Connexion and the Bible Christians should be added to the Deaconess Committee and the Uniting Conference was asked to implement this. The members of the Committee who were members of the Uniting Conference were asked to act as a watch Committee to safeguard its interests.[22]

The question of the insurance of the Sisters needed to be addressed and a committee was set up to study the problem, including the possibility of joining a Friendly Society. It was agreed that 'the Bowron House Sisters & servants be insured in the Connexional Insurance Office if possible on the same terms as the Book Room staff . . .' After the 1907 Union the Committee decided in 1912 that because 'of the small allowance the Sisters receive . . . the whole contribution for the Sisters to the Insurance Society be paid by the Committee'. After further consideration it was agreed that each Sister should be free to decide which 'approved society she

---

21. *UMFC Mins. of Conf.* (1904) p.263
22. UMDIMins I pp.7, 10, 13

would join'. Here the matter rested until the National Health and Insurance Act came into being. Then, at first, the Institute paid the Sisters' contribution but, in 1926, when there was an increase in the rate levied, it was agreed that the Sisters should pay 6d per week as the finances of the Institute could no longer subsidise them. However, in 1929 'the Ministry of Health . . . [decided that the deaconesses were] not entitled to be insured under the National Health Insurance & Contributory Pensions Act as employed contributors'. This decision caused the Institute Committee several problems and it decided that any Sisters who were eligible 'must become Voluntary Contributors . . . in order to maintain their rights . . .'; that those not eligible 'must join some other Society and so make provision against sickness etc.'; that any who did not make any provision should not have a claim on Institute Funds; and that to help with this extra cost the allowance should be raised to £2.12s.6d. per month.[23]

The United Methodist Deaconess Order (1907-32)

The new Superintendent Minister appointed to Pimlico Mission in 1908 was the Rev. A. G. Goodwin and because the cost of living in the area was high it was agreed to try to provide him with £90 a year. It was also regarded as 'absolutely necessary' for a Sister to be appointed to the Mission if the progress of the work was to be maintained. Sister Lillie Davis, who had been working at Pimlico, decided to leave the sisterhood and as apparently (no reason given) her work there had not been satisfactory she was allowed to resign immediately. The Minutes state 'she had returned her costume' – this seems to imply that the deaconess uniform was the property of the Institute rather than belonging to the individual Sister.[24] By 1910 the Pimlico Mission was once again in financial difficulties and it was resolved that the matter of the Mission's finances should be referred to the Home Mission Committee as the Deaconess Institute funds could not be used for it. That there were still problems in the Pimlico Mission and with its relationship with the Deaconess Institute is apparent in 1913 when it was resolved

> That the Warden, the Trustees of Pimlico Church, and Rev. J. H. Blackwell, Mr. Deadmarch & Rev. W. P. Austin be a committee to consider what methods

---

23. UMDIMins I pp.6, 7, 11, UMDIMins II pp.225, 227, 230, 329, 334-35
24. UMDIMins I pp.34, 35, 37; cf.pp.53-54

should be adopted in dealing with this matter, the committee being given power to act. Rev. T. J. Cope to act as convenor of the Committee.

As a result of a Special Meeting on 10th October 1913 it was agreed that the relationship between the Pimlico Church and the Deaconess Institute should be dissolved as Conference had 'connected' Pimlico and Victoria Churches with the Fulham Circuit and that the Rev. T. J. Cope should act as Secretary and Treasurer of the Pimlico Trust until the Quarterly Meeting. Various financial adjustments and questions relating to the renewal of leases were to be made. So the long association of the Deaconess Institute and the Pimlico Mission came to an end.

A sign of the development of the Deaconess Institute within the United Methodist Church came with the proposed closer relationship between the Institute and the Connexional Home Mission organization. The Plymouth Conference of 1909 accepted this closer relationship and granted £150 to the Institute.

Then the decision of the Secretary of the Institute to retire after the Institute reached its 21st year led to several organizational changes. The Treasurer, Mr Bowron, resigned unexpectedly in March 1911. As the Minutes record Mr J. Bowron had been 'the first treasurer of the Deaconess Institute which office he held for 21 years. He was a most generous supporter of the work and was the close & loyal friend of our revered founder the Rev. T. Cope'. He remained a member of the Committee until two years before his death, when he left the country to live with his daughter in Honolulu. He died in New Zealand in the spring of 1929.[25] In May 1911 the Consultative Committee, perhaps rather daringly, suggested:

> Inasmuch as the Institute is a Women's Organisation it would be very appropriate to have a woman as Treasurer. It was therefore Resolved that the Chairman & Secretary be requested to wait upon Mrs. Wm. Mallinson & ask her to allow her name to be forwarded to the Conference in nomination for the Treasurership.[26]

However, apparently the President appointed the Rev. A. Crombie to act as interim Treasurer until the 1911 Conference, so the Institute

---

25. UMDIMins II p.337
26. UMDIMins I p.92

Committee recommended that this period be extended to the 1912 Conference. One wonders if Mrs. Mallinson was ever approached and whether she refused or whether the idea of a woman Treasurer was anathema to the full Committee and the Conference! Ultimately Dr. A. E. Cope was nominated in 1912. It was evident that with both a new Treasurer and Secretary there were likely to be a number of changes and so the Lady Superintendent for the last 17 years, Miss Bushnell, felt she should offer her resignation.

Miss Bushnell's Resignation Letter

Dear Mr. Cope,

As it is probable your retirement . . . may involve changes in the working . . . as well as fresh workers being introduced . . . it may be the household management is amongst the proposed changes and that it will be thought advisable to have a new matron. As I would not on any account stand in the way . . . I take this opportunity of placing my resignation as Lady Superintendent in your hands.

You can understand that after seventeen years of constant and very deep interest in every person and every incident in the work of the Institute it is with deep sorrow I think of leaving the work & beginning in a sense a new life.

For several reasons this fresh start does not look very inviting to me, amongst others I have not been able out of my salary to save much for the coming days. However, He who chose me years ago for this work can if it should be necessary make a fresh opening for me. . . .

With kind regards, Believe me, Yours truly, A. M. Bushnell

Source: United Methodist Deaconess Institute Minutes (1906-17) pp.107-08

The Home Mission Committee Secretary, the Rev. John Moore, requested a joint meeting with the Bowron House Committee to discuss 'the future arrangements for working' and this special meeting convened in December 1911. After a resolution of thanks to the retiring Secretary various suggestions were made on the matter which resulted in the following resolutions:

> That in the opinion of this Committee a Minister should be set apart as the Secretary of the Deaconess Institute.
> It was further Resolved: That a sub Committee be appointed which shall consider

1. The relation of the Institute to the Home Mission Committee

2. Whether it be possible for the Minister & his wife to reside in the home 25 Bolingbroke Grove, and to serve as the Secretary and Lady Superintendent respectively

3. Or whether the Secretary must live in a separate house and a Matron be appointed to manage Bowron House.

4. Any other matter connected with the Institute.

and the sub-committee was elected.[27] A meeting of the sub-committee was held on 11th June 1912 at which it was recommended that Miss Bushnell's resignation be accepted, that an appreciative resolution of her service be sent to Conference and that a 'suitable Annual Monetary provision be made' for her. This was settled at 26 guineas per year. With regard to the Secretaryship it was resolved:

1. That arrangements be made for the new Ministerial Secretary to reside at the Institute, Bolingbroke Grove, the Secretary's wife to act as Matron.

2. That in the opinion of the Committee the present Institute is adequate for the above and for the other purposes of the Institute with slight alterations such as a little experience will suggest to be advisable.

Several names were suggested as Secretary with the Rev. Henry Smith being the favourite. The relationship of the two committees – the Institute and the Home Mission – was felt not to be very satisfactory as, although Home Missions had representatives on the Institute Committee, the reverse was not so. It was agreed that a more equitable arrangement was needed. However, when the Special sub-Committee met again in June there was an unresolved divergence of opinion, but eventually the matter of the Secretary and the future of the Institute was settled by the full Committee with the following resolution:

1. That inasmuch as the resolutions of the Publishing House Committee, if adopted by the Conference, will open the way for the Rev. Hy. Smith to serve the Deaconess Institute in addition to his other duties this Committee earnestly requests the Conference to appoint the Rev. Hy. Smith Secretary of the Deaconess

---

27. UMDIMins I pp.106-08, 109, 118-21, 125

Institute believing this to be the most effective method of serving the Institute and reducing the Connexional Expenditure. The Institute will thereby secure an efficient Secretary and the Connexion a reduction in the number of the Departmental Officers.

2nd Resolution

That this Committee which has always striven to work in co-operation with the Home Mission Committee will be pleased to fall in with any reasonable arrangement that will give unity to our Home Mission Organisations & promote mutual help and Connexional progress. It will at all times be a gratification to the Committee to send Sisters to Home Mission stations at the request of the Home Mission Committee.[28]

The Rev. Henry Smith was involved with the Publishing House as Editor and apparently there needed to be financial cut-backs at the Publishing House, so it seemed that if he could become Secretary of the Deaconess Institute and reside at the Institute while still editing the *United Methodist* newspaper and if the Rev. Henry Hooks could edit the *United Methodist Magazine* money would be saved. However, the Home Mission Committee, being anxious for a closer relationship with the Institute, opposed this suggestion and floated the idea that Ranmoor Theological College, Sheffield should be used as the Deaconess Institute. There was much debate in the Conference at Hanley on 10th July 1912, but the appointment of Henry Smith as Secretary was finally approved. In June 1913 it was decided that the title of 'The Secretary' should be dropped in favour of 'The Warden'. Alterations were made to 25 Bolingbroke Gardens to accommodate Mr. and Mrs. Smith. Then in October 1912 Sister Constance was appointed as Home Sister with responsibility 'to attend to the subscriptions list, to assist the Lady Superintendent, to do deputation work and act generally under the direction of the Secretary and that her allowance be increased to £25 per year'. Her various visits to churches proved very successful in promoting the interests of the Institute. The linking of the Institute with the Publishing House meant that arrangements had to be made about expenses, with the Institute agreeing to one half of the Connexional Assessment, namely £123.8s.0d, for the first year.

---

28. UMDIMins I pp.121-22

The 1912 Conference had suggested that the Deaconess Institute Committee should unite with four other committees to form a Connexional Committee. This was discussed fully and resulted in the following resolution:

> 1. That this meeting is of the opinion that the best method of working this Institution would be through a Committee specially appointed for the purpose by the Conference.
>
> 2. That if the method named in the above resolution should be deemed inadvisable, this Committee expresses its judgement that the next best arrangement would be that the Deaconess Committee should form part of a separate Home Mission committee, with lady representatives upon it.
>
> 3. That should the plan suggested in resolution 2 be found impracticable at present, this Committee is willing to fall in with Dr. Packer's suggestion that the Deaconess Committee should be one of the committees formed out of the General Connexional Committee (*Minutes* 1912 pp.35-36); but this Committee is emphatically of the opinion that as the Institution has to deal with deaconesses and needs constant supervision members should be co-opted on the suggested Deaconess Sub-Committee from the London District, and a number of these should be ladies.[29]

Mr Cope maintained a close association with Institute for many years after his retirement from the Secretaryship right up to his death on 10th February 1927.

The Second Secretary [First Warden]: The Rev. Henry Smith (1912-18)

The new Warden outlined the plans he had to raise funds for the Institute which included 'the issue of special letter, the securing a Vice President in each district who might help to form a local committee & arrange an Annual Meeting, the visitation of the churches, special meetings at the Institute, and an Appeal to the whole Connexion for £200 before the end of April'. These proposals were endorsed.

---

29. *UMMins. of Conf.* (1912) pp.35-36; UMDIMins I pp.139-40, 141-42, 148

In June 1913 a sub-committee was set up to consider ways of providing a Retiring Fund. At the first meeting it was decided to get information about the National Children's Home Retiring Fund and to 'tabulate the record of the Sisters from the beginning of the Institute as to years of service and the causes which led to any of them ceasing their connection with the work' and to circulate this information to the members of the Committee. Details were also collected of the Wesley Deaconess Order, the Mildmay and the Bible Women and Nurses' schemes. All the information thus gathered was submitted to the Rev. George Parker, the Secretary for Assessed Funds, for his consideration. On 11th February 1914 the Committee received a not very encouraging reply, about setting up a scheme along the lines of other existing schemes, unless there was a considerable sum of money to meet any payments. Mr. Parker suggested:

(a) Arrange with some reliable Company for special terms.

(b) Let each deaconess pay a fixed amount of the necessary premium and the balance by the Committee.

(c) Get the Company to take on <u>all</u> your present deaconesses at a <u>level</u> rate.

(d) New deaconesses to pay premium according to the age at entry.

(e) If you strictly limit the benefits to
(a) Superannuation after continuous service of say 30 years.
(b) To one cash payment if health completely unfits for continuous service, after say 10 years service you should not have any very great premium to pay.

(f) The number who will complete 30 years' service will be few. . . The serious cost would be if you attempted to provide annuities for those who may be physically unable to continue and have not completed say 30 years.

Mr. Parker went on to suggest that the deaconesses should be 'encouraged to take up midwifery' so that they had something to fall back on if the strain of their deaconess work became too much. After studying this reply the Committee resolved to obtain quotations from several Insurance Companies along these lines. The

Warden contacted four, but only the Norwich Union Life Assurance Company and the Standard Life Assurance company were able to give quotations. After correspondence about the details and cost the Warden felt that 'a scheme which involves <u>fixed yearly payments</u>' would be very expensive and that a 'better plan would be to raise a capital sum, to be called the Retiring Allowance Fund . . .' from which an annuity could be bought for a sister who 'became unfit for work after 20 or 30 years' service' at the cost of about £200 which would ensure £13 per year after 20 years' service or £22 per year after 30 years' service. Again Mr. Parker's views were sought and this time he responded favourably. Then in June 1915 Mr. William Mallinson, J P offered to give £100 a year for five years to the fund in memory of his wife if the Institute would raise an equal amount. The offer was accepted with gratitude. In November 1916 the Warden received a letter from 12 Sisters, who evidently were feeling very concerned about the financial situation in which they found themselves and very worried about how they would fare in times of sickness for they wrote, suggesting that after '15 years service' the allowance should be increased to £2.8s.0d. per month, after 10 to £2, after five to £1.10s. emphasising that their present allowances did not 'leave any margin whatever for making any provision for the future'. They also commented that the present 'cost of goods', presumably exacerbated by the First World War, made their allowance quite inadequate. The letter implied that often the Sisters, in the course of their work, needed to give monetary support to needy people. Further, they felt that the seven shillings and sixpence Insurance money was an added burden, especially where churches did not provide accommodation. They urged the Committee to provide a Retiring Allowance, to ensure that the Sisters had better accommodation where they could have peace and quiet in which to prepare for their work and have opportunity for relaxation. In conclusion, they acknowledged that times were difficult because of the war and therefore they were willing to wait for the increases until January 1917. The very fact that 12 Sisters could send such a letter surely indicates that they were suffering considerable financial difficulties. The Committee was sympathetic and sent a reply to each of the 12 setting out the position and assuring them that they were doing their best and 'making progress though slowly' and hoping 'that none of us will fail in patience until we realise our ideal'. However, they could not resist a slight dig by pointing out others had suffered too and how much had been achieved!

Extract of Reply to Twelve Sisters' Letter 1916

Others have toiled and suffered. The first Secretary served for nearly sixteen years without fee or reward and for many years no Sister received more that £1.6s.8d. per month. But we have advanced from that state. And we have purchased, furnished, and paid for the house in Bolingbroke Grove.

The next step was the establishment of a Superannuation Fund. But the Union of the denominations came and while waiting for the new Churches to become familiar with the Institute and its claims preliminary steps were taken for the formation of a Sisters' Retiring Allowance Fund. Then the war broke out.

Notwithstanding this adverse event something has been done . . .

In view of these things and of the difficulty of carrying them through during and immediately after such a dreadful war the Committee appeal to the Sisters to exercise further patience, especially as the Committee intend as soon as the superannuation fund is arranged to revise the whole financial conditions of the Sisters' services . . .

Source: United Methodist Deaconess Institute Minutes
(1906-17) pp.275-76

In February 1918 the United Methodist Warden wrote to the Wesley Deaconess Institute Warden requesting information about that organization's Retiring Allowance Fund so that 'in view of possible Methodist reunion we shall all be desirous of approximating as closely as possible to your scheme'. In response Bradfield sent him a copy of the 1917 Report of their Registered Friendly Society and a copy of the rules of the Society. After much debate a resolution was sent to Conference outlining two schemes for the Retiring Allowance, one suggesting that payment should start at 55 and the other at 60. Conference agreed that if funds permitted payment should start at 55. The scheme would come into operation in September 1919.[30]

It was decided in June 1913 that money received through legacies should be put in a special Legacy Reserve fund which was opened at the London City and Midland Bank, Sheffield with a deposit of £300. A Helpers' League was formed in 1914 to encourage Women's Work in the United Methodist Church, 'for

---

30. UMDIMins II pp.3-5, 30, 34-39 cf 54-55, 57, 77, 85, sheets between pp.155 & 156 cf.pp.158-59, 259-60.

befriending girls & young women who come up to London from our provincial churches and Sunday Schools and for securing further assistance in the development of the work of this Institute'.[31] Until 1913 the Sisters had been known by their Christian names, but it was now recommended that when Sisters joined the Institute their surnames be added.

Meanwhile the general work of the Institute went on, with 40 evangelistic missions being arranged for the autumn of 1913 and the Sisters being appointed to circuits and churches throughout the denomination. However, in September 1914, it was reported that only 30 requests for missions had been received and the Warden 'feared that the number of Missions would be much smaller than last year in consequence of the unsettlement of Church work caused by the War'. In the autumn of 1915 Sister Kathleen was released from St. John's Ambulance work and went to the military hospital in Malta.

In October 1913 it was agreed that T. J. Cope's manuscript 'The Hand of God in the history of the Deaconess Institute' should be printed 'on good paper and sold at the price of one penny per copy' and that *Ministering Women* should be reprinted. *The Hand of God* was reissued in 1920 'as it was felt that much good would result therefrom'. When in February 1923 it was discovered that '1200 sheets of *Ministering Women* were lying at the Magnet Press' and that the Institute was going to be charged for storage it was decided estimates should be obtained for binding them as a paperback edition to which the Rev. T. J. Cope would add an addendum on the 'Retiring Fund'. This edition was to be sold at one shilling.[32]

It seems as if the appointment of Henry Smith as Warden and Connexional Editor was an annual one until 1913 when the Conference suggested that a longer term would be helpful. After discussion the Institute resolved:

> 1. That should the Conference of 1914 designate the Rev. Henry Smith as Connexional Editor until 1918 the Deaconess Institute Committee will be willing to continue the present arrangement.

---

31. UMDIMins I pp.164-65, 185, 186, 192, 213, 214
32. UMDIMins I pp.169, 172-73, 179; UMDIMins II pp.96-97, 102, 163, 166

> 2. That taking all the circumstances into consideration the Deaconess Institute Com. does not see its way to depart from the present financial arrangements in reference to the Warden.

Then, in 1916, a special committee, consisting of four members from the Home Mission Committee and five from the Deaconess Institute, was instituted to 'bring recommendations as to the Warden to be appointed at Conference 1918'. The report suggested that the supervision of the Institute should be undertaken by the Home Mission Secretary, the Rev. John Moore, who would live in London, with the day-to-day running being in the hands of a Lady Superintendent and a local House Committee, and that an assistant should be appointed to help the Home Mission Secretary. It was observed that this arrangement would also be economical. The 1917 Conference agreed and John Moore was duly appointed as Warden. Mr. Mallinson bought a house, 68 Thurleigh Road, Wandsworth Common, for Mr. Moore's use. So the ties between the Deaconess Institute and the Home Mission Committee were strengthened.

The deaconesses were usually 'set apart' for their work, but in 1915 there is the first reference to 'a public consecration service' being held. Then, in April 1917, Sister Mary Payne and Margery Westby were to be received as 'fully accredited' deaconesses, but a note was added: "As the usual meeting of deaconesses is not being held in connection with the Anniversary it was resolved that the ordination of Sisters Mary Payne & Margery Westby be deferred a year.' This is the first use of the word 'ordination' in the official United Methodist Deaconess Institute Minutes.

Two ladies, Lilian Bartholomew, a deaconess in the Newcastle Children's Mission, and Lily Cowmeadow, a former Bible Christian evangelist, were accepted as Auxiliary Sisters. Lilian Bartholomew was eventually received as a full Sister in June 1918. After about 12 years working in this country the Foreign Missions Committee requested the 'loan' of Sister Lilian for four years to work in Africa after which she could 'resume service at home'. The Foreign Missions Committee would pay all her Retiring Fund contributions while she was with them. The Deaconess Committee agreed, but asked that if she suffered 'any breakdown or injurious effect [in] health owing to her work in Africa, the F. M. should deal generously & sympathetically with her'. The case of Lily Cowmeadow is especially interesting as showing that, although at 47 she was well beyond the normal age limit for acceptance, the Institute was flexible enough to appreciate her long service record and accept her 'as an Auxiliary Sister for 12 months'. She resigned in 1918.

Report on Lily Cowmeadow

Miss Cowmeadow is of Bible Christian ancestry and became a member of that church in early childhood. Desiring some definite form of Christian service she offered herself to the Salvation Army and for seven years, till 1898, was engaged in the Army's Rescue work. Breaking down in health under the strain, she went to visit relatives in America for twelve months. She then took up evangelistic mission work for nine years in the Bible Christian Church, being commended to the Churches for such work by the Conference. She then for several years took up mission work among the Methodist Churches of Australia under the auspices of Conferences and District Synods. Returning to this country just over two years ago she took up evangelistic mission work again, mainly among ex-Bible Christian churches. During the year just closed she has had charge of our Hastings Circuit under our Home Mission Secretary, the Rev. John Moore.

Source: United Methodist Deaconess Institute Minutes
(1906-17) pp.261-62

In anticipation of Mr. Smith's retirement and the changes because of the appointment of the Home Mission Secretary, the Rev. John Moore, as Warden it was agreed that a job description for the Lady Superintendent should be drawn up, so Smith wrote to Bradfield asking for a copy of the Wesley Deaconess College's regulations. Bradfield replied that there were none, but that they had a Home Sister in charge of the housekeeping, while his wife was always on hand for advice and consultation and to deal with pastoral concerns with regard to the students. So Sister Constance, who had been the Home Sister at the Institute, was appointed as Lady Superintendent and Sister Agatha became the Home Sister.

Warm tribute was paid to the retiring Warden, the Rev. Henry Smith and his wife and he was presented with some bookshelves.

Lady Superintendent's Duties 1918

1. To make the Institute as home-like as possible . . . and to develop to the utmost the idea of the Sisterhood.
2. To take entire responsibility for the domestic arrangements . . . and keep all necessary accounts . . .
3. To maintain the reputation of the Institute . . .
4. To be responsible for ordering and supplying the uniform . . .
5. To cooperate cordially with the Warden and the Committee . . . in promoting the interests of the students and of the Institute . . .

Source: United Methodist Deaconess Institute Minutes (1917-32) pp.40-41

The Second and Third Wardens, the Rev. John Moore, (1918-20), the Rev. Tom Sunderland, (1920-22)

With the closer liaison between the Institute and the Home Mission Committee many financial matters had to be resolved. A special committee considered several points, namely, that as the new Warden was also Home Mission Secretary, there would be no charge for his services or for his assistant, but £26 should be allowed to Mr. Moore for office heating, lighting and wear and tear, that if a Women's Home Mission Guild Secretary be appointed and, she happened to be a deaconess, she should be released from her appointment, that the Lady Superintendent, Sister Constance, should be paid £40 per year, that the churches should pay more (£36 per year and £1 to the Retiring Fund) for the services of a deaconess and that, until more students were admitted into the Institute, those deaconesses working in London should reside at 25 Bolingbroke Grove. There were two further matters which are of special interest, the first being that the Warden 'had arranged for Sister Eva to be sent to Barrow-in-Furness in place of a minister at a minimum payment of £100 for the year'. Then, secondly, 'that the Sisters of the Primitive Methodist St. George's Hall Mission, Old Kent Road, should be given facilities to take lectures along with our own students at the Institute . . .'. This latter arrangement continued for a number of years. There was evidently close co-operation between the United Methodists and the Primitive Methodists, because, in 1927, it was reported that a request from the Primitive Methodist Scarborough Circuit for a Sister had been granted.

John Moore intimated in March 1920 that he intended to retire as Warden and also as Home Mission Secretary and the Rev. Tom Sunderland succeeded to both posts. During his term of office he was instrumental in linking the Institute with the Mallinson Road Church which provided more scope for practical training. Then a joint committee of the Institute and the Home Mission resolved 'that the Warden shall be appointed at the Conference of 1922 and shall also be minister of Mallinson Road Church and reside in the Institute until the needs of the Institute make that course impracticable'. The Home Mission members of the Joint Committee agreed to accept the nominee of the Deaconess Institute Committee as the next Warden.

The last United Methodist Warden – the Rev. R. W. Gair (1922-32)

It was decided to approach the Rev. R. W. Gair to become Warden for five years from 1922, to which request he agreed, if he could be released from his appointment at Paradise Road Church. When this was settled it was resolved that he should be paid £50 above the minimum superintendent's stipend, plus free residence in the Institute, which was valued at £100. The Institute also agreed to pay half the connexional assessment and the Warden was to contribute £140 'in lieu of food, lighting and gas etc.'. As Mr. and Mrs. Gair would be living in the Institute the position of Sister Constance as Lady Superintendent altered, so it was arranged that, as compensation, she should be credited with 10 years' service, and that her superannuation be £50 per year with the caveat 'that this did not set a precedent for superannuation'.[33]

In May 1923 it was reported that there were 37 Sisters in the work with six students in training and that the training period had been extended to two years. In July 1924 it was proposed that the Institute should be enlarged, presumably because of the shortage of accommodation. This is emphasised by the note that five candidates should be accepted as 'student probationers, if necessary, sleeping out arrangements be made for one or two'. In November 1924 a number of deaconesses were working in central Missions and Gair pointed out that

---

33. UMDIMins II pp.113, 126, 130, 139, 142 sheet inserted between pp.149 & 150

> For such centres deaconesses are essential, and leaders
> in like areas will do well to heed the recommendation
> of the 'Commission for Aggressive Work' . . . and
> consider the possibility of having the full-time service
> of a trained woman. It seems necessary to repeat again
> that our student deaconesses are now receiving two
> years' training for this work, which includes practical
> church and school work, under the direction of the
> Warden, in the thickly populated area of our Mallinson
> Road Church, as well as a sound course of studies.[34]

There seems to have been an increased demand for help with
missions in the spring of 1925 and as no deaconesses were available,
it was decided to allow senior students to go out in pairs for a few
weeks.   No more is heard of the proposed extension, though
alterations and renewals were undertaken in 1926.   1927 brought
financial problems, chiefly due to the industrial depression,
especially in the mining industry, which affected collections at
missions and donations from contributors, but also by the necessity
to carry out urgent repairs to the Institute.

   In 1929 the Deaconess Institute Committee urged the Home
Mission Committee to recommend Conference to reappoint the Rev.
R. W. Gair as Warden and minister of the Mallinson Road Church,
with an increase in salary of £25 per year.

Designation of Warden – The Rev. R. W. Gair 1929

Mr Gair has the fullest confidence of all members of the [Deaconess
Institute] Committee and it is their strong conviction that Mr. Gair's
knowledge of all the work will be of untold value in the negotiations
which must take place in view of Methodist Union.

Source: United Methodist Deaconess Institute Minutes (1917-32) sheet
inserted between pp.335-36

Methodist Union

   Towards the end of the decade, as the prospect of Methodist
Union drew nearer, the question of the rôle of the deaconess
organizations and their place in the unified Church had to be
considered.   A joint meeting of the interested parties of the

---

34. MSS Cuttings *The United Methodist* (6th November 1924) p.546

Wesleyan Methodist, the United Methodist and the Primitive Methodist Churches was arranged for 11th January 1927 at which, after a full and frank discussion, it seemed that 'there is no insuperable barrier to the union of the Sisterhoods'. There matters rested until the Churches decided on Union. Dr. Maltby, Warden of the Wesley Deaconess Order, visited the United Methodist Institute in early 1930 to discuss a scheme for uniting the organizations and this was followed by a visit of Gair and the London Sisters to the Wesley Deaconess Convocation in Wesley's Chapel. Then, in June 1930, Mr. Gair was invited to join the Wesley Deaconess Committee at the candidates' weekend in Ilkley and, although he was unable to accept, the invitation had been appreciated and shows that there was mutual goodwill on all sides towards working together. Co-operation between the two organizations developed as the two Wardens were invited to each other's committee meetings and a joint committee was formed which met on 8th January 1931. Here information was given about 'the present position of the deaconess work in the three different churches'. It was felt important that all the deaconesses' appointments should be made by the 'authorised (sic) department' and that allowances should be standardized. It was agreed that deaconess work should be an 'autonomous department'; that it should be administered by a General Committee; that for the present Ilkley College and Bolingbroke Grove be maintained with House Committees; that the period of training should be at least two years, including practical experience and that, in view of the differences in financial arrangements, the Wesley Deaconess 'scale and method be adopted as soon as practicable'. As there would be a year between the Uniting Conference in 1932 and the first united Conference in 1933 it was decided that a sub-committee consisting of Dr. Maltby, Mr. Gair and Mr. Wiles (Primitive Methodist Home Mission Secretary) should be empowered to deal with any details during that period. The Report of 1931 summed up the Union discussion thus: 'Union is being prepared for in a spirit of goodwill which is finding expression in the fellowship of the Sisters of the three Churches, and between the wardens and committees.'[35]

---

35. UMDIMins II pp.257-58, 264, 373, 376, 381, 384, 388, sheets between pp.389-90, 391, sheets between pp.395-96 cf. *The United Methodist* (14th May 1931) p.234

Methodist Union – The Deaconess Work

It was reported that the membership of the Wesley Deaconess Order is about three hundred and that the work is a separate department of the Church, governed by a Connexional Committee.

In the United Methodist Church there are about fifty deaconesses, the work being a part of the Home Missions Department.

In the Primitive Methodist Church, no connexional responsibility is taken for the Sisters, of whom there are about twenty. About ten are trained at St. George's Mission, New Kent Road, but other churches engage their workers and make their own arrangement with them as they wish. There is no Retiring Fund, nor a recognised standard of allowance. The Manchester Mission, West London Mission, and some other Missions in the Wesleyan Church were named as being in the same position.

Source: United Methodist Deaconess Institute Minutes (1917-32) – sheets inserted between pp.389-90.

Union raised practical questions: such as the accommodation at the Institute and the residence of the Warden, but one of the main problems was the difference in the Retiring Allowance Funds and, in December 1931, an Emergency Committee was set up to deal with this and any other situation which might arise. The committee convened on 16th February 1932 and recommended to the deaconess Institute Committee, that it was important that the traditions of the United Methodist Deaconess Institute be maintained; that there should be a London base for training, especially for practical experience, with Bolingbroke Grove being that centre and that this would mean the provision of a house for the Warden until such time as two wardens were not required. With regard to the Retiring Allowance Fund it was felt that the fund could pay a much larger pension than previously and the Warden submitted a list of Sisters who would be eligible in the next few years to the next meeting .[36]

---

36. UMDIMins II sheet between pp.413 & 414

With Union, as we have seen earlier, came the revision of the service for the consecration of deaconesses in the Wesley Deaconess Order and Dr. Maltby invited two United Methodist members to join this committee.[37]

Finally, an interesting comment by Gair in his report on the Institute in 1931 shows the attitude of the United Methodist Church towards the ministry of women:

> There is a distinct tendency on the part of the Churches to shift the balance of the Sister's service away from the more domestic side, and make it nearer the kind of work expected of the ordinary minister. The call for women in the ministry may not be very vocal yet, but the demand for women to do much of the work of a minister is insistent, and is increasing; and there are churches today humming with life, the centre of which is a deaconess.[38]

The last meeting of the Committee took place on Thursday, 21st July 1932 when the hope was expressed that Methodist Union would 'be marked by an effort in evangelism, and we have Sisters well qualified to conduct such Mission services in town or country'. The Committee concluded its business with a resolution thanking God for the work of the Deaconess Institute over the years and looking forward to the contribution its deaconesses would make to the unified Church.

The Deaconess Institute: Last Committee   21st July 1932

This Committee, meeting on 21st July 1932, for the last time under the name of the United Methodist Church, places on record its thankfulness to Almighty God for His unfailing guidance and continued blessing during the history of the Deaconess Institute from its inception in 1891.

It recalls with joy . . . the steady growth and progress of the Sisterhood with its increasing forms of ministry, through which the churches have been enriched, homes brightened, and lives brought into Christian discipleship.

The Committee further expresses its thankfulness for the unblemished record of the characters of nearly two hundred women who have

---

37. UMDIMins II p.396 cf. chapter 11
38. *The United Methodist* (14th May 1931) p.234

> passed into the ranks of the Sisterhood, and reaffirms its conviction and belief in the Divine Order of the Ministry of Women, praying that in the power of the Spirit our Sisterhood may make a great contribution to the effectiveness of the witness of the Methodist Church into which we shall pass on 20th September under the Act of Union.
>
> *Source:* United Methodist Deaconess Institute Minutes (1932-35) p.21; MSS cuttings book (R. W. Gair) loose article

The United Methodist Deaconess Institute probationers, taken at Bowron House with the Warden, Rev. R. W. Gair and Mrs. Gair, 1932-33

Front Row: *Sisters Dorothy Tremberth, the Warden, Mrs. Gair*
Centre Row: *Sisters Margaret Harwick, Doris Sheen*
Back Row: *Sisters Florence Davenport, Rosalind Watts, Ann Ireland BA*

Training

The basic training for the United Methodist Free Churches deaconesses in 1891 covered Biblical and Theological studies, First Aid and Nursing, General Reading and practical work. However, when the work was fully established and recognised by the Church the Consultative Committee, in June 1907, recommended that the training period should be two years, the first year of which would be spent in Bowron House and the other in active work as a probationer and that no Sister would be 'fully accredited until she has proved her suitability by a year of service in a church or circuit'. It was agreed, in light of the 1907 Union, to revise the curriculum of studies in order to achieve the maximum efficiency and the Rev. Richard Pyke, Dr. Jones and the Secretary were charged with this task. They arranged the curriculum and timetable and instituted an examination programme for the end of the year. It seems that the following subjects were covered: Theology; Bible Study; First Aid and Nursing; Elocution; Methodist History; United Methodist Church Polity with Lectures on visitation, Mothers' Meetings, Boys and Girls' Guilds, Benevolent and Relief work and 'the ideal Deaconess' also the students were to attend Dr. Campbell Morgan's Bible Lectures. So the Sisters trained at Bowron House received a very good grounding in general education as well as the more specialized areas which would be useful for their work within the church and community.

Subjects & Results of Exams – September 1910 Maximum Marks 100					
Sisters	Old Test Hist	Theology	Eng. Grammar	E. Lang & Compos	First Aid Injured	Nursing
Frances	75	95	94	80	Certifi	Certifi
Rose	62	86	81	72	Certifi	Certifi
Reno	27	49	75	72		
Annie	58	86	85	77		

Comment:
Sister Frances had been in the Institute for two years; Sisters Rose and Reno for one year and Sister Annie for six months. Special allowance should be made for Sister Reno who had missed many lectures through personal and domestic afflictions.

Source: United Methodist Deaconess Institute Minutes (1906-17) p.77

Just before the 1907 Union it was resolved that if any Sister became engaged to be married the Committee should be informed and if her fiancé was a member of the church in which she was working, then she would be moved, unless there were exceptional circumstances. It is obvious that the deaconesses had to resign when they married and there are also cases where the Committee was unhappy that a Sister had not served for long before she left to marry. The implication is that two years' service minimum was expected.

So many women were offering as candidates that it was decided 'that in the opinion of the Committee it is not desirable to undertake the training of ladies for the office of deaconess who are over 30 years of age except under very special & exceptional circumstances'. The Committee adhered fairly rigidly to this dictum, and many were turned down on age grounds, others because it was felt that their health would not stand the strain of the work and yet others because of their educational standards. Dr. A. E. Cope, son of the Institute's founder, was the medical advisor and examined each candidate. By 1910 candidates had a formal interview and were asked about 'their conversion to God, the work they had done for Christ, the books they had read, the branch of work they preferred, their health, & their call to the work of a deaconess'. There are many reports on candidates, students and the Sisters inserted in the Minutes of the Deaconess Institute and these shed a great deal of light on the courses of study, the standard expected and the ongoing training of the deaconesses.

In 1924 it was decided that a written test should be given to the candidates before they appeared for interview. Of the 12 applications that year, two were rejected outright, one because of age and the other 'seeing we have so many candidates from our own churches' (she was a Primitive Methodist), four were rejected because they were too young or did not reach the required standard, but they were 'left with the option to apply again should they so desire'. The remaining six were admitted to the Institute as students.

Candidates 1924		
B. Allott	20	Manchester
Papers G	Ref G	not musical. elocution
M. C. Attrill	21	Portsmouth
Papers V. G.	Ref G	good speaker, not musical
E. Collin	22 Aug.	Leicester
Papers G.	Ref G	preacher, sing & play
D. H. Chrimes	22	Northwich
Papers G	preacher, Home or Foreign musical	
M. Crickmay	30	Walthamstow
Papers V. G.	Ref G.	not musical, elocution
E. Hotchen	24 or 5	Manchester
Papers V.G.	Ref G.	preacher, musical
E. M. Lipscomb	22	Portsmouth
Papers V.G.	Ref G.	trained as nurse, play & sing
L. Mitchell	22	Leeds
Papers F.G.	?	not musical, elocution
J. Symms	20	Northwich
Papers M.	Ref G.	preacher, musical
M. A. T. Thompson	23	N. Shields
Papers G.	Ref G.	preacher
Miss Sellar	38	Walthamstow
Miss Baldwin	Primitive Methodist	
Source: United Methodist Deaconess Institute Minutes (1917-32) p.195		

Once admitted the students underwent a very comprehensive course of study. For example, the New Testament course in 1916-17 aimed at covering the whole of the New Testament 'to show the development of Xtn. life over against the background of the Graeco-Roman life in the 1st century'. The tutor was the Rev. Evelyn Clifford Urwin, MA, BD (an ex-Free Methodist minister stationed at Brixton) who seems to have been a very demanding teacher. He reported on the progress of his students:

> On the ground of industry and hard work, both students are to be heartily commended, but in point of efficiency Miss Jackson has very considerable lee-way to make up. She doubtless suffers from a very inadequate equipment, though at some points she shows to better advantage. I do not doubt that she has the makings of a very useful worker.[39]

Supplementary Reading for the New Testament Course 1916-17   The Rev. E. C. Urwin

It ought to be added that the N. T. reading has been supplemented by the reading of a Life of Jesus, 'Jesus in History and Experience' (Swanwick Free Ch. Fellowship), by various parts of introductions in the Century Bible, art. in H. B. D. and the One-Vol. Commentary (Dummelow) and by Whyte-Melock's 'The Gladiators' & Lytton's 'Last Days of Pompeii' to illustrate 1st.

Source: United Methodist Deaconess Institute Minutes (1917-32) p.21

In addition to the more academic studies the students received training in elocution and public speaking to help them with work in the churches. From a comment about a probationer deaconess in June 1918 it seems that the Institute encouraged students with public speaking ability to take up 'with zeal and persistency the Local Preachers' Studies arranged by the denomination' and she was told 'that her acceptance as a fully accredited deaconess' would depend on the success with which she did this during her second probationary year.

---

39. UMDIMins II pp.21, 27

Public Speaking Course   **Letter Heading 1918**

MR. G. BOWER CODLING

(Author of 'The Public Speaker's Training Course')

TEACHER OF

ELOCUTION AND DRAMATIC ART, PUBLIC SPEAKING
AND READING, RECITATION, AND VOICE PRODUCTION

CLASSES AND PRIVATE LESSONS IN TOWN AT

                                  53 Moyser Road,

King's Weigh House Club,   Streatham S. W.16

Thomas Street, Oxford Street, W.1   LONDON

(Opposite Selfridge's, and one minute's walk

from Bond Street Tube Station)

Source: United Methodist Deaconess Institute Minutes (1917-32) p.61

In May 1922 the Consultative Committee, which dealt mainly with the selection, training and supervision of the deaconesses, was faced with an unusual problem. They received an application from a Mrs. Devey and decided 'to recommend Mrs. Devey's acceptance with the idea of a short period of training in the Institute and an appointment in the autumn'. So she was 'received as a deaconess on trial and temporarily appointed to Battersea Park'. However, in July it was resolved with regard to 'Sister Violet'

> that Rev. H. Smith and Rev. R. W. Gair be a Committee to interview Mr. Devey of Wolverhampton, and report to this Committee the results of their interview.

At its meeting in August 1922 the Consultative Committee was presented with 'a long statement from Sister Violet' (not extant) and after hearing it the Committee decided

> that the Warden should communicate with Mr. J. A. Devey with a view to securing his consent to Sister Violet continuing her calling as a deaconess, and that if such consent be clearly given an appointment should be made for the Sister.

The matter ended in September when the General Committee, with one dissenting vote, decided on the following resolution:

> The Committee of the Deaconess Institute having considered the circumstances brought before it, and with the sense of its responsibility to the Denomination regrets that it cannot see its way clear to accept the services of Mrs. Violet Devey as a deaconess.
>
> It desires to express its high appreciation of her Christian character and eminent abilities, and wishes her every possible success and blessing in the future, praying that she may have the Divine Guidance in the solution of her life's problem.

This episode raises several questions, such as, was she a widow or separated from her husband; was Mr. Devey her father-in-law or her husband; was there a marriage break-up; was there opposition from her family? Unfortunately, it is impossible for us now, with the information available, to answer these questions and it would be interesting to have the full picture and also to know what happened to her.[40]

The Institute and its medical advisor, Dr. Cope, were very caring about the sisters who became ill in the course of their work, but two incidents in particular deserve mention. First, when the Consultative Committee received a letter from the House Surgeon of the Cancer Hospital reporting that Sister Lois had 'been too ill to attend for Electrical treatment' and had now returned home to her sister in Louth, they were very concerned and instructed the Warden to cover any costs involved and to assure her family that they would give her any help possible. Then, Miss Ireland was a probationer student who had a slight speech defect, but obviously her commitment to the Sisterhood and her ability deserved special consideration and the committee was anxious not to lose her services, so she continued her training.

---

40. UMDIMins II pp.134-35, 136, 138, 145, 146, 147, 150

Report on Miss Ireland

In the case of Miss Ireland who possesses exceptionally fine gifts as a student and musician, a young woman of real culture, but with a slight defect of speech the following resolution was passed, after considering a special report from Dr. Cope & Mr. G. B. Codling – that Miss Ireland be continued as a student and that the Warden shall explore the possibilities of Miss Ireland serving in a tutorial and secretarial capacity.

Source: United Methodist Deaconess Institute Minutes (1917-32) p.368

After two years' training the Sisters were appointed to a circuit or church, but a careful oversight was kept on them and their work, with reports being sent to the General Committee. Discipline was quite strict, for example, due to a mix-up of dates Sister Annie in 1914 had been 'double-booked' to take missions in Laisterdayke, Bradford and also at Ridsdale in the Bellingham Circuit. On discovering his mistake the Warden requested the circuit and the Ridsdale Church to accept a different date, but they refused. Having consulted the Chairman and Vice Chairman of the Institute, it was decided that the original arrangement with Laisterdayke must be honoured. The Warden conveyed the decision to Ridsdale and instructed Sister Annie to go to Laisterdayke, but she declined. The Consultative Committee resolved that Sister Annie should be told 'that the deaconesses are absolutely at the disposal of the Committee . . . as to their appointments and that if a similar declinture occurs again on the part of Sister Annie it will be deemed to be her resignation'. In another case, Sister Gladys had obviously not fitted in well at Ecclesfield, Sheffield because some of the circuit officials complained to the Warden at the 1926 Conference. Sister Gladys was asked for her side of the story, but this did not sway the committee who decided she should not remain there. The Warden was asked to write to her and tell her that 'in view of the fact that there has been trouble in previous churches where she has been appointed, we suggest that she be more tactful'. One wonders if she was getting a little disillusioned with the Sisterhood or whether it was family circumstances because, in May 1929, she requested permission to leave the Chester Circuit and for leave of absence 'to go home from August to the end of December in order to become acquainted with her father's business'. Permission was refused at that time, but, being granted a year's absence 'for personal reasons' later that year, she then asked for her travelling expenses home to Norwich![41] Perhaps another example of her lack of tact!

---

41. UMDIMins II pp.242-43, 247, 339, 345

Letter   **Sister Gladys**

The Warden read a letter from Sister Gladys who has been granted a year's absence from work (in response to her request) for personal reasons. In the letter she said her expenses from Chester to her home in Norwich were £3. 1. 3. and implied the Committee would pay them. After careful consideration, seeing Sister Gladys had gone home for the convenience of herself and family, the Committee decided to inform her that it is not the custom to pay expenses under such circumstances and that we cannot establish such a precedent.

Source: United Methodist Deaconess Institute Minutes (1917-32) pp.354-55

Another deaconess who was warned about her work was Sister Ida to whom it was pointed out 'that unless more successful reports of her work came to hand her continuance in the Sisterhood would have to be seriously considered'. Then Sister Barbara was a first year or junior student who had been accepted in 1924. Evidently she had not lived up to her initial promise as her examination results in 1926 left much to be desired, so 'owing to her general unfitness for the work' she was refused admission to the second year of training. From these few examples it is obvious that a high standard of behaviour, commitment and work was regarded as paramount.

Examination results 1926					
	Theology	Child Psychology & Sunday School Work	O.T. Literature	Pyschology & Personality	Sermon
Possible marks	100	50	50	100	
Senior Students					
Sister Rhoda	94	48	50	90	Very Good
Sister Elsie	92	44	50	80	Good
Sister Eunice	91	17	50	75	Good
Junior Students					
Sister Mildred	84	42	48	90	Excellent
Sister Barbara	64	37	46	65	Fair
Sister Monica	61	39	39	63	Very Fair
Sister Linda	61	40	39	60	Very Fair

Source: United Methodist Deaconess Institute Minutes (1917-32) p.246

In December 1925 the Warden reported that he had arranged for Miss Margery Westby to give six lectures on 'Social Work and Subjects'. A. Margery Westby, who was fully accredited in 1917, had had to resign, owing to the death of her father after nearly three years' service, in 1918, so if this is the same lady presumably she would be able to draw on her own experiences and therefore know how best to angle her lectures to the work in which the Sisters would be engaged. Then, in 1926, Miss Saul, a member of the General Committee, with the blessing of Dr. Cope, arranged to give 'rhythmic exercises to the students at her own house free of charge'.[42] So the training of the United Methodist Deaconesses was wide ranging, covering the needs of body, mind and spirit.

At the Anniversary in 1929 the Sisters had requested a scheme of studies for continuing their training after they left the Institute but, although the proposal was referred to the Tutors, there is no indication that anything was formally arranged. Perhaps this was deferred as the prospect of uniting with the Wesleyan Deaconess Order would mean that there could be a common scheme put in place before too long.

In October 1933 Gair contributed a note about the ex-United Methodist Section to *The Agenda* in which he remarked that for the first time ever some Sisters were on the Reserve List. However, he felt that this was chiefly because of the upheaval and reorganization following Methodist Union, especially as regards circuit work. He rejoiced in the closer links that Union had brought and felt that 'the fellowship is very precious'.[43]

The Primitive Methodist Deaconesses

Unfortunately, there is very little information about the Primitive Methodist Deaconesses, but it seems that the Rev. James Flanagan (1851-1918) was the prime mover in the establishment of the Women's Settlement connected with St. George's Hall in Bermondsey when he was minister (1892-1905) in Southwark Mission (later called the South-East London Mission). Although there is a lengthy and fulsome obituary of him in the *Primitive Methodist Minutes of Conference* of 1918 it makes no mention of this side of his ministry.[44] The Mission had been started in 1872 by

---

42. UMDIMins II pp.29, 32, 223, 228
43. *The Agenda* (October 1933) p.5
44. *Primitive Methodist Minutes of Conference* (1918) pp.258-60

a few enthusiastic Christians, but, although much self-sacrificing work was done in the neighbourhood, the area was a very difficult run-down one. Then, in 1891, Conference's attention was drawn to a certain James Flanagan who was working with much success as missioner in Nottingham. He was persuaded to enter the Primitive Methodist ministry and duly appointed to the Southwark Mission. There Flanagan found that Trinity Street Chapel was gloomy and depressing and the area rife with poverty and degradation. It seemed an impossible task, but, in 1897, the site of a 'disreputable drink shop known as "The Old Kent Tap" became available. It was acquired from the Corporation of London and a Mission, to be named St. George's Hall, was built there. It was opened on 4th January 1900. Flanagan worked tirelessly to raise funds for the project, and also to meet the needs of the people in the locality. He started a Waifs' Festival for the children, a 'Ministry of Old Clothes' for the needy, a Brass Band, a Gymnasium, Girls' Institute, Young Women's Parlour, Lodging House and various other social services. Flanagan had the idea of setting up a Women's Settlement soon after St. George's Hall was erected and to that end he engaged Nurse Blackburn and Sister Louie, who were to visit the sick, care for the needy, persuade the local children to come to the Sunday School, hold prayer meetings in people's homes and encourage young women to avoid temptation. On the whole the two were made welcome by the people and so Flanagan determined to establish a permanent Settlement. His idea met with disapproval from some people in the Connexion, but was welcomed by others. He appealed for help in *Light and Truth* – a local free newspaper – with the result that he was able to rent a house in the Old Kent Road as headquarters for his Sisters, where they were trained and where he met with them and their helpers every Monday for prayer, to exchange experiences and offer encouragement. This house served as a Mission house from which the Sisters visited the sick, helped the needy, conducted prayer meetings and, in particular, worked with the young women of the district. Many of the stories found their way into the pages of *Light and Truth*. The Settlement was formally recognised in 1901. The freehold of St. George's Hall was offered to the Missionary Committee by the London Corporation for £3,500, as long as it was purchased within seven years. When it was realized that four of those years had gone by the Conference decided to appoint the Rev. Joseph Johnson (2) to St. George's Hall and set James Flanagan free to raise the necessary money. During his time at the Hall Johnson and his wife bought, adapted and furnished a permanent Sisters' Settlement at a cost of £900. The Settlement was self-supporting and trained young intelligent women to be Sisters of the People. As it became established well-wishers contributed to its cost. The Sisters received nine months' training, including instruction in anatomy, medicine and nursing. If they were not needed to work in the Southwark Mission, then they were available to take appointments in circuits or churches.[45]

As we have seen, the Primitive Methodist Sisters attended some lectures at the United Methodist Deaconess Institute as part of their training, but most likely they 'learnt on the job' in practical situations. In 1919 the Rev. Raymond Taunton, writing in *The Aldersgate Magazine* about the South-East London Mission, said:

> Women are very necessary at St. George's Hall and you find them there, hard at it. The Sisters – Elsie, May, Dora, Mabel, Isabel, Eva and Kathleen – are alike in purpose penetrating into the neighbourhood . . . with invisible love and with the visible signs of it, carrying light into darkness; and each one has also an individuality which means some specialised service to the Mission, besides adding to its human wealth all marshalled, to the praise of the watchful, by Sister Elsie, the Sister-in-Charge. An additional motherly touch of great value comes from Mrs. H. J. Taylor who loves to be active in all this work for its own sake, and who has the confidence of the Sisters and all the women of the Mission. She and her husband – the 'chief' – the Rev. H. J. Taylor, give a fine lead, regarded from any viewpoint. The Mission has a heart; the women form a large part of the heart; Mr. Taylor forms the rest of the heart, and he is certainly the mind of the Mission.[46]

A typed duplicated manuscript gives a little flavour of what life was like for the Primitive Methodist Sisters living in the Sisters' Settlement of St. George's Hall:

---

45. *The History of the Primitive Methodist Church* (H. B. Kendall, n.d. ?1902?) 2 vols. Vol ii pp.513-16; *The Life of James Flanagan* (R. W. Russell, 1920) p.147-49
46. *The Aldersgate Magazine* (October 1919) p.691

SISTERS' SETTLEMENT AND TRAINING
HOME RULES AND REGULATIONS

1.   Each Sister, it is hoped, will renew her consecration to God each day; redeem all spare time for the cultivation of her mental and spiritual life; carefully study the word of God with the best helps available, that she may be thoroughly instructed in all good works and ready for possible calls to larger service.

2.   Each Sister is required to keep a Diary of the number of visits made in her district; to note particulars of special cases of interest, to record all such cases in the Day Book supplied by the Sister-in-Charge.

3.   Each Sister during her term of training must consider herself on probation; permanent service altogether depends on the possession of suitable gifts, general adaptation and fitness for the work, and on suitable openings presenting themselves.

4.   Each Sister is required to act both in private life and public service in harmony with the spirit and purpose of the Settlement, remembering that each one holds in keeping the character of all.

5.   It is expected that all Sisters be mutually considerate and helpful; avoid everything that irritates and tends to create discord, and 'By Love Serve one another'.

6.   No Sister may neglect or change any part of her authorised work, but must consistently, in the fear of God and as an honourable woman, attend to her district and the other duties allotted to her.

7.   Each Sister is expected to be an example of personal cleanliness and neatness, and is required to make her own bed, keep her room neat and clean and have it ready for inspection at any time. She must be willing to undertake such household duties as may be necessary and as desired by the Sister-in-Charge.

8.   No Sister is to remain in the Settlement between the hours of 10 a.m. and 12.30, 2.30 and 4.30 except by the sanction of the Sister-in-Charge; these hours must be given to visiting or taking services, or such work as is allotted by the Sister-in-Charge and every hour must be accounted for in the daily record.

9.   No Sister is to be out of residence later than 10.30 p.m. without the knowledge of the Sister-in-Charge and the permission of the

Superintendent. All lights in the Settlement to be out by 11 p.m. Reading in bed is strictly prohibited.

10. No visitors are allowed except by the knowledge and consent of the Superintendent and Sister-in-Charge.

11. Any complaints as to management, rules, food, work etc., should be made in person or in writing to the Superintendent.

12. ORDER OF THE DAY
    7.15 a.m. Getting up Bell
    8.00 a.m. Breakfast
    8.30 a.m. Prayers
    10.00 a.m. District Visiting
    12.30 p.m. Dinner
    2.30 p.m. District Visiting or special work
    4.30 p.m. Tea
    5.30 p.m. Fill in diary
    6.30 p.m. Such work as is allotted by the Sister-in-Charge for each evening on the first five days of the week.

13. Promptness in everything is absolutely necessary.

14. No Sister is to visit in any District other than her own without permission of the Sister-in-Charge.

15. Each Sister when away from the Mission must inform the Sister-in-Charge as to where she is going and with whom she is to spend the time.

16. In the interest of general satisfaction in the Mission no Sister is expected to accept an invitation to have a meal or join in a Social Gathering in the home of any member of the Mission. Permission to accept such invitations can only be given by the Superintendent and then only for exceptional reasons.

17. No Sister is to visit members or adherents of the Mission excepting such as live in their own district.

18. Each Sister is expected, when considered qualified, to take such Mission Services in any Church seeking their aid. The remuneration for such services to be arranged by the Superintendent, such remuneration to be applied to the Funds of the Sisters' Settlement. All services by Sisters away from the Mission to be arranged by the Superintendent.

19. Each Sister is expected to advocate the cause of the Settlement on every suitable occasion and to solicit tactfully, gifts of

money etc. All such gifts to be handed to the Superintendent for official acknowledgement.

20. While Saturday is an off day for all Sisters, it is expected that the morning will be given to some form of study about which the Superintendent may be expected to ask for information at any time.

21. Any wilful contravention of the above requirements will seriously affect the relationship of any Sister concerned, to the Mission.

On Behalf and by Order of the
Sisters' Settlement Council.[47]

At Union, as noted previously, the Primitive Methodist Sisters were not able to join with the other deaconesses immediately as they were not a connexional organisation, though they had received some official recognition from the Primitive Methodist Home Mission Committee, but they were welcomed into the fellowship and, in 1934, 24 Sisters came into the combined Order.

Sister Gladys P. Barran was one of the Primitive Methodist Sisters of the People who came into the Wesley Deaconess Order in 1933 and in October 1952 she wrote in *The Wesley Deaconess Magazine* about her memories of Methodist Union.

Memories of a Union	**Sister Gladys P. Barran**

I have before me as I write, one of my most treasured possessions. It is the badge of the Wesley Deaconess Order. It is shabby now, some of its enamel is missing and the pin is crooked, but to me it is very precious. It was a gift, handed to me by Dr. Maltby nearly twenty years ago. It is a constant reminder of the joys and blessings that have come to me down the years through the Fellowship of the Order. I am one of the fortunate people for whom Methodist Union has been *all* gain. Sometimes I think I stand in an unique position regarding Union. Brought up in the Primitive Methodist Church, I became one of its deaconesses. During my training at St. George's Hall I shared lectures with the Sisters of the United Methodist Church at Bowron House. Then, in 1932, came Methodist Union. The next year Dr. Maltby, in the name of the deaconesses of the Wesleyan Church, invited us to share Convocation with them at Sheffield. It was an

---

47. MS typed sheet

unforgettable experience. There was an odd assortment of bonnets and hats, costumes and long coats, but in spite of outward appearances there was an underlying unity. It was with the sense of belonging to a wonderful fellowship that I returned to my work. The inspiration of those days, and friendships made then have remained with me down the years.

During the months which followed machinery was set up to bring us into a United Order. This was accomplished at Birmingham Convocation 1934, when I became the proud possessor of my first badge. We were not 'taken in'; a term which has sometimes been used when speaking of Union; we were one body in Christ. Our sick members too were accepted, and love and care and a sense of security not known before, has been given to them during years of infirmity. I remember at the close of that Convocation, meeting the Rev. R. W. Gair (Warden of the United Methodist Deaconess Order). 'Well, Sister,' he said, 'And what do you think about it?' I replied, 'If Union could begin at the level on which we have moved this week there would be very few problems ahead of us.'

The next year, 1935, I had the inestimable privilege of studying at the College, Ilkley. The Order owes more than it can ever say to the Wardens and Sisters who have staffed the College for the past fifty years. Lectures are important and are on a high level (indeed one student coming to Ilkley remarked that the standard of lectures was at least as high as those to which she had been accustomed at University). But it is the quality of the life maintained there that has been the moulding influence of so many lives. The Fellowship of the Order is, to my mind, an extension of the life of College.

I remember our first Ordination Service, for I was an Ordinand that year. (Up to that time Deaconesses had been 'Consecrated').

I look at my badge, and I remember this sequence of events and thank God for the Wesley Deaconess Order and its College at Ilkley.

GLADYS P. BARRAN.

Source: The Wesley Deaconess Magazine (October 1952) pp.14-15

It is surely significant that within the same decade ministers of all three branches of the Methodist Church should have realised the important part that women could play in helping their ministry and established organizations to achieve this. Work desperately needed to be done among the women and children and seemed to be a particular service suited to dedicated trained women. They were right and the women achieved great things.

Chapter 10

Changing Fashions: The Deaconess Uniform

Although it may seem a little odd to catalogue the evolution of the Wesley Deaconess Order uniform, it was an integral and important part of the ethos of the Order and also of the United Methodist Deaconess Institute. It identified the Sisters and aided them in their work. It was adapted and altered to meet changing circumstances and social conditions.

Sister Grace: Wesley Deaconess Uniform, 1890s

Stephenson in *Concerning Sisterhoods* explained that he had been against a specific dress for his deaconesses until he had observed for himself the benefit of it during the Franco-Prussian War, when the Kaiserswerth Sisters were recognised and respected wherever they went. He felt that a distinctive uniform would not only open up more opportunities for service, but would also form a protection for his deaconesses against unwelcome attentions. So Stephenson decided that when, his deaconesses became Probationer-Deaconesses – after their three months' probation – they should wear distinctive clothes which would mark them out, but would also mean that there would be no obvious difference 'in the association of women, some of whom may be wealthy, others of whom may have only the allowance for necessary expenses made to them by the association itself'. A uniform would also settle the matters 'of taste, and present(s) to all onlookers an example of Christian modesty and propriety in dress'.[1]

In pursuit of this object a sub-committee in 1897 decided that deaconesses should have an allowance of at least £20 per annum and that £16 of this should be in cash 'with material for two dresses, a cloak or jacket and two bonnets'. However, some Sisters felt the question of allowances should be reconsidered as 'that the amount of uniform offered was in excess of their requirements', so the sub-committee agreed that deaconesses already recognised should have

---

1. *Concerning Sisterhoods* pp.70-71

the option of accepting the new arrangement or keeping to the previous one, but that new members would receive a cash allowance and some uniform.[2]

In 1906 *Flying Leaves* sought to answer questions about the Order and one was about why the deaconesses dressed alike. A threefold reply was given:

(a) It is desirable that people should recognise them as servants of the Church, and members of their Order.

(b) It is desirable that the dress and whole appearance of a woman so employed by the Church, should be neat, quiet, and lady-like.

(c) Her uniform enables her to go safely night and day among persons, and into places, where she would not be safe in private clothing.[3]

Sister Sara:
Wesley Deaconess
Uniform, 1890s

The value of a recognisable uniform was illustrated when a deaconess had unexpectedly to fill the pulpit in a small Methodist chapel in the Yorkshire Dales, where the preacher failed to arrive.

Blue and White to the Rescue

. . . A lonely little Methodist Chapel. Congregation, a few people from neighbouring farms, and half a dozen summer visitors.

No preacher! . . . At length two or three hardy ones step outside . . . Scarcely have they done so, when one . . . cries, 'Isn't that a blue veil with white stripes?' and she points to a group of three slowly and comfortably approaching, of whom one wears the distinctive veil, now floating out like a banner of hope. 'You are a Wesley Deaconess, aren't you?' 'Yes.' 'I thought so.' and turning to her two companions, she says, 'Now we're all right.' Turning to the Wesley Deaconess she says, 'The preacher has not come. Please take the service.' . . . It is well for people to know that a blue veil with white stripes declares a Wesley Deaconess.

Source: Flying Leaves (October 1905) p.326

---

2. WDIMins I pp.39, 46-47, 54
3. *FL* (November 1906) p.170

Sister Lillie Gustard, entered Wesley Deaconess Order 1905; consecrated 1905 note stripe on her veil

Early pictures of Wesley Deaconesses indicate that they wore full length, long sleeved, dark, front buttoning tucked dresses, with white collars and cuffs, while on their neatly piled up hair they had a dark bonnet which tied under the chin, often with a veil. For some of their work long aprons were worn.[4] A typescript states a Uniform was preferable to 'miscellaneous modes of dress, and this was a long grey dress, a grey apron (to symbolise service), and a bonnet and veil' and it adds that there was a story that after Stephenson's retirement, Mrs. Bradfield, the new Warden's wife, 'was heard to say that she couldn't understand where all the grey dusters were appearing from in the college'. (The students had obviously had enough of the grey aprons.)[5]

Writing in 1959, Mildred Homer recalled the pioneer days of the Order when she started work in Bethnal Green, London in January 1893. She found that, of necessity, much of her work consisted of nursing and that she was very thankful for 'the ample white apron provided'.

Nursing in Bethnal Green, 1893   Sister Mildred Homer

Who will blame me then, if, after 'practising' for a few years without killing anyone, even with some light measure of success, with amusement came the vision of myself putting up outside the Mission Hall my plate engraved upon it "M. H. the two penny doctor!"

Source: The Wesley Deaconess Magazine (December 1959) p.3

Mildred added that in the early days the uniform was supplied chiefly to act as a protection in dangerous areas. While at times it served this purpose, at others 'the long veil hanging behind' was a temptation for ill-intentioned people to throttle the wearer as she herself had found out, when attacked by a woman.

---

4. *HH* (1892) pp.138, 150, (1894) p.59, (1895) p.233
5. Typescript lent by the Rev. Margaret Stanworth (Sister Margaret)

A Student Song! – Tune: Unison

Deaconesses arise, and put your bonnets on strong in the uniform supplied by Doctor Stephenson.

Source: The Wesley Deaconess Magazine (December 1959) p.5

The Order was nothing if not practical and a picture of Sister Gertrude Nettleship in the 1898 *Highways and Hedges* shows her in a uniform appropriate for her work in Ceylon, accompanied by the observation:

> The picture . . . shows her in her Deaconess costume, which of course has to be modified to the requirements of a tropical climate. She wears thin material, the colours of which are a reversal of those worn in England. Instead of blue dress, with white cuffs and collars, she wears a white dress with blue cuffs and collar. Her head gear is a kind of helmet of cork, to protect the head from the tropical sun.[6]

It was an indication that the Wesley Deaconess Institute was well established when the need was felt for there to be a distinctive badge. The small consultative committee, set up in November 1901, recommended that a Maltese Cross should be the Badge of the Order.

First Wesley Deaconess Order Badge – 1901

. . . the upright and the transverse being of blood colour, and the circle of white. On the circle are the words 'To seek and to save that which is lost.' . . . On the transverse are the words 'For Jesus' Sake', . . . On the upright is the figure of the Dove, . . . And surely no emblem for such a work could be more beautifully fit than the brooding Dove, which reminds us always of the Spirit of Power. To this we add, on the lower transverse, an open Bible: for if the Spirit is the energy of our work, the Word of God is its instrument.

Source: Wesley Deaconess Institute Minutes (1895-1910) pp.102, 109, *Flying Leaves* (September 1902) p.131

---

6. *HH* (February 1898) pp.42-43

After 12 years' service a star pendant with the word 'true' was to be awarded and Sister Ruth Northcroft was the first recipient of this distinction at the 1902 Convocation. Deaconesses who had served for 21 years were to receive one with 'faithful' on it. A similar badge to the deaconess badge, but with a blue instead of a white circle was available for 'Associates of the Deaconess Order', those women who were sympathetic to the Order's work and who helped with its fund-raising, for the modest sum of one shilling.

First Wesley Deaconess Order Badge, 1901

Once the Wesley Deaconess Order had settled down in its new home in Ilkley it evolved its organisation, a pattern of training and numerous domestic matters. So in May 1903 a revision of both the arrangements for the provision of the Wesley Deaconess uniform, which had previously been supplied by the Children's Home, and a change in the outfit itself was proposed. Apparently material for the uniform used to be sent to each deaconess and then she was responsible for the making up of the outfit, but now it was proposed that Hepton Bros. of Leeds should both supply and make up the materials with Mr. Holtby of Bradford supplying the collars and cuffs and H. W. Lee and Co. in the East End of London providing the bonnets direct. This arrangement would release the College from the necessity of having to stock and dispatch these items. The comparative cost of the old and new arrangement meant a saving of one halfpenny per outfit!

Regulations respecting uniform – 1903

I **Students in Residence at the College**
shall receive during the year for use in District Work:

One Cloak.
One Bonnet.

II **Students before leaving the College**
shall receive the following ('Grey') Uniform, which Uniform shall last until Consecration, i.e. 18 Months' Outfit:

1 Two Grey Dresses.
2 One Cloth Jacket.
3 One Bonnet.
4 A Second set of Bonnet Trimmings.

---

5 Four Aprons.
6 Six Linen Collars and One Celluloid Collar.
7 Six Pairs of Cuffs and One Pair of Celluloid Cuffs.
8 Four Lawn and Two Silk Ties.

III <u>In the Month of March, before Consecration</u>
the usual yearly allowance of ('Blue') Uniform will be provided. This must last until the end of the following May 12 months, i.e. 13 Months' Outfit:

1 Material for One Dress:
   (a) Serge or
   (b) Heptonette

2 One Made Outer Garment per year which shall be either:-
   (a) Heptonette Cloak, or
   (b) Winter Cloth Jacket, or These three classes of Garments
   (c) Summer Jacket of to cover together three years' wear.
      (i) Serge or
      (ii) Heptonette.
3 One Trimmed Bonnet.
4 Second Set of Trimmings for the Same.
5 Material for Two White Linen Aprons.
6 Four Linen Collars.
7 Four Pairs of Cuffs.
8 Two Silk and Four Nainsook Ties.
9 Extra Veil.

Source: Wesley Deaconess Institute Minutes (1895-1910) pp.143-45

Wesley Deaconesses, 1903

A brief aside, in a report of the 1903 Convocation, notes that at a meal 'The students (still privileged to wear pretty blouses, for they do not adopt indoor uniform till their College year is ended) waited kindly and deftly. One wonders if the anonymous writer had a passing regret for 'ordinary' clothes![7]

By 1907, when there were 15 deaconesses overseas, it became evident that the uniform originally designed for the British Isles was not suitable for warmer climates so another detailed review took place and the regulations were 'to be firmly enforced both at home and abroad'.

Uniform regulations – 1907

I. For countries with temperate climates.

A. For Consecrated Deaconesses.
1. A plain navy blue dress of serge or cravenette, made without trimmings or ornamentation: the bodice to be made with a Bishop sleeve: white turned down collar, outside cuffs, and white bow.
2. A navy 'Wesley' cloak, or jacket supplied.
3. A bonnet trimmed with navy velvet, with velvet strings, and a veil of navy silk with the white stripe, which is the distinguishing mark of the Order.

N.B. A plain navy cotton dress may be worn in the heat of summer.

B. For Probationers.
1. A plain grey dress of cravenette or serge, made without trimmings or ornamentations, with white turned-down collar, outside cuffs, and white bow.
2. A navy 'Wesley' cloak, or jacket.
3. A bonnet and veil like those of the Consecrated Deaconesses.

N.B. A grey cotton dress may be worn in the heat of summer.

C. For Student-Probationers.
1. A 'Wesley' cloak, with bonnet and veil worn on Sundays, and for District work.
2. A grey dress (provided by the student) for Sundays and special occasions.
3. A grey apron and cape, with collar and cuffs, worn over private clothes for week days, during the time of residence in College.
4. A 'Probationer dress' is supplied in advance before Convocation.

---

7. *FL* (June 1903) p.85

II. For Countries with Tropical and sub-Tropical climates.
A. <u>Full Dress</u>. The navy blue uniform with cuffs, collars, bow and bonnet, as worn at home, only the dress to be made of thin cashmere.
B. For afternoon wear, Sundays and visiting. White drill skirts, with plain white muslin blouses, navy belts and bows, Plain straw shade hat, trimmed simply with white washing silk or a helmet.
C. Working dresses may be worn. Blue-grey gingham skirts, with zephyr blouses to match, with blue belt and white bow.

Source: Wesley Deaconess Institute Minutes (1895-1910) pp.296-97

The whole ethos of the Deaconess Order was eminently practical, in training, uniform, work and outlook. In 1908 it was suggested that 'uniform be supplied according to a price list, to the amount of £3 per annum'. The *General Regulations 1908* stipulate that the 'distinctive uniform of the Wesley Deaconess Order includes a blue veil with white stripes'. The students provided their own clothing while at College, and they were instructed that 'a grey dress must be brought for Sunday wear and for District visiting. It

Sheffield Convocation, June 1912: note the striped veils

must be similar in colour and style to the Probationers' uniform . . . A bonnet and cloak will be provided by the College without charge. Students must see to it that their dress shall at all times be simple, quiet, and unobtrusive, and their whole appearance befitting the calling for which they are offering themselves.' The Probationers' uniform consisted of 'a plain grey dress, the material for which is provided by the Institute, with white turned-down collar, outside cuffs, and white bow, a navy-blue cloak or coat, and the bonnet and veil of the Order. In hot weather, a grey cotton dress my be worn.' The Deaconesses' uniform was navy-blue, otherwise it was similar to that of the Probationers. The badge of the Order, presented at Consecration, was worn as part of the uniform. In 1909 it was made clear that the deaconesses' veils were the property of the Institute and must be returned when a Sister resigned.

Wesley Deaconesses with the Warden, the Rev. William Bradfield and Mrs. Bradfield, 1910

In May 1914 one of the pen-portraits of deaconess work was given by Muriel Murphy who, because of ill-health, had been obliged to give up ordinary deaconess work, but who had, to her great astonishment, found a new field of service in charge of the Uniform Department at Ilkley. She explained that the Department had been set up because the possibility of 2,000 Wesley Deaconesses scattered throughout the United Kingdom dressing alike was very remote: given individual taste and different suppliers! She commented: 'It was tried and found 'not possible'.

Uniform Department, Ilkley, 1914   Sister Muriel Murphy

As I had never had business training or such experience of any kind, the thought of Ledgers, Cash Books, Invoices, Stock Books, not to speak of piles of correspondence struck terror to my heart. But in spite of —

> 'Books to the right of her,
> Boxes to the left of her,
> Labelled and numbered,
> Hers not to flinch and fly,
> Hers but to dare and try,
> Into the Uniform Office
> Plunged one of the two hundred.'

'Well', I thought, 'if it is my lot for the present to "abide by the stuff", I must put my best into it', and one of our junior Sisters quoted to me a remark I had made to her when she was about to take her first meeting, 'God's commandment is God's enablement', and told me to put in practice my own precept. And certainly I have found it true . . .'

Source: Flying Leaves (May 1914) pp.80-81

A practical issue raised by the 1916 Convocation was the possibility of wearing 'plain uniform' during hot weather, but of even more interest is

Hats. The question of a plain hat for the hot weather, (and specially for deaconesses who had much cycling) was again considered; and permission was given to wear a simple hat in cases where it was needed; the bonnet to be carried on the cycle in cases where meetings were to be taken.[8]

---

8. RConv. (31st May 1916)

It is likely that the First World War had something to do with these requests and also with the further ones when Convocation of 1921 asked that the long service badges in future be plain, but continued to be presented at Convocation and that the uniform be 'modernised'. The resolution on the uniform indicates the deaconesses' wish for more practical, yet distinctive, clothes which would enable them to carry out their duties, but which would not make them feel too old-fashioned:

1. An alternative uniform was unanimously recommended.

2. That a plain sailor felt hat was considered the most suitable; that there be a voluntary choice of shape; and that the hat, in two or three sizes, be available at the Uniform Office.

3. That there be a five-striped ribbon round the hat; small or 'pin stripes'.

4. That a badge on the hat is not necessary if the striped ribbon be used.

5. That a soft collar: Polo or Peter Pan: be worn.

6. That the question of cuffs be optional.

7. That a navy blue tie be worn with the addition of the badge.

8. That the blouse be of blue cashmere: plain shirt pattern: to be supplied from the College.

9. Probationers to wear grey dress and blouse; navy hat; grey tie; and blue coat.[9]

Perhaps this was a sign of the times and the growing status of women which had developed during the war years when many women had taken over men's jobs while they were away fighting. Many deaconesses during those years had been in situations and done work which would have been unthinkable when the Order started or even when the first uniform regulations were formulated, so this new uniform request was essentially a practical one from the people involved. The following year Convocation requested that the grey uniform for probationers should be abolished in favour of all deaconesses wearing blue – again a practical measure to save money, but a final decision having been postponed for further consultation, the result was that it was retained. An alteration to the

---

9. RConv. (31st May 1916)

badge was agreed in 1924 after considerable discussion. The new badge would have the words 'Wesley Deaconess Order' in place of the motto and the words in the centre would be removed. In the July *The Agenda* informed the deaconesses that 'those who wish for straw hats can now obtain them – either in the shape and size of the Panamas which were on view at Convocation, or in the same shape as the felt and velours – but in tagel straw'.[10]

Convocation in 1926 set up a small working party to consider details of the uniform and it reported the following year and suggested that 'the wearing of a hat with a badge be recognised as official uniform equally with the bonnet'. The question of uniform was obviously a prickly one at this time because it was pointed out by some of the deaconesses that it 'was a difficulty to many outside the Order'. It was felt that 'as the time to discuss these matters was hopelessly inadequate' an extended committee should meet at Ilkley to try to resolve the difficulties. The following resolution was passed unanimously at the 1927 Bolton Convocation:

> This Convocation desires to record its sense of the value of the recognised Uniform of the Order. It suggests that when the alternative Uniform is worn, the hat shall be a plain uniform shape, in which case it would be considered equally as official uniform as the bonnet.
>
> It is also of the opinion that, whereas for some years several members of the Order in special circumstances have not worn the Uniform, these exceptions should be approved and regularised, and the same liberty extended to any others joining the Order in the future, whose work would be better served by such freedom.

Uniform matters continued to be debated in Convocation as the Order sought to bring its image up to date and so, in 1929, the use of a Ribbon, with the Order's Badge woven on it, to be worn on the Uniform Hat was approved, as also was the option of a Uniform Blazer with the 'W.D.O.' monogram.[11]

---

10. *The Agenda* (July 1924) p.8
11. *The Agenda* (June 1928) p.4, (May 1929) p.8; (June 1929) p.11

The Badge in Spain, 1930　　　　**Sister Isabel Adams**

I had a brief holiday . . . I made my way to the tiny village and entered a shop to buy postcards. The shopkeeper, a Spaniard, noticed my badge and asked if it was religious, was I a Protestant. I replied that I was an evangelical Christian, that I did not use the word Protestant because Roman Catholics also protest. The words on the badge are 'to seek and to save that which was lost'. He had never heard the Gospel, never read the Bible. I promised to send him a Bible on my return to Barcelona. After a rather hurried talk, he asked me to write the words down for him. I did so in Spanish. Then he asked for them in English. The Bible was sent, also a letter explaining where to begin to read, etc. Since then I have heard from him, saying that 'That which was lost has been found'. I am proud of my badge, and cherish it, for the many opportunities it gives me of telling that Jesus found me.

Source: The Agenda (May 1930) p.13

The United Methodist Deaconess Uniform

The United Methodist Deaconess' uniform was very similar to that of the Wesley Deaconesses, though some wore a long dark skirt with a white blouse. Although veils were apparently expensive and funds short it was decided in December 1909 to keep them as they were a distinctive feature of dress.[12] In 1911 dissatisfaction was expressed by some deaconesses, especially those stationed at a distance, as they were unable to 'try on' their uniform cloaks and so it was decided to follow the Wesley Deaconess Order's practice and 'send the Sisters the money that they may purchase cloaks for themselves, but that the Sisters be instructed they must conform to the Committee's pattern cloak, and that they must keep their respectable appearance'.[13]

One of the duties of the Lady Superintendent, as set out in her job description in 1918, was to be responsible for the ordering and supplying of the uniform and it is noted that

---

12. See Smith, (list of illustrations) p.6; UMDIMins I p.68
13. UMDIMins I pp.103, 103-04, 104-05

The present regulations as to uniforms are as follows:
Each Sister must be supplied with –

1. A summer cloak and a winter cloak once every two years.
2. A bonnet, collars & cuffs every year and a veil twice a year.[14]

Apparently the veils were made of gossamer as, in 1923, Mrs. Gair, the Warden's wife and Lady Superintendent, reported that it was difficult to obtain and so she was authorised to get samples of other materials and consult with other ladies about them. They duly chose a more suitable material and also agreed that the present style of the cloaks should be kept. Perhaps there had been some laxity or rebellion against the wearing of uniform for in July 1924 the Warden was asked in his next monthly letter 'to enforce the Committee's rule that when Sisters are on duty they are expected to wear the uniform of the Sisterhood as provided'. Cost, rather than modernisation, seems to have been the major fact in abandoning the cloaks for in 1926 the best quotation for summer cloaks was £2.18.6 whereas coats could be obtained for £2.10.0. The colour was to be navy blue and it was reported that 'the new coats had given great satisfaction among the Sisters'.[15] As fashions changed so the question of the style of the bonnet was raised and again the Ladies Committee consulted and recommended that:

1. That a change in the style of the bonnet is desirable.
2. That the sample submitted in grey with the three fold front be adopted but that the veil should be a lighter shade to bring it into harmony with our own shade of grey.
3. The ladies also wish the Committee to make a very strong request to the Sisters to wear the whole uniform when on duty.

So it was agreed that bonnets costing 17s 6d. each should be purchased.[16] Writing in April 1926 Gair commented that 'The grey veil is the distinctive feature of the uniform of the United Methodist Church Deaconess and the women who wear it are, after training, set apart for the work of our churches.'[17]

---

14. UMDIMins II p.41
15. UDMIMins II pp.170, 177-78, 199 (cf.253); 229, 232, 237
16. UDMIMins II pp.322, 323, 325
17. MSS Cuttings Book (Gair) 7th April 1926

United Methodist Deaconess Badge

By 1917 the Institute felt well enough established to consider having a long service badge and the Warden was asked to explore the idea. This resulted in a series of letters between Smith and Bradfield, Warden of the Wesley Deaconess Institute, seeking first permission to use 'the same motto as you use, provided we adopted a different design'. Smith commented that, personally, he would like also to use 'the two words you use in the bars given after 12 and 21 years' service respectively, but that is asking too much' and he felt that, looking ahead to a union of the Methodist churches, it would be good if all the Methodist deaconesses had the same badge. Bradfield replied that his Committee had no objection to the use of their motto by the United Methodist Deaconess Institute.[18] As Smith wrote to Bradfield, in February 1918, he had left the matter of the badge and motto in abeyance 'in view of the action taken by your last Conference (Wesleyan) encouraging interchange of thought and information between the Methodist churches with a view to seeing if a way can be found for Methodist union' and was now wondering if permission might be granted for the United Methodist Institute to use the Wesley Deaconess badge and bars 'if we gave them to our Sisters on precisely the same rules as you do'. Although he realised he was asking a great deal he pointed out that the difference in the veils worn would distinguish the members of each order. However, Bradfield replied that his Committee and the deaconesses themselves were unwilling for their badge to be used.

Methodist Union

With the coming of Methodist Union in 1932 and the uniting of the deaconesses from the three branches of the Church, the question of uniform was important, but the emphasis put on it by some members of the press, especially one lady reporter, implied that it was the most important matter to be discussed at the Sheffield Convocation! Apparently, Dr. Maltby was not amused and 'gave the Press a severe castigation' for making such a fuss about a 30 minute discussion. The reports in *The Methodist Times and Leader* and *The Methodist Recorder* are worth quoting:

> They have come from all parts of England, and with their picturesque uniforms . . . Those uniforms have caused quite a flutter. On Saturday morning there was . . . a discussion as to the distinctive attire of the Order

---

18. MSS letters 26th April 1917, 23rd June 1917; UMDIMins II pp.5, 10

> ... As things are at present you can see at a glance which section of Methodism members of Convocation were formerly associated with. There is a strong sentiment in favour of uniformity in these uniforms, but it is impossible to get 300 women to settle quickly whether Sisters shall wear hats or bonnets, veils grey or blue, or no veils ...[19]

and

> These Sisters were undeniably proud of the uniform that proclaimed their friendliness and service to the people. Of its variety, a glance over the assembly afforded convincing proof. But should the uniform be uniform – a 'common' dress worn by all alike? ... Of types of uniform, one recognised the dual coloured bonnet introduced by Mrs. Hugh Price Hughes on the formation of the Sisters of the People at the West London Mission 40 years ago. Ilkley appears to favour a blue felt or straw hat. The phalanx of United Methodists were distinguished by grey cloaks and similar head-gear. The Primitive Methodists of the London Mission wore a navy cloak with a close-fitting head-dress, which had on the front a gold cross.[20]

Convocation was asked to suggest a distinctive dress, preferably one which would not be too dissimilar to the previous uniform worn by the separate orders, so that people would still be able to recognise the Sisters. A sub-committee consisting of four Wesleyans, three United Methodists and one Primitive Methodist, together with Mrs. Maltby, Mrs. Bradfield, Mrs. Gair and others was appointed. The recognised uniform of the Order decided upon was:

> (1) <u>Head dress</u>. A bonnet (as sample) with navy veil, three fine stripes round the crown and down the centre of the veil; with the alternative of a plain felt hat bearing the recognised hat band of grey-bordered navy and woven badge.
> (2) <u>Dress.</u> Plain navy dress, white collar and cuffs, white tie if bonnet worn or navy tie with hat. In the case of probationers the dress to be grey.

---

19. MS Cuttings Book (Gair) *The Methodist Times and Leader* loose sheet 27th April 1933
20. MSS Cuttings Book (Gair) *The Methodist Recorder* loose sheet 27th April 1933

(3) <u>Coat</u>. To be plain navy.

Other details to be left to the good taste of the individual.[21]

The Wesley Deaconess Order had had a centralised uniform department at Ilkley from which the Sisters ordered the basic items and this was kept open.

After 10 years as a Wesley Deaconess, Sister Edith Walton remembered her ordination at Sheffield in 1944 when 'I put away the grey uniform of a Probationer and for the very first time wore navy-blue'. Of necessity the normal Wesley Deaconess uniform rules had had to be relaxed during the war years, but, in 1947, it was decided to review the position and a Uniform Committee, which

Uniform of the 1940s/1950s: Sisters Kathleen Share; Joyce Wakely, Amy Leeworthy, Elsie Maynard and Dulcie Foss

reported each year, was set up. A proposal the following year to abolish uniform altogether failed to find a seconder at Convocation and the report of the uniform committee, after full discussion and some amendments, was carried. The uniform was now to be:

1. Uniform for official wear be navy blue dress with stiff white collar and stiff cuffs and navy tie . . . Navy coat and hat to be worn.
   As an alternative, for wear <u>not</u> on official occasions, a navy costume with a white shirt blouse and navy tie, could be worn by ordained deaconesses only.

2. For those who care to do so, a storm cap may be worn during the winter months, but not for official wear.

3. A summer frock of navy tricoline or some similar material with white collar and long sleeves can be worn, but if worn for official occasions, a stiff white collar and tie, and stiff white cuffs must be used.

---

21. RConv. 1933 (22nd, 24th, 25th, 26th April); WDOMins III p.5 (7th June 1933); *The Agenda* (April 1933) pp.9-10

4. The colour of stockings for official wear should be grey.

5. The wearing of a navy, or navy and white scarf is recommended for uniform.

6. A navy felt hat should be worn, but the bonnet is still uniform wear for those who prefer them, until the present stock of veils is exhausted.[22]

When one compares this uniform list with earlier ones it is possible to see how the Order had adapted to modern conditions, both with regard to practicality and the change in the spheres of work, and yet maintained a distinctive dress. At the same time Sister Dorothy Farrar's proposal that the new badge for probationers be 'a red cross bar bearing the words "Wesley Deaconess Order" in gilt letters' was accepted.

Although a navy or a navy and white scarf was permitted the deaconesses wished to have a special uniform scarf, if possible with a grey stripe, and so enquiries were made in the 1950s for a suitable washable navy and silver one that would cost no more than 27/6. At the same time it was felt that £3 was not sufficient to cover the cost of uniform and so Convocation sent a recommendation to the General Committee asking for the levy to be raised to £6, with a review in two years' time.[23]

In 1953 a proposal that the 'storm cap', used when cycling, should be discontinued in favour of a beret was carried, only to be rescinded the following year, when it was decided that either the storm cap and a navy beret could be used for cycling, but on 'unofficial occasions only'. The same year and again in 1954 the wearing of 'nylon' stockings and collars was discussed and also the making of uniform dresses: apparently very few deaconesses wished to have their dresses 'ready-made' at a cost of £1.18s.1d., many preferring to make their own. Hence Sister Lily Dodds, in charge of the Uniform Department, agreed to obtain a 'selection of patterns for uniform dresses and one basic pattern which could be adapted'. The majority of the deaconesses were obviously both cost-conscious and handy with their needles! A later session of the 1954 Convocation agreed with the Convocation Committee recommendation that

---

22. Mins. of Conv. (May 1947) pp.76, 78, (April 1948) pp.86, 88-89, 93-95 cf. (May 1949) p.103
23. Mins. of Conv. (April 1950) p.118

as an alternative to the dress and coat, deaconesses may wear a costume with white shirt blouse and tie (not on official occasions). Or a summer dress with soft collar and long sleeves or sleeves to the elbow – with the understanding that short sleeves are for unofficial occasions. (Stiff collar and cuffs to be worn on official occasions.)[24]

A sign that the uniform regulations were becoming rather more relaxed by 1959 is shown when it was agreed that 'the members of the Order must use their own discretion in the interpretation of "a plain navy hat bearing the recognised hat band of grey bordered navy, and woven or metal badge" '.[25]

There was a major development in 1967, when the Uniform Committee sent a recommendation to the Convocation Committee that there should be considerable change to the uniform and to the uniform regulations.

Uniform, 1967

1. That uniform should in future be the same for probationers and ordained Sisters.

This was agreed . . .

2. That the vote should be a definite 'Yes' or 'No' . . . A majority of 2/3 needed.

3. That the 'running-down' period for the present uniform be two years.

The suggested new uniform was shown to Convocation and was accepted by a clear majority . . . Thanks of Convocation were expressed to Hardy Amies and to the Committee.

Source: Minutes of Convocation (1936-69) (April 1967) pp.3-4

A possibility of more modern design for the Wesley Deaconess Order Badge had been considered for several years, but, in 1967, 'three specimen badges were handed round Convocation. It was agreed that the same badge, in two sizes, be used as a pendant or brooch and on the hat'. The proposal that the Maltese Cross design should be accepted was carried by 167 votes to 52.[26]

---

24. Mins. of Conv. (April 1953) p.148, (May 1954) pp.154, 159
25. Mins. of Conv. (April 1959) p.208
26. Mins. of Conv. (April 1967) p.6

Uniform, designed by Hardy Amies, modelled by Sister Jean Baillie at Convocation 1970

Updating continued when it was reported, in 1968, that the nearest pattern to the prescribed uniform was 'Simplicity' Pattern No.6621 and that there was a Heatherlands jumper in the same blue as the Order's colour. Sister Dora Dixon modelled a summer dress in sailcloth and a hat in buckram and linen, but not everyone was convinced about the dress and other materials were suggested, so it was agreed to look into the possibility of 'having uniforms in plain Crimplene or Terylene'. However, the summer hat was accepted, with the badge to be worn on the left side of all hats. A large majority approved of the proposal that Probationer and Student deaconesses should be entitled to wear the brooch badge.[27]

Margaret Stanworth remembers a navy blue dress with stiff white collar and cuffs, a navy tie, navy felt hat and navy coat and that the Student Probationers wore grey dresses, white collars and cuffs with a Probationer's badge. She commented that the collars and cuffs were originally of stiff starched linen, but later of plastic which was 'easier to keep clean, but hot to wear!'. As the navy and the grey uniform was quite similar to that worn by District Nurses, Sister Margaret said the deaconesses were often taken for nurses.

Wesley Deaconess/Nurse   Sister Margaret Stanworth

In my first appointment as a probationer in Exeter, I remember being called to a road accident – because the lady who rushed up to me thought I was a nurse. (I fled to the nearest telephone box and rang for an ambulance!)

On another occasion, in a later appointment in Manchester, I was waiting at a bus stop (no cars for us in those days!) outside a hospital where I had been to visit someone. A hearse drove out of the hospital, and the driver stopped and offered me a lift. He said 'You don't mind the body in the back, do you, nurse?'

Source: MSS letter: Sister Margaret Stanworth (August 2000)

---

27. Mins. of Conv. (April 1968) p.4

The later royal blue uniform avoided this confusion with nurses and was much easier to wear, if not so distinctive. The Warden explained that at the 1975 Convocation he was only too thankful to vacate the chair and hand over to the Vice President, Sister Margaret Stanworth, when the question of uniform was being discussed. On this occasion the question was not whether it was a good or bad thing to wear uniform, or the colour or shape, but simply the difficulty of supply. Consequently, it was agreed that a blue dress would suffice as 'uniform' if necessary. Mr. Galliers observed that there was a deeper significance to this decision than merely that of dress: the work in which the deaconesses were engaged was much more varied and very different from what it used to be and this was reflected by alterations in the uniform.

Sister Margaret Stanworth,
Vice President of the Wesley Deaconess Order 1975-76

Chapter 11

Women in the Church/Ministry Debates with special relation to the Wesley Deaconess Order

Three important decisions taken at the 1909 Wesleyan Methodist Conference had in some degree an impact on the Deaconess Order. First, a small committee was appointed to revise the 'Service for the full reception of Deaconesses into the Order' and it was hoped that the service would gain connexional recognition. The new Order was presented to the 1911 Conference and printed in the *Minutes of the Wesleyan Methodist Conference.* Secondly, the Conference voted in favour of the admission of women to Conference and although it had been referred to the Synods there seemed little likelihood of it being rejected. Interestingly, the Warden, William Bradfield comments that 'although we well know that a great many good women have no sort of desire [to go] . . . we think that the Church will do well to remove an unnecessary and irritating restriction'. This was indeed done at the ensuing Conference. Then thirdly, 'the regulations with regard to women preaching (were) referred to the consideration of the Committee of Law'. Here he commented that the regulations certainly needed amending, but there was no fear that the evangelistic work of the deaconesses would be stopped or that any moves would be made to impose the ministry of women on those who did not want it. The regulations were duly amended in 1910.

It is well known that during John Wesley's lifetime he had allowed women to give exhortations and, eventually, he had permitted certain women to preach if they had an 'extraordinary call', but after his death the 1803 Wesleyan Methodist Conference passed a resolution: 'We are of the opinion that, in general they [women] ought not.'[1] This did not mean that women stopped preaching altogether in Wesleyan Methodism, but *officially* there were no women preachers.[2] However, certain deaconesses who had a special aptitude did preach and even Stephenson admitted right from the beginning that in certain circumstances they might take services. Now in 1910 the Wesleyan Methodist Conference deleted

---

1. *WMMins. of Conf.* (1803) (1862 ed.) p.187
2. See chapter 2 fn.1

the 1803 phrase 'address only her sex', but an addendum was inserted restricting their preaching to neighbourhoods in which there was no special opposition. The Order's General Committee's resolution of 20th September 1910, presumably prompted by the Conference deliberations on the subject of women's preaching, is of great significance:

> Resolution re Women preaching:
> The Committee having heard the new regulations of Conference with regard to women preaching, gives its sanction to the preaching of the following deaconesses, who have already either been engaged as Deaconess-Evangelists, or have been accustomed from time to time to take services, where required to do so: [15 are listed] . . .
>
> With regard to all further applications, the Committee resolves that in the case of any Deaconess who feels called to preach, and asks for authorisation, the matter shall be brought before the Committee by the Warden, provided he is satisfied that she has the necessary gifts, that she has read Mr. Wesley's Sermons, and that she believes and preaches our doctrine. All authorisations to preach shall be for the ensuing year, and subject to the annual review of the Committee. No authorisation shall be renewed unless the Warden is satisfied that the Deaconess applying for it is doing some theological reading, and keeping up a living acquaintance with New Testament studies.
>
> N.B. It is distinctly understood that the authorisation of the Committee only entitles a Deaconess to preach, where she is desired to do so by the Superintendent of the Circuit in which the service is to be held.[3]

This Resolution shows that a very strict eye was kept on the suitability and competence of any deaconess wishing to preach and she was required to do a considerable amount of extra studying. Thereafter, until women were accorded equal rights as local preachers with men and those deaconesses who had been preaching were accredited, deaconess preachers were named in the Order's Minutes as approved by the Warden. An interesting comment in December 1915 was that Bradfield, in reporting that he had given

---

3. WDIMins I pp.366-67; cf. *FL* (September 1910) pp.124-25, (October 1910) p.141

authorization to Sister Maud Gent, stated that she 'was taking the place of a minister who had gone to the War – the first case that had occurred'. In 1915 she was stationed in the Glasgow (North-West Mission) Circuit where the minister the Rev. J. Forster Holdsworth was a Chaplain 'responsible for the pastoral oversight of Wesleyan Soldiers in the Army and Seamen and Marines in the Royal Navy'.[4]

As was noted earlier seems a little strange to find the 1920 Conference, which appointed W. Russell Maltby as Warden, also directing 'the Committee of the Wesley Deaconess Institute . . . to consider during this year the desirability of the appointment of a suitable woman as Warden of the Institute . . .' However, the Order felt that it was important to have a minister as Warden and so the status quo was maintained.

Debates in the 1920s

During the 1920s there was much debate in Methodism about Women and the Ministry and Women's Work in the Church. This had apparently been brought to a head in 1922 when a woman candidate for the ministry had been nominated by a superintendent minister and unanimously endorsed by the Quarterly Meeting, but because it was deemed to be contrary to Wesleyan Methodist regulations she was not allowed to proceed. By 1922 Methodism had become aware, without doubt largely through the work of the Wesley Deaconess Institute and the Women's Auxiliary, of the increasing scope and growing importance of women's work. So the Conference appointed a Committee 'to consider the whole question of the admission of women to the Ordained Ministry, to the work of a Deaconess and kindred forms of service . . .'.[5]

It is surely significant that the Warden of the Wesley Deaconess Order was made convenor of this Committee, tacitly acknowledging the valuable work of the organisation and his own personal commitment to women's involvement in all aspects of church life. William Bradfield, the former Warden, was one of the Committee of 18 ministers. The 1923 Conference received the Committee's interim report and reappointed it 'with power, if it think well, to meet along with the corresponding Committee appointed by the Representative Session' which had realised 'the importance to the Laity of our Church of the relation of women to

4. *WMMins. of Conf.* (1915) p.503, (1916) p.547
5. *WMMins. of Conf.* (1922) p.272; cf. *The Agenda* (June 1928) pp.9-14

the ministry'.[6]   Maltby was also the Convenor of that Committee which included eight laymen and seven women, one of whom was a deaconess, Sister Esther Taylor.

At the end of December 1922 Maltby reported to the Institute's General Committee that in January there was to be an informal gathering in London of people concerned with Women's Work in Methodism to consider:

> 1.   A new appeal for the service of Christian women in many forms.

> 2.   The possible provision on a new scale for training in the Christian Service, whether as voluntary workers in the church, or set apart for some special vocation.[7]

A year later more meetings, both formal and informal, were held on both subjects with representatives, including three deaconesses, of the Wesley Deaconess Order in attendance.   The Committee's Report, presented to the 1924 Conference, stated that due to the great changes 'in the work and status of women' and now that there were many more openings for women it was necessary for the Church to have a reassessment of women's rôles in Methodism. The Committee could see no real reason for women to be disqualified from 'any function of the Ordained Ministry . . . merely on the ground of (her) sex'.   Although this was so in principle there were practical difficulties.   The Committee also felt that many women were now reacting so strongly against not being allowed to enter the ministry that their talents were being diverted into other channels and thus a great resource was being lost to the Church.   It was noted that there was much work in Methodism which lay women could do and that trained and educated women had a vital part to play.   The Committee rebuked the Church for making not the best use of its women and believed that there should be a 'Ministry of Women parallel to the Ministry of Men . . . equally recognised by the Church, held in the same honour, trusted with adequate authority, and united by the same bond of fellowship'.   Rather daringly, perhaps, it recommended that 'in certain cases of outstanding service on the part of women whom the Church has called, they should be formally ordained to such a ministry.'   Further it stated that women missionaries and deaconesses 'should have the full recognition as colleagues with the ordained ministers .. .'.

---

6.   *WMMins. of Conf.* (1923) p.87
7.   WDIMins II p.190

Finally the Committee recommended that a Standing Committee on Women's Work should be appointed with the following remit:

1. To advise women desiring to fit themselves for better Christian service;
2. To watch for possible opportunities of women's service in the Church;
3. To open up opportunities of training for such workers;
4. To report to Conference generally on such questions as are dealt with in this Report.[8]

A Standing Committee consisting of 12 ministers, 10 women, including one deaconess, Sister Esther Taylor, and two laymen, with Maltby and Miss M. V. Hunter as Convenors was duly appointed. The Representative Session of the 1924 Conference adopted the Report, but the Pastoral Session, while giving general approval 'in view of the many difficult questions involved' remitted the Report for further consideration to 'a Committee consisting of the Ministerial Members of the 'Standing Committee on Women's Work', appointed by the Representative Session, plus six more ministers. The Committee reported their findings to the next Conference, namely, that women, subject to certain provisos, should be admitted.

Report to 1925 Conference

. . . a report approving the admission [of women] to the ministry substantially on the same terms as men and by the same procedure subject to certain conditions which concerned finance, training and marriage.

Source: The Agenda (July 1928) p.11

Although the 1925 Conference received the Report on 'Women and the Ministry' and reiterated its belief that there was a growing rôle for trained women in the Church; that the changing social perception of that rôle necessitated a serious rethink about admitting women to equal colleagueship with men and that there was no fundamental reason why they should not be admitted to the ordained ministry but 'Both our organisation and traditions, however,

---

8. WDIMins II p.200; *WMMins. of Conf.* (1924) pp.94-97, 301; cf. *The Agenda* (July 1923) pp.5-8, (January 1924) pp.6-7, (September 1924) pp.2-6

interpose serious practical obstacles to the admission of women to an itinerant Ministry such as ours, which do not immediately admit of any complete solution.' So, yet again, the Report was returned to the Committee with an additional instruction 'to prepare a Statement showing the Biblical grounds on which the new departure is based'.[9] Apparently the Committee came back in 1926 with proposals in much the same terms, including a set of procedures to be followed if a woman believed she had a call to enter the ministry, training and reception into full connexion. It also made suggestions for overcoming the practical difficulties, especially those of marriage and maintenance. The Representative Session adopted these proposals with a confirming resolution, but the Pastoral Session did not and issued a conflicting one. Therefore, neither was confirmed by the Legal Conference, but were reported to both sessions of the 1927 Conference which resolved that in the circumstances the whole matter needed further serious consideration and remitted it to the Standing Committee on Women's Work. The poor unfortunate President placed in this dilemma was none other than the Rev. Dr. W. Russell Maltby, the Warden of the Wesley Deaconess Order and the Convenor of both Committees.

Women's Work and Women and the Ministry

Resolutions upon 'Women and the Ministry' were adopted by the Representative and Pastoral Sessions respectively which, in the judgement of the President, were in conflict with each other and were therefore not confirmed by the Legal Conference. The Resolutions will be reported accordingly to the respective Sessions of the next Conference.

Source: Wesleyan Methodist Minutes of Conference (1926) pp.144, 472 cf. (1927) pp.80, 295

The 1927 Conference received the Report of the Standing Committee on 'Women's Work' and was then directed

> to explore the possibility of suggesting such arrangements as shall secure larger opportunities for the exercise of the gifts of consecrated women in the service of Christ, and the further development of the existing Diaconate of women in the Ministry of the Church. Such Committee shall confer, if desired, with the Committee appointed by the Representative Session.[10]

---

9. *WMMins. of Conf.* (1925) pp.276-77
10. *WMMins. of Conf.* (1927) pp.80-81; *The Agenda* (July 1928) p.113

The Committee was reappointed, with the addition of six ministers and six lay members, to continue discussion of three of the original purposes, with the fourth one being altered to read:

4.   To report to Conference on questions relating to the work of women in the Church.

It was instructed to prepare and issue a pamphlet during the year on 'How Women can Serve the Church'. In 1929 the Conference, having received the Report, invited the 'other Methodist Conferences to join with it next year in appointing a joint Committee, to consider the question and to report to the three Conferences'.[11] The Standing Committee on Women's Work delivered its final report to the 1930 Conference and was then discharged, while the three Conferences appointed their representatives to the Women and the Ministry Committee.

The Committees concerned with the discussions on women's rôle in the Church held meetings and Maltby was very involved with both. He took pains in *The Agenda* to keep the deaconesses well informed of the various developments. It is obvious that he was a passionate advocate for women being accorded a rightful and proper place in the Church, and felt that it should be recognized that 'the traditional subordination of women is fast passing away, and a new colleagueship between men and women workers, on equal terms, is emerging'.

Women's rightful place in the Church   The Warden

. . . the Church ought to concern itself about the recognition it gives. It belongs to the health of the Church to offer due scope and due honour to its workers, especially those who take the hardest part. So if I could, I would shout in every drowsy ear and fret every easy conscience until Methodism turned and reflected on the place we expect women to occupy in the great service. The Church ought to entrust responsibility freely to competent women without waiting to be badgered about it or shamed into it . . . Churches and Missions are now often asking for Deaconesses with 'initiative', but they would be surprised to learn in how many instances in the not distant past 'initiative' was regarded as a disturbing inconvenience.

Source: The Agenda (September 1924) pp.2-6

---

11.   *WMMins. of Conf.* (1929) pp.71-72

Sister Esther Taylor, the deaconess on the Standing Committee, read a Memorandum on the Ministry of Women to the 1923 Convocation. This contained a suggestion for 'a common training centre for all women workers such as: S. School workers, capable of leading meetings, Girl Guide officers, girls' club work, qualified Class leaders, local preachers, social welfare workers'. The Warden developed the theme and an interesting discussion ensued resulting in the following resolution being passed and sent to those who had drafted the Memorandum:

> The members of the Wesley Deaconess Order, realising the need of a centre for the adequate training of women for every form of Christian work, are in full sympathy with the ideals set forth in the Memorandum & are ready to co-operate in any such advance.

It was also requested that 'some steps might be taken to gather together the women representatives of the different organisations in Methodism to explore the avenues of service which are opening to women'. This idea of a Special Women's Committee to represent the women's organizations of the Methodist Church was eventually taken up in 1954. The General Committee backed the suggestion of the Wesley Deaconess Order, the Women's Work and Women's Fellowship forming a Standing Committee to liaise and negotiate with other women's organizations. The Order's representative would be Sister Dorothy Farrar. A year later she reported that the Central Committee for Women's Work was operational with Sister Margaret Statham and Miss Walton as joint secretaries, while she was Chairman, and that it looked likely to be more useful that had at first been envisaged.

When the 1924 Convocation met in Wesley's Chapel there was much debate on 'the future of women's work & especially the relation of the Wesley Deaconess Order to a "wider ministry of women"' and the following Resolution was passed:

> Convocation recognises that a new situation has arisen. It welcomes the possibility of wider opportunities and more adequate recognition of the place & service of Women Workers in the Church.
> The members of Convocation realise that in the Wesley Deaconess Order there is already a nucleus for a large & more varied body of Christian workers. They believe that the line of future development is indicated in the existing organisation, fellowship and status of the

Wesley Deaconess Order. They would be glad to co-operate with others in framing whatever new policy might be required for the future.[12]

Maltby reported to the 1926 Convocation on the deliberations of the Women and the Ministry Committee and said that the Conference would consider the following resolution:

> That any Department of Methodism which had anything to do with Women's Work, may recommend to a Supt. Minister that a certain woman worker should be a candidate for the ministry. In doing so that particular Dept. must undertake the provision of that woman's livelihood during her life.[13]

Other informal discussions were taking place as well. For example, a small conference was held in Manchester in April 1927 'to talk over the possibilities of closer fellowship between the branches of Women's Work' and its recommendations passed to the Deaconess Committee for its December meeting included:

> 1.   It would be valuable if a Circuit Recognition Service were the rule for every Deaconess going to a new appointment.
>
> 2.   The time is ripe for asking that Wesley Deaconesses should be ex-officio members of the Representative Session of the Synod.
>
> 3.   The names of those received yearly into the Order should be printed in the Agenda and Minutes of Conference. The question of printing the Deaconess appointments in the Minutes should be considered again.
>
> 4.   The Associate members might be used to greater advantage . . .
>
> 5.   The recognition of the Church might be extended to other workers . . . who satisfied certain requirements.[14]

Although the Committee approved of them it did not feel it could make any definite proposals (presumably to the Conference Committee).

---

12.   RConv. (29th May 1924) cf. quoted in *The Agenda* (February 1928) p.4
13.   RConv. (27th June 1925)
14.   WDIMins II p.242

A meeting of the London Deaconesses at the Leysian Mission in December 1927 considered 'the future of the Order and its relation to other branches of women's work in the Methodist Church' and concluded that 'all kinds of work have been commenced and partly recognised and organised, but with little attempt at correlation and with very little idea of an ultimate policy'. The inference is that this needed to be addressed urgently and that the Wesley Deaconess Order by virtue of its very existence had a vital part to play. Indeed, Maltby commented in *The Agenda* in June 1928:

> All these discussions relate to the admission of women to 'the ministry', and, it might be argued, are not our immediate concern. But the Deaconess Order is already a ministry, and such proposals as are now under discussion do affect our Order and our work.[15]

The 1927 Convocation debated thoroughly several Notices of Motion, but two in particular were relevant to the question of the place of deaconesses within the ministry and life of the Church. Although agreement was expressed Convocation did not feel able to put forward definite resolutions – maybe they were too radical! The two in question were, first:

> 2. That we should send a resolution to Conference that every Wesley Deaconess should be an ex-officio member of the Representative Session of the Synod in the District in which she is appointed.[16]

This question of Deaconesses attending Synod ex-officio was raised again in 1929, but again without a resolution being forwarded. However, Sisters 'elected to attend the Representative Session of Synod in the usual way' were urged to accept.

The second Notice of Motion was even more radical, namely,

> 3. That we send a Resolution to Conference that in exceptional cases, such as village chapels, small missions, etc. where ministers are rarely appointed to preach, the Deaconess should be permitted to administer the Sacraments.[17]

---

15. *The Agenda* (February 1927) pp.2-3; (June 1928) p.13
16. RConv. (23rd May 1927)
17. RConv. (23rd May 1927); (discussed and rejected again in 2001)

In 1930 the permitting of deaconesses to administer the Lord's Supper in special cases was raised again, but the Warden felt 'that such an empowerment would be a breach of Methodist Law, and to approach Conference now would be highly inadvisable'. So the matter was dropped.

The Deaconess Convocation held at Ilkley, 4-9th June 1928, heard a review of the whole position from the Warden in light of the Report being submitted to the forthcoming Conference. After considerable discussion a resolution was agreed:

> The members of the Wesley Deaconess Order, assembled in Convocation, give thanks to God for the Order to which they belong, and the wide opportunities of service they have found there. They desire, for the sake of the service to which they are dedicated, that more scope and freedom in the direction of their work should be entrusted to Deaconesses, and a more secure place in the organisation of the Church.
>
> They recognise that God is calling women everywhere to fresh service. Believing as they do, that the time had come for the Church to recognise this development, by opening the ordained ministry to women, they welcome the proposals now under consideration by the Wesleyan Methodist Church.
>
> The Order will give its wholehearted and unqualified support and fellowship to any woman, whether of its own number or not, who by virtue of her opportunities, gifts and calling, is able to take the full ministerial training and receive ordination. Fully realising that this step is a venture fraught with possibilities and uncertainties, the Order believes that the Church should go forward in that spirit of adventure and faith which is the life of Methodism.[18]

By 1928 the Conference, especially the Pastoral Session, had rather grudgingly accepted that:

> 1.   Women who believe they are called of God to a wider and fuller Ministry of the Church than now obtains among us, may secure the sanction of the Conference under the following regulation:

---

18.   RConv. (7th June 1928) cf. *The Agenda* (May 1930) p.10

> 2.   A woman who believes herself called of God to
> the Christian Ministry in our Church may offer under
> the same regulations as apply to men . . .

The rest of the Report was approved in general, but the Committee was asked to look again at such points as marriage, training, probation and finance before provisional legislation could be considered. When it came to 1929 Methodist Union was appearing on the horizon and so to a certain extent the Conference was able to shelve a thorny subject by resolving that both Reports should be received and that the other Methodist Conferences be invited to join with it the following year to appoint a joint committee to consider the question and report to the three Conferences. The committee was to consist of 20 Wesleyan Methodist, 10 Primitive Methodist and 10 United Methodist members. In 1930 these are listed and comprise 10 ministers, five women, five men with Maltby as Convenor. No deaconess is included. Did Conference feel that Mrs. Bradfield, ex-Lady Superintendent, and Maltby provided adequate representation? In 1930 the Report of the Standing Committee on 'Women's Work' was received and the Committee discharged. The Committee on 'Women and the Ministry' was reappointed in 1931, with the Rev. G. E. Hickman Johnson joining Maltby as Convenor, but the Conference specifically requested:

> 3.   . . . the Deaconess Committee, in conjunction with
> the Committee concerning Women and the Ministry to
> consider the whole question of the status of the
> Deaconesses and their position under the constitution of
> the united Church.[19]

The Wesleyan Conference meeting for the last time received the Report of the Committee, which had also convened for the last time under Maltby's guidance, and referred it to the Uniting Conference, which simply also received it and asked the Committee to report to the next Conference. So the 1933 Conference:

> 2.   having considered the reports from the Synods on
> Women and the Ministry, is of the opinion that there is
> not sufficient support for the scheme to justify
> procedure into the main project at present; it notes,
> however, with satisfaction the desire of many Synods to
> develop the existing ministerial work of women.
>
> 3.   The Conference thanks the Committee on Women
> and the Ministry for its services and discharges it.

---

19.   *WMMins. of Conf.* (1929) pp.71-72, 260, (1930) pp.87, 73 (19), 83-84, 261

The Ministerial Session agreed with the Representative Session's resolutions, but wishing to appear positive in view of the 'widespread changes in the whole position of women . . . is deeply concerned that the Methodist Church should respond worthily . . . and . . . when the question is again before the Conference, make all such adjustments in our organisation as will give to women called of God full scope for the exercise of their ministry'.[20] So Methodism, in its own inimitable way, accepted the work of women, but declined to give them the official status that their work deserved, and the position so remained for many more years, until 1973.

Post union debates on the status of the Wesley Deaconesses (Women's Ministry)

The General Committee in June 1933 endorsed the paragraph from the Report of the Women and the Ministry Committee:

> It must be acknowledged that our Church has hardly given to these workers the recognition and the scope which they ought to have. So far as the Deaconesses are concerned they are inadequately represented on the Committee which administers their affairs; they are not provided for in the circuit and district organisation of Methodism; their allowances have to be found after all other ordinary circuit and Connexional demands are met, with the result that the dropping of a Deaconess is often the easiest retrenchment, and work which is amongst the most needy is the first to be abandoned, or curtailed.[21]

Convocation that same year had obviously been concerned about the low profile of the deaconesses as among the notices of motion was one asking for the list of deaconess appointments to be printed in the *Minutes of Conference*. Dr. Maltby felt that unfortunately this was highly unlikely, but expressed the hope that it would be printed in the *Methodist Recorder*.

At Union it became necessary for a new *Book of Offices* to be compiled and a committee, which reported to Conference each year, was appointed. In 1935 the question of a service for the 'ordination' of deaconesses was proposed and six members of the Deaconess Committee were invited 'to meet a Sub-Committee of the Book of

---

20. *Mins. of Conf.* (1934) pp.102, 249
21. WDOMins III pp.5-6

Offices, to discuss a revision of the Deaconess Consecration Service with a view to incorporating it in the new book of Offices'. Three ministers and three deaconesses were chosen. The new order of service was tried out at Convocation on 24th April 1936. It is interesting to note that among the first group of Wesley Deaconesses to be *ordained* using this new service was Sister Dorothy H. Farrar. Miss Dorothy H. Farrar had been involved with the Order for a number of years as a tutor and on a number of committees, but in March 1936 she applied to be admitted to the Order and was gladly accepted. Following the service opportunity was given for discussion about the revised service and a number of suggestions were passed to the committee for consideration before the order of service should be presented to Conference. The new book was authorised for use by the Newcastle-on-Tyne Conference, July 1936 and so for the first time in March 1937 the Sisters to be admitted into full membership of the Order were described as 'Candidates for Ordination and it was agreed that they should be Ordained at the forthcoming Convocation'. Until 1900 students who had completed their probation had been 'recognised', but from 1901 they were 'consecrated'.

Sister Dorothy H. Farrar:
Vice Principal and Tutor

Another important step towards raising the status of deaconesses was their recognition as local preachers. Back in 1918 women had been granted equal recognition as men and the following year women preachers, including Wesley Deaconesses, who had 'already been preaching' were received 'upon full plan without further examination'.[22] However, not all deaconesses were recognised local preachers, and, as we saw earlier, annual permission 'to preach' was given by the Warden. In 1937 Dr. Maltby felt that the situation ought to be clarified and so he had discussions with the Rev. F. A. Farley, the Local Preachers' Connexional Secretary, and reported the following facts:

> 1. Most of our Students have had no opportunity of coming on the Local Preachers' Plan in their own Circuits.

---

22. *WMMins. of Conf.* (1918) p.85; (1919) p.271

2. The Students while at College are constantly called upon for preaching appointments in the neighbourhood. The average number of appointments supplied from the College is about 50 each quarter.

3. Many of our Deaconesses are required to take preaching appointments in the Circuits where they are stationed. Further the work they are doing in many instances is indistinguishable in principle from preaching. If they are fit for the one they are fit for the other.

4. The position therefore should be regularised. But the procedure devised and suitable for young and untrained people is unsuitable and improper for those who have been Connexionally recognised and set apart for the work of Deaconesses.

5. The Committee therefore suggest the following rule to be presented to Conference:

A Deaconess who has received the full course of training at Ilkley, and is certified by the Deaconess Committee as an acceptable preacher may be accepted by a Local Preachers' Meeting on full plan without further examination'.[23]

In late 1940 again the question of the status of deaconesses was considered. Dr. Scott Lidgett was anxious to see their status raised and, having had conversations with the Rev. W. Harold Beales as Warden, brought a resolution to Conference that '(1) the status of Deaconesses should be defined and (2) a Committee be appointed to look into the matter'. The resolution was duly endorsed by the 1941 Conference with the Special Committee's terms of reference being:

To enquire into the status of the Order of Wesley Deaconesses, and especially to examine what changes should be made in order to improve the Connexional status of the Order, to give increased recognition and security to the Deaconesses, and to assist the extension of this invaluable work.[24]

---

23. WDOMins III pp.55-56
24. WDOMins III p.133 cf. *Mins. of Conf.* (1941) p.67 where the phrasing is '. . . to inquire into the Constitution of . . .'; cf. file of 'Minutes of special committees' (11th September 1941-20th May 1942)

Several members of the Deaconess Committee were on the Special Committee so that the Order's interests might be fully represented. A copy of the proposals drafted was sent to the Deaconess Committee for consideration and in February 1942 it agreed that comments be submitted to the Special Committee on (1) the procedures for considering candidates involving local Circuit Quarterly Meeting, (2) the function of Convocation, (3) the oversight of probationers, (4) ordination, (5) unemployment, (6) invitations and (7) to be members of the Representative Session of Synod. The Committee also raised a number of other concerns because 'the whole question of the work and status of women in the modern world is forcing itself on the attention of every responsible body . . .'. These were that (1) historically many of the women who entered the Order had been 'leisured and educated' and 'not entirely dependent upon it for their livelihood', but this was no longer the case, (2) there were now many more openings for women which combined vocation and a livelihood, (3) deaconesses were not being given the same 'adequate scope, responsibility and freedom' in the Church as women in secular professions and (4) Conference should consider giving fully trained and competent deaconesses greater responsibility, for example, oversight of villages to build up such causes. In response to the final area of concern of the Special Committee – that of finance, particularly regarding '(a) The Administration & Training Account', (b) The allowance to Sisters retiring between the ages of 55 and 60 and (c) The meagre allowance to Sisters in the active work, due to rising costs and the payment of income tax' – the Warden reported that appeals had been made to the Methodist Finance Board and to the Rank Trust, and promises received which would help to improve the situation.[25] The Report of the Special Committee was duly presented to the 1942 Manchester Conference and adopted. The Warden and his predecessor were especially delighted with the first of the General Resolutions which affirmed the Wesley Deaconess Order as a vital part of the Church deserving an honoured place in Methodism. Both Beales and Maltby regarded it as 'a Charter for the Sisters of the Order'.

---

25. WDOMins III pp.112, 118, 133-38 cf. pp.167, 174, 192-93, 3rd July 1944, 16th March 1945; *The Agenda* (August 1942) pp.3-5, 12-13, 14-17

> ## Charter for the Sisters of the Order – 1942
>
> In particular the Conference declares that the Deaconess Order should be better known, honoured, and used than it has been in the past. Ordained Deaconesses are not to be regarded, any more than Ministers, as employees. The only right relation is an honourable colleagueship, in which no gifts of leadership and insight need be denied their exercise, and a deaconess shall have scope and freedom to do the work for which she has been trained and ordained.
>
> *Source: The Agenda* (August 1942) p.4

It seems likely that this discussion about the status of the Wesley Deaconess Order and the changing rôle of women in the world led once again to the reopening of the debate on Women and the Ministry. *The Agenda* of July 1944 contained a small, but significant 'Note. – Sisters and other friends will be interested to know that, for the first time in the history of the Order, Deaconesses ordained this year will be received by Conference into Full Membership of the Order. They will be received in Conference early on Tuesday afternoon, 18th July .' Then, in December the same year, the Warden reported that the Conference Committee on Women and the Ministry was preparing its report and would welcome their opinion. The scheme was referred to a special meeting of the Executive Committee, plus the Deaconesses serving on the General Committee, on 16th March 1945. A resolution was passed:

> Although . . . the scheme may have some unfavourable repercussions on the Wesley Deaconess Order, we nevertheless resolve generally to approve . . . because it embodies the principle for which we have long contended, namely women in the ministry. We also wish to affirm our conviction that the whole ministry shall be open to women.
>
> We do, however, wish to draw attention . . . to the following points . . .
>
> 1. When women candidates are under consideration, we suggest that the possibility of there being women as well as men on the July Committee.
>
> 2. It was also suggested that when the training of women candidates for the ministry is under consideration, some consultation with the Deaconess College might be valuable.

<u>Ordination.</u> The Committee having been asked to consider the meaning of the Ordination of Deaconesses, the following definition was agreed to:

1. <u>Office</u>

Ordination is the solemn setting apart by the laying on of hands, of women called to life-long service in a recognised ministry of the Methodist Church. This office has its sanction in the Church as described in the New Testament.

2. <u>Service of Ministration</u>

The ministry to which a Deaconess is solemnly ordained is in the main pastoral, and may include the services outlined in the President's charge. It should be observed that the pastoral vocation may or may not include a call to preach.[26]

Following the resolutions of the 1945 Conference the Conference Committee on Women and the Ministry circulated an enquiry to the Deaconesses seeking the views of the 1947 Convocation on the resolutions to be presented to Conference. After much thoughtful discussion Convocation approved by a large majority the resolution that 'women who believe themselves to be called of God and prove themselves to have the fitness and the gifts for this Ministry' should be ordained to the Ministry of the Word and Sacraments. However, it wished to change the wording from 'Men and Women in the Ministry shall have the same status and shall receive allowances on the same scale' to '. . . shall have the same responsibility, freedom and scope' preferring not to discuss allowances, and agreed that 'The marriage of a woman minister shall involve her resignation from the ministry, unless, in special circumstances and on application of the person concerned, the Conference shall determine otherwise'. As Convocation had agreed that women should be admitted to the Ministry of the Word and Sacraments it followed that it rejected a second resolution that there should 'be a parallel Ministry of the Word and Sacraments designed only for women . . .'.[27] The Conference Committee had also put forward seven 'suggestions' to be considered, four of which met with Convocation's approval, namely, the recommendation of candidature, examination by Synod, ordination at Conference alongside men and eligibility to be members of the Ministerial

---

26. WDOMins III (12th December 1944), (16th March 1945) cf. Mins. of Conv. (April 1945) pp.61, 64; *The Agenda* (September 1946) p.4
27. for full text and voting see Mins. of Conv. pp.78-80, cf. *The Agenda* (July 1947) p.4

Sessions of Synod and Conference under the same arrangements as men. However, it felt that each candidate should be assessed on merit and, while it agreed that women should be trained at one of the theological colleges, it deemed a special consultative committee to be unnecessary. However, all the years of discussion were to no avail as the 1948 Conference received the report but declined 'to declare its willingness to receive for Ordination to the Ministry of the Word and Sacraments, women who believe themselves to be called of God to this work'.[28]

During March 1945 there had been a rather acrimonious series of letters and articles in the *Methodist Recorder* about the Wesley Deaconess Order, in which it was suggested that girls should not be encouraged to become deaconesses because the salaries were so low and general conditions of service poor. Replies, from the Warden, some deaconesses and others, refuting the allegations were published. The matter was discussed at Convocation and proved not to have been accurately dealt with in the Margaret Harwood column and hurtful to the Order. The Warden said that he was taking the matter up at the next Board Meeting of the *Methodist Recorder*, but he hoped that 'perhaps in the long run we (the Order) might get some slight good out of this correspondence, but at the moment it has done us some real disservice'. Convocation passed a Notice of Motion to be included in the account of Convocation published in the *Methodist Recorder*:

> Convocation . . . desires afresh to express their gratitude to God for their calling as Deaconesses and for the opportunities of service which it affords. They also wish to thank the many who during the years have given time and labour without stint to the work of administration and to caring for the interests of the Sisters. They believe that in the times immediately ahead there is a most urgent need for the service of such trained and qualified women as the Fellowship of the Wesley Deaconess Order can provide, and they earnestly hope for the co-operation of the Methodist people as a whole in giving to all Deaconesses full scope and freedom to do all their calling requires in the service of Christ.[29]

---

28. *The Methodist Church Conference Agenda* 1948 pp.141-43; *The Methodist Church Ministerial Session of Conference Agenda* 1948 p.9; *Mins of Conf.* (1948) pp.50, 162
29. *Methodist Recorder* (8th, 15th, 22nd March); Mins. of Conv. (April 1945) pp.59-60, 63; cf. also *The Agenda* (July 1945) pp.1-5 for reference to the

There is a significant sentence in the Warden's Report to the General Committee on 16th December 1955, when he commented 'that in many new appointments deaconesses were being called upon to do the kind of work complementary to that of a minister'.[30] So it looks as if the status of deaconesses was now being recognized and this may also have had an influence on the future as regards training and appointments.

In the late 1950s there was much discussion in the British Council of Churches and the Methodist Faith and Order Committee about the place of women in the Church and the Warden, the Rev. T. Morrow, felt it was essential for the Wesley Deaconess Order to clarify its thinking on this topic. So the Order's Report to the 1958 Conference, in view of this discussion on the ministry and ordination, included mention of 'the institution of probationer studies', and made 'reference to the question of Ordination and status of the deaconesses within the Methodist Church'.[31] One wonders if this institution of probationer studies indicated that the training of deaconesses was becoming more akin to that of ministers and that the thorny question of deaconess status was lurking in the background bearing in mind the resurrected discussion of the place of women in the Church. So Convocation wished it to be made clear how important the studies were and how much they would be taken into account when the question of ordination occurred. This importance was reiterated in later years and it was emphasised that failure to complete these satisfactorily was liable to result in deferment of ordination. In their discussions on the ministry and the meaning of their ordination the Faith and Order Committee also included the ordination of deaconesses and as they had requested the opinion of the Order, both the General Committee and Convocation set up special sub-committees to look at this. There was a very important and lengthy debate in the 1960 Convocation about 'women in the ministry and the status of the Wesley Deaconess Order'. The Warden gave a résumé on the Committee's thinking indicating that

> There seemed to be general agreement that there was no theological reason against women in the ministry; the main difficulty that Conference had experienced in the past was the practical difficulty. The questions in their mind were: how many members of the Order

---

correspondence, which covered status, colleagueship, allowances, lodgings, appointments etc.
30. WDOMins IV 15th December 1955
31. WDOExec. Com. Mins. 27th February 1958

would desire to be in the ministry if there were women in the ministry, how would it affect the Wesley Deaconess Order; if they were talking about the status of the Order, how far would the Order feel that there was full justification for every ordained deaconess to have the right to administer the Sacraments?

Nowadays almost every deaconess was called to the ministry of the Word and dispensations were given to deaconesses, but could the Order fulfil its ministry if it had that, not as a dispensation, but as a right?

Sister Dorothy Farrar put forward some suggestions remarking that the question of women in the ministry might be rejected altogether and that no women might feel called of God to enter the ministry. She felt that the ministry in its present form

was not meant for women, although the Order had been granted some of its privileges such as administering the Sacraments. Ours was a pastoral ministry, given to prayer and the inner life. If, however, we believed that God calls women into the ministry, what must the Church do about it?

In the ensuing debate questions about the difference between ministers and deaconesses in full pastoral charge; what difference would it make if deaconesses had the right to administer the sacraments; and what effect Methodism's move to unite with the Anglican Church had on the question of women in the ministry were raised. It was also asked 'if the committee had discussed deaconess ordination, as it was felt that it would be better if we knew what we were ordained to'. It was suggested that the charge to administer the sacraments might be added to the ordination service. In concluding the debate Morrow reminded Convocation that to be allowed to administer the Sacraments should not be regarded as 'a step up. If we are called to do such work, it is a sacrament linked with the sacrament of the washing of feet, and not therefore a matter of status at all'.[32] At the next Convocation the debate was continued and the following points emerged:

1.   That the vast majority felt that the door should be open for women to enter the ministry.

2.   That Convocation believed this, whatever its impact on the work of the Order might be.

32.   Mins. of Conv. (May 1960) pp.217-18

3.   That deaconesses must not think in terms of 'status', but in terms of ministering.

Sister Margaret Statham gave a digest of the Report on Women in the Ministry at the 1962 Convocation and after a general discussion it was agreed that the following statements should be included in the Order's Report to Conference:

> The members of the Wesley Deaconess Order assembled in Convocation express their thankfulness that God had called this Order into being and their belief that in its membership many have in the past and will in the future find the full exercise of their calling. They would, however, affirm their conviction that the full ministry of the Word and Sacraments should be open to such women as are called thereto, and whose call the Church is able to confirm. The implications of these two beliefs can be left in God's hands.[33]

In 1969 the Cardiff (Canton) Circuit sent a Memorial to Conference asking:

> for a working party to be set up to study the structure (including stationing) and Function of the Wesley Deaconess Order, the meaning of deaconess ordination and the possibility of ordination taking place at Conference, and the place of the Wesley Deaconess Order in the life of the Methodist Church of Great Britain today.

It was pointed out that the words 'such a study to include the Anglican approach' had been omitted from the memorial as printed. After discussion it was agreed that during the coming year deaconess groups should be asked to consider the following questions and report to the 1970 Convocation:

> (1) What is the place of the Deaconess Order in the life of the Church to-day?
>
> (2) What is the work of a deaconess within the Order?[34]

---

33. Mins. of Conv. (April/May 1962) p.7
34. Mins. of Conv. (April 1969) p.3

This Convocation set up a working party to consider the re-structuring of Convocation. Then, quite naturally, Convocation in 1972 was very concerned about how the opening of the Presbyteral Ministry to women would affect the Order and asked the General Committee, which agreed, to present the following resolution to the Conference:

> The Wesley Deaconess Order meeting in Convocation, aware that the Ministry of the Word and Sacraments may be open to women, requests the Methodist Conference to direct the Faith and Order Committee to examine the meaning of both presbyteral and diaconal ministries.[35]

However, apart from a reference in January 1973, that the Warden told the General Committee about the 'changes taking place in the Order, and of the work of the Faith and Order Committee on the nature of the diaconate' nothing more is reported. It therefore seems likely that, in view of all the reorganisation necessitated through the integration of the Order into the Division of Ministries and the problems which arose with regard to stationing now that a number of deaconesses had entered the presbyteral ministry, plus the setting up of the working party in 1976 referred to in chapter 6, the matter was overtaken by events. It was agreed that the Wesley Deaconess Order pensions of those who were accepted for the presbyteral ministry should be 'frozen' from that date until they reached retiring age and that balances left in any individual deaconess's uniform account should be returned.[36]

So after many years, much debate and argument, women were admitted into the presbyteral ministry. Although many Conference Committees and Conferences had admitted that, in principle, there was no reason against the ordination of women they had long hesitated to take the final step. The Anglican-Methodist Conversations forced the 1965 Conference to shelve the matter once again as, at that time, the Anglican Church was resolutely opposed to the ordination of women and it was seen to be an insuperable barrier to any hope of the two Churches coming together. However, when the Conversations failed the Conference finally accepted the admission of women into the presbyteral ministry in 1973 with the first ordinations in Britain taking place in 1974.

---

35. WDOMins. IV 12th June 1972
36. WDOMins. IV 12th January 1973; WDOFinance Com. Mins 20th September 1972, 25th September 1973

Chapter 12

The Wardens and their special contribution

Over the years there were seven Wardens of the Wesley Deaconess Order and five of the United Methodist Free Churches, later the United Methodist Church. A brief look at each will give some idea of their contribution to and impact on the Order.

The Rev. Thomas Bowman Stephenson, DD, LLD, (1890-1907)

Thomas Bowman Stephenson, the youngest of six children, was born at Red Barns in the Newcastle-on-Tyne Circuit on 22nd December 1839 into the Wesleyan Methodist ministerial family of John and Mary Stephenson. After attending schools in Bedford, Louth and Dudley, at around the age of 14 he went to Wesley College, Sheffield, and when a revival 'broke out' there Thomas became convinced that 'I must give my life to the work of Christ'.[1] While at Wesley College Stephenson started to prepare for his London University Matriculation examinations, and

The Rev. Dr. Thomas Bowman Stephenson: Founder of the Wesley Deaconess Order and First Warden (1890-1907)

needing time to continue his studies, he went to Gateshead to supply for a minister who had become ill. There he felt a definite call to the Wesleyan Methodist ministry and, accepted as a candidate in 1858, was sent to Richmond College.[2] Richmond's close proximity to London meant the students were able to go to a variety of meetings there and hear many great preachers. The remarkable oratory and spirituality of W. Morley Punshon and the passionate advocacy of Temperance by John B. Gough had a profound influence on Stephenson, who became a powerful preacher, valuing many different elements of worship, and also a dedicated Temperance worker.

---

1. Bradfield p.26
2. Frank H., Cumbers ed., *Richmond College 1843-1943* (Epworth, 1944) pp.129-30

After college, stationed in Norwich, Stephenson quickly showed the characteristics which were to stay with him for life: he built up ecumenical relations, and eagerly embraced new ideas for evangelism, even holding services in a theatre in Norwich and in St. Andrews' Hall. Possessing a remarkable singing voice and having a deep love of music Stephenson made full use of his talents in his evangelistic services, later training the choirs of The Children's Home, which toured the country, and writing a number of hymns and tunes himself.[3] After two years in Norwich Stephenson was sent as a missionary evangelist to the Manchester Grosvenor Street Circuit, where he started a successful social gathering for poor working families on a Saturday evening. It was the time of the Lancashire Cotton Famine and many people in Lancashire and Yorkshire were starving as the American Civil War (1861-65) had severely affected trade. A Society 'to plead the cause of freedom', as represented by Abraham Lincoln and the Northern States of America, was formed and the Free Trade Hall became the venue for many meetings in which Stephenson took an active part. Here is evidence of the concerns which continued throughout his life and formed the basis of his ministry and future work in The Children's Home and the Wesley Deaconess Order.

Stephenson's reception into full connexion and ordination at the 1864 Bradford Conference was quickly followed by his marriage to Ellen Lupton, whom he had first met at the age of 14, when his father was minister in the Bramley Circuit, near Leeds. In 1865 the Stephensons moved to the Bolton (Bridge Street) Circuit, where Thomas had charge of Fletcher Street Church, a very large church with a Sunday School of 1,600, including 400 adults. With his love of music Stephenson delighted in the fine organ and great singing of the congregation, but once again his social concerns made themselves evident and one of the first things he did was to start a 'Union for Christian Work' with the evangelistic aim of reaching out to all classes in the community. He also instituted a system of house-to-house visiting and his social gatherings, with lectures, were well attended. The Sunday night mission services held 'for people who had not clothes of sufficient respectability to make them willing to go to the chapel' were very successful. Other evangelistic and social concern enterprises included cottage and open-air services, an Adult Spelling Class and the publication of a church magazine called *The Monthly Greeting*. This latter is particularly important because, in the September 1868 issue, there is mention of 'Miss

---

3. *HH* and *FL* passim

Entwistle, our deaconess' and that she had been 'indefatigable' in visiting as well as holding a weekly Mothers' Meeting. Stephenson's biographer and successor as Warden of the Wesley Deaconess Order, William Bradfield, rightly comments:

> It is much to notice that a woman was employed and set apart for the work, and supported whilst doing it, but it is certainly striking and unusual that she should be called a 'deaconess' as in 1868 the use of that word in connexion (sic) with English Protestant churches must have been rare indeed.[4]

Theodora (later Sister Dora), the only child of the Stephensons, was born while they were in Bolton. Stephenson had expected to move to Leeds (Oxford Place) Circuit, but the Rev. Benjamin Gregory's appointment as Connexional Editor left an unexpected vacancy in Lambeth and Stephenson was sent there, in 1868, to take pastoral charge of the chapel in Waterloo Road, situated opposite the Main Line Station (London and South-West Railway). Many people passed along Waterloo Road each day and as the chapel stood about 30 feet back from the road this seemed an ideal place to hold open-air services. Each evening services and Temperance meetings were held, with music and Stephenson's singing proving to be great "crowd-pullers", and, because he was not afraid of experimenting and his preaching was often topical, many stopped to listen. As many lives were touched Waterloo Road Chapel became very popular; however, close by was 'The New Cut', a notorious, very crowded slum. The people, especially the children, who lived there and the conditions in which they lived concerned Stephenson greatly. In Bolton he had been considering starting a Children's Home, so now here in 'The New Cut' he found his life's work. He wrote:

> I soon saw little children in a condition which made my heart bleed. There they were, ragged, shoeless, filthy, their faces pinched with hunger, and premature wretchedness staring out of their too bright eyes, and I began to feel that now my time had come. Here were my poor little brothers and sisters sold to Hunger and the Devil, and I could not be free of their blood if I did not at least try to save some of them.[5]

---

4. Bradfield p.51
5. Bradfield p.78

Thomas Bowman Stephenson was a man with a vision: a vision of providing care for the many poor and homeless children to be found living in terrible conditions on the streets and in the poverty stricken areas of London and, later, other large towns. To fulfil that vision he needed 'Sisters' to care for the children in The Children's Home, but then his horizons enlarged and he realised that there was work to be done, by dedicated and trained women in the circuits and churches throughout Methodism, so the idea of a separate Order of Deaconesses was born.

For 17 years Stephenson guided the infant movement, overseeing its inception, its training, including the branch houses, its development into a useful organisation with its own officers, tutors, Convocation, uniform and badge, its move from London to Ilkley, and its acceptance by the Wesleyan Methodist Conference as a Connexional Institution. He battled with financial difficulties to maintain the Institute, to provide reasonable allowances for the deaconesses, adequate sick pay and removal expenses and started the long complicated process which resulted in the setting up of a superannuation fund. He encouraged the recruitment of Lady Associates to help income. Stephenson coped with building problems to get Ilkley College established, he fought long and hard to get his deaconesses properly trained and accepted, he saw their numbers grow from two in July 1890 to 173 in 1907, and their being used in circuits, churches and Missions, particularly in work among women and children. Women with an aptitude for public speaking were encouraged to become Deaconess Evangelists who travelled the country, conducting missions and preaching, in the days well before Wesleyan Methodism officially sanctioned women preaching. Many deaconesses undertook specialised nursing courses, gaining good qualifications and so becoming Deaconess-Nurses. Stephenson was also instrumental in starting the overseas work when the Order was able to respond to requests from South Africa (1894) and Ceylon (1897) for deaconesses to work in those countries. In addition to everything else Stephenson wrote, at first a few pages in The Children's Home Magazine, *Highways and Hedges,* and then started and edited the Order's own magazine, *Flying Leaves.* The magazine contained various articles, hymns and lists of Bible readings which all contributed to the on-going education of the deaconesses. He was Chairman of the Halifax and Bradford District (1905-07) and President of the Wesleyan Methodist Conference in 1891.

Eventually ill-health forced Stephenson to relinquish the Wardenship on doctor's orders in 1907, but he left, knowing that his vision had been realized and that a well-established Order passed into the capable hands of his successor.

The Rev. William Bradfield, BA, (1907-20)

The Rev. William Bradfield was an ideal successor to Dr. Stephenson, being well aware of his vision and of the work being done by the deaconesses. He had long had connections with, and interest in, the Wesley Deaconess Order from the time when he was stationed in Leicester (1891-99).

The Rev. William Bradfield: Second Warden (1907-20)

William Bradfield was born into a Methodist home at Kingsclere on 15th December 1859. After a childhood dogged by ill-health he preached his first sermon in 1879 and was nominated as a candidate for the Wesleyan Methodist ministry in 1881. However, as Conference was unable to accept any candidates for the home work, he had to wait, but eventually spent four years at Headingley College, and, in his last year, he was 'sub-tutor' and obtained his University of London BA degree. After serving in Sunderland and York Bradfield was stationed in Leicester, where he engaged in much evangelistic work and came to appreciate the work done by the Wesley Deaconess Order, having close connections with Calvert House, the Deaconess Training House. From Leicester Bradfield went to Oxford and to Cambridge: in both cities he became very involved with university life and delighted in sharing different points of view and opinions. Appointed as Warden of the Wesley Deaconess Order in 1907 Bradfield combined this post with the Chairmanship of the Halifax and Bradford District for 13 years and when he resigned as Warden he became the separated Chairman of the District.

First Impressions	The Rev. William Bradfield

It is true I had considerable familiarity with the work of the Wesley Deaconess Institute from 1892 to 1899 in Leicester, but what I was acquainted with was, as it were, a little girl in short frocks and her hair down, while the Deaconess Institute of today is decidedly a grown-up young lady! . . .

I am glad of the opportunity to say that the principles upon which Dr.

> Stephenson has founded this Institution, and the lines upon which he has developed it, approve themselves to my judgement as sound, wise and reasonable, and that I have no fear of being placed in the difficulty of feeling compelled to alter and rearrange what he has planned. I can gladly, and with all my heart, administer the Institution on these lines, and shall hope to be permitted to develop it still farther in the same directions.
>
> *Source: Flying Leaves* (October 1907) p.138

As the second Warden, Bradfield's main task was one of consolidation and development. Under his able stewardship the property was modernised and some additional building projects put in hand. Financial matters were given a more secure footing: by making economies, asking for more realistic remunerations from circuits for the services of the deaconesses, seeking grants from the Connexion and instituting ways of raising additional funds, increasing the number of Associates and subscribers. He also overhauled some parts of the original constitution to make it more appropriate to the growing Order. However, possibly the two areas in which Bradfield's contribution was most marked was in teaching, especially biblical teaching, and in persuading Methodism of the importance and significance of women's ministry for the future. As previously noted, in 1909 Conference took three important decisions – to revise the Reception Service, the admission of women to Conference and on women preaching – all of which affected the Wesley Deaconess Order, and the Warden was involved with these issues.[6]

As Bradfield's tenure of office covered the period of the First World War he naturally was greatly concerned about the deaconesses who found themselves in many very different and often dangerous situations. He felt great responsibility for those taking the places of ministers who had joined the forces, those working in various capacities with the armed forces, and especially with their families, those working with women who had taken men's jobs in factories and who often found themselves in alien environments and for those who were isolated overseas.[7]

Having guided the Order through the difficulties of the war William Bradfield retired in 1920, but his 13 years as Warden and

---

6. see chapter 11
7. see chapter 2

careful management of everything connected with the Order left the organization in a healthy and stable position for his successor. Unfortunately, he did not live long to enjoy his retirement as, after a short illness, he died on 4th January 1923. Sister Esther Taylor, Secretary of the Order, commented:

> I shall never forget . . . the first time he talked business matters with me . . . What then struck me most forcibly about him was . . . his patience and serenity . . . His patience was immense. He could wait, especially if big issues were involved . . . He rested in God and he could wait patiently for him . . .
>
> Looking back over the time I worked with him, it is his bigness that stands out – big brain, big heart, big soul . . .
>
> He spent himself unstintingly in work for the Order . . . The establishment of its finances on a sound and secure basis, the steady emphasis laid on the status of the Deaconess and her rightful place in the Church, the insistence on a 'call to service', and the clear note of evangelism were all marks of his administration.
>
> He had a genius for figures . . . He was an expert financier, who could have made his fortune on the Stock Exchange . . .
>
> We knew we had a great man with us, but we didn't just admire his greatness from a distance. He was so human; he was near to us; our interests were his; our welfare his concern. He sympathised with our hopes and our fears, he shared our troubles and he let us share with him. He belonged to us and we loved him with all our hearts.[8]

Tribute to William Bradfield (1859-1923)
Rev. Dr. W. Russell Maltby

There were 156 deaconesses when he was appointed Warden, and there were 277 when he resigned. But the increasing numbers were not the measure of his work. He saw the meaning of this ministry and understood its significance for the future. He guided the whole Church in successive steps of recognition, because he saw the vision of a Ministry of Women, parallel to the Ministry of Men, and complementary to it, and worthy of the best service that the women of Methodism could give. When he left the work, an Anglican authority

---

8. *The Agenda* (February 1923) pp.7-11

> who knows our Deaconess Order better than most Methodists do, described it as the 'finest body of organised women workers in all the Churches'. If these words were justified, it was largely Mr. Bradfield's doing.
>
> *Source: The Agenda* (February 1923) p.3

The Rev. W. Russell Maltby, DD, (1920-40)

The Rev. Dr. William Russell Maltby: Third Warden (1920-40)

The announcement of the Rev. Dr. W. Russell Maltby's appointment as the third Warden came in a telegram from William Bradfield to the Order – 'Maltby, Praise the Lord'.[9] William Russell Maltby, the son of the Rev. William Maltby, was born at Selby on 5th December 1866. Educated at Woodhouse Grove and Kingswood Schools he qualified as a solicitor in 1892, and, accepted as a candidate for the Wesleyan Methodist ministry, he spent one year at Headingley College before being sent on supply to Dewsbury and Newcastle-upon-Tyne. After over 20 years in circuit, including three (1907-10) at Manchester (Gravel Lane), where doubtless he came into contact with the deaconesses serving there, he was appointed as Warden of the Wesley Deaconess Order in 1920. Previous to this he had become close friends with William Bradfield through their participation in the Cliff College Conference in 1918, which was a five-day retreat for ministers and led to the formation of the 'Fellowship' movement. Its purpose was to train lay leaders and *Manuals of Fellowship* were produced for these Schools of Fellowship, a number of which were written by Maltby himself or his brother, T. R. Maltby, a master at Kingswood School, who, from time to time when W. R. Maltby was absent from the Wesley Deaconess College, stood in for him.

Bradfield and Maltby   **J. Alexander Findlay**

Wilfred Moulton . . . once told me that the two most powerful minds he had ever encountered outside . . . 'academic circles' were those of William Bradfield and Russell Maltby, the one a steam hammer, the other a rapier. Both were formidable debaters at Conference, both

---

9. *The Agenda* (Christmas 1946) p.3

> became wardens of the Deaconess College, Ilkley, and chairmen of the Halifax and Bradford District, but they were as unlike each other as two men could be. Nevertheless, their love for one another was unaffected by widely different temperaments and opinions . . . Hour after hour they talked, argued, even contradicted one another, yet remained two inseparable friends, struggling towards the same goal.
>
> *Source: William Russell Maltby: Obiter Scripta* (selected and arranged by Francis B. James, with an appreciation by J. Alexander Findlay, 1952) p.3

Maltby took three months to assess his new job before presenting his thoughts on future developments: more accommodation in College to enable the establishment of a two-year training course, with practical experience, and training made available to other paying students. He gained the backing of the General Committee for a building programme and a publicity drive for candidates and funds. So, yet again, this Warden had to contend with property and finance matters, just as had his predecessors.

In the late 1920s and early 1930s Maltby became deeply involved with the negotiations for Methodist Union, especially as they affected the Wesley Deaconess Order. Fortunately relations between the Order and the United Methodist Institute were very good, as were those with the Primitive Methodist authorities, so that there was relatively little difficulty in uniting the Orders when Methodist Union became a reality in 1932.[10]

As noted in chapter 8 when Maltby restarted the Order's magazine under the title *The Agenda,* he determined that, as well as information about the Order and reports from the deaconesses, it would contain practical articles to help the deaconesses with their work. So suggestions were made for organising and running Bible Classes, Junior Classes, Guilds and Reading Circles. He nearly always wrote an 'editorial' which was meant to be informative, helpful, but thought-provoking, so that the readers could grow in their own knowledge and faith and be enabled to pass it on. *The Agenda* also contained many prayers and verses composed by Maltby. Although he only published two books, those and his other writings, including the Fellowship Manuals, emphasised the importance of a personal relationship with Christ and influenced countless readers. To the Sisters he wrote personal letters of encouragement and support, often enlivened by humour: letters which showed a deep insight into their work and needs.

---

10. see chapter 6

> **Letter to one going to a difficult appointment**
>
> **The Warden**
>
> I hope you will leave some things to the Lord. If you could for one hour a day live like a cabbage, with no concern for other cabbages, or your growth and greeness (sic), there would be wisdom in that.
>
> *Source: The Agenda* (December 1940) p.9

Another issue with which Dr. Maltby was deeply concerned was the whole question of women and the ministry and women's work in the church. He had become convinced that Methodism was not making the best use of its women workers and that the Church was exploiting their 'willingness to do all the work of a minister (except the administration of Holy Communion) under conditions which would never be tolerated by their male colleagues in the ordained ministry'. So when he became Warden he followed in Bradfield's footsteps in making 'a determined effort to do for the deaconesses what they were too selfless to do for themselves, to raise the status of the Order and improve their prospects when the time came for them to retire through old age or sickness'. His pension scheme was described by one judge as an economic 'master-piece'. As Findlay commented, 'Maltby had certainly not been trained in the law for nothing.'[11] By the 1920s, the whole of Methodism had become aware of the important work done by the Wesley Deaconess Order and the Women's Auxiliary and the Conference set up committees to consider the matter in depth. Maltby was appointed convenor of two committees and this meant a great deal of work, many meetings, protracted negotiations and much diplomacy. In particular, when as President of Conference (1926-27) he had to deal with contradictory votes from the Pastoral and Representative Sessions on the Report on 'Women and the Ministry'.[12] Sister Bessie Higgins well summed up Maltby's work in this field when she wrote:

> He had a vision of men and women working in true partnership for the Kingdom of God, bringing their joint gifts to the service of the Church. Our best tribute to him will not be in words, but in deeds, in a renewed dedication to Christ and the work of His Kingdom.[13]

---

11. *William Russell Maltby: Obiter Scripta* (selected and arranged by Francis B. James, with an appreciation by J. Alexander Findlay, 1952) pp.11-13

12. see chapter 11

13. *The Agenda* (December 1940) p.9

As Dr. Maltby was a prominent figure, beyond British Methodism, he was involved with more wide-reaching organizations. In 1923 he visited West Africa and was able to see, at first hand, the work of the Missions, colleges and schools, especially those where deaconesses were stationed. He participated in conferences arranged by the Young Men's League and the Student Christian Movement, being especially concerned with evangelistic work in the universities. J. Alexander Findlay related how, when Maltby rose to give his speech, someone at the Glasgow Quadrennial Conference said, 'Who is that male deaconess?' When Maltby had finished all the man could find to say was "Good God!" ' Four years later at the Edinburgh Quadrennial Findlay heard someone ask the then Archbishop of York, William Temple, '. . . Your Grace, what religious leader has most effectively appealed to the student-classes in recent years?' Immediately Temple replied, 'Without any exception of any sort, unquestionably Maltby.'[14] Maltby's connection with the Student Christian Movement led to an invitation to make a lecture tour on their behalf to India, Burma and Ceylon in 1926. In 1928 he gave the Burwash Memorial Lecture in Canada and the Australian Methodist Conference invited him to be the first Cato lecturer in 1935.

Although he had intended to retire as Warden in 1938 Maltby was persuaded to stay until 1941, but ill-health forced his resignation in 1940 and he became a supernumerary minister. However, contact with the Order was not entirely severed as Maltby retired nearby the College and was able to give lectures, write for *The Agenda* and, for some years, he acted as one of the Order's Treasurers. The 1940 Report to Conference pointed out that during his years of office the Deaconess Order had been enlarged to include not only the ex-United Methodist and ex-Primitive Methodist Deaconesses, but also the Manchester Mission Sisterhood and that he had 'fought untiringly the cause of the unattached and unpensioned workers of Methodism and now practically all our Churches and Missions are staffed from the Wesley Deaconess Order.'[15]

---

14. *William Russell Maltby: Obiter Scripta* p.15
15. *The Agenda* (December 1940) p.7 cf. *The Methodist Church: Conference Agenda* (1940) p.245

> ### Retirement of the Rev. Dr. W. Russell Maltby
> The Committee wish to record their deep gratitude for the service given to Methodism by the Rev. W. R. Maltby, D.D., as Warden of the Wesley Deaconess Order from 1920 to 1940. He has brought to this work spiritual leadership of a high order, a genius for teaching the truth of the Christian faith, and the power of offering Christ to the mind and heart of his hearers. His year as President of the Wesleyan Methodist Church and his travels all over the world have made him widely known and loved. The Order has been immeasurably enriched by his continued contact with the Universities and by the great esteem in which he is held by other Communions. His insight into the hopes and aspirations of women and his sympathy with the difficulties arising in their work have been a cause for thankfulness to hundreds of women inside and outside the Deaconess Order. But he has been and is most deeply loved by those to whom he has been Teacher, Pastor, and Friend, and to whom he has truly fulfilled the best meaning of the word 'Warden'.
>
> *Source:* Wesley Deaconess Order Minutes(1932-47) p.106 cf.
> *The Agenda* (December 1940) p.7

The Rev. Dr. W. Russell Maltby's Wardenship had put the Wesley Deaconess Order firmly 'on the map' of the Methodist Church. Having brought the deaconesses of the branches of Methodism happily and successfully together and been a passionate advocate for women's ministry he passed an Order, proud of its place in the worldwide Methodist Church, into the safe hands of the Rev. W. Harold Beales.

A prayer-poem of Maltby's entitled 'A Greeting', which was reprinted in *The Agenda* on his retirement, seems to sum up not only his own attitude to his life and work, but also that of his beloved Wesley Deaconess Order:

> Peace with Adventures,
> Labour and a light heart,
> A sense of Vocation and a Sense of Humour,
> A Mind girded, but not tense,
> Alert, but not anxious.
> Employed but not busy,
> Strenuous, but well rested.
>   In a word,
> Grace to you and Peace from God our Father,
>   and the Lord Jesus Christ.
>
>   W. R. M.[16]

---

16. *The Agenda* (December 1940) p.11

The Rev. W. Harold Beales, MA, (1940-52)

The Rev. W. Harold Beales, the son of a minister, was born in Bingham, Nottingham in 1886. He had a pre-collegiate year in Cheltenham before going to Didsbury College in 1907, after which he served in the Severn Valley Mission, Cheltenham, Bath, Bristol, Cambridge and London (Finsbury Park) Circuits. While in Cambridge (1924-30) Beales inspired some undergraduates who formed 'The Cambridge Group', which met together in fellowship meetings, retreats and for projects of Christian action. This movement, also encouraged by Maltby,

The Rev. W. Harold Beales: Fourth Warden (1940-52)

developed into the later 'Methsocs', which spread into universities and colleges countrywide. This passionate fervour for stimulating fellowship and Christian action led to a roving commission, working under the auspices of the Home Mission Department, for the next six years. In 1940, on the premature retirement of his friend Dr. Maltby, Beales became Warden of the Wesley Deaconess Order, but an arrangement was made whereby he continued some work for the Home Mission Committee. As the new Warden Beales took up where Maltby had left off, but in very difficult circumstances: the Second World War had broken out in 1939 and by 1940 many Wesley Deaconesses were in 'front line' appointments. During the First World War Beales had been a pacifist and suffered much criticism, which he took with 'unfailing good humour', so to find himself faced with supporting deaconesses working in wartime conditions must have been a considerable personal strain.

A short 'Monthly Letter' had been circulated among the deaconesses to supplement the larger intermittent magazine and on 30 August 1940 Mr. Beales wrote his first message in which he said he 'had never come to any work in my life with such a sense of privilege'; that despite his retirement Dr. Maltby would still be 'near to us all' and that 'this message comes with an unsentimental offer of friendship'.

> **The Warden's Dream**   **The Rev. W. Harold Beales**
>
> . . . if the Order is realising the New Testament dream for it, it is an evangelical Fellowship of the Holy Spirit, its inner secret such a love as the world has seen only in Jesus Christ. My wife and I are not in that Fellowship yet; but we want to be. So this message comes with an unsentimental offer of friendship – as far as ever it is possible for individual friendship. May we claim yours in return? In the encouraging strength of such a relationship we can all go forward. For these are no ordinary times – all around us danger, yes, but immense opportunity! We have not only got a Gospel; it becomes daily clearer that we have got the only Gospel there is!
>
> *Source: Monthly Letter* (30th August 1940)

Writing in the first magazine to appear for a year Beales confessed that he was at a complete loss about what he was expected to say, but that he had 'been deeply impressed by the intimate fellowship which exists between staff and students here'. He felt that all the Methodist Colleges should be 'Homes of God where the relationships are family relationships . . . already that is true of this one. It is a benediction to live in it.'[17] These first messages from the new Warden set the tone for his emphases during his term in office: fellowship, relationships and evangelism were fundamental. His ministry to the deaconesses was essentially personal and pastoral as the many letters exchanged show – he was deeply concerned about the individual needs and concerns of each of his Sisters. Beales was a great letter writer and by that means gave great support to the deaconesses, especially with those in trying circumstances encouraging them to 'fag at it' when faced with difficult colleagues and situations and also, as Sister Yvonne Hunkin further remembers, he was fond of quoting, 'When God closes a door, he opens a window.' He was touched by a letter, in 1950, from one deaconess whom he had had to send, in his own words, 'to one of the hardest, perhaps one of the least obviously rewarding stations' in which she wrote: 'There are enough puzzles and problems here to frighten a Dutchman; but we plough on, and life's got a bloom on it. I would not change it for a King's Ransom.' He commented, 'I could make a sermon on that! But isn't it splendid?'[18]

---

17. *The Agenda* (December 1940) pp.3-4
18. I am indebted to Sister Yvonne for the loan of Monthly Letters from W. H. Beales

The war was chiefly responsible for the non-appearance of *The Agenda,* but the 1940 Report to Conference reported a total of 393 deaconesses and that

> The tension which preceded the War and followed its outbreak has necessarily thrown new duties upon the Deaconesses. Some have followed evacuated mothers and children into new areas: some have found their premises commandeered and their customary work curtailed, but fresh opportunities have been disclosed.[19]

The 1941 Report to Conference celebrated 'what has been in many ways the greatest year which the Order has ever known. Most of our sisters are at work in the blitz areas. Many have lost all that they had, four have given their lives. The message that comes from all of them is the same – that this hour of national crisis has been the hour of their most wonderful opportunity. God had indeed opened for them "a great door and effectual".'[20] Unfortunately the financial side was extremely depressing and worrying with a very large deficit. So Beales, like all his predecessors, had to cope with considerable financial worries, but in these years war conditions exacerbated the problem. Added to this was the likelihood of potential candidates and indeed deaconesses being 'called up' for National Service, so Beale appealed to Associate Members, ministers and Methodism in general to seek out suitable candidates. However, he emphasised that the word 'suitable' must be underlined! A simple first test would be to enquire whether this 'candidate would be a truly welcome addition to the staff in one's own Circuit or Mission'.

1942 brought a great boost to the Wesley Deaconess Order when, at long last, the Report of the Special Conference Committee on Deaconess Work was presented to the Manchester Conference and accepted. Dr. Maltby had been very deeply involved with the discussions and both he and Beales were thrilled that at long last the deaconesses were to be accorded their rightful status.[21]

---

19. *The Methodist Church: Conference Agenda* (1940) p.245
20. *The Methodist Church: Conference Agenda* (1941) p.235
21. See chapter 11; *The Agenda* (August 1942) pp.1-5, 12-17

Conference 1942   **The Rev. Dr. W. Russell Maltby**

It [the Special Report on deaconess work] was formally moved by the Warden, and Dr. Lidgett then rose to second it. Dr. Lidgett was, I think, at his best. His heart was wholly in the business; he had taken trouble to know the facts and he spoke with courage, with humour and immense weight. 'If I had my way,' he said, 'I would double the number of deaconesses and put them in every crowded centre.' ...

When Sister Helen Styles 'ascended the tribune,' a friendly minister was moved with pity and said 'Poor thing!' But a knowledgeable neighbour answered 'Don't worry. She can do it.' ... Sister Helen did not weaken it; she carried it on and the friendly minister withdrew his pity and murmured approval when she was done. She wasted no words, used no synthetic unction. Her plea for candidates and the right kind of candidates was very effective, and her reference to the meagre superannuation allowance a Deaconess receives at 60 years of age – £52 a year – moved the Conference.

Source: The Agenda (August 1942) p.12

To return to the deaconess 'at war', many were stationed in difficult and often dangerous positions, working in city Missions and churches, braving the blitz and bombs which devastated many of the country's major towns – London, Birmingham, Coventry, Manchester, Hull and Liverpool – facing hardship and danger along with their people, showing remarkable bravery, courage, fortitude, endurance and cheerful good humour. Others found themselves in unusual situations: taking the places of ministers who had joined the forces; serving with and in the armed forces; working in factories, often in ones making munitions, which raised moral problems for some of the women; providing help for families anxious about loved ones. All these circumstances tested the deaconesses' faith and must have inevitably raised questions and one can imagine how much of a strain this must have been for the Warden too. A strong, loving caring company of friends and colleagues was extremely important to sustain them by prayer, fellowship and with constant encouragement. This 'back-up' the Order provided, through various communication channels, not least the personal letters from the Warden himself, which enabled the Wesley Deaconesses at home and abroad to keep in touch, encourage and support one another.

> ## Report of the Wesley Deaconess Order, 1942
>
> A feature . . . has been the newness of it. The War is bringing special appeals and unusual opportunities . . . One of the first twelve women to be appointed for assistant-chaplain work in the A.T.S. is a Wesley Deaconess. Several Sisters have already begun work in munitions hostels . . . A growing number are engaged in club-organisation or leadership under the National Youth scheme. Thus the Order is steadily extending its ministry and influence beyond the borders of Methodism . . . While from one point of view these developments give cause for congratulation, from another they are not so happy. For they mean that openings which offer the greatest scope for initiative and enterprise are tending increasingly to occur outside rather than inside the Church . . . It urges the Conference to consider further responsible openings for trained and competent Deaconesses. As one example . . . it would be reasonable in the present condition of our work in many villages to give to some Sisters the responsibility of several villages where their leadership and their pastoral gifts would make all the different to the health of the cause and work of God . . .
>
> *Source: The Methodist Church: Conference Agenda* (1942) p.161

It was during Beales' Wardenship that Linnburn, the property next door to the College, was acquired as a hostel, so that more candidates could be admitted and trained.[22] The stringencies of the war years had meant that Sisters who had retired or resigned had not been replaced so now, in 1946, extra accommodation was needed for more students. Also the social climate had changed and more openings were evolving as Beales explained:

> . . . Appointments . . . have had to be given up; and just when they have needed her ministry most, Churches and Missions have had to be left without a Deaconess altogether. Meanwhile new calls have been coming to us with increasing frequency. Some of these have arisen out of war difficulties . . . others have been associated with programmes of advance, offering fine and satisfying opportunities for permanent service . . . we are challenged to certain specialised forms of ministry, youth work, moral welfare work, etc., and we want to play our part worthily . . .[23]

---

22. See chapter 6
23. *The Agenda* (January 1946) pp.1-2

Another property which came into the ownership of the Order during Beales' time was the Holiday Home at Worthing where deaconesses and other women workers could have the benefit of rest, relaxation and sea air. The pension situation had been improved and a start made towards the provision of a home for aged deaconesses. This was a matter which greatly concerned Beales and at one stage his 'dream' looked like being fulfilled, but it was not to be at that time.[24] Just before he retired from the College he pleaded for help to provide such a home.

Dream for Aged Deaconesses   **The Warden**

I want you, if you will to consider the case of so many of our beloved Sisters who are reaching or have reached old age. Everyone of them is a single woman. By the time that they retire their relatives are thinning out . . . quite a few . . . have no relatives at all . . . they must live, for the most part, in lodgings . . . [too high prices; too small a pension] . . . We *must* do something about it if we can. It would, of course, widen the appeal of the Order itself. You would be surprised if you knew how many girls come to us against their parents' wishes . . . There can be no doubt that many girls are persuaded not to come. We lose people some of who might have served the Church well. But that is not my basic reason for wanting to see more done for our retired Sisters. It is that they *are* our *Sisters*, members of *our* family, our relatives in Christ and his Church. During years of faithful and sacrificial ministry they have never let their family down; and, now, when they are old, the family cannot let them down.

Source: The Wesley Deaconess Magazine (December 1951) pp.3-4

The format of the magazine of the Order was modernized and it was renamed *The Wesley Deaconess Magazine* in 1950, but, on the whole, the content remained much the same with various articles, news of the College and the deaconesses, many written by the Sisters themselves. Beales wrote his last editorial in the new magazine just before he retired. He reflected on his time as Warden: how much the Order had 'given' to him; how much he had learned from the deaconesses' ministry; how many risks and challenges there had been, how much real, true, fellowship he had found, but how much more there could be – in the Order and in the Church. In the same issue, the Vice Principal of the College, Sister Dorothy Farrar, wrote a tribute in which she remarked that the Warden had

---

24. See chapter 8

always seen his colleagues as his friends with whom to share burdens and joys. Not only was he a teacher, but also an evangelist, who was 'sure of his Gospel', full of faith and 'a representative Methodist of "Catholic Spirit", in fellowship with all the followers of Christ, yet refusing to compromise his principles in well-meant efforts to hasten reunion'.[25]

The Rev. W. Harold Beales, MA   Sister Dorothy Farrar

He brought to us also, something without which any Warden might as well resign at once, but he brought it in a measure so rich that it strengthened, supported and often rebuked us all. It is this: he believes as few men believe, in a ministry of women in the Church of God. He saw the work of a deaconess as something sacred because it was of God, and the disappointments and problems which are bound to arise in the course of a twelve years' guidance of several hundred women in the service of Methodism has never changed his reverence for our work. To look at our ministry through his eyes seems to make it richer and more precious to each one of us.

Source: The Wesley Deaconess Magazine (July 1952) p.6

The same year as Beales retired and went back to live in Cambridge, having passed on the Wesley Deaconess torch to his successor, the Rev. Thomas M. Morrow, the College at Ilkley celebrated its Golden Jubilee. Beales contributed an article to the Jubilee number of the magazine looking over the 50 years, noting that his first contact with the Order was with the rather austere Jeanie Banks, who he soon realised '*knew* the Saviour whom she so quietly and compellingly offered'. He commented that many of the 'early Deaconesses were gifted women coming from gifted families. They are still coming. One of them (Sister Dorothy Farrar) is Vice-President of the Conference this year.' He concluded by asserting that 'The Order was and is part of His redemptive purpose in Christ.' As such it should 'move forward into an unhampered strength to its second half-century of glorious service'.[26]

Sister Margaret Statham, as the Administrative Secretary at Ilkley, worked closely with Beales during his 12 years there and came to appreciate his meticulous grasp of all the details connected with the deaconesses' appointments and their welfare, and his deep

---

25. *WDMag.* (July 1952) pp.5-6
26. *WDMag.* [College Jubilee Number] (October 1952) pp.5-6

concern both for those in the active work and those who had retired. When he died, 17th September 1967, she added her own personal tribute to the many others.

The Rev. W. Harold Beales   Sister Margaret Statham

As Warden of the Order he was concerned for the welfare of every member, whether in active work, in sickness, or in eventual retirement. He was also concerned about the Order as a whole and its place in the life of the Church, and indeed the whole area of the ministry of women. For himself, though, it is doubtful whether he ever thought of men and women as in separate categories: they were just people – interesting people – the people of God.

Those who were his colleagues at Ilkley, those who came to him in any kind of need, and indeed the whole company of those who were members of the Wesley Deaconess Order while W. H. Beales was Warden, remember with gratitude his leadership, his friendship, his lovable (sic) human qualities, and that something extra which can perhaps only be described by the word 'saintliness'.'

Source: MS Tribute by Margaret Statham

The Rev. Thomas Manser Morrow, MA, (1952-64)

The Rev. Thomas M. Morrow was born in Kennington, London on 23rd May 1908 and entered the Wesleyan Methodist ministry in 1928. Following one year on the Reserve List he went to Cambridge and then after 20 years in circuit became the fifth Warden of the Wesley Deaconess Order in 1951. Morrow was Chairman of the West Yorkshire District from 1965 until his death in 1974.

The Rev. Thomas M. Morrow:
Fifth Warden (1952-64)

In Morrow's first editorial, almost as soon as he had arrived, he wrote of his debt to his two predecessors: to Maltby, who conducted a Youth weekend in his home circuit, which caused him to accept 'God's call to discipleship and service', and to Beales, who had a profound effect on him during his time in Cambridge:

If you ask me if I believe in Apostolic succession, I can only answer that God laid his hand upon me through two great Apostles of his Word. Every friend of the Order will have cause for gratitude to God for the ministries of past Wardens. I thank God for W.R.M. and W.H.B.[27]

When the next issue appeared, eight months later, Morrow had had chance to become familiar with the job and to know the deaconesses. He had been deeply impressed, and indeed moved, by Convocation and especially the Ordination Service and by the 'Conversation on the Work of God' session, when many speakers had related how God was working in different situation. He commented: 'Thrilling things *are* happening. God *is* using the Order in His work. This is also clearly reflected in the scores of letters I have had from Superintendents writing in the most glowing terms of the vital work that Deaconesses are doing in Churches and Missions. Methodism has every right to be proud of its Cinderella.'[28]

At last Beales' dream came into being when a house in Cleethorpes was bought, on very generous terms, as a Home for Retired Sisters and one can imagine how this must have rejoiced his heart. Albemarle opened in November 1953 with the official ceremony in the following March, but to the regret of all present Mr. Beales, 'who had dreamed a dream and seen a vision', was unable to be present.

Conversation Overheard   **The Warden**

Not long after our Home for Aged Deaconesses at Cleethorpes was opened, the following conversation was overheard from two passers-by: 'Who lives in that big house now?' 'I'm not sure, but I think it's a home for Archdeaconesses.'

Perhaps we would apply the adjective 'Arch' to the residents at Albemarle House, but if an Archdeacon is superior to a deacon, then presumably an Archdeaconess is a superior kind of deaconess!

Source: The Wesley Deaconess Magazine (December 1959) p.1

However, at the other end of the spectrum there had been a worrying fall in the number of candidates offering for the Order and

---

27. *WDMag.* [College Jubilee Number] (October 1952) p.3
28. *WDMag.* (June 1953) p.2

Morrow constantly urged ministers, Associates of the Order, circuits and churches to publicize its work, seek out possible candidates, and support it with prayers and gifts.[29] Demand for deaconesses far exceeded supply in the 1950s and the Warden had to explain that the shortage of candidates and the two-year training programme for the successful ones meant that, regretfully, many requests had to be refused. In support of his oft repeated and urgent plea for the seeking out of suitable candidates Morrow told how many times he had been made aware of women who would have offered as candidates 'if only they had known about the Order when they were young enough'.

Qualifications for a Deaconess Candidate   The Warden

'In . . . this magazine there are several moving witnesses to the response that people have made to the call of God. They have been written by people with very varied gifts and temperaments, and they were called from very varied occupations. That is surely one of the glorious things about the Order, its infinite variety of gifts. Deaconesses wear uniform, but there is no uniformity about the people themselves. If you are wondering just what qualities are needful in a candidate . . . let this suffice — a sense of the call of God to service, a love for God, a love for people, an ability to benefit from College training, physical fitness, a warm heart and a thick skin!

Source: The Wesley Deaconess Magazine (December 1953) pp.2-3

From time to time, as with all the previous Wardens, property considerations forced themselves upon the notice of the Order, so in 1954 the bedrooms and the Library were updated, but a more serious matter arose in 1956. A fire, a small thing in itself, led to the discovery that the chimney which served the central heating system was dangerous. The further inspection revealed that the building needed a major structural overhaul to ensure the safety of the residents: for a while it seemed as if the closure of the College and rebuilding elsewhere might be the only option, but fortunately it did not come to that.

Colleagueship was very important to Morrow and particularly as it affected the deaconesses. He felt that happy team work in all situations could produce lasting results. The Order had been conscious for many years that some people regarded the ministry of

---

29. *WDMag.* (June 1953) p.3

the deaconesses as a 'second class' one and that due value was not given to their vocation, training, dedication and commitment. The earlier Wardens had fought to raise the status and profile of the Wesley Deaconess Order and to ensure that the deaconesses were given the position they deserved. Morrow followed this line by insisting that colleagueship was vitally important for Methodism, and indeed wider ecumenical relationships, if its full potential was to be achieved.

Colleagueship   **The Rev. Thomas M. Morrow**

One of the most rewarding, and, at the same time, one of the most difficult sides of our work is colleagueship, whether it be with ministers, fellow deaconesses, or lay helpers. It is rewarding, for happy team work can produce results more lasting and more successful than individual effort. But it is difficult simply because a deaconess has to face peculiar problems. She has no normal home life as have her lay helpers, she has often nobody with whom she can share her deepest problems as has a minister. It would be impossible to estimate the debt of the Order to those understanding colleagues who give such rich help to the deaconess.

Source: The Wesley Deaconess Magazine (July 1954) pp.2-3

Following discussion in the 1963 Convocation a Special Committee on Training was set up 'in view of the demand and opportunities presented by our society today' to consider 'the whole method of training'. The initial report covered the purpose of training; the standard of training; the curriculum; the length of training, staffing and the place of training. However, as there was to be a change of Warden in 1964 it was decided that the incoming Warden ought to share in any final decisions and so the Committee was reappointed to continue its deliberations.[30]

Tribute to the Rev. Thomas M. Morrow, the retiring Warden, was paid in the 1964 Report to Conference:

> Though coming younger than his predecessors to this position he reached the College equipped with a first class theological education, a wide knowledge of Circuit work and very considerable administrative

---

30. WDOMins IV 24th June 1963, 22nd June 1964; Report of Training Committee (duplicated Report n.d.); Minutes 12th November 1963, 6th January 1964, 2nd March 1964 cf. chapter 8

experience; all this has enriched his work. His lecturing has been of a high order especially in a field of particular interest to him i.e. Church History. During a period of change and transition he has ably represented the Department in Conference and carefully watched the best interests of the deaconesses throughout the Connexion. In his dealings with individuals he has manifested sympathy, integrity, patience and discretion. In himself he has revealed deep humility and a willingness to sacrifice all personal interests to what he has felt to be the good of the Order and of the Methodist Church as a whole.[31]

Mr. Morrow died on the eve of the 1974 Conference and as the Order's Magazine commented, those who were his students remembered him 'with thankfulness and affection. His balanced judgement, wise counsel and personal care for many people was deeply appreciated. To this must be added the scholarship and insight he brought to lecturing and tutorials.'[32]

The Rev. Geoffrey Litherland, MA, BD, (1964-72)

The Rev. Geoffrey Litherland was born in Knutsford, Cheshire on 9th January 1911. From Altrincham Grammar School he went to St. John's College, Cambridge and then taught Chemistry and Mathematics in Liverpool. He entered the ministry in 1935, training at Wesley College, Headingley. After 22 years' experience of Methodism in England in 1957 he was appointed Principal of Queen's College, Nassau in the Bahamas at a critical stage in its development. His mission was two-fold: to move the College from its dilapidated buildings in the centre of Nassau to a new site and to make it a racially integrated establishment. His obituary notes his success:

The Rev. Geoffrey Litherland: Sixth Warden 1964-72)

In the face of much opposition, difficulties and delays the school was built and under his guidance became a centre of excellence in academic, artistic and sporting

---

31. WDOMins III 22nd June 1964
32. *A Way of Serving* (Autumn 1974) p.1

spheres for black and white Bahamian, Greek, Chinese, American and British children. After he left the island the science block was appropriately named the Litherland Laboratories.[33]

The reasoned statement to the Conference requesting his appointment as Warden of the Wesley Deaconess Order contains the following: 'throughout his ministry he has shown himself to be a strong and wise leader and a good pastor and preacher, and has won the respect of his people and his colleagues. For four years he was Chaplain to Southlands College. In his present work in Nassau he has proved to be a most effective administrator, as a student and a leader, he would bring to this work a well trained mind and proved ability.'[34]

Litherland inherited the Special Committee set up by the previous Warden to look at all aspects of the future training for Wesley Deaconesses. As he had been kept abreast of all the discussions and recommendations of that Committee the change of Warden meant that the deliberations continued along much the same lines.[35] The Warden emphasised that, although some people might argue that these new ventures in training tended to be rather more academic, 'the basic aim of the new programme is *the development of the whole personality, within the discipline and devotion of community life, with a view to the richest possible ministry in the world by doing and by being.*'[36] So deaconess training was now to be three years, some lecture courses were to be shared with the ministerial students at Headingley and it was hoped that many of the deaconess students would 'work towards some external examination'. Practical training was also to be developed with outside lecturers visiting to share their experiences and a wider range of 'field work' being offered to enlarge the scope of the students' knowledge of the outside world. That the 'spiritual' side of College life was vitally important went 'without saying'.

---

33. *Mins. of Conf.* (1992) p.57
34. WDOMins IV 2nd April 1963
35. WDOMins IV 24th June 1963, 22nd June 1964; Report of Training Committee (duplicated Report n.d.); Minutes 12th November 1963, 6th January 1964, 2nd March 1964, 11th December 1964; cf. chapter 8 pp.15-16
36. *Doers of the Word* (June 1965) p.4

> ## College Life and Training   The Rev. Geoffrey Litherland
> I don't think I need to say very much, because it goes without saying that we believe that God is right in the centre of it all. Friends may rest assured that though we may not use some of the familiar religious words so freely, this is at the heart of our planning and of all we do. Our training is not to be regarded as 'technical training' or 'further education', but as training of the total personality through the daily encounter of the individual with God in a community which aspires to be the Body of Christ in its local environment.
>
> *Source: Doers of the Word* (June 1965) p.4

Another matter which came to the fore during Litherland's time as Warden was whether Wesley Deaconesses in the active work should be permitted to do work outside the normal deaconess appointments and still remain as members of the Order. It was realised that this was likely to be an increasing development and so the decision was taken to examine the whole question. The appointed sub-committee resolved that 'Special Ministries . . . to make the most of opportunities not only within the circuit but in modern fields of evangelism outside . . .' should apply to the Order just as much as to ministers and that the Order should be ready to appoint suitable deaconesses as, when and where opportunities arose, providing certain conditions were met.[37]

Yet another problem Litherland had to deal with was a resolution passed to the General Committee from the 1965 Convocation relating to Ordination and Marriage:

(1)   The offer of a candidate for ordination as a Deaconess is for life.

(2)   Ordination into the Deaconess Order is for life.

(3)   Ordination is terminated only by resignation, not by marriage.[38]

A sub-committee and a working party were set up to consider this and eventually it was agreed that 'in principle marriage need not entail resignation from the Deaconess Order'. However, it was deemed necessary for the General Committee 'to implement a scheme with suitable safeguards whereby ordained Deaconesses may remain members of the Order on marriage'.[39]   A further

---

37. WDOMins III 22nd June 1964, 11th December 1964; Sub-Committee 1965;
38. WDOMins III 17th December 1965 cf. Mins. of Conv. (1965) p.4
39. WDOMins III 20th June 1966: cf. chapter 8

resolution from the 1965 Convocation suggested that deaconesses who had served for a number of years might be granted sabbatical leave to engage in further study or training. The General Committee responded positively and requested the Finance Committee to look into possibility of providing bursaries to this end.[40]

However, a major headache came when it was learned that the Ministerial Training Committee was reviewing the training of ministers and the future of the theological colleges. Anything which affected Headingley College would obviously have an impact on the College at Ilkley, especially now that there were closer ties between the two. It was a very unsettled period, but when finally the decision was made to close Headingley, Litherland had to explore other possibilities for the training of the Wesley Deaconesses and eventually he had to oversee the Order's move to Birmingham: first to near Handsworth College and then, when that amalgamated with the Anglican Queen's College, to Edgbaston.

The final year of Litherland's Wardenship saw the commencement of the restructuring of Methodism's national organisation amid concerns that the Wesley Deaconess Order should not lose its particular identity. Having been reassured that a satisfactory arrangement had been reached Litherland retired in 1972 leaving the new Warden to implement the restructuring and to work through the implications of the opening of the Presbyteral Ministry to women.[41]

The Rev. Brian J. N. Galliers, MA, BD, MTh (1972-80)

The Rev. Brian James Newby Galliers was born in London on 30th April 1931. He received his ministerial training at Wesley College, Headingley, Leeds (1951-54) and after one year at Romford returned there as Assistant Tutor for two years before spending the next 15 years in circuit. In 1972 Mr. Galliers was appointed as Warden of the Wesley Deaconess Order, during which time he presided over vast changes as Methodism and the Order worked through the new structures, the

The Rev. Brian J. N. Galliers: Seventh Warden (1972-80)

---

40. WDOMins III 17th December 1965 cf. Mins. of Conv.(1965) p.7
41. See chapter 12

many new ideas about diaconal ministry and the impact on the Order of the opening of the presbyteral ministry to women.

The Future   **The Rev. Brian J. N. Galliers**

. . . a meeting . . . asked me to speak about the future of the Order. I did my best; we have no crystal ball, and it had to be sanctified guesswork; but when I had finished the cry was not 'Things weren't like that in the old days'; but 'If God can do that – Amen!' For me that typifies the spirit of the Order; it is realised that change must come, but that change is neither resisted nor resented. It is seen as the hand of God.

It is in that light that the acceptance of 21 members of the Order into the ministry by the 1973 Conference must be seen. There is no silent feeling that these have deserted; there is general thankfulness that the Church has opened for them what they feel to be the true fulfilment of their ministry. And although that number represents about one-eighth of our circuit strength, there is certainly no fear that this spells the beginning of the end.

Source: A Way of Serving (Autumn 1973) p.3

The Order was now part of the newly formed Division of Ministries and this meant considerable alterations in the organization and training. Of necessity there was a great deal of administration to be done, decisions to be taken, lectures to be prepared and given, counselling offered, public relations – preaching, speaking at meetings, publicizing the Order and its work – to be undertaken. However, in spite of all these 'business' meetings the Warden's chief concern was for the welfare of the deaconesses. Many deaconesses were now working in and with 'outside' organizations and so much of the deaconess ministry was very different from the earlier years. During his first year as Warden Galliers travelled widely to meet the deaconesses and to share their experiences – both the joys and the difficulties and concluded that, whatever else, he would 'not die of boredom!'.

First Impressions 1972-73   **The Warden**

I am immensely impressed by the dedication of the deaconesses of Methodism. Most of them ask nothing more than to be found places where they can work within the circuits. This may mean working in a large building in the centre of one of our cities . . . in twilight areas of

> the city . . . on . . . tough housing estates . . . whilst, in an entirely
> different surrounding, it can be discouraging to drive over one
> hundred miles on a Sunday and preach three times, to congregations
> which number less than twenty in total.
>
> Our women accept these situations as part of their Christian
> discipleship and ministry, and accept them gladly. I have heard very
> few 'moans' . . . but where complaints have been made, they have
> related less to the difficulties of the work than to the lack of
> colleagueship . . .
>
> I am also impressed by the commitment of those deaconesses whose
> ministry is in the Sectors . . . for them this is not a running away from
> circuit life . . . It is a genuine desire to serve Christ within a particular
> professional sphere, and at the same time to build up a relationship
> with the Church.
>
> *Source: A Way of Serving* (Autumn 1973) pp.1-2

During the years before the Order ceased recruiting there were
a number of misconceptions within Methodism and so the Warden
had often to assure the churches that 'the Wesley Deaconess Order
is still very much alive – and kicking!'. He pointed out that in 1976
there was a training programme in Birmingham, that the Order was
'over 300 strong, with almost 100 deaconesses in Methodist circuits
and others serving in places abroad and in sector work in Great
Britain'. It was true that it was a time of change and that a number
of deaconesses had entered the presbyteral ministry, but there were
many others who felt that God had called them to be Wesley
Deaconesses.[42]

1977-78 was a year of decision when the Board of the Division
of Ministries recommended to the Conference the ceasing of
recruitment to the Order; that its future rôle be redefined and that
consideration be given to the establishment of a new Order of lay
service in the Church. Convocation accepted the recommendations
'as a creative way forward both for the Order and the Church'.

> **The Future? 1978**   **The Warden**
>
> It was felt . . . that by ceasing recruitment . . . and by wholeheartedly
> sharing with the Division of Ministries in seeking to discover what
> alternative type of organisation might be best suited to the needs of

---

42. *A Way of Serving* (Autumn 1976) pp.2-3

> Methodism today, we would be responding to the guidance of God. The future might bring a 'wider' order, which could include men and women, and not necessarily be limited to those who are able to offer themselves to an itinerant ministry; or it could bring a 'narrower' order, in which a few people might try to find new ways of expressing the ideals of poverty and obedience; or it might even be felt that there is no longer a place for such an order or diaconate within the Methodist Church . . .
>
> One thing must be made very clear indeed. The work of the Wesley Deaconess Order will go on . . . Even though numbers of 'active' members of the Order will decrease, there will still be such members working . . . In addition, the life of the Order as a whole, and its work of prayer and its spirituality in general, will still (I believe) enrich Methodism, and indeed the whole Church.
>
> *Source: A Way of Serving* (Autumn 1978) pp.2-3

When the Order ceased recruiting in 1978, and those students who were in training completed their courses in 1981, new plans had to be made. A smaller property was purchased as the headquarters of the Order; Mr. Galliers moved to a circuit appointment elsewhere in Birmingham and was no longer full-time Warden, but continued as Ministerial Secretary, while Sister Yvonne Hunkin, as the first 'Deaconess Warden', took over the day-to-day running of the Order. Two years later, in 1982, Galliers became Chairman of the London North-East District.

> **'A continuing contribution'   The Rev. Brian J. N. Galliers**
>
> . . . there are at least four areas where the Order has an important contribution to make to Methodism in the early eighties.
>
> (1)   It will witness to the value and importance of *the ministry of the deacon*. Deaconesses have emphasised the importance of ministry *to people* . . .
>
> (2)   There is an *availability* about deaconess ministry which is important for the church . . .
>
> (3)   . . . the *spirituality* which is often spoken of as the characteristic of the Order. People were taught how to pray, in the days of training at Ilkley; and I hope – and believe – that others have been similarly helped in the years at Birmingham. Methodism is famous for its 'activity': it always needs those who can help it rediscover 'the practice of the presence of God'.

> (4)   There is a *broadness* in the ministry of the Order as a whole
> . . . our 'marrieds' . . . now have (contacts), often with people right
> outside the Church and with whom they would never have made
> contact during their days as circuit deaconesses. Their commitment
> to Christ and their practical training are enabling them to minister in
> this wider way, and this could be of significance to the Church as a
> whole.
>
> *Source: A Way of Serving* (Autumn 1980) pp.3-4

Mr. Galliers steered the Order through one of the most difficult periods in its long history. There were closer links to be established with The Queen's College and here the fact that he was very ecumenically minded and open to all the varied nuances emanating from the different denominations was a great asset. His teaching, both in College and at Convocation, was very scholarly and clear. Then came Methodist restructuring and here Galliers guided the Order into the new Division of Ministries and 'interpreted the Order to colleagues there and in the Conference'. When discussions were taking place about the future of the Wesley Deaconess Order and the way ahead was very unclear his deep, clear thinking and guidance, as well as endless patience and understanding, helped everyone to face the future, whatever that might be. By presenting all sides of countless arguments and discussions he was able to ensure that all involved were sensitive to the many varied feelings, apprehensions and hopes of the Order. The Warden was very supportive of the Order: his understanding, kindness, consideration, thoughtfulness and friendship reassured many deaconess who were feeling hurt and anxious. He is remembered as an able communicator, both in official negotiations and on a personal, pastoral level with a deep concern for people as individuals, ever willing to listen.[43]

---

43. I am indebted to several deaconesses and others who worked closely with Mr. Galliers for their helpful comments.

The United Methodist Free Churches/United Methodist Church

The Rev. Thomas John Cope (1891-1912)

The Rev. Thomas J. Cope, founder and first Secretary/ Warden of the United Methodist Free Churches/United Methodist Deaconess Institute, (1891-1912)

The United Methodist Free Churches, as indicated in chapter 9, established a Deaconess Institute at much the same time as did Thomas Bowman Stephenson. The Rev. T. J. Cope, who was the prime mover in this, was born at Lostwithiel on 16th March 1838, the eldest of 10 children. He entered the ministry of the United Methodist Free Churches in 1861 and served in various circuits in different parts of the country. Then in 1890 he was appointed to Westmoreland Street Church, Pimlico, London, where, like Stephenson in Lambeth, he was appalled by the poverty and deprivation and determined to do something about it. His vision was to provide evangelistic and social activities for the neighbourhood and out of this grew the Deaconess Institute because he could see the value in having 'good women set apart to minister to the people in their homes, in such ways as only women can . . .'. Cope persuaded the 1891 Annual Assembly to accept Bowron House as a Connexional institution for the training of deaconesses and a committee was appointed to deal with the selection of candidates, the curriculum and staffing. In due course Cope negotiated closer ties between the Deaconess Institute and the Home Mission Committee and prepared the organization to become an integral part of the United Methodist Church at the 1907 Union. He continued as Secretary of the Institute until 1912, the year of the Institute's 'coming of age'. For 21 years Cope had guided the infant organization and seen it grow both in size and usefulness, especially in the fields of nursing and evangelism. He was described as the Deaconess Institute's 'Secretary, its very soul, [and] its ceaseless driving force'. He died on 10th February 1927.[44]

The Rev. T. J. Cope and the Deaconess Institute

The man and the Institute are indissolubly associated in the history of the Methodist Free Church (sic) and of the United Methodist Church.

---

44. See chapter 9; Smith, Swallow & Treffry, pp.33, 61-62, 121-22

With those who know either history, to think of Mr. Cope is to think of the Deaconess Institute and to think of the Institute is to think of Mr. Cope . . . His youngest son, Mr. Vincent Zachary Cope, has said very truly that – four things characterised his father – first, his optimism; second, his unbounded energy; third, his great faith; fourth, his vision . . . He believed. He prayed. He dreamed Dreams. He saw visions. He heard God's voice speaking to him directly. Because of all this he felt he must begin the Deaconess Institute . . .

Source: The Story of the United Methodist Church (Smith H., Swallow J. E., Treffry W. eds, 1932) pp.61-62

The Rev. T. J. Cope   The Rev. Henry Smith

. . . the Deaconess Institute was born in Mr. Cope's brain and heart. He rocked its cradle. He watched with care and deep solicitude over its often-menaced childhood. He directed its steps and fostered its development. He toiled for it prodigiously. He served it with unstinted sacrifice. At length he saw it become strong and able to take a worthy part in the evangelistic life and activities, first of the United Methodist Free Churches, then of the United Methodist Church. Only when it attained to fullness of vigour and promise did he hand it over to the care of others. But he did not then cease to love the child of his heart and brain . . .

Source: Ministering Women (Smith, H. 2nd ed.)
[Appendix – 'Foreword'] pp.211-12

The Rev. Henry Smith (1912-18)

The Rev. Henry Smith was born in Pendleton, Manchester in 1857. He entered Ranmoor, the Methodist New Connexion Theological College in Sheffield in 1877 and, after serving as a circuit minister for 27 years, he became Connexional Editor, having responsibility for both the magazines and the newspaper. He held this post, first in the Methodist New Connexion and then in the United Methodist Church, until 1922. On Cope's retirement in 1912 Conference appointed Henry Smith as the second Secretary of the Deaconess Institute and the following year the title was changed to 'Warden'. Mrs. Smith became the Lady Superintendent and when the First World War broke out the Warden opened a 'Help During the War Fund' and his wife formed a 'Lady Helpers' League'. The income from these enabled them to pay off a £300 debt on the current account, to meet the everyday running costs of the Institute, in spite of increased expenses and loss of income due to the war, and still hand over a balance to their successors. However, the most important development during Smith's period of office was the establishment of a Retiring Fund. This had been long desired, but, time and again, circumstances had delayed it; however by the 1918 Conference he was able to report that nearly £1,500 was in hand towards the Sisters' Retiring Allowance Fund. Links with the Wesley Deaconess Order were further strengthened when information about the Retiring Fund and the post of Lady Superintendent of the training houses was shared. Smith filled many Connexional offices, including being President of the United Methodist Church (1920) and Connexional Secretary, (1925-32), thus having much to do with Methodist Union. When he retired from his official duties Smith returned to circuit work in Brighton until he superannuated in 1925. He died in Brighton on 22nd February 1939.[45]

Retirement of the Warden and Lady Superintendent, the Rev. and Mrs. Henry Smith, 1918

The Committee record(s) its sense of the valuable services they have rendered.

The Sisters who have been trained . . . have found in him an unfailing example of devotion to life's highest ends. His oversight of their studies, at once intelligent and sympathetic, has contributed in no small way to their efficiency. In all the Sisterhood he has taken a wise and kindly interest, giving advice, sympathy or help as the circumstances demanded.

. . . special mention should be made of his strenuous efforts to secure a Retiring Fund for the Sisters . . . and with this part of the Institute's history his name ought to be permanently associated . . .

Mrs Smith has shown herself more than equal to the duties and responsibilities of her position . . . The domestic side has been specially difficult during the last four years, but she has faced the situation with capacity and courage.

Source: United Methodist Deaconess Institute Minute Book (1917-32) p.64

For the Deaconess Institute, his lasting memorial is the book, *Ministering Women,* which he wrote to tell its story and of the work of its deaconesses.

---

45. See chapter 9; Smith, Swallow & Treffry, pp.61-62; *Mins. of Conf.* (1939) pp.32, 98, 160; UMDIMins II p.86

> **The Deaconess Institute**   **The Rev. Henry Smith**
>
> We have no better Home Mission work being done in the Denomination than that done by our deaconesses, and it deserves the utmost support and fervent prayers of our people.
>
> *Source: Ministering Women* (Smith, H. 2nd ed.)
> [Appendix – 'A Delightful Development.] p.216

The Rev. John Moore (1918-20)

The Rev. John Moore entered the ministry of the United Methodist Free Churches from Claremont Church, Burnley in 1876. He spent two years in the denomination's theological college in Victoria Park, Manchester before serving in circuit ministry for many years, both in his original denomination, during which he was Secretary of Ashville College, Harrogate, and in the United Methodist Church. In 1903 he was appointed Home Mission and Church Extension Secretary until 1907 when he became the Home Mission Secretary of the United Methodist Church, which post he filled for the next 12 years. In the years before the First World War Moore had issued the very effective 'Home Mission Call', but all the usual evangelistic activities suffered greatly after the outbreak of war, as the Deaconess Institute reports show, with a great decrease in missions undertaken. In 1918 Moore added the Warden of the Deaconess Institute to his other duties and soon it became an integral part of the work of the Home Mission Committee. He also put the Sisters' Retiring Allowance Fund on a solid basis. His concern for the deaconesses' welfare and work went far beyond the 'academic' interest which might have been expected from his office as Home Mission Secretary.

> **Retirement of the Warden, the Rev. John Moore, 1920**
>
> The Committee . . . record . . . their high appreciation of the many and valuable services he has rendered before and during his tenure of that office. They rejoice that through his influence the Institute is now recognised as an integral part of the Home Mission Organization, and by his advocacy of its claims has secured such generous response that the larger scheme for the 'Retiring Fund' was speedily assured. His personal interest for the Sisters in their work and tender regard for them in their sickness won for him a warm place in all their hearts . . .
>
> *Source:* United Methodist Deaconess Institute Minute Book (1917-32) p.86

Moore was President of Conference in 1919 and retired in 1920, when for three years he acted as bursar at Edgehill College before going to live in Sheffield where he died on 23rd September 1931.[46]

The Rev. Thomas (Tom) Sunderland (1920-22)

The Rev. Tom Sunderland was born in Warley, Halifax in 1863, entering the United Methodist Free Churches ministry and training at Victoria Park College from 1885-88. After 19 years in its ministry and 13 in the United Methodist Church, he became Home Missionary Secretary in 1920, in which post he served until 1928, achieving much evangelistic co-operation between all the branches of Methodism. As Home Mission Secretary Sunderland also became Warden of the Deaconess Institute for two years. Then, on the sudden death, in 1927, of the Rev. George Parker, the Secretary of the Ministers' Superannuation and Children's Funds, the 1928 Conference appointed Sunderland as his successor. During Mr. Sunderland's time the Institute was linked with the Mallinson Road Church, with the Warden being resident at the Institute, but also the minister at the church. This afforded more opportunities for the deaconesses to gain practical experience.[47]

Retirement of the Warden, the Rev. Tom Sunderland, 1922

The Committee . . . desires to put on record its appreciation . . .

It recognises on the one hand, the difficulties under which he carried out the duties by reason of the addition of the work of the Sustentation Fund to the already heavy responsibilities of the office of Home Mission Secretary, and on the other, it expresses its appreciation of the vision and courage with which he initiated and carried through the new policy by which the Institute and Mallinson Road Church were linked together and thus provided a better opportunity for the practical training of the Deaconesses.

Source: United Methodist Deaconess Institute Minute Book (1917-32) p.160

Sunderland died on 14th November 1935 in London.

---

46. See chapter 9; Smith, Swallow & Treffry, pp.45, 85-86; *UM Mins. of Conf.* (1932) pp.39-40; UMDIMins.II p.86
47. See chapter 9; Smith, Swallow & Treffry, pp.27-28, 60-61; *Mins. of Conf.* (1936) p.188

The Rev. Robert William Gair (1922-35)

The Rev. Robert W. Gair was born in the early 1870s and entered the ministry of the United Free Methodist Churches from Houghton le Spring, having trained at Victoria Park College, Manchester (1895-97). After 25 years' circuit ministry in both that and the United Methodist denomination Gair, who was already in the London, Brixton Circuit became Warden of the Deaconess Institute, combining those duties with being minister of Mallinson Road Church. He was the last United Methodist Warden (1922-32) and each month wrote to all the United Methodist Deaconesses, enclosing their salary cheque, giving news of the work of the Institute, of the Sisters and their appointments: this monthly letter served instead of a magazine.[48]

The Rev. Robert William Gair, United Methodist Deaconess Institute Warden (1922-32)

First Monthly Letter　　　　　**The Rev. R. W. Gair**

As this is my first letter to the Sisters, I wish to assure them that the relationship into which Mrs. Gair and I are entering is from the first a sympathetic one. The call to this work came as a great surprise to me and as the appointment carries the duties of Minister at Mallinson Road as well as Warden of the Institute, the responsibilities are weighty. However, I take up the work with joy and hope. Some of the Sisters are personally known to me, having been students in the class which it has been my privilege to take for seven years, whereas others would only be recognisable by the veil. Then I am familiar with work of the Sisters having had a Deaconess during my eight years at Paradise Road; and while my sympathies have been with the Sisterhood since I entered the ministry, I can also say that with the years my appreciation of their work has grown. I begin my work therefore with an admiration for the Institute and its traditions, and with great confidence in the Sisters, and it will be the aim of Mrs. Gair and myself to make the life of the Sisters as happy and useful as possible. We feel the Sisters will not fail us in loyalty.

Source: Monthly Letter from R W. Gair (14th September 1922)

---

48. Copies of these letters survive (14th September 1922-11th July 1935)

Mr. Gair had a vital rôle to play in the history of the Institute – in that decade he saw the number of deaconesses increase, the training period extended to two years and was very involved in all the arrangements for integrating the United Methodist deaconesses into the unified Wesley Deaconess Order when the various branches of the Methodist Church came together in 1932. Gair worked very closely with Dr. Maltby of the Wesley Deaconess Order and the Rev. George Edward Wiles, the Primitive Methodist Home Mission Secretary, to ensure that all the deaconesses from the three branches were happily settled in the Wesley Deaconess Order and the Methodist Church.

The Rev. R. W. Gair   **United Methodist Deaconess Institute Committee**

The committee hereby places on record its grateful appreciation of the services of the Warden, the Rev. R. W. Gair, during the past the years. It realizes that the present high tone of the Institute is largely due to his devotion, unbounded energy and unfailing courtesy.

He has won and retained the confidence and affection of the Deaconesses who have ever found in him a wise guide and sympathetic friend.

By inaugurating a Conference Meeting he has awakened the interest of the Churches in the work of the Deaconess, and the strong financial position of the Retiring Allowance Fund is a witness that the movement has won a place in the hearts and minds of our people.

Source: United Methodist Deaconess Institute Minute Book (1932-35) (21st July 1932) p.22

Gair continued to serve as Warden along with Dr. Maltby until 1935. Then he became one of the joint secretaries and went into circuit in Rochdale, where he acted as Chairman of the Bolton and Rochdale District. He died suddenly on 12th December 1938 after a serious operation.[49] Many tributes were paid to Mr. Gair, but two, rather different ones, show a many faceted character who was greatly appreciated.

The Warden of the Wesley Deaconess Order, the Rev. Dr. W. Russell Maltby, having endeavoured with Mr. Gair to bring about a successful union of the Deaconess Orders, expressed appreciation of his attention to detail and sympathetic understanding of the many nuances involved in such negotiations.

---

49. See chapter 9; chapter 6; *Mins. of Conf.* (1939) p.207; *The Agenda* (December 1938) p.10, (March 1939) pp.6, 13-16

> ### Tribute: the Rev. R. W. Gair   The Warden
>
> I who knew him in the many details of business and policy which the union of the two Orders involved, had more opportunity than most to see and admire his qualities and to prize his friendship. He could be utterly loyal to the fellowship which he had served so well, but his loyalty had no narrowness nor any intrusion of jealousy of others; always fair-minded, magnanimous, friendly, and a good counsellor in any difficulty.
>
> *Source: The Agenda* (March 1939) p.6

Miss M. Ireland (Sister Ann) had spent six years at Bowron House with Mr. and Mrs. Gair and, for five of those, she had been Mr. Gair's secretary and therefore felt that she had a close relationship with him and indeed with his whole family.[50]

> ### Tribute: the Rev. R. W. Gair   (Sister Ann)
>
> Religion was the mainspring of his life, and what a splendid virile religion his was! He had no time for mawkishness; his faith was lived out in service. He had a very rich and happy ministry and one crowned with success, particularly among young people. The Methodist Church was very dear to him, especially his own 'bit' of it. He once said to me that he felt that his ministry had been made up of 'Unions' — first, the Union of 1907, and later the larger union of 1932. In both cases he had to face new situations and cope with new conditions. His attitude to these denominational changes was delightfully human. Originally he had belonged to the 'Free Church' section, and he always regarded it as 'the best of the bunch' in the 1907 Union; just as in the 1932 Union he undoubtedly felt that the United Methodist Section was the little leaven in the lump! But he was generous in his praise of the other sections, and the thought of precedence never seemed to enter his head. So long as he could render service he was satisfied.
>
> *Source: The Agenda* (March 1939) pp.15-16

Each of the Wardens played their part and all made a vital contribution to the life, work and history of the Deaconess Order in their various ways and it is best to let these accounts stand on their own merit as tribute to their endeavours to foster the place, and status of women's ministry within the Methodist Church.

---

50 See chapter 9 pp.360-61

Conclusion

The Impact of the Wesley Deaconess Order

In the 1936 *Order of Service for the Ordination of Deaconesses* the President of Conference says these words to the deaconesses about to be ordained:

> You have learned, Sisters, during the years of your training and probation how various and exacting are the services which your calling will require of you. It may fall to you to preach the gospel, to lead the worship of a congregation, to teach both young and old; you may be required to feed the flock of Christ, to nurse the sick, to care for the poor, to rescue the fallen, to succour the hopeless, to offer friendship, even at cost, to many who, but for you, may never know a Christian friend. But in all this you must be true evangelists of our Lord Jesus Christ translating your Gospel into the language of personal service, that it may be better understood, not reckoning your ministry complete till those whom you serve can say, 'Now we believe, not because of thy speaking; for we have heard it for ourselves, and know that this is indeed the Saviour of the world.'
>
> You will remember that you are one of an Order whose members must be jealous for its good name, honouring and helping one another, ready at all times to take up each other's work, and loyally to carry it on. You must be prepared to go where you are needed, and to leave the place where you are needed less, in order to go to the place where you are needed more. Above all, you will remember that you are, first and last, the servants of the Lord Jesus Christ, and that all your service is rendered to Him.[1]

The Wesleyan Methodist Church had been very male dominated, especially in its higher courts, right from the beginning. Although in many local congregations women were in the majority there were relatively few female office holders. Wesley had adopted

---

1. *The Order of Service for the Ordination of Deaconesses* (1936) pp.12-13

a fairly pragmatic approach to every situation, allowing women as class leaders and even permitting them to preach if they had an 'extra-ordinary call', but post-Wesley the hierarchy took a more rigid stance with the result that women were sidelined. However, it was obvious that there was much work to be done, especially among women and children, in the poorer parts of cities and in rural areas and that it could, in many cases, best be done by women. To hand was a great untapped resource – the women of Methodism. The non-Wesleyan connexions had already both realized, and indeed used, their womenfolk to great effect as evangelists, preachers and 'social workers'.

So Thomas Bowman Stephenson first organized the Sisters of the Children to care for the needy children and then the Wesley Deaconesses to extend the work among women and children in the churches. Meanwhile the United Methodist Free Churches had come to see the value of women's work and set up their own Deaconess Institute. There were also other local initiatives, often connected with the city Missions and the Forward Movement, but that is another story.

At first it was an uphill struggle to convince some people of the importance of this work, but soon the results spoke for themselves and more requests for deaconesses were being received than could be met. The numbers grew and the work spread throughout the country and then overseas. It was obvious that the Orders – both the Wesley Deaconess and the United Methodist Free Churches – were meeting a need. There were things that trained women could do which male ministers could not, there were new fields of service to be explored. The danger was that the deaconesses would be used as an inferior 'ministry' and it was this that the Wardens were anxious to counteract. The deaconesses were carefully selected, highly trained and well supervised – they deserved to have a high status in the life of the Church and to enjoy good colleagueship with their male ministers and the Wardens were determined that this should be recognized by the whole Methodist Church.

All the deaconesses had undergone basic first aid courses, including some midwifery, as part of their training. They kept a medicine cupboard from which they could dispense simple remedies and deal with the minor ailments and emergencies they came across during their district nursing work. However, some deaconesses had specialized in the medical field and felt that that was their calling. The Deaconess-Nurses had, in many cases, obtained good qualifications and were as well trained and experienced as any in the nursing profession and better than most! To these qualifications was added their Christian faith, devotion and dedication which ensured that their nursing skills were enhanced by a deep loving care and concern for their patients.

Although, officially, Wesleyan Methodism did not permit women to preach there had always been some who did and the Wesley Deaconess Order had a number of women who were authorised by the Warden, on a yearly basis, to preach. However, there were some deaconesses whose main activity was evangelism. The Deaconess Evangelists travelled the country conducting missions, but it was not done haphazardly. Careful preparations were made and adequate follow-up procedures put in place, so that the fullest benefits could be reaped and the converts and enquirers integrated into the local churches. The Bible Christian (part of the United Methodist Church in 1907) and the Primitive Methodist Connexions had always had women travelling preachers and so it is not surprising to find that the United Methodist Deaconess Institute laid a greater emphasis on evangelism than did the Wesley Deaconess Order. When Wesleyan Methodism officially allowed women to be local preachers those deaconesses with an aptitude for public speaking naturally joined their ranks. As the years passed evangelism took a rather different form when some deaconesses engaged in 'caravan ministry', by taking the caravans into villages and later onto new housing estates to meet the people on their own ground.

Both World Wars had a significant effect on the Order, allowing the deaconesses greater opportunities and freedom – opening areas hitherto closed to women, so deaconesses worked with women drafted into the forces and factories and their families; became chaplains; helped internees and evacuees, as well as doing sterling service in the towns and cities which suffered in the Blitz and cared for many who had lost loved ones either while on active service or as a result of enemy action.

Then as time passed the nature of the work changed and a number of deaconesses became involved in different social ventures. In the early days much work had been done in the city slums, fighting poverty and drunkenness or in 'Rescue work', but also tackling the same problems in rural situations. In the great 'Central Missions' era deaconesses were the mainstay of work among women and children. More recently deaconesses spread their wings and worked as professionals in hospitals, prisons, universities and schools and ecumenical situations as well as in the modern, but more traditional appointments in Missions, circuits and churches.

Overseas work became a very important facet of deaconess ministry. In particular, in Hindu and Muslim countries the deaconesses could go where no male missionaries could. They broke down the religious and cultural barriers which surrounded the women, going into the closed zenana communities and providing both nursing and teaching to isolated women and girls. Often their care of these women opened up the way for a wider acceptance of missionary enterprise among the men as well. Close co-operation with the Women's Auxiliary meant an extension of missionary activity in many countries.

One of the criteria for candidates wishing to enter the Wesley Deaconess Order was that they should be intelligent, willing to learn and 'teachable'. All the deaconesses were, to some extent, teachers, and taught in Bible Classes and Sunday Schools throughout the Connexions. It is important to realise that 'teaching' often meant giving instruction in the fields more associated with school education and not just imparting biblical knowledge. However, a number, including graduates, felt specifically called to be Deaconess Teachers, and were highly trained educationalists, so they were able to staff schools, particularly in overseas appointments.

The impact of the Deaconess movement on the Methodist Church has been incalculable. Without it Methodist Church life would have been infinitely the poorer. Writing a Foreword to the second edition of *The Hand of God in the History of the Deaconess Institute of the United Methodist Church,* the then Warden, the Rev. Tom Sunderland, used words which seem to epitomise all the Deaconess work in the Methodist Church:

> Here is a story of vision and achievement . . . This . . .
> is both history and prophecy. It links up a grateful
> memory with the rapture of a forward look. 'Hitherto
> the Lord hath helped us: henceforth He will not fail us'
> has been the keynote for every stage of the movement.
> For all Christian institutions, today is the goal of
> yesterday and the starting point of tomorrow.[2]

---

2. Cope p.3

Postscript
Deacon Christine Walters

Death and Resurrection

To be a Wesley Deaconess in the late 1970s and early 1980s was a painful experience. As membership rapidly decreased it felt like being on a sinking ship, because many deaconesses offered for the presbyteral ministry, which had been newly opened to women, and so candidates were few and then non-existent. During this time, the Deaconess Warden was Sister Yvonne Hunkin and the Rev. Brian Galliers, followed by the Rev. Edward Lacy, were the Ministerial Secretaries. It became difficult to persuade the Methodist Church that deaconesses were still available, that it was only recruitment which had ceased. It seemed as though instructions had been given to let the Order die quietly and both the number and variety of appointments decreased. For the deaconesses it became a time of being a 'remnant people', of 'dying' that new life could come: all thoroughly good biblical principles which can be seen more clearly with hindsight.

By 1986 there was growing evidence that God was still calling people to diaconal ministry. To become a lay worker employed by a circuit was the only avenue open officially to serve the Church, but some found that this rôle, however satisfying and fruitful, was not enough: God was calling them to a lifelong commitment and they needed the Church to test this call. The decision to reopen the Wesley Deaconess Order for both men and women candidates was made at the 1986 Methodist Conference in Stoke and emerged from a debate on a report entitled *The Ministry of the Whole People of God*. The report had come from a working party set up to explore possible ways in which the ministry of all God's people could be better released for the service of the Church and the world.

Sister Sheila Parnell was Warden of the Order when it was reopened to receive offers from men and women who felt called to diaconal ministry and she, with others, set up new candidating and training processes. The first group of candidates produced students who trained at many venues from September that year, and, from 1988, the Order was again able to offer the Church an increasing number of deacons for stationing and service.

So the resurrection of the Order happened and, at the same time, many questions had to be faced. Should the new members of the Order be ordained, as had the Wesley Deaconesses? If so, should it be at the annual Convocation as previously or at the Conference? As there were now men in the Order, it could hardly continue to be called the 'Wesley Deaconess Order', so what should be the new name and what the design of the new badge? As a result, at the 1988 Conference, the Order was renamed the Methodist Diaconal Order and a new badge of Celtic design introduced. A new Ordination Service was produced with ordinations taking place at the Methodist Conference. So the 1990 Cardiff Methodist Conference celebrated the first ordinations of the new Order and, at the same time, rejoiced in the 100th anniversary of the Wesley Deaconess Order.

Another question which arose during this time concerned the status of deacons within the Church. Wesley Deaconesses, although ordained, were treated as lay people by the discipline and practice of the Methodist Church. As the years had passed, the reality, at congregational level, was that they were treated as equal and complementary to ministers. For many years the training of deaconesses had been similar to that of ministers, although the focus of their work had been different. It was also realised that, unlike ministers, deaconesses, and now deacons, were not so visibly under the discipline of the Conference: that the Order was a religious order had taken precedence, and it was perceived that its members were only under the discipline of the Order. In fact this was far from how it worked out in practice!

The 1989 Leicester Conference set up a group under the auspices of the Faith and Order Committee to look at the theological and practical implications of whether deaconesses/deacons were lay or ordained. The Convocation of 1991, after much consultation, agreed that members of the Methodist Diaconal Order should be recognised as an order of ministry, as well as a religious order. This was endorsed by the 1992 Conference, which accepted the Faith and Order Committee report that the Church should recognise that there was an order of presbyters (ministers) *and* an order of deacons.

A consultative process, within the Diaconal Order, and with the Church, was put into action, which, with a Connexional Committee, handled the many changes the Conference needed to make to its practice and discipline and to the Deed of Union of the Methodist Church. This meant consulting widely within the Church and within the Order itself and then rewriting most of the legal documents of the Church to include the Diaconate. A climax was reached at the 1998 Scarborough Conference, with the historic moment of receiving all ordained members of the Methodist Diaconal Order (by then all called deacons) into Full Connexion. At the same time, the Conference affirmed the Order's Rule of Life and it was visibly seen that the Order is both an order of ministry and a religious order.

The result was that this brought the Order into a closer relationship with and made it more accountable to the Conference than in the early days. The Methodist Diaconal Order headquarters remain in Birmingham, but candidature, training, stationing and discipline processes are closely linked to that of presbyters. For the first time the Methodist Church acknowledged it had a distinctive/permanent Diaconate – men and women serving alongside presbyters and lay people, enabling the Church to fulfil its calling of the servant ministry of Christ.

The 'new' Methodist Diaconal Order has brought huge change to its members. Men as well as women, a wider representation of ages, although we could do with many more younger members. We are a dispersed community and have a simple Rule of Life and Prayer daily to link us together. Regional groups meeting wherever possible; the monthly letter from the Methodist Diaconal Order headquarters, our annual Convocation, which deals with business, similar to that dealt with by the Ministerial Session of the District Synod, as well as further training all help keep us in touch. An ongoing process within the Diaconal Order is that of working together in a consultative way, making decisions by consensus wherever possible – because we believe that our ministry in church and community life needs to reflect this way of working alongside people.

So the story continues as God goes on calling men and women to diaconal ministry. The glorious heritage and spirituality of the Wesley Deaconess Order has been subsumed into the new Order. We still have many types of people: the 'quiet' and the 'loud' characters; the 'behind the scenes' type and those who find themselves 'up front'; – people of faith and courage willing to be pioneers. The ministry of the present day deacon is not much different from that of the Wesley Deaconesses, but we serve in a very different society. The tradition continues of being people prepared to work at the edges of church life: flexible in ministry, 'go-between' people, offering the friendship of Christ, especially to those who are unable, or unprepared, to step through the doorway of the church. We are thankful that the Methodist Church has recognised this ministry in new ways, especially during a time when God has been renewing the Diaconate of the Church across the denominations, worldwide. In this context, the Wesley Deaconess Order, now the Methodist Diaconal Order, has been seen as a pioneer.

Christine Walters
Warden: Methodist Diaconal Order 1989-98
Vice President of the Methodist Conference 1994-95

St. James Road, Birmingham:
the present Methodist Diaconal Headquarters

Important Dates

Some major dates and events – further details are to be found in the text itself.

1869   The Children's Home opened

1890   The Rev. Dr. Thomas Bowman Stephenson wrote *Concerning Sisterhoods*
            Wesley Deaconess Institute (Order) started

1890-1907   Rev. Dr. T. Bowman Stephenson – Warden of the Wesley Deaconess Order

1890   Mewburn House, London, opened
            First recognition service for Wesley Deaconesses (Sept)

1891-92   The Rev. Dr. T. Bowman Stephenson President of the Wesleyan Methodist Conference

1891   Bowman House, Norwich, opened
            United Methodist Free Churches Deaconess Institute started

1891-1912   Rev. Thomas J. Cope – Warden of United Methodist Free Churches Deaconess Institute

1891   Bowron House, Pimlico, London, opened
            United Methodist Free Churches Deaconess Institute Constitution adopted

1892   Calvert House, Leicester, opened

1894   Deaconess House, Gravel Lane, Salford, opened
            Work in South Africa started (March)
            Wesley Deaconess Institute Constitution adopted

1897   Work in Ceylon started (August)
            Sister Christian Hughes went to New Zealand (September)

1900	Dr. Stephenson resigned as Warden of The Children's Home
1901	*Flying Leaves* magazine started (September)
	Maltese Cross adopted as badge
	First Lady Associates
	Doddington Convalescent Home opened
	St. George's Hall, (Primitive Methodist) Bermondsey, opened and the Rev. James Flanagan engaged two ladies as 'Sisters', who were based in rented house in the Old Kent Road.
	Sisters' Settlement formally recognised by the Primitive Methodist Home Mission Committee.
1902	First Convocation of Wesley Deaconess Order, Leeds (April)
	Wesley Deaconess College, Ilkley opened (October)
1903	United Methodist Free Churches Deaconess Institute moved to Bolingbroke Grove, Wandsworth
1904-05	Leeds Sisters joined the Wesley Deaconess Order
1904	Work in West Africa started (September)
1905	Work in China started (March)
1907-20	Rev. William Bradfield – Warden of the Wesley Deaconess Order
1907	Work in India started (September)
	The United Methodist Church formed from the United Methodist Free Churches, Methodist New Connexion and Bible Christian Connexion
1909	United Methodist Deaconess Institute linked with the Home Mission organization
1910	Wesleyan Methodism officially sanctioned women preaching
1912	Death of the Rev. Dr. Thomas Bowman Stephenson (16th July)

1912-18	Rev. Henry Smith – Warden of the United Methodist Deaconess Institute
1914-18	World War I
1915	*Flying Leaves* magazine ceased
1918-20	Rev. John Moore – Warden of the United Methodist Deaconess Institute
1920-40	Rev. Dr. W. Russell Maltby – Warden of the Wesley Deaconess Order
1920-22	Rev. Tom Sunderland – Warden of the United Methodist Deaconess Institute
1922-35	Rev. Robert William Gair – Warden of the United Methodist Deaconess Institute
1922	*The Agenda* magazine started 'Restawhile', the holiday home, opened (December)
1923	Death of the Rev. William Bradfield (January 4th)
1925	Deaconess work started in Rhodesia
1926	Rev. Dr. W. Russell Maltby – President of the Wesleyan Methodist Conference
1928	Work in the West Indies (Jamaica) started
1930	Work in Kenya by the United Methodist Deaconess Institute started
1932	5 Queen's Road, Ilkley acquired as Warden's residence (July) Methodist Union – The Wesleyan, Primitive and United Methodist Churches came together as The Methodist Church (September)
1933	First united Convocation of Wesley Deaconess Order and the United Methodist Deaconess Institute (April)

1934	Primitive Methodist Sisters received into the Wesley Deaconess Order
1936	Manchester and Salford Mission 'Sisters of the People' received into the Wesley Deaconess Order
1939	Maltby Wing opened at Ilkley College West Indian Deaconess Order started
1940-52	Rev. W. Harold Beales – Warden of the Wesley Deaconess Order
1940	Jubilee of the Wesley Deaconess Order
1939-45	World War II
1945	Linnburn acquired as a hostel annexe to Ilkley College
1946	Worthing Holiday Home opened (July)
1949	*The Wesley Deaconess Magazine* started
1951	Rev. Dr. W. Russell Maltby died (July 9th)
1952-64	Rev. Thomas M. Morrow – Warden of the Wesley Deaconess Order
1952-53	Sister Dorothy H. Farrar – Vice President of the Methodist Conference
1952	Jubilee of the opening of the Deaconess College at Ilkley (October)
1953	Albemarle, Cleethorpes, retirement home, opened (October) South African Deaconess Order established
1960-67	Linnburn leased out
1960	'Restawhile' closed
1964-72	Rev. Geoffrey Litherland – Warden of the Wesley Deaconess Order

1964	*Doers of the Word* magazine started
	Sector work authorized
1965	Lectures with Headingley Theological College students
1965-66	Deaconesses who married permitted to remain in the Order
1967	Death of the Rev. W. Harold Beales (17th September)
1967-68	Closure of Wesley College, Headingley, Leeds
1968	Ilkley Deaconess College closed and sold (June and October)
	Wesley Deaconess Order moved to Birmingham to study at Handsworth Theological College
1970	Amalgamation of Handsworth (Methodist) and The Queen's (Anglican) Colleges
1971	Opening of the Wesley Deaconess Order's headquarters, Ilkley House, Pritchatts Road, Edgbaston, Birmingham
1972-80	Rev. Brian J. N. Galliers – Warden of the Wesley Deaconess Order
1973	*A Way of Serving* magazine started
	Opening of the presbyteral ministry to women
	Methodist restructuring
1974	Death of the Rev. Thomas M. Morrow (25th June)
	Albemarle, the retirement home, closed
1978-79	Recruitment into the Wesley Deaconess Order closed
1980	Worthing Holiday Home closed
	Ilkley House sold
	26 St James Road, Edgbaston, Birmingham acquired
1986	Order reopened as the Methodist Diaconal Order for both women and men

Bibliography

The official Deaconess records – Minutes, Records of Convocation, deaconess diaries, lists of appointments, rolls of members and reports – and other primary sources, such as the Conference Agendas and Minutes and the various magazines, noted in the text are not listed here, but many will be found in the Methodist Archives and Research Centre, (MARC) The John Rylands Library, Deansgate, Manchester M3 3EH, though some are in private hands.

Printed Sources

A hundred years on and . . . A Renewed Order 1990

An Alphabetical Arrangement of Wesleyan Methodist Ministers . . . with their Circuits (various dates)

Banks, J., *The Story So Far: The first 100 years of the Manchester and Salford Methodist Mission* (1986)

Barber, B. Aquila, *A Methodist Pageant* (1932)

Beckerlegge, O. A., *United Methodist Ministers and their Circuits* (1968)

Bradfield, William, *The Life of Thomas Bowman Stephenson* (1913)

Chambers, Wesley A., *Not Self – But Others: The Story of the New Zealand Methodist Deaconess Order* (Wesley Historical Society (New Zealand), Proceedings No. 48, August 1987)

Cope, Thomas J., *The Hand of God in the History of the Deaconess Institute of the United Methodist Church* (n.d.)

Cumbers, F. H., ed., *Richmond College 1843-1943* (1944)

Findlay, G. G. and Holdsworth, W. W., *The History of the Wesleyan Methodist Missionary Society* volume 2 (1921)

Garlick's Methodist Registry 1983

Hymns & Psalms (1983)

James, F. B., ed. *William Russell Maltby: Obiter Scripta* (1952)

Kendall, H. B., *The History of the Primitive Methodist Church* 2 vols. (n.d.)

Leary, W. *Directory of Primitive Methodist Ministers and their Circuits* (1990*)*

Lenton, J. H., '"Labouring for the Lord": women preachers in Wesleyan Methodism 1802-1932 – a revisionist view', in *Beyond the Boundaries: preaching in the Wesleyan tradition,* ed. Richard Sykes, Oxford 1998

Milburn, Geoffrey and Batty, Margaret, eds. *Workaday Preachers: The Story of Methodist Local Preaching* (1995)

Ministers and Probationers of the Methodist Church . . . with the Appointments . . . (various dates)

Rupp, G., Davies, R. E., George, A. R., *The History of the Methodist Church in Great Britain* volume 3 (1983)

Russell, R. W., *The Life of James Flanagan* (1920)

Smith, Henry, *Ministering Women: The Story of the Work of the Sisters connected with the United Methodist Deaconess Institute* (n.d.) [1st and 2nd editions]

Smith, Henry, Swallow, John E., Treffry, William, *The Story of the United Methodist Church* (1932)

Stephenson, T. B., *Concerning Sisterhoods* (1890)

The Methodist Hymn Book with Tunes (1904)

The Methodist Hymn Book with Tunes (1933)

The Methodist Local Preachers' Who's Who 1934

The Order of Service for the Ordination of Deaconesses (1936)

Vickers, John A., ed., A *Dictionary of Methodism in Great Britain and Ireland* (2000)

Newspapers

The Free Methodist (1890-1907)

The Joyful News (1890-1900)

The Methodist Recorder (1890-)

The Methodist Recorder – Winter Numbers

The Methodist Times and Leader (1932-37)

The Methodist Times (1890-1932)

The United Methodist (1907-1932)

Secondary sources

By His Daughter, (Dorothea Price Hughes), *Life of Hugh Price Hughes* (1905)

Fry, Ruth, *Out of the Silence: Methodist Women of Aotearoa 1822-1985* (Christchurch, New Zealand, 1987)

Mantle, J. Gregory, *Hugh Price Hughes: A Strenuous Life* (1903)

Oosthuizen, Constance M., *Conquerors through Christ: The Methodist Deaconesses in South Africa* (1990)

Senior, Geoffrey R., (translated with an introduction), *A Chinese Diary: Some events during 1926-7*, by Rev. Tan Chin-ching (2000)

Senior, Geoffrey R., *The China Experience: A Study of the Methodist Mission in China* (1994)

Index

Deaconesses are indexed under surnames. Those who are referred to by Christian name only and who therefore cannot be positively identified are omitted from the index.

Findlay, Rev. William H., 122,
123-24, 158-59
Fishe, Alice C., 299
Fisher, Bessie, 86
Flanagan, Rev. James, 363-64
Flint, Frances, 302
Flower, Gertrude A., 140, 142
Flying Leaves, 8, 106, 139, 244
Foot, Lady, 226
Fordsburg, South Africa, 107
France, 238
Freer, Sarah, 52-53, 55, 274,
296, 316
quoted, 9-10, 275
Freetown, Sierra Leone, 130-31
Furniss, Dorothy (Mrs.
Constantine), 207
Furniss, Eileen, 93, 94-95

Gair, Rev. R. W., 256, 257,
311(2), 350-51, 352, 359,
363, 449-51
quoted, 354, 449
Galliers, Rev. Brian J. N., 269,
271-72, 315, 389, 439-43
quoted, 51, 440-43
Gent, Maude, 392
quoted, 27-28
Gilbert, Rev. J. E., 311
Goodwin, Rev. A. G., 337
Gosling, Nellie, 274
Gossling, Mary, 238
Goudie, Rev. William, 138
Gould, Ellen, quoted, 67-68
Gould, Rev. John, 274, 290
Graham, Margaret, quoted, 83,
83-84
Grant, Rev. E. W., 114
Graves, Rev. George, quoted, 53
Greenwood, Miss, 223
Greenwood, Mabel and Nellie,
319-21
Gregory, Rev. A. E., 305
Gridley, Vera, 227
quoted, 226
Gustard, Lillie, portrait, 372

Hackney Wick Mission, 285-86,
289
Hagen, Yvonne von, 114
Haigh, Winifred, 129, 136
Haiti, 222-23
Bird's College, 222
Hall, A. Mary, 140, 141
Hamilton, Miss C., 176
Hampsthwaite, 80
Handsworth College,
Birmingham, 266-68, 315, 439
Hankow, 204, 206
hospital, 195-99, 206, 209-10
Harmes, Gertrude, 93, 94
Harpur, Louie, 53-54
Harris, Flora, 134
Harrison, Evelyne, 88, 89
Harrison, H. B., 279
Hartley, Rev. Marshall, 109
Hassan, Mysore, Girls'
Orphanage, 185-86
Hatchard, May, 139
Hawken, Lucy, 110, 113, 278-79
portrait, 113
quoted, 15, 23
Hawkins, Rita (Mrs. Williams),
11-12, 243, 293, 297, 316
quoted, 9
Hayden, Easter, 164, 170, 171,
172, 174
quoted, 166-67, 175
Headingley Theological College,
Leeds, 265-66, 314, 437,
439
Heard, Bessie, 187, 188, 190
Hellier, Annie M., 178-79
Herd, Helen, 42-43
Higgins, Bessie, quoted, 422
Higson, Miss, 309
Hinckley, 26
Hindle, Dorothy, 21
Hodge, Rev. Dr. S. R., 193, 194
Hoffman, Fraulein, 300
Holdsworth, Rev. J. Forster, 392
Holiday Homes, 319-22
Holloway, Jessie, 136, 138

471

Melling, Miss, 300
Mellows, Mary, 211
Methodist New Connexion, 73
Methodist Recorder, 408
Methodist restructuring, 270-72, 439
Methodist Union, 256-57, 309-10, 351-54, 421
Mewburn House, London, 16, 243-44, 294
Meyer, Mrs. Lucy Rider, 284, 298
Middlebrook, William, 291
Middleton-on-Tees, 80
Miller, Jean, 264
Millican, Maud, 188, 200, 201, 203, 204, 207
Mitchell, Lillie, 68
Moore, Rev. John, 339, 347, 348, 349-50, 447-48
moral welfare, 16, 44, 190
Morley, Mabel, 220
Morley, William, 212
Morrow, Rev. Thomas M., 262, 263-65, 409, 410, 432-36
   quoted, 435
Morton, Mary, 223, 227
Moss, Adela, 178, 179-85, 186-87, 188, 322
   quoted, 180, 181, 182, 182-83, 183-84
Mountford, Bessie (Mrs. Hutchinson), 194
Murphy, Muriel, quoted, 378

National Children's Home, 152, 240, 293, 316
Nenguba, Rhodesia, 115
Nettleship, Gertrude, 150-54, 162, 166, 171-72, 173, 373
   portrait, 98, 149, 158
   quoted, 151, 152
New Zealand, 212-21
Newbury, Northbrook Street, 65
Nicholls, Clara, 33
Nicholson, Doris, 321
Nizamabad, India, 188

Northcroft, Ruth, 54, 55, 250, 277(2), 278, 279-80, 282-83, 322, 374
   quoted, 280, 283
Norwich
   Bowman House, 53, 274-76
   workhouse, 14
Nottingham, Albert Hall Mission, 19
nursing, 23-25, 120-21, 141, 143, 416, 453-54; *see also* Ellareddypett; Hankow; Puttur; West Africa
Nuttall, Rev. Ezra, 102

Oats, Evelyn, 99-113, 295
   portrait, 110
   quoted, 100, 101, 105, 107(2), 109, 110
Oglethorpe, Jean, 82
Okyne, Rebecca, 147
Oosthuizen, Constance, 114
ordination/consecration, 347, 354, 402-03, 407, 409, 411, 438, 457-58

Palmer, Eva, 85
Palmer, Evelyn, 88, 89
Parker, Rev. George, 343-44
Parnell, Sheila, 49, 254, 456
Parris, Mary, 80
Parsons, Bessie, 65
Passmore, Annie Elizabeth, 300
Passmore, Edith, 30
Perkins, T. E., 316
Peru, 232-34
Peters, Edna, 42
Phillipson, Rev. Oliver, 264
Pitts, Elizabeth Ann (Annie), 305
Platts, Dorothy, 145
Plymouth, Stonehouse, 46
Polkinhorne Florence, 308
poor, work among, 9-12, 25-26, 32-33, 37
Posnett, Rev. Charles W., 182
Posnett, Rev. Joseph, 276

Trimmer, Rev. and Mrs. George
J., 150, 155
quoted, 151, 154
Trineman, Nora, quoted, 44-45
Trinidad, 225
Tunstall, Dr. A. C., 305
Twentieth Century Fund, 297

uniforms, 27, 46, 220, 241-42,
260, 337, 370-89
badge, 244, 368, 373-74,
380, 381, 386, 387
United Methodism, 37-41,
71-76, 119, 203, 337-
51, 353, 381-83, 444-51
Helpers' League, 345-6
Home Mission Committee,
340-42, 347
insurance of Sisters, 336-37
training, 355-63
uniform, 381-82
United Methodist Free Churches,
34-37, 68-71, 326-37,
444
University and School
Chaplaincy, 48-50
Urwin, Rev. Evelyn Clifford,
358

Vandersteen, Vera,
portrait, 273
Vanner, James E., 294
Vinson, Charlotte, quoted, 55-56
Volckman, Isabelle, 322

Wade, Rev. Wilfred, 262
Waights, Rev. Kenneth L., 269
Wakely, Joyce, 47
quoted, 95-96
Waller, Dr. David J., 294
Walters, Christine, 254
Walters, Elsie, 146-47
Walthamstow, UMC, 37-38

Walton, Miss, 397
Walton, Edith, 385
Ward, Elsie, 231
Ward, Michael, 47
wartime, 84-97
Boer War, 84-85, 103-08
Chaplain's assistants, 92-93
World War I, 85-88, 233,
379, 418
World War II, 88-94, 260-61,
425, 427-29
Watson, Marjorie, 224, 225
Webb, Muriel, 203
Weddell, Sara, 18-19
Wellington, New Zealand, 218
Wesley, John, 452-53
Wesley Deaconess Institute
1940 Jubilee, 259-60
attendance at Synod, 399
Committee, 256-57
constitution, 295
and Order, 2-3
types of work, 7-8, 33-34,
122, 242; *see also* blind;
evangelism; industrial
chaplaincy; moral
welfare; nursing; poor;
prison visiting; preaching;
social work; teaching;
temperance; wartime;
youth work
woman Warden, 253, 319
see also allowances;
candidates; ordination;
qualifications; retirement;
training; uniforms
Wesley Deaconess Magazine,
430
West Africa, 120-49, 423
teaching, 130-37, 142-44
West Indies, 222-30
Westall, Maud, 85
Westby, Miss Margery, 363